SOCIAL WORK RESEARCH AND EVALUATION SKILLS

Social Work Knowledge
Frederic G. Reamer, Series Editor

Social Work Knowledge
Frederic G. Reamer, Series Editor

Social work has a unique history, purpose, perspective, and method. The primary purpose of this series is to articulate these distinct qualities and to define and explore the ideas, concepts, and skills that together constitute social work's intellectual foundations and boundaries and its emerging issues and concerns.

To accomplish this goal, the series will publish a cohesive collection of books that address both the core knowledge of the profession and its newly emerging topics. The core is defined by the evolving consensus, as primarily reflected in the Council on Social Work Education's Curriculum Policy Statement, concerning what courses accredited social work education programs must include in their curricula. The series will be characterized by an emphasis on the widely embraced ecological perspective; attention to issues concerning direct and indirect practice; and emphasis on cultural diversity and multiculturalism, social justice, oppression, populations at risk, and social work values and ethics. The series will have a dual focus on practice traditions and emerging issues and concepts.

David G. Gil, *Confronting Injustice and Oppression: Concepts and Stategies for Social Workers*

George Alan Appleby and Jeane W. Anastas, *Not Just a Passing Phase: Social Work with Gay, Lesbian, and Bisexual People*

SOCIAL WORK RESEARCH AND EVALUATION SKILLS

A Case-Based, User-Friendly Approach

Frederic G. Reamer

Rhode Island College

Columbia University Press

NEW YORK

Columbia University Press
Publishers Since 1893
New York   Chichester, West Sussex
Copyright © 1998 by Columbia University Press
Library of Congress Cataloging-in-Publication Data
Reamer, Frederic G.
    Social work research and evaluation skills : a case-based, user-friendly approach /
Frederic G. Reamer.
        p.   cm.
    Includes bibliographical references and index.
    ISBN 0–231–10222–4 (cloth : alk. paper)
        1. Social work education—United States. 2. Social service—United States—Research.
3. Social service—United States—Statistical methods. 4. Social service—United States—
Statistical services. 5. Evaluation research (Social action programs)—United States. I. Title.
HV11.R34 1998
361.3'2'071073—dc21   97–37983

⊗

For Deborah, Emma, and Leah

Special thanks to my wife, Deborah, for her wonderfully useful commentary and suggestions, and to my friend, Peg Patterson, whose imaginative and creative cartoons help bring many of the book's concepts to life

CONTENTS

PREFACE

Recently I saw a television commercial for Oldsmobile cars. Perhaps you've seen it, too. The main point of the commercial, as I saw it, was to convince viewers that "today's" Oldsmobile is new and different, a radical departure from the Oldsmobile of yesteryear that many of us remember and associate with our parents. In fact, the commercial's tag line was "It's not your father's Oldsmobile."

I suppose this book's preface is a bit like that commercial. One of my goals is to convince you that this research-and-evaluation book is a bit different from those that have been in the field for some time. Existing research and evaluation textbooks may be well-written texts, but students rarely describe them as "interesting" or "engaging."

Over the years, when teaching social work research and evaluation courses, I've discovered that students are much more likely to learn research and evaluation concepts when they are presented in the context of the kinds of social work practice situations that students will encounter in real life. Because social workers have traditionally learned various concepts by reviewing and discussing cases, wouldn't it make sense, I thought, to extend this venerable case study approach to social work research and evaluation?

And that's more or less how this book came about. After years of using case material to teach social work research and evaluation concepts, I decided that I would put these ideas between two covers. I'm convinced that if social workers learn important research and evaluation concepts in the context of case material, they will be more likely to understand and use them.

Toward this end, I begin with an overview of a comprehensive family service agency, Mt. Washington Family Services. Throughout the book, I discuss various programs run by this agency and various challenges facing the agency's social work staff and administrators, to make the research and evaluation concepts seem more real. Every example is based on actual experiences in the social work field.

My hope is that this approach will help readers picture how research and evaluation concepts can be, and actually are, used in real life. With this approach, I think, the relevance of research and evaluation concepts and tools will be clearer than they would be if I were to present a more traditional overview of them. I know that the skillful use of these ideas can help people with the kinds of problems that social workers address. I've seen it happen. For me, research and evaluation skills are as much a part of social work practice as are other practice skills such as relationship building, assessing, interviewing, counseling, community organizing, advocacy, administration, and policy formation. Used competently and judiciously, research and evaluation can have a profound effect on social workers' ability to help individuals, families, groups, organizations, and communities.

And that's the reason for social work.

SOCIAL WORK RESEARCH AND EVALUATION SKILLS

I

THE RELEVANCE OF SOCIAL WORK RESEARCH

AND EVALUATION SKILLS

Start where the client is. Every social worker has heard this expression at some time, whether in an introductory social work practice course, field placement, or continuing education. Starting where the client is has become a maxim in the profession. That is, it's best not to impose your own preconceived agenda on your clients.

Although this practice concept is used almost exclusively in clinical social work, I've learned that it also is relevant to every other area of social work practice, including research and evaluation. Now don't get nervous. I'm not about to turn this into a clinical relationship. What I am trying to say is that even with this topic—research and evaluation—I think the best bet is to begin with an assessment of the issues, challenges, goals, and resources that you bring to this task.

But I'm at a distinct disadvantage here. Since you and I are interacting via the printed word, I can only guess at your background in the study of social work research and evaluation; we can't have a conversation.

The alternative is to speculate about your perceptions and attitudes based on my many years of contact with social work students who have taken research and evaluation courses, and this can be a bit risky. After all, you may or may not be similar to other social work students I've taught. If you're not, I would be making the mistake of inappropriately generalizing to a group of people from a sample of data. (Now you've just been exposed to your first research and evaluation concept: sampling error. More about that later.)

But as researchers say, data are data. I would be foolish to ignore what I've learned from the legions of students who have taken social work research and evaluation courses, just as experienced clinical social workers would be foolish to ignore lessons learned from the legions of clients with whom they've worked.

What have I learned? Not surprisingly, social work students bring diverse attitudes to research and evaluation courses (there's a second research and evaluation concept: statistical dispersion). Some students approach these courses enthusiastically. They've taken similar courses elsewhere and found them to be intellectually challenging. They also see that the course content is relevant to their professional practice. Other students, however, are terrified of these courses and dread taking them. Some of them had miserable experiences with other research courses and may have had some difficulty grasping the material. The course content may seem about as exciting as watching grass grow, paint dry, or parking meters expire. Finally, some students are ambivalent about research and evaluation courses. They have some understanding of the material's potential value but also some anxiety about mastering all the concepts. There may be some other variations on these themes, but in my experience these are students' most common reactions to beginning their research course.

Perhaps you see yourself in one of these categories. If you're genuinely interested in this course, eager to explore its relevance to your career, and reasonably confident of your ability, all I can say is . . . *mazel tov* (that's Yiddish for congratulations). But if you have knots in your stomach and would prefer to use this book only as a doorstop, please, please, please, give me (and your instructor) a chance. You may find this hard to believe, but I've taught hundreds of students who have started research and evaluation courses with similar feelings (I think some of them came to the first class with one of those air-sickness bags available on airplanes) and walked out of the last class feeling remarkably relieved that (1) the material was reasonably interesting, (2) the concepts and skills are relevant to what real social workers do for a living, (3) there's a way to learn research and evaluation skills and have some fun, (4) 1 and 2, (5) 2 and 3, (6) 1 and 3, or (7) all of the above.

My objective is to get you to the point—if you're not already there—that you're willing to admit that social work research and evaluation are essential to competent practice. I am going to do this by making this material as interesting and relevant as possible. Instead of presenting it in the way it usually is— with fairly abstract overviews of theoretical concepts and occasional applications to practice-based situations—I will begin with real case material to show you just how important research and evaluation concepts really are. After I set the stage, by describing a social service agency facing some challenging issues, I will introduce a wide range of research and evaluation concepts and explore their relevance to this multiservice agency. I think this approach will bring these otherwise abstract concepts to life and help you see how they pertain to actual social work practice.

THE AGENCY

Imagine that you are a caseworker in a local family service agency—the Mt. Washington Family Service Agency—which has provided social services in your community for more than fifty years. In fact, Mt. Washington is one of the oldest social service agencies in the region.

Mt. Washington offers a wide range of services to the local community: individual, couple, family and group counseling, services for senior citizens (day care, respite care, homemaker assistance), foster care services (casework and counseling services to children in foster care, foster parent recruitment and training, case monitoring), adoption services (preadoption counseling for birth and prospective adoptive parents, information and referral, postadoption counseling), refugee resettlement services, outpatient substance abuse treatment, and family life education (workshops on a variety of topics, such as parenting, family relationships, intimacy, adoption, and coping with stress).

Like many family service agencies, Mt. Washington receives funding from a variety of sources, both public and private. Some clients pay fees for the services they receive. In addition, the agency has contracts with several public agencies to provide specific services. For example, Mt. Washington has a contract with the state child welfare agency to recruit and train foster parents. It also has a contract with the local school district to provide social services, including counseling and crisis intervention, to several area schools.

The agency also administers several grants, one of which is from a local private foundation and provides funds to work with pregnant and parenting teenagers who have substance abuse problems. Another grant, from another private foundation, provides funds to help recent immigrants who are having difficulty with housing, employment, isolation, and so on.

Mt. Washington employs a large number of staff. In addition to agency administrators, the professional staff has several program directors, casework staff, and group workers. Most of them have BSWs and/or MSWs, although several have a master's degree in another human service field, like counseling or education. The agency also employs many paraprofessional and support staff. The paraprofessionals do not have a college education or formal social work or social service training. They often help deliver concrete services (for example, delivering meals to and visiting with homebound elderly clients or helping recent immigrants find affordable housing). The agency's support staff provide a variety of secretarial, accounting, and custodial services.

As a caseworker, you have a number of responsibilities. You spend about 60 percent of your time providing counseling services to individuals, couples, and families. In addition, you must coordinate the agency's family life education program, which means working with a steering committee of social service professionals from the community to develop a family life education curriculum, to plan workshops, and to identify workshop leaders. Your family life education responsibilities take up about 25 percent of your time.

The remaining time in your schedule is spent supervising two undergraduate social work students from a nearby college who are completing their required field placements at Mt. Washington. One of the students works exclusively with recent immigrants who need assistance with housing, employment, health care, and child care. The second student divides her time between the program for pregnant and parenting teenagers and assisting you with Mt. Washington's family life education program.

One of the clients you have been serving is a single mother, Ms. E. Ms. E. has a nine-year-old son, Toby, who is in the fourth grade. Toby's teacher and the principal at his school referred him and his mother to a neurodevelopmental pediatrician because of difficulties Toby was having in school. According to his teacher, Toby was having trouble completing written assignments at his desk, paying attention to the teacher when she spoke to the class, and staying in his seat. Toby's teacher described him as "very fidgety and all over the place."

The pediatrician examined Toby thoroughly and concluded that he had symptoms of Attention-Deficit/Hyperactivity Disorder, or what is commonly known as ADHD (American Psychiatric Association 1994). That is, Toby manifested inattention, hyperactivity, and impulsivity that interfered with his ability to function in school. The pediatrician prescribed medication that is often used to control these symptoms, and she also referred Toby and his mother to Mt. Washington for counseling. In the pediatrician's experience, it often is useful for parents to consult with a social worker to learn new ways to cope with their child's ADHD. Such counseling focuses on helping parents learn ways to manage their child's behavior and deal with the stress in parenting a child with special needs.

You have met weekly with Ms. E. for three months. Initially, the two of you concentrated on specific behavior management techniques that many parents of children with attention deficit and hyperactivity problems find useful. These techniques use simple behavioral principles, such as positive reinforcement, to help strengthen children's appropriate behavior.

After several weeks, you sense that Ms. E. is distraught. Although she says that the new behavior management techniques seem to be helping, Ms. E. also says that she is feeling "blue" and "depressed," that she has been feeling this way "for months, maybe even a year. I just don't know what's wrong with me. I just feel so sad so much of the time."

Once you and Ms. E. feel confident that she is properly using the new behavioral management techniques with Toby, you agree that it would be useful to spend some time on Ms. E.'s own distress. Ms. E. reports that her difficulties with Toby are part of the problem, but not all of it. In addition, Ms. E. says, she cannot stop feeling guilty about her divorce from Toby's father. She also is very worried about her finances; she is behind in her rent and owes a lot of money on two credit cards.

During the next seven weeks, you spend most of your sessions with Ms. E., helping her deal with her feelings of depression. Although you devote some time during each session to discussing Toby's behavior, most of the time is spent on Ms. E.'s own difficulties. The two of you decide to focus on several issues from Ms. E.'s experiences in the family in which she grew up. You also use a variety of intervention tools that are sometimes useful in treating depression, drawing primarily on cognitive techniques you learned in a recent continuing education workshop on the subject.

At the end of the third month of your work with Ms. E., the clinical director at Mt. Washington asks you to prepare a progress report. The clinical director would like to know where things stand with Toby and Ms. E. One reason she wants a report is that the agency's clinical director is concerned about the clients in this particular case, and she also wants to be certain that sufficient progress is being made with Toby and Ms. E. to justify your continued involvement with them. In addition, the clinical director wants to ensure that the agency's resources are being used effectively; she's feeling some pressure because of the agency's growing waiting list.

How would you assess the effectiveness of your work in this case? In particular, how would you assess both Toby's and Ms. E.'s progress?

THE ROLE OF RESEARCH AND EVALUATION IN SOCIAL WORK

Toby's and Ms. E.'s case is not unusual. It involves a social worker who has designed and implemented an intervention plan for clients with several problems. The problems to be addressed are the child's difficulties in school and the mother's psychological distress, so the social worker designed and implemented an intervention strategy for both the child's and the mother's needs.

In every case, regardless of the clients and problems, social workers must be concerned about the effectiveness of their efforts. Accordingly, assessing the effectiveness of social work intervention is one of the principal purposes of social work research and evaluation. This is true whether one is engaged in direct practice—such as work with individuals, couples, families, or groups— or indirect practice—such as community organizing, community planning, or agency administration. Whether one is helping an individual client cope with symptoms of depression, working with a group of adolescents struggling with a substance abuse problem, providing psychotherapy to a family in the midst of a contentious divorce, organizing tenants of a public housing development, or administering a community mental health center as its executive director, a social worker must, at the very least, attempt to answer a fundamental question: Are my efforts working and achieving the results that I and my clients are seeking?

How you answer this question will be a major focus of our discussion in subsequent chapters. In short, you need to know how to identify indicators of effectiveness, gather information about them (usually referred to as *data*), and analyze and interpret the results.

Evaluation—whether of clinical intervention with individual clients, families, couples, and groups or of entire programs—is only one of several purposes of social work research. A second function is determining how well significant needs are being addressed in the communities where the social workers work. Imagine, for example, that as the person responsible for organizing Mt. Washington Family Service Agency's family life education program, you are concerned that very few people of color or ethnic minorities from the agency's catchment area have attended workshops. This is particularly troubling to you, since, according to the most recently published census data, nearly 40 percent of the local population are people of color and ethnic minorities.

In light of your concern, you think it would be useful to conduct a needs assessment to gather more information about this problem. That is, you want to survey a sample of people of color and ethnic minorities in the community to determine their needs for family life education, their knowledge and perceptions of Mt. Washington's family life education program, their interest in participating in family life education workshops, possible obstacles to their participation, and so on. Your goal at this point may not be to evaluate the effectiveness of the family life education workshops but, rather, to carry out a family life education needs assessment with respect to people of color and ethnic minorities. Hence in addition to evaluation, a second purpose of social work research is conducting needs assessments.

Now let's imagine that as part of your work with Toby, you would like to design an effective intervention to help Toby's schoolteacher manage Toby's disruptive behavior. In particular, you would like to help Toby's teacher learn how to increase the likelihood that Toby will complete assigned tasks in school (for example, reading, arts and crafts projects), pay attention to the teacher when she is talking to the class, and remain in his seat. As a conscientious professional, you know that it is important to consult the latest research literature to help you design the most appropriate intervention. You make time in your busy schedule to go to the local university library to conduct a comprehensive literature search concerning classroom-based interventions designed to manage the behavior of children who have been diagnosed as having attention deficit disorder with hyperactivity.

Your literature search turns up lots of recent journal articles and book chapters summarizing studies evaluating clinical interventions with schoolteachers to help them better manage students' problematic behavior. Each publication includes a conceptual overview of the topic studied, the research questions addressed, the research methodology (research design, sampling, data collection instruments and techniques), the results, and a discussion of the findings' implications. Your task is to review this empirically based literature and determine which research findings are relevant to Toby and his schoolteacher. That is, you should read through these publications for evidence of the effectiveness of various clinical approaches and their suitability for use with Toby and his teacher.

A third function of social work research and evaluation is thus enabling social workers to draw on empirically based literature to develop guidelines for practice. Of course, to use empirically based literature, you must understand the technical aspects of the studies discussed. That is, you will need to know how to assess the appropriateness of the research design, sampling procedures, data collection methods, and data analysis. The information contained in this book should help you do that.

Now let's take your work with Toby, his mother, and his teacher one step further. You have been active in your state's association of school social workers. Although you do not work full time as a school social worker, you do spend a considerable amount of time providing services to area schools as part of Mt. Washington's contract with the local school district. As a result, you have found it helpful to participate in activities sponsored by the state association of school social workers.

You recently received a flyer announcing that the national association of school social workers, with which the state association is affiliated, is sponsoring a major conference on effective clinical interventions with children with attention deficit problems. The flyer invites recipients to submit abstracts summarizing intervention approaches, to be presented at the conference. The flyer indicates that preference will be given to empirically based proposals, that is, proposals based on research evidence concerning the effectiveness of the author's clinical intervention. The flyer also states that presenters will be invited to submit reports of their clinical research to a prominent national journal for publication. The goal is to share information with school-based social workers nationally about effective clinical approaches with students who have attention-deficit difficulties.

After reading this flyer, you decide to use your work with Toby, his mother, and Toby's teacher as an opportunity to gather data for possible presentation at the national conference and publication. A fourth function of social work research and evaluation is, therefore, knowledge creation and dissemination. Social workers need to know how to carry out a research or evaluation project, from beginning to end, and to write up the results for formal presentation and publication.

In summary, the four main functions of social work research and evaluation are

1. to assess the effectiveness of interventions,
2. to conduct needs assessments,
3. to draw on empirically based literature and findings to inform and provide guidelines for practice,
4. to create and disseminate knowledge for use by other professionals.

Let us now examine each of them. This discussion will provide a valuable foundation for the remainder of the book, in which we will review the concepts, tools, and techniques needed to conduct social work research and evaluation.

ASSESSING THE EFFECTIVENESS OF SOCIAL WORK INTERVENTION

Every social worker knows that it is important to think about the effectiveness of her or his work. After all, wouldn't it be odd if social workers were not preoccupied with the outcome of their efforts?

How should social workers determine the effectiveness of their work? This is a straightforward question, but unfortunately, the answer is quite complicated. For many years, social workers did not regularly use research tools to evaluate the effectiveness of their interventions, but this does not mean that until recently social workers did not do any research related to the profession. Quite the contrary. As we shall see shortly, social workers have always been involved in various kinds of research. Only since the 1970s, however, has there been a concerted effort to include all social workers—not just researchers—in the ongoing evaluation of practitioners' work.

I don't want to inundate you with tons of historical detail about social work research. It is important, though, for you to know something about the changes in social work's relationship to research—especially with respect to practice evaluation—since the formal inauguration of the profession in the late nineteenth century. Understanding this historical context can help you appreciate the role of research and evaluation in contemporary practice.

I believe there have been four phases in the history of social work research. The first began with the start of the profession itself. During the charity organization society era, many social workers believed that "scientific philanthropy" would enable professionals to understand the nature and causes of poverty or "pauperism" and that the scientific method could be followed to study and understand the treatment of individual cases (Reid 1987; Zimbalist 1977). In the early twentieth century, the classic writings of luminaries such as Edith and Grace Abbott, Jane Addams, Gordon Hamilton, Florence Hollis, Florence Kelley, Julia Lathrop, and Virginia Robinson influenced social workers' thinking about the importance of studying social work practice scientifically (Orcutt 1990; Tyson 1995).

Perhaps the best-known benchmark during the early twentieth century was the publication of Mary Richmond's *Social Diagnosis* (1917), which described the phenomenon of social diagnosis as an extension of scientific problem solving. Also, the early-twentieth-century social survey movement constituted one of the era's most ambitious efforts to apply scientific methods to troubling social problems.

The movement led to the second phase, using social science research methods to study both the social problems of interest to social workers and the success of various interventions. Many social work educators, and a smaller number of practitioners, began using research methods that had been pioneered in disciplines such as psychology, sociology, and, to a lesser extent, political science. For example, social work researchers conducted studies of poverty, casework effectiveness, delinquency prevention, and multiproblem families (Tyson 1995; Zimbalist 1977). Often these studies and research projects were carried out on a large scale, with large samples of clients, complex data collection methods, and multiple sites.

Although many of these studies produced important and useful results, most social workers had difficulty relating to them. For one thing, most social workers had received only a modest education in social work research methods and, therefore, were not able to understand fully, or might have been intimidated by, the complex research studies. Also, because many of the better-known studies were carried out on a large scale with the results reported as trends for groups of clients, social workers may have been frustrated in trying to apply findings from these studies to their day-to-day work with individual clients, families, couples, and so on.

By the late 1970s, social work was clearly in a new phase of its development in regard to research. Before this time, social workers' training and education concerning research depended heavily, often exclusively, on designs and methods borrowed from disciplines such as psychology and sociology. There was very little social work literature on research methods, one exception being Norman Polansky's (1960) edited collection of articles about social work research. Not until about 1980, however—nearly eight decades after social work's formal beginning—did the profession begin to see the publication of a critical mass of research texts written by social workers for social workers (see, for example, Atherton and Klemmack 1982; Bloom and Fischer 1982; Grinnell 1981; Jayaratne and Levy 1979; Reid and Smith 1981). No longer was the profession almost entirely dependent on research texts written primarily for practitioners in other fields. Instead, for the first time in the profession's history, social workers had access to a range of publications based on social work values, practice principles and priorities, and examples.

During this time, a number of social workers were also becoming concerned about the limitations of some of the research methods commonly used in the social sciences and frequently adapted for use in social work research and evaluation (Reamer 1993; Tyson 1995). I will have more to say about this later, but in short, a number of social workers began to question the validity of attempts, using traditional social science designs and tools, to measure empirically the kinds of phenomena with which social workers are concerned. A common criticism was that social workers (and social scientists) exaggerate the ability of many conventional research tools to measure the effectiveness of social work interventions and also such things as mental health, self-esteem, community well-being, and organizational health. These doubts led to intense debate in the social work community about the validity of widely embraced approaches to research and evaluation.

This period marked a significant turning point for social work. Since then, many social work scholars and practitioners have developed a wide variety of research and evaluation tools to help social workers in the field. The emphasis has shifted from training social workers to understand research designs, data collection techniques, and data analysis procedures that tend to be used primarily by academic researchers (based on large samples and complex methods that typically are not feasible for most social workers and that may not provide the richest, most meaningful information for practitioners) toward training social workers to use a variety of manageable, practical, and relevant research and evaluation tools.

This brings us to the current phase in the development of social work research and evaluation, and the one around which this book is organized. This phase emphasizes educating social workers to understand how they can use research and evaluation concepts, skills, and tools in their day-to-day practice. We know now that research and evaluation are forms of practice. For many years, social workers viewed research and evaluation as activities only for social work researchers, people who were separate and distinct from social workers in the field who had direct contact with clients. To a great extent, this was an accurate perception. Until relatively recently, much of the research in social work was done by academic social workers or persons employed as researchers. For many practitioners, the fruits of these efforts were interesting but separate from the demands of everyday practice.

Now, however, social work educators routinely emphasize the integration of research and practice and the use of research and evaluation as research tools. As we will see in our discussion of activities at the Mt. Washington Family Service Agency, research and evaluation have practical purposes and can facilitate the delivery of services.

First let's think of ways in which research tools can be used to assess the effectiveness of services offered by the Mt. Washington staff. One way is to use clinical research tools to monitor and evaluate the effectiveness of work with an individual client (or couple or family). How can you find out whether Toby's behavior has changed during the time you have worked with him and his schoolteacher? How can you find out whether your interventions, separate from other events in Toby's life, caused these changes? Similarly, how can you find out whether your work with Toby's mother, Ms. E., has made her feel less depressed and whether your intervention accounts for this change?

To monitor and assess client change—whether it concerns behaviors, feelings, life circumstances, or thinking patterns—you need to understand a variety of research techniques, generally referred to as *clinical research tools*. We will discuss these in more detail later.

You can also imagine a variety of ways in which other services and programs

at Mt. Washington might be evaluated. Remember I said that you spend a portion of your time at the agency coordinating an ambitious family life education program. This program includes a large number of workshops offered to
community residents. Shouldn't you find out whether these workshops are
useful and effective? Consider, for example, a workshop on parenting skills
that you regularly offer. Participants typically include parents who are having
difficulty managing their children and so are eager for advice and information
about behavior management. The workshop has six, one-hour sessions.

How would you find out whether the participants' knowledge of parenting
skills and behavior management techniques has improved as a result of the
workshop? How would you determine whether the parents' skills actually have
changed? Clearly, you would need some practical knowledge of program evaluation, including information and skills that can be helpful whether you are
evaluating a relatively small workshop offered as part of an agency's family life
education program or a very large social service program, such as a delinquency prevention project, with hundreds of clients, multiple sites, and various intervention approaches.

CONDUCTING NEEDS ASSESSMENTS

It is not hard to imagine the situations in which the staff at Mt. Washington
might need to rely on information provided by needs assessments. Earlier I
pointed out that a needs assessment might explain why so few community residents of color and ethnic minorities have participated in Mt. Washington's
family life education programs, their social service needs, and obstacles they face
in getting those needs met. This information can then help the Mt. Washington
staff identify the relevant issues and design a strategy to address them.

But there are many other possibilities as well. For instance, needs assessments might be advisable for Mt. Washington's refugee resettlement program.
This program gives the Mt. Washington staff an opportunity to address
important issues in the community. Even without data from a needs assessment, we know that many refugees have difficulty with language, employment, housing, health care, child care, education, loneliness, and culture
shock. It would be irresponsible to offer services without basic information
about the number of refugees who might need assistance, the particular problems that refugees in Mt. Washington's surrounding area often encounter, the
refugees' current circumstances (for example, sources of income, housing situations, support networks), and their interest in receiving assistance. To deliver
these services, the Mt. Washington staff must have the kind of information

that can be provided only by a well-designed needs assessment. This would also be true of many other programs offered by the agency.

USING RESEARCH KNOWLEDGE TO GUIDE PRACTICE

Earlier I explained why it was important for you to consult the published literature on the effectiveness of interventions designed to help teachers manage the behavior of children with attention deficit problems. Thus before helping Toby's teacher learn behavior management techniques, you should have a good grasp of the current state of the art, that is, what the research literature says about what is and is not effective. Why waste your time implementing an approach for which there is no or little evidence of effectiveness? Why not concentrate instead on techniques that have been found to be helpful? To get this information, you need to know how to locate relevant studies and findings and how to assess their quality and relevance to your particular practice situation.

This kind of knowledge, based on prior research, can be helpful for several other services offered by Mt. Washington. For example, think about the agency's contract with the state child welfare agency to recruit and train foster parents. The state child welfare agency depends on Mt. Washington to place abused or neglected children in high-quality foster homes. Thus there is considerable pressure on Mt. Washington's staff to recruit prospective foster parents and to offer appropriate training and supportive services to them. High turnover among foster parents is a costly problem, not only in financial terms (that is, the cost of recruiting and training new foster parents), but also with respect to the loss of experienced, reliable foster parents who are available when placement needs arise. In addition, Mt. Washington's administrators should run this program well in order to retain the agency's contract with the state child welfare agency. Clearly, it is in everyone's interest—that of the state child welfare agency, the foster parents, Mt. Washington, and, most important, the children—to enhance the quality of foster care recruitment, training, and retention efforts and to help prevent foster parents from leaving the pool.

What can the Mt. Washington staff do to strengthen their foster parent recruitment and training program? One possibility is to ask comparable agencies in the state and throughout the nation to help locate effective recruitment and training programs. One problem with this approach is that it can be time-consuming, inefficient, and unreliable. It takes a great deal of time to track down and chat with colleagues locally and out of state. In addition, this approach yields, at best, anecdotal information, some of which may be biased by the storyteller's perceptions. That is, this kind of informal survey might produce testimonials about a particular agency's "wonderful" (or "rotten") approach but whose actual effectiveness—in regard to foster parent satisfaction and retention, for example—has not been determined. This does not mean that seeking anecdotal information is a waste of time. Such details about individual programs—"informal case studies"—can be quite valuable. But if an agency really wants to be thorough, it makes much more sense to conduct a carefully designed, comprehensive literature review.

A more efficient and productive approach would be for the Mt. Washington staff to find published (and unpublished) literature on the subject. They also could contact national child welfare organizations, such as the Child Welfare League of America, which could recommend effective models that could be implemented at Mt. Washington and could suggest pertinent research and evaluation literature. It would make sense for Mt. Washington's staff to consider the results of studies of foster parent recruitment and training efforts (for example, see Kadushin and Martin 1988:363ff). Indeed, the agency might be able to save a lot of time, effort, and money by reviewing the existing research and evaluation literature on the subject.

The same holds for Mt. Washington's substance abuse treatment services. Like many multipurpose social service agencies, Mt. Washington offers a number of substance abuse treatment options, like short-term counseling and crisis intervention, long-term outpatient counseling, and group counseling.

Would it be appropriate for Mt. Washington's administrators merely to instruct staff to design and deliver any old substance abuse treatment program that makes sense to them, without having them first search for and analyze the relevant research and evaluation literature? Of course not. This makes no more sense than a cardiologist's treating patients without first evaluating the research and evaluation literature pertaining to their medical conditions or symptoms. This would be unthinkable (and clear evidence of malpractice).

To be able to review and use the literature competently requires special skills. As I noted earlier, social workers need to know how to carry out a comprehensive literature review, understand the technical aspects of the research methodology used to conduct studies, and judge the relevance and the quality of published reports. We will discuss these sorts of skills throughout the book.

CREATING AND DISSEMINATING KNOWLEDGE

It is one thing for social workers to understand the importance of evaluating the effectiveness of their work, conducting needs assessments, and drawing on available and relevant research and evaluation literature. But is this enough? Is it enough to use research and evaluation skills in one's work with individual clients or in one's own social service program? The simple answer is no.

We just discussed how important it is for social workers to search for and consult the research and evaluation literature relevant to their practice. Where can they find this knowledge? Obviously, someone has to conduct the research for other social workers to use. Although a significant portion of this research is conducted by academic social workers (faculty in social work education programs) and staff in various research institutes, more and more of it is being conducted by practitioners in the field, either by themselves or in collaboration with academic researchers. It does not take a genius to figure out that if this research is not conducted and published, it will not be available for others to use. Thus even though it is necessary for social workers to use research and evaluation skills as part of their own practice and with their own clients and programs (working "retail," we might say), it also is important for social workers—especially those on the profession's front lines—to consider ways of generating and disseminating new knowledge for widespread use (working "wholesale"). Here social workers must master special skills and concepts, so they, too, will be on our agenda throughout this book.

RESEARCH AND EVALUATION AS A PART OF PRACTICE

Over the years, social workers have changed the way they think about research. Once upon a time, most social workers believed that research was done by "someone else" and had little direct relevance to practice. More recently, however, social work research and evaluation have taken on a different meaning. We now have a much better understanding of some of the practical ways in which research and evaluation can influence our work with individuals, couples, families, groups, organizations, and communities. We now believe that social work research and evaluation are part of our practice, in much the same way that assessment skills, counseling techniques, community organizing, and grant writing are practice skills. Hence, research and evaluation skills need to be learned and mastered so that they become part of the well-trained social worker's collection of knowledge and skills.

Social workers are educated to think about solving their clients' problems, whether the clients are individuals, couples, families, groups, communities, or agencies. During the first century of social work's formal existence, a wide range of problem-solving strategies were developed. Although social workers define the problem-solving process in different ways, most practitioners and scholars acknowledge that it has several components and steps: defining the problem to be addressed, setting the goals, assessing them, developing an intervention plan, implementing it, evaluating the progress toward attaining the goals, and terminating the process.

In most respects, the steps in social work research are the same as these. The social worker concerned with research and evaluation must decide on the research question(s) and develop a sound research design or plan to investigate it.

It should be easy to see that practice and research not only are quite similar on the surface but also are intertwined. It no longer makes sense to view social work research as separate from practice. Social work research and evaluation are practice.

2

UNDERSTANDING RESEARCH AND EVALUATION QUESTIONS

Now let's take a step back and think more about the various kinds of research and evaluation questions that social workers encounter. In every social service setting—whether in a small community-based agency, school, prison, psychiatric hospital, rehabilitation center, large public welfare program, comprehensive mental health center, or private practice—there are dozens of issues that need to be explored. It is not unusual for social workers—including caseworkers, clinical directors, policy aides, and administrators—to complain about their need for additional information to perform their jobs well and about the lack of time available to gather this information. Sometimes this problem is only a lack of time. In many instances, however, social workers may not know how to identify the information that is worth gathering in the first place. This, too, is a specialized skill that every social worker should have. Thus, before devoting a great deal of time to explaining the technical aspects of research and evaluation design and the methodological tricks of the trade, social workers must learn how to determine which information is worth obtaining.

Over the years I have found it helpful to think about this challenge in two ways. First, it is useful for social workers to think carefully about the kind of information they need to perform their various duties. More specifically, what is social workers' primary goal when they set out to collect information by using research and evaluation skills? Second, what is the focus of their research and evaluation? Do practitioners emphasize those issues and questions related to work with individual clients, families, groups, communities, organizations, or social policy? By considering these two dimensions together—goal and focus—we can get a good grasp of the kinds of research and evaluation relevant to practice.

THE GOALS AND FOCI OF SOCIAL WORK RESEARCH AND EVALUATION

Most social workers have three possible research and evaluation goals, the first of which is *exploration*. Social workers do exploratory research when they first begin to gather information. Remember that I am not talking here about social workers who are full-time researchers—they are fish that swim in a different bowl! No, I'm talking about mainstream social workers who work in real agencies with real clients. Frequently these practitioners need to collect exploratory information (or data) to help them in their work.

Let's consider some typical examples at the Mt. Washington Family Service Agency. In chapter 1, I mentioned that Mt. Washington offers a variety of adoption-related services, such as information and referral services for people interested in adoption, preadoption counseling for prospective birth parents and adoptive parents, and postadoption counseling. A major goal of the agency's program is the recruitment of adoptive parents for children with special needs (for example, children who are over age three and children who have mild-to-moderate behavioral or health problems).

The information and referral service is particularly popular. The social worker in charge of the program, Dawn S., and her staff receive a fairly constant stream of telephone calls from couples and single persons interested in adopting children. Typically, Mt. Washington's staff offer these people a free initial consultation session, during which the staff provides an overview of adoption options, the agency's adoption program and services, parenting issues in raising adopted children, legal issues, and fees.

Dawn S. is concerned that about a third of the prospective adoptive couples and individuals who contact the agency about becoming clients do not return after the initial consultation, that some of these prospective clients may be dissatisfied with Mt. Washington's services or approach to adoption. They may have spoken to different service providers and decided to work with another agency. Or maybe after the initial consultation, some of these couples decided, for a variety of reasons, not to follow through with the adoption.

Whatever the reasons, Dawn S. is concerned. She and her colleagues spend a lot of time providing initial consultations free of charge. Although Dawn S. regards this is an important service, she cannot deny that it is costly for the agency. Prospective adoptive parents who decide to become Mt. Washington clients do pay fees that cover nearly all the agency's adoption service expenses. But because an estimated 30 percent of the people who receive initial consultations decide not to return as formal clients, Mt. Washington's staff are working many unreimbursed hours of service. Even though this may be a generous and valuable service, the agency cannot afford the continued expense.

As a result, Dawn S. decides that it would be useful to contact some of the people who attended the initial consultation but did not return as formal clients. She would like to ask them about their experience with Mt. Washington, their reaction to the initial consultation, the impact of the consultation on their views about Mt. Washington's approach to adoption, their contact with other social service agencies that also provide adoption services, and their future plans regarding adoption. In Dawn S.'s opinion, this kind of information might help the agency's staff enhance the likelihood that the individuals who participate in the initial consultations will return to the agency as full-fledged clients.

At this point, Dawn S. is not in a position to interview many individuals and couples. For one thing, she is planning to conduct these interviews herself, and her time during the next couple of months will be quite limited. In addition, before she decides to contact more people for interviews, she would like to know whether such interviews are likely to produce useful information. If the interviews do prove valuable, Dawn S. plans to ask agency administrators at Mt. Washington about using agency funds and staff to conduct a more ambitious survey.

Dawn S. decides to look through her files to identify about six couples and individuals who had the initial consultation in the last six months but who have not contacted the agency since then in regard to becoming formal clients. After she compiles this list, she jots down a few questions to ask them:

1. When did you first think about adopting a child?
2. At what point did you decide to contact the Mt. Washington Family Service Agency about its adoption program?
3. In general, were you satisfied with the services you received from Mt. Washington? Why or why not?
4. Are you still considering adoption?
   a. If not, why not?
   b. If so, are you working with another agency? May I ask which one?
5. I notice that you did not return to Mt. Washington for services after your initial consultation. Would you be willing to explain why you did not return?
6. We always are interested in improving our services to our clients. Were there aspects of the services you received from Mt. Washington that you particularly liked? Some that you did not like?
7. Could you suggest specific ways in which we might respond better to people who come to Mt. Washington for information about adoption?

I won't take time now to comment on the appropriateness of the topics addressed by these questions, the sequencing of the questions (the order in which they would be asked), or their wording. Although all that is important, I will wait until we describe in more detail the construction of questionnaires. For now, let's just say that this set of questions and Dawn S.'s approach to gathering this information are a nice example of the kind of exploratory research a social worker might carry out in an agency setting. Dawn S. does not want to conduct a large-scale study with a large number of people, a comprehensive interview instrument, and so on. For the moment, she simply wants relatively informal feedback from a small group of people who have had contact with Mt. Washington and who have decided not to return for additional services.

This kind of exploratory research is practical and, in most cases, manageable. Sometimes exploratory projects lead to bigger, more comprehensive studies, but other times social workers are satisfied with the outcome of these more modest efforts. In this case, if the small number of interviews proves to be fruitful, we can imagine that Dawn S., or another agency staff member, might decide to expand the research to include more people (researchers would say a larger *sample*) and a longer, more detailed set of questions (a more comprehensive *interview instrument*).

A second goal of research in many social work projects is *description*. Let's suppose that a clinical supervisor at Mt. Washington, Deborah L., is concerned about clients' changing patterns of use of the agency's counseling services. Although many of the agency's clients have some kind of mental health insurance coverage, insurance and managed care companies have been placing more and more restrictions on the use of counseling services. This trend also seems to be changing the way in which Mt. Washington's social workers provide counseling.

Deborah L. has chatted informally with a number of her clinical staff, who suggest that most clients are being treated for a shorter period of time than in past years. These clinicians report that they are now more inclined to use intervention approaches designed for short-term treatment. Based on her observations and informal conversations with staff, Deborah L. thinks it is advisable to gather information more systematically with regard to changes in Mt. Washington's service delivery pattern. The results, she believes, are likely to have important implications for the agency's intake criteria, intervention approaches, staffing patterns, and budgeting.

Given the importance of the information, Deborah L. and her administrative colleagues think it would be a mistake to rely entirely on exploratory information. At a staff meeting, they agree to collect information more comprehensively. The agency's administrators decide to assign funds to carry out a *descriptive study*, whose primary purpose is to gather detailed information to create an accurate profile, or snapshot, of the phenomenon being studied.

In this case, how would the staff carry out a descriptive study? As a first step, they would list the topics about which they wanted information. Possibilities include the length of intervention (such as the number of weeks) for each clinician's cases during a certain period of time, the nature of the presenting problem(s) in these cases, the services provided, the client's and worker's assessment of change in the status of the client's problem(s), the client's and worker's feedback concerning the adequacy of the number of sessions, and the payment source (for example, insurance, self-pay). In addition, it might be useful to ask the agency's social workers for their own opinions about changes in the delivery of clinical services. Background information about the social workers could also be included, such as their length of time with the agency, educational and employment history, and preferences concerning schools of thought and intervention approaches.

The main purpose of this survey is to *describe* the changing characteristics of clinical cases over time (perhaps over a two-year period), the clinical social workers' opinions of these changes, and background information about the social workers. Descriptive information from clients also would be useful. Descriptive studies of this sort can be enormously helpful, particularly when administrative staff and clinical directors are trying to anticipate changes in the field that could affect the agency's staffing needs, financial stability, priorities, and mission.

The third goal guiding much social work research is *evaluation*. The principal purpose of social work is to intervene in clients' lives (individuals, families, couples, groups, organizations, communities) to bring about some kind of meaningful change. It should be obvious, therefore, that social workers have an obligation to evaluate whether, and the extent to which, their efforts make a difference.

Consider, for example, one of the Mt. Washington Family Service Agency's substance abuse treatment programs. This program uses a particular treatment approach with those clients who have a history of chronic cocaine abuse. The treatment model combines psychoeducational, cognitive, and behavioral techniques designed to reduce and, eventually, eliminate cocaine use. The psychoeducational element is teaching clients to understand the physiological dimensions of their cocaine abuse, the nature and causes of their addiction, and the environmental triggers of their own drug abuse. The cognitive element is discussing with clients their thinking patterns, particularly their distorted perceptions of their substance abuse. Finally, the treatment's behavioral element uses the principles of extinction and positive reinforcers to prevent further cocaine abuse. The agency's cocaine abuse treatment program lasts for eight weeks. The program has been in existence for almost six years and has enrolled approximately 450 clients.

It is important to know whether this treatment approach is effective, but in a case like this, exploratory and descriptive research projects won't quite do the trick. Although anecdotal or exploratory information gathered from a small group (or sample) of participants might be somewhat useful and provide some valuable insights and observations, this sort of information alone would not offer enough detail to enable the Mt. Washington staff to assess the program's effectiveness. Similarly, a carefully conducted descriptive study won't suffice. The staff might indeed want to gather a lot of descriptive information about the substance abuse treatment program. I can think of lots of reasons that they might want such descriptive details as the number of clients served, the clients' substance abuse and treatment histories, and their demographic characteristics (the term *demographic* usually refers to information such as race, ethnicity, age, sex, educational background, socioeconomic status, and marital or family status). But this kind of information, valuable though it may be, would not enable Mt. Washington's staff to answer the most pressing question, Does our program work? To answer this question, the staff must design an *explanatory* or *evaluative* project whose principal goals are to *explain* the extent to which changes in clients' cocaine use are a result of the Mt. Washington program, as opposed to other factors, and to *evaluate* the effectiveness of this particular treatment approach or model.

The social workers' goals are, therefore, what shape the nature of their research. In some instances, relatively modest exploratory projects may lead to more ambitious and comprehensive descriptive or explanatory/evaluative projects. In many cases, however, social workers simply turn to whatever research activity makes sense at the moment, without considering whether a particular research project will evolve into something "bigger and better." This makes sense. Most social workers do not organize their professional work around major research agendas. Rather, most are preoccupied with helping their clients enhance the quality of their lives (or communities, organizations, and so on). The challenge is to discover how to use research and evaluation skills to pursue those goals.

Remember, though, that the distinctions among exploratory, descriptive, and explanatory/evaluative research reflect only one of two ways to think about social work research and evaluation—the social worker's primary *goal* (whether to explore, describe, explain, or evaluate). The second way has to do with the *focus* of the social worker's professional work with clients.

There is no simple way to describe what social workers focus on in their work. Some focus on individual change, and others focus on policy formulation. Some social workers focus on mental health problems, and others focus on drafting legislation to provide funding to prevent homelessness. Clearly, social workers' research and evaluation are in large part a function of the focus of their efforts. It would help if we could find a convenient way to classify these various foci.

I find it useful to think of three major "focus" categories. The first is what most social workers call *direct practice*, or work focused directly on individual clients, couples, families, and small groups. Most social workers are involved in direct practice, in the form of casework and counseling. Similarly, much of social work research and evaluation is focused on issues related to direct practice.

The second focus category is social work with *communities and organizations*. The former includes community organizing and the development of community-based services (such as the formation of a network of housing or mental health agencies to enhance the group's lobbying power with state and local officials, or the formation of an anticrime task force among residents of a particular neighborhood). The latter includes organizational development and consultation (such as consulting with a social service agency's board of directors to improve its services or working with administrators to resolve the chronic conflict among staff or to help the staff appreciate their clients' cultural and ethnic diversity).

The third focus category is somewhat broader and includes activities related to *social welfare policy*. Here social workers might participate in formal lobbying, policy formulation, and policy implementation with respect to a variety of issues, such as public welfare, health care, the state's spending on human services, social work licensure, or civil rights legislation to protect people who are HIV positive.

A TYPOLOGY OF SOCIAL WORK RESEARCH AND EVALUATION

Now let's put together our discussion of research and evaluation goals and focus, to help us understand the wide range of research and evaluation possibilities in the profession.

Each of the three foci lends itself to research on the three goals we just

Focus of Social Work Research and Evaluation

	Direct Practice	Communities and Organizations	Social Welfare Policy
Exploration	*1*	*2*	*3*
Description	*4*	*5*	*6*
Explanation/ Evaluation	*7*	*8*	*9*

Goals of Social Work Research and Evaluation

FIGURE 2.1   A Typology of Social Work Research and Evaluation

defined. In figure 2.1 we see how the three goals and the three foci intersect, creating nine different combinations (or cells).

Let's look at some examples of the kind of research and evaluation corresponding to each of these nine combinations that might be carried out at the Mt. Washington Family Service Agency. In cell 1 we find the intersection of exploratory research and direct practice. An example is a social worker working with several Mt. Washington clients who have serious eating disorders, such as anorexia nervosa or bulimia. The social worker has had a hunch for some time that many of them have histories of sexual abuse that must be addressed in order for the treatment of the eating disorder to be successful. Although this social worker is not in a position to conduct a major study of this phenomenon, she wants to know whether there is a connection between sexual abuse and the development of eating disorders. She therefore decides to ask her clients a few simple questions about their sexual abuse history and asks each one to complete a simple, easy-to-administer scale that explores this issue. This is the kind of exploratory research that might influence the social worker's intervention approach (of course, the social worker should also consult the relevant literature to determine whether prior research and theoretical discussions suggest a link between sexual abuse and eating disorders).

Cell 2 contains the intersection of exploratory research related to work with communities and organizations. Here we can return to our earlier example concerning Mt. Washington's family life education program and the lack of attendance by local ethnic minorities and people of color. Before starting to study the issue, the director of the agency's family life education program may want to ask a relatively small number of ethnic minorities and people of color in the community to talk with him informally about the agency's program. However, the social worker probably wouldn't want to spend much time finding a representative sample; that task would be more appropriate to a larger-scale study. The social worker also might not want to spend much time developing a formal interview instrument but, instead, a shorter length of time formulating a few questions to ask a small group of community residents. Their answers might provide some initial insights that could then lead to the development of a larger study with a bigger, more systematically drawn sample and a more comprehensive interview guide.

In cell 3 we have the intersection of exploratory research and social welfare policy. Suppose that the associate director for administration at Mt. Washington, Nancy C., is concerned about the amount of stipend that the state child welfare agency gives to foster parents. In her experience, some foster parents drop out of the program because the stipend does not cover the actual expenses of raising a foster child.

Nancy C. decides that it is time to do something about this problem. She and her boss, the agency director, think it would be a good idea to contact other family service agencies that have contracts with the state child welfare agency to find out whether they are having similar difficulties. Perhaps the agencies together could make some changes. Nancy C. recognizes that first she needs more information and so decides to telephone a handful of her counterparts in other family service agencies to see whether they also believe that the amount of the stipend affects the retention of foster parents. Nancy C. settles on a half-dozen agencies located in different parts of the state and also draws up a short list of fairly simple questions to ask her colleagues. The questions have to do with the number of foster care cases the agency typically handles, feedback or complaints that agency administrators have received from foster parents about the stipend, and administrators' views of whether the stipend's size causes foster parents to leave the program. Nancy C. plans to use this preliminary information to get a sense of the extent of the problem and to gauge her colleagues' interest in resolving it. Nancy C. thinks that this information may be sufficient to begin to organize family service agencies across the state. But she also realizes that she may need to survey a larger number of agency administrators and collect more detailed information to persuade the state to change its stipend. Nancy C. thus decides to wait until she has completed this modest exploratory survey before proceeding with a more ambitious study.

Cell 4 contains the intersection of descriptive research and direct practice, where we find the information needs of a clinical social worker at Mt. Washington, Judy S. Judy S.'s caseload typically includes individuals with chronic mental illness. Most of her clients have been diagnosed with some form of schizophrenia and have been hospitalized in a psychiatric facility at some point in their lives; many have been hospitalized many times.

For some time, Judy S. has speculated that several of her clients seem to be manifesting symptoms of depression in addition to periodic symptoms of schizophrenia. In retrospect, Judy S. believes that she, and perhaps her colleagues, has not been attentive enough to her clients' symptoms of depression.

Judy S. thinks it would be a good idea to begin collecting some information about her hunch, so in the following week, she begins to administer a simple depression assessment scale to all her current clients and each new client. The depression scale takes about five minutes to complete and is easy to score. The instructions accompanying the instrument explain how to interpret the results for clinical purposes, that is, the cutoffs for placing individuals into different clinical categories (no, mild, moderate, or serious concern). Judy S.'s plan is to summarize her clients' depression scores when she has accumulated seventy-five sets of results. She wants to see the variation among clients, possible patterns, and correlations between the depression scores and the clients' demographic characteristics and psychiatric histories. Judy S. does not plan to gather conclusive information to help her explain whatever patterns she finds, if any. Rather, she is primarily interested in better understanding her clients' clinical needs so that she can formulate an appropriate intervention plan. This is exactly the kind of purpose that descriptive information related to direct practice can serve.

Now let's look at cell 5, the intersection of descriptive research and work with communities and organizations. We'll return to the ongoing concern at Mt. Washington about the lack of participation by local ethnic minorities and people of color in the agency's family life education program. Staff members agree that to attempt to address this problem, perhaps through an organized outreach effort and better public relations, they need to have some basic information. How many different ethnic and racial groups are represented in the community? In what numbers? How has the community's ethnic and racial mix changed in recent years?

How would you gather this kind of descriptive information? One way would be to use recent data compiled by the U.S. government. Another option is to contact the planning department in the local city and/or county. The staff there may have some information about the community's ethnic and racial profile. Many local governments routinely collect this sort of information for planning purposes. Your principal goal is to collect solid descriptive information to help the Mt. Washington staff understand more about the various population groups and also to learn more about their cultural norms and values that may affect their participation in Mt. Washington's family life education program.

In cell 6, we have a combination of descriptive research and social welfare policy. Suppose one of the nagging local problems for many people living in the Mt. Washington community is the lack of affordable housing. For a variety of reasons, the area's housing costs have escalated rapidly, and many low- and moderate-income people have had difficulty paying rent and buying houses in the area.

One of Mt. Washington's social workers, Andrew R., is a member of a task force that has been meeting for several months to devise a strategy for the state's housing finance agency and the governor's policy office to make housing more affordable. The task force has talked about asking for a larger pool of subsidized mortgage money for first-time, low-income home buyers and also for some kind of state-sponsored rent subsidy program. The task force members agreed that they need to back up their proposal with some solid descriptive information about the nature and extent of the housing problem. They decide to collect information concerning changes in local rents during the past twenty-four months, changes during this period in the ability of local residents to qualify for a mortgage to purchase an average-priced house, and changes in the number of local residents who spend more than 30 percent of their income on housing. The task force can get much of this information from public agencies or by examining rents advertised over time in the local newspaper.

Cell 7 contains the intersection of explanatory/evaluative research and direct practice. Of the different possibilities here, one concerns the Mt. Washington clients we encountered in chapter 1, Ms. E. and her son, Toby. Recall that Ms. E. sought counseling because of Toby's behavioral difficulties in school. As the clinical social worker, you decided to help Toby's teacher learn new behavior management techniques that prior research suggests can be effective with children who have attention deficit problems.

After you meet with Toby's teacher and help her develop an intervention strategy, the two of you decide to evaluate the effectiveness of this approach. You know that one possibility is to use what is commonly known as a *single-case* or *single-subject design* (we will learn the specifics later). This is a tool that can be used in practice to help determine how well an intervention is working with one client.

Another possibility for this cell (7) is a project designed to evaluate the effectiveness of an intervention approach with a larger number of clients. Consider, for instance, Mt. Washington's substance abuse treatment programs. In recent months, because of budget shortfalls, the agency has begun using a *group* approach, rather than one-on-one counseling, for some clients who have problems with cocaine abuse. Groups are less expensive to treat and, for some clinicians, are a preferable approach to substance abuse treatment.

The clinical director of the substance abuse programs at Mt. Washington believes that the agency should compare the effectiveness of the individual-counseling and the group-counseling approaches. The agency plans to continue using both approaches for the foreseeable future. One possibility is for the staff to evaluate these two approaches formally, to assess differences in relapse prevention, client and staff satisfaction, and cost.

Cell 8 combines explanatory/evaluative research and work with communities and organizations. A good example is Mt. Washington's program to provide transitional housing to a group of single mothers and their children. Women who participate in the transitional housing program have been on welfare for at least three years and are interested in moving off public assistance and into private-sector jobs. The program is designed for women who are willing to participate in educational and vocational programs and counseling during the time they spend in their subsidized housing unit. The program also offers child care while the mothers are busy with their education, training, and counseling activities.

Each mother agrees to remain in the program for two years, at the end of which they are expected to obtain private-sector employment and unsubsidized housing.

The transitional housing program has operated for six years, and forty-three women have completed the program. Fourteen mothers either dropped out of the program on their own or were asked to leave (usually because they did not comply with one or more program rules or requirements).

To date, however, no one has conducted a formal follow-up of the program participants to find out what has happened to them since leaving the program. Mt. Washington's board of directors has asked the agency's executive director to arrange a formal evaluation. Using funds provided by a local foundation that has helped support the transitional housing program, and also some of Mt. Washington's own resources, the agency contracted with a social worker employed by a research and consulting firm to conduct the follow-up study. The study conducts follow-up interviews with all the program participants, including those who did and did not complete the program. The research staff collect detailed information about the participants' current status (for example, employment, income, housing situation) and their perceptions of the program's strengths and limitations. The research staff also explore the transitional housing program's success in enabling the mothers to become independent.

The final cell (9) is the intersection of explanatory/evaluative research and social welfare policy. In many instances, this sort of research is carried out on a large scale by sophisticated research institutes, "think tanks," and academicians. They might examine the impact of national welfare reforms, the effectiveness of state or federal substance abuse prevention policy, and the outcomes of different educational and social service models designed to reduce teenage pregnancy.

It is possible for the staff of a family service agency, such as Mt. Washington, to participate in this kind of research. Although Mt. Washington, an agency of modest size, may not embark on large-scale policy research on its own, it can be an active participant. One way to do so is to serve as one of the local sites for a large, multisite study. In many instances, broad-based policy research depends on the involvement of local sites, particularly when the study focuses on the services and/or populations served by local agencies. For example, Mt. Washington might join a multisite study of substance abuse prevention policy, in light of the agency's active involvement in substance abuse prevention and intervention. The agency might also become a local site for studying strategies to prevent teenage pregnancy. For this to happen, of course, agency staff must collaborate with others evaluating social welfare policy.

APPLIED AND BASIC RESEARCH

Let's pause for a moment and reflect on what we've done. At this point we know some of the ways in which research and evaluation activities apply to social work practice. It should be clear that research and evaluation often are essential to good practice. I described examples of ways in which information relevant to sound practice—whether with individuals, families, couples, groups, communities, organization, or policymakers—can be obtained via well-conducted research and evaluation. The kind of research and evaluation that social workers choose depends on their specific goals: to explore, describe, or evaluate/explain some aspect of their work.

This approach to social work research and evaluation is different from that taken by researchers who are less interested in obtaining practical information to be used for specific purposes (such as more efficiently delivering services to a single client, evaluating a particular program's effectiveness, or conducting a needs assessment before embarking on a new set of services). What I have described is an *inductive approach* to research and evaluation. The inductive approach identifies pressing problems or information needs in social work settings (for example, welfare offices, community mental health centers, rehabilitation centers and hospitals, schools, prisons, nursing homes, private practitioners' offices) and then brainstorms ways in which research and evaluation tools, of the sort we will learn about in this book, can be used to find out this information. That is, the social worker begins with needs that arise in practice and moves from there to appropriate research and evaluation tasks.

An inductive approach contrasts with a *deductive approach* to social work research and evaluation. A deductive approach typically begins with a theory or hypothesis that, in the researcher's judgment, should be tested. A theory is a systematic attempt to explain phenomena or facts. Social work scholars and practitioners construct theories to guide their practice. They might be interested in theories that attempt to explain phenomena such as why some people, but not others, become clinically depressed; the effect of executive directors' administrative style on staff productivity; factors that increase the likelihood of clients' changing; causes of poverty; and the relationship between community residents' racist attitudes and the incidence of hate crimes.

Some theories are ambitious and formal, for example, a theory concerning the relationship between the use of paradox in family therapy and client change or the relationship between client empowerment and the likelihood of escaping poverty. Other theories are much more informal and personal. Indeed, sometimes the term *theory* is used rather casually to refer to social workers' individual hunches about the way things work in practice. For example, I might have a "theory" about why a particular social worker on my staff is having difficulty completing certain administrative tasks. You might have a theory about why illegal drug activity is increasing in your neighborhood. A staff member at Mt. Washington might have a theory about the reasons that foster parents drop out of a program. What all theories have in common is that they try to explain and/or predict phenomena.

Theories typically generate hypotheses about the relationships among specific phenomena. In principle, a *hypothesis* is a claim or an assertion that something is true. In social work, hypotheses often make some claim about the effectiveness of a particular intervention approach or the causal relationships concerning a variety of social conditions and individual functioning. An example is that the higher the incidence is of community residents' racist attitudes in the Mt. Washington community, the higher the incidence of hate crimes will be in the community. Or court-ordered treatment of alcoholism is less likely to be effective than voluntary participation in alcoholism treatment. Both hypotheses make a claim about the relationship between phenomena. In principle, these claims can be tested. That is, we should be able to design a study and gather data to determine whether these hypotheses are true. The results may have some implications for practice.

Ideas for testing theories or hypotheses often reflect the researcher's academic interests. An example is a social work researcher who may be interested in exploring possible correlations between individuals' family-of-origin issues and anxiety disorders. This interest may be based on the researcher's earlier work experience and her familiarity with literature suggesting a possible connection between these phenomena. She may not be working with this population now but may have an academic interest in the causal connections between the two phenomena. Ultimately, she may be interested in the practical relevance of her work, but for now, she is interested only in generating knowledge for knowledge's sake.

Another example of the deductive approach is a social work researcher interested in the relationship between executive directors' administrative style, as portrayed in a well-known typology of administrative styles appearing in the literature, and staff morale in various human service organizations. This researcher may be interested in raising the staff's morale and would like to discover some useful insights into the impact of executive directors' administrative style. He may have no explicit interest in any particular human service agency; rather, he is interested in locating appropriate human service organizations that can participate in the study. Whether these agencies are likely to benefit directly from the study may not be important to him.

Using a deductive approach, the researcher moves from the general to the specific, that is, from a broad, conceptually based or theoretical concern to an attempt to explore empirically that concern in one or more settings. The aim is to create knowledge in the grand sense, as opposed to the aim of an inductive approach, whose goal is to gather information for a practical purpose.

As I mentioned earlier, social workers' views of the role of research in the profession have changed over the years. One of the most significant changes is the increasingly widespread recognition that most social workers need research and evaluation that can be directly and practically applied to their work—that is, inductive research and evaluation. Most practitioners have less need to learn about the theory construction and hypothesis testing that are more consistent with a deductive approach. This is not to minimize the value of knowledge created for knowledge's sake or the value of theories and hypotheses. But in the practice world, where most social workers function, practitioners need a solid command of research and evaluation skills with immediate relevance and application. Although theory and hypothesis testing are important to social work, the main purpose of this book is to teach social workers the practical skills and knowledge to enable them to use research and evaluation tools in their practice.

THE ANATOMY OF RESEARCH AND EVALUATION QUESTIONS

One of the most important skills for social workers to learn is the ability to formulate questions that may be answered using research and evaluation. Social workers are trained to identify compelling issues related to clinical practice, agency administration, community organization, and social welfare policy. Historically, however, social workers have not received comparable training to help them recognize when research and evaluation can help them carry out their professional responsibilities. Just as social workers need considerable education and apprenticeship to learn how to recognize complex clinical, organizational, community, and policy phenomena, they also need training to recognize and pursue opportunities to incorporate research and evaluation into their practice.

What does a social worker need to learn about research and evaluation? Many things, among which are the ability to formulate relevant research and evaluation questions or issues, design the appropriate methodology to collect pertinent information or data, analyze and interpret this information, and present the results in a way that is applicable to practice.

Let's take a closer look at the components of a question or issue that lends itself to research. Earlier in this chapter we stated that the clinical director of the substance abuse treatment program at the Mt. Washington Family Service

Agency wanted to know whether there was a difference between two approaches, individual and group counseling, with respect to clients' substance abuse problems. That is, does one of these approaches lead to a better outcome? The answer to this question is likely to have important consequences for the agency's treatment philosophy and approach, intake criteria, staffing patterns, and budget.

What I have just presented is the research and evaluation question: Is there a significant difference between the effectiveness of the individual- and group-counseling approaches to substance abuse treatment at the Mt. Washington Family Service Agency? This is a practical question, the answer to which is likely to have important implications for the agency. It is essential in social work that research and evaluation questions address issues that matter, as opposed to abstract or pie-in-the-sky issues that may have little or no relevance to practice. Social work is a profession dedicated to helping vulnerable clients, and so practitioners should not waste their time on abstractions that have nothing to do with the profession's core mission.

Embedded in this fairly straightforward question concerning the relative effectiveness of two counseling approaches to substance abuse treatment are several elements that are often found in research and evaluation questions. First we have *variables*, the phenomena or concepts that we study. In this example, we have two general variables, treatment approach and outcome. The clinical director of Mt. Washington's substance abuse treatment program wants to know whether there is a connection between these two variables.

Our other examples of research and evaluation activities at Mt. Washington focus on other variables. The example of Toby E. and his mother focuses on the variables of classroom intervention and behavior. That is, one of your goals as a social worker in this case would be to work with Toby's teacher to help her learn behavior management techniques that might improve Toby's classroom behavior. Similarly, the example of the effect of the state's stipend for foster parents on the retention rate also has two variables: the state's stipend and the retention rate.

To conduct research and evaluation, social workers need to be able to measure the phenomena and concepts that they are investigating. Without good measures, how could we find out about the concepts and variables we are examining? For example, it's fine to say that we are interested in whether Toby's schoolteacher's intervention had an effect on his classroom behavior. But if we don't have a good measure of his classroom behavior, what good does it do to ask the question?

Formulating good measures of concepts and variables requires *operational definitions.* We use operational definitions to help us move from rather abstract concepts—such as classroom behavior or self-esteem—to specific, concrete, and measurable indicators.

Take the example of evaluating the effectiveness of two different treatment approaches for the outcome of participants in Mt. Washington's substance abuse treatment program. How would we operationalize the variable of treatment approach? In this case, the variable, or concept, of the treatment approach is operationalized in the form of two specific techniques, individual and group counseling. More specifically, the operational definition of individual counseling is counseling given weekly by a social worker to one client at a time. Each weekly session lasts for fifty minutes. The operational definition of group counseling is counseling given weekly by a social worker to six to eight clients who meet together. Group sessions last for ninety minutes.

We also must operationalize the variable of treatment outcome. Usually, evaluations of the effectiveness of substance abuse treatment programs focus on, at the least, the participants' relapse rates. Studies operationalize relapse rates in different ways. Examples are the number of alcoholic drinks consumed or illegal drugs taken each week during a follow-up period (one year, say) after the termination of the treatment program and the number of readmissions to a substance abuse treatment program. Social workers can be, and should be, creative when they operationalize variables. In addition to relying on "hard" data, such as the actual number of drinks consumed (assuming we can obtain valid, accurate data on this), social workers should also routinely consider obtaining information from the clients themselves, about their perceptions of the services they received, significant events in their lives, and other information that conveys the clients' views of their outcome. Although some critics allege that such information is too "soft" and subjective, in my view it is no less valuable or relevant. In fact, some of the most useful information I have obtained in program evaluations has been based on clients' perceptions and opinions. It is true that such data must be analyzed carefully and that possible biases need to be taken into account, but this also is true of so-called hard data that allegedly provides "objective" information about a program's outcome.

Now let's look again at the example presented earlier concerning one of Mt. Washington's clinical social workers, Judy S., who wanted to determine the extent to which the clients on her caseload were manifesting symptoms of clinical depression. The key variable here is clinical depression. How would we operationalize that? We have several choices. One is to look for a standardized depression scale or instrument that is used for clinical purposes. A *standardized instrument* is one that has been developed and tested for a specific purpose. Standardized instruments measure a wide range of phenomena, including self-esteem, eating disorders, the quality of marital and parent–child relationships, employee burnout, and substance abuse.

In many instances, social workers construct their own measure, because there is something they do not like about the available standardized instruments or because no standardized instrument exists that measures exactly what the social worker wants to measure. (Later on I will have much more to say about how social workers can assess the quality and appropriateness of standardized instruments and how one designs one's own instrument.)

In addition, the social worker in this case, Judy S., might ask her clients for their subjective descriptions of their feelings and moods, that is, their own "stories" about their life. This information is *qualitative* data.

Learning how to operationalize variables is a challenge. There are no simple tricks of the trade; experience tends to be the best teacher. There are, however, some guidelines that social workers can follow to get started. First, identify the *directly relevant* indicators of a variable. If Judy S. is interested in measuring her clients' symptoms of depression, she must identify those aspects of their depression that are relevant to symptoms of it. Would it make sense to operationalize the concept of depression by gathering information on clients' perceptions of the quality of their job or their marriage? Certainly, clients' feelings about their jobs and marriages may be related to their feelings of depression, but questions about jobs and marriages in themselves do not directly relate to depression. This information may help explain why clients feel depressed but is not a good operational indicator of the concept of depression. It is too indirect and would require Judy S. to make inferential leaps about the relationship between the quality of one's job or marriage and one's feelings of depression.

It would be much better to identify commonly accepted symptoms of depression and to create questions that pertain directly to those symptoms (or find a standardized instrument that does the job). How should a social worker do this? What I would do is blitz the literature on depression and take good notes on the conventional thinking about the kinds of behaviors and attitudes manifested by people who are feeling depressed. Presumably this literature is based on the latest research evidence regarding symptoms of clinical depression, such as thinking about suicide, loss of appetite (or excessive eating), loss of interest in sexual activity, feeling blue or down in the dumps, and having difficulty sleeping (or sleeping excessively).

After I had listed what appeared to be good indicators of the concept, I would move to the second criterion of a good operational definition: the indicators must be *clear and unambiguous*. Most of us would agree that "loss of appetite" and "loss of interest in sexual activity" are clear and unambiguous. But what about "feeling blue or down in the dumps"? Is this one clear and unambiguous? My guess is that all of us have some general understanding of what this question means, but it doesn't seem quite as clear and unambiguous as "loss of appetite" and "loss of interest in sexual activity." Although it may be necessary at times to include operational indicators that are somewhat vague—because no better indicator exists—as a general rule, you should try to stick with indicators that are crystal clear and unambiguous.

Finally, the indicators must be *measurable*. Some operational indicators are easy to measure. If Judy S. were to gather demographic information about her clients' sex, age, and ethnicity, her job would be easy. We don't need a graduate degree in demography to figure out how to measure "male," "female," years (age), and ethnic origin (although we might quibble some about which ethnic groups to include).

But look what happens when we get to an operational indicator like "thinks about committing suicide." How do we measure this? I bet that if we put ten experienced social work researchers in a room (now there's a scary thought) and asked them to find a good way to measure the extent to which Judy S.'s clients at Mt. Washington think about committing suicide, we would end up with many different proposals. I doubt that all the social workers would agree. One possibility is a question like "During a typical week, how often do you think about committing suicide?" The response choices might be "never," "once or twice," and "three or more times." Another possibility is "Please indicate the extent to which the following statement describes your feelings: Sometimes I think about committing suicide." The response choices might be "a great deal," "somewhat," and "not at all." Still another possibility is to use an agree–disagree scale, asking clients to indicate the extent to which they agree or disagree with a statement like "Committing suicide is a good solution to my problems." The response choices would be "strongly agree," "agree," "disagree," and "strongly disagree."

It is also possible that one of those social workers in the room would reject the idea of using one of these scales. She might prefer what is called an *open-ended question*, which asks clients to describe, in their own words, the extent to which they think about committing suicide. This qualitative approach is equally legitimate.

Recently I read a summary of a project designed to create a list of outcome indicators related to work with vulnerable children and their families—children who grow up in poverty, children who have been abused or neglected, delinquent children, children with psychiatric or substance abuse problems, and the parents of these children. One of the project's goals was to produce standardized operational definitions of key variables, so that the results of programs designed to help children and families could be compared. Some of the outcome indicators were fewer school dropouts, truants and suspensions; less incidence of poverty, inadequate housing, school-age pregnancy, substance abuse, sexually transmitted diseases, out-of-home placements, child abuse, suicide, homicide, and arrests; greater self-sufficiency; and increased rates of high school completion.

All these seem to be reasonable outcome measures that might be used to monitor or evaluate a program at Mt. Washington providing services to vulnerable children and families in the community. For the most part, these indicators seem to be relevant, clear, unambiguous, and measurable.

Why do I say "for the most part"? I have no doubt about the indicators' relevance. All of them seem to be tied directly to the basic welfare of children. That's not the problem. Furthermore, most of the indicators seem fairly clear, unambiguous, and measurable. Assuming that the data are available from local public or private agencies (for example, welfare agencies, school departments, criminal justice agencies, health departments)—and that the data are valid and reliable—indicators such as dropout rates, high school completion, school-age pregnancy, and arrests should be just fine.

But what about an operational indicator like self-sufficiency? How does one define self-sufficiency? Is it indicated by parents' employment status, family income, housing circumstances, access to a car, the extent to which a child is involved in an enmeshed relationship with his or her parents, a psychological "feeling" of independence, or what? Various social workers are likely to define this concept differently. That's one problem, although it is not insurmountable.

Another problem is coming up with hard data on the variable. Assuming that social workers could agree on a precise, clear, and unambiguous definition of self-sufficiency, where would the data come from? Public and private agencies do not routinely gather all this information, although they may collect some of it. Thus social workers would have to find practical ways to measure the variable.

As we will see later, even variables that seem easy to operationalize may present a problem. For example, suppose we are interested in the extent to which a program at Mt. Washington reduces the incidence of delinquent acts committed by youths participating in the program. At first, it might seem easy to measure delinquency; we simply rely on arrest records from the local police department.

But before we know it, we've got a problem—actually, a couple of problems. One is that the police never find out about lots of delinquent acts because in many cases the victims decide that it's just not worth the trouble to report an incident. Those data never show up in the police department's statistics.

In addition, arrest figures can be inaccurate. Sloppy record keeping may lead to a distorted profile of local delinquency rates. Hence, arrest data can be misleading. What we have here, then, is a good illustration of what may appear on the surface to be good, solid, and reliable information with which to operationalize a variable—arrest data obtained from a law enforcement agency. It sounds good, and it has an authoritative ring of authenticity, doesn't it? When we scratch beneath the surface, however, we discover problems that raise questions about how measurable this phenomenon really is.

The main point is that some variables are easy to operationalize, some are moderately difficult to operationalize, and some are so hard to operationalize that you're tempted to scrap the whole project (when this happens, it's usually a good idea to do something mindless like washing dirty clothes or watching a silly television program, and return to the daunting task once your blood pressure has gone back down). Consulting with colleagues can be enormously useful. I am continually amazed at how helpful it can be to get my colleagues' opinions on operational definitions (and just about all other aspects of the research and evaluation process). Despite my experience in the field, sometimes I just miss the obvious or fail to consider reasonable options—or I could just be having a bad day and need the benefit of my colleagues' better judgment.

Some research and evaluation projects focus on only one variable. For example, if Judy S. is interested only in the extent of clinical depression among her clients, she would be focusing on only one variable.

Frequently, however, social workers are interested in more than one variable. Maybe Judy S. is interested simultaneously in her clients' depression symptoms, self-esteem, and use of illegal substances. Each of these variables should be operationalized.

Another possibility, one that occurs quite often in social work, is that practitioners are interested in exploring the presence of a *causal relationship* between variables. This makes sense in light of the frequency with which social workers introduce an intervention (the cause) to bring about a change (the effect). This is the case in the example of Mt. Washington's substance abuse treatment program. The program's clinical director wants to know whether there is a causal relationship, or a cause-and-effect relationship, between the agency's two treatment approaches (individual and group counseling) and outcome (less frequent or reduced substance abuse).

CAUSAL RELATIONSHIPS IN SOCIAL WORK RESEARCH

Understanding the nature of causal or cause–effect relationships in social work is tricky. First let's get some terminology out of the way. The variables that we treat as the cause of something are *independent variables*, and the variables that we treat as the effect, or outcome, of the intervention are *dependent variables*. In our example, the treatment approach (individual versus group counseling) is the independent variable (the cause), and the relapse rate is a dependent variable (the effect or outcome).

For many causal relationships, it is important for social workers to understand the possible influence of *antecedent* and *intervening variables*. As the prefix of antecedent suggests, an *ante*cedent variable is one that "comes before" or precedes an independent variable and influences the independent variable. In contrast, an *intervening variable* is one that "comes between" the independent and dependent variables; thus the independent variable has a causal influence on the intervening variable, which, in turn, has a causal influence on the dependent variable.

This probably sounds rather abstract, so let's consider an example. Let's go back to the case of Toby E., whose mother and teacher were having some difficulty managing his behavior. According to Toby's mother, Toby is often aggressive with her and with other children. That is, he has a tendency to push, shove, and hit when he gets frustrated or doesn't get his way.

One day, Toby's social worker was reading the local newspaper, in which was an article whose headline read "Study Results: TV Watching and Aggression Linked in Children." Toby's social worker read the article with considerable interest, not only because of her involvement with Toby and his mother, but also because she frequently had cases of children with problems with aggressive behavior.

According to the newspaper article, prominent researchers at a well-known university extensively studied the causal relationship between television watching and aggressive behavior. They gathered data on the number of hours a large sample of children watched television and how often they engaged in aggressive behavior with other children in a playroom used for the study. The article reported that there was "strong evidence of a connection between children's television viewing and aggressive behavior. Children who watched more television were much more likely to engage in aggressive behavior than children who watched less television."

The newspaper article included reactions from several local schoolteachers, parents, and counselors. According to one of the counselors interviewed, "This is a profoundly important study. Many of us have sensed for quite some time that violence on television stimulates aggression in children. Clearly, we must do something to reduce children's exposure to these TV shows."

The implication of the newspaper article is that there is a causal relationship between television viewing and children's aggression. In the study, the independent variable is television watching, and the dependent variable is aggression. The independent variable was operationally defined as the number of hours each child watched television during an average week (parents recorded children's television-watching patterns), and aggression was operationally defined as the frequency of specific behaviors displayed by the children in the playroom. These behaviors were pushing, hitting, biting, kicking, and yelling at other children (trained observers recorded the frequency with which these behaviors occurred).

Assuming that the newspaper article accurately reported the study's methodology and findings (not always a safe assumption, I have learned), what are the implications? Specifically, what relevance might these findings have for Toby's social worker?

My guess is that many social workers would conclude that this study's results suggest that an effective way to reduce the occurrence of children's aggressive behavior is to reduce the amount of television they watch (particularly programs containing violence and acts of aggression). There may be, in fact, some merit to this line of reasoning, but based on this study, can we say this for sure? Clinically, is this the wisest path to travel down? Is the most appropriate intervention working with a child's parents to reduce the amount of time the child watches television? I doubt it.

Why not? This little scenario is a good example of the reasons that social workers should understand antecedent and intervening variables and the nature of causal relationships. Let's assume for the moment that the study's results do in fact support a strong correlation between television watching and children's aggressive behavior. Is it safe to assume that this is a strong causal relationship?

As we will see in a moment, there is an important difference between *correlational* and *causal* relationships. What is the likelihood that the main cause of the children's aggressive behavior is watching television? Let's think this through—first, the possible differences between children who watch a lot of television and those who do not. What might account for this difference? Perhaps the parents of children who do and do not watch a lot of television have different parenting styles. Perhaps the parents of children who watch a lot of television are less likely to read to their children or encourage them to play indoor and outdoor games. Children who watch a lot of television are more sedentary and thus have fewer opportunities to release pent-up energy. Perhaps these children live in more chaotic households where the television is used as a convenient electronic babysitter. Some of their aggressive behavior in play with other children may reflect this lifestyle. If this is true, should we be surprised that children who watch a lot of television are more likely to engage in aggressive behavior?

I cannot prove, of course, that these factors really account for much of the children's aggressive behavior—to do so would require an entirely different study. But I think I have raised some important doubts that a social worker reading this newspaper article must consider. If I am right, we have here some antecedent and intervening variables that are related to these more obvious independent (the television watching) and dependent (the children's aggressive behavior) variables. Perhaps the parents' lifestyle and parenting style influence the amount of television the children watch. If that is so, the parents' lifestyle and parenting style are antecedent variables. That is, they have some causal influence on the independent variable with which we began our analysis. In turn, large amounts of time spent watching television may lead to a buildup of children's unspent energy, which may then be expressed in the form of aggressive behavior during play with other children. If this is so, the buildup of the children's unreleased energy is an intervening variable. That is, the energy is influenced by the independent variable (the time spent watching television) and, in turn, influences the dependent variable (the children's aggressive behavior). This possible relationship is displayed in figure 2.2.

How should a clinical social worker account for this? A social worker who is shortsighted and interprets the study's results superficially might be inclined to work with parents to reduce the amount of time their children watch television. Perhaps this would have some beneficial effect. But how effective is this approach likely to be if the bulk of the problem is related to the way the parents rear their children (an antecedent variable)? It might be more constructive for a social worker to attend also to parenting skills. Better parenting skills may have longer-lasting effects if the antecedent variable—parenting skills— has more to do with the children's aggressive behavior than does the amount of time the children spend watching television.

You can see how important it is for social workers to understand the nature of causal relationships and how easy it is to confuse correlation with causation. Many phenomena are correlated, but evidence of correlation is not evidence of causation. To illustrate: If I were to arise each morning at 5:00 A.M. and beat a drum in my backyard, I bet light would appear in the sky not too long there-

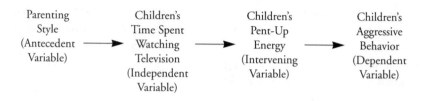

| Parenting Style (Antecedent Variable) | Children's Time Spent Watching Television (Independent Variable) | Children's Pent-Up Energy (Intervening Variable) | Children's Aggressive Behavior (Dependent Variable) |

FIGURE 2.2   Hypothetical Causal Relationship

after. In fact, I bet there would be a perfect correlation between my drum beating and the appearance of light. Does that mean that my drum beating *caused*
the appearance of the light? Of course not. Another way to state this is that
correlation does not imply causation. Correlation is an essential component of
causation (two phenomena must be correlated if there is a causal relationship
between them, right?), but by itself, correlation is not sufficient evidence of
causation. (Academicians like to say that correlation is a necessary but not a
sufficient condition of causation.)

Let's apply this thinking to the situation at Mt. Washington in which the
clinical director of the agency's substance abuse treatment program wants to
compare the effectiveness of individual and group counseling. Suppose these
treatment approaches are implemented with different groups of clients. Mt.
Washington's staff somehow measure the relapse rates of the two groups' participants, and the results suggest that the group-counseling approach is more
effective. The participants in this group had a 19 percent lower relapse rate
than did the clients who received individual counseling.

Can we conclude therefore that these results are evidence of a causal relationship between the treatment approach (the independent variable) and the
outcome or relapse rate (the dependent variable)? It is tempting to say yes,
given the correlation between treatment approach and outcome.

Not so fast! This conclusion could be wrong because of the influence of
other variables. One of the things we need to ask is whether the clinical pro-
files of the two groups' clients were comparable. Although there was considerable variation within both groups, were the groups' overall substance abuse histories, family circumstances, demographic characteristics, and so on similar? If
the answer is no, we have a major problem.

Let's assume that when the clients were assigned to the two groups by the
social worker conducting the intake interviews, he tended to assign to the
"individual-counseling" track the more serious cases (those with longer sub-

stance abuse histories, more extensive prior treatment experience). The intake interviewer may have been benevolently biased in that she believed that the more serious cases required more intensive help and that this help was more likely to be forthcoming in individual counseling. If this is what happened, the cases assigned to group counseling may have been less severe and perhaps more responsive to treatment. In this respect, the deck may have been stacked from the beginning in a way that favored the group-counseling approach. It would be difficult to determine whether the superior results for those who participated in group counseling were caused by the treatment approach itself, whether these cases were less serious to begin with and the clients less likely to have relapses, or both. As we shall see later, there is a way to design a study to avoid this confusion.

How do we know whether we ever have evidence of a causal relationship in social work? Three main conditions must be met to demonstrate that a causal relationship exists.

1. The independent variable (the cause) must precede the dependent variable (the effect) in time.
2. There must be a correlation between the independent variable and the dependent variable.
3. All other possible causes must be ruled out and accounted for.

The first condition is not very complicated. After all, how could one variable cause another if the first did not precede the second in time? Obviously, to argue that children's television watching causes them to behave more aggressively, you must have evidence that the television viewing occurred before the aggressive behavior. Similarly, if staff members at Mt. Washington want to demonstrate that their group-counseling approach to substance abuse treatment is superior to their individual-counseling approach, the intervention (the independent variable) must precede the outcome (the dependent variable, measured by the relapse rate) in time.

So far, so good. But what about the second condition—that there must be evidence of a correlation between the independent and dependent variables? This one is only slightly more complicated. If we argue that children's television viewing causes their aggressive behavior, we must be able to present evidence of a strong correlation between these two variables.

What is a correlation? A correlation occurs when an increase or decrease in the value or magnitude of one variable is associated with an increase or decrease in the value or magnitude of a second variable. Notice that I said "associated with." I did not say that an increase or decrease in the value or magnitude of one variable *causes* an increase or decrease in the value or magnitude

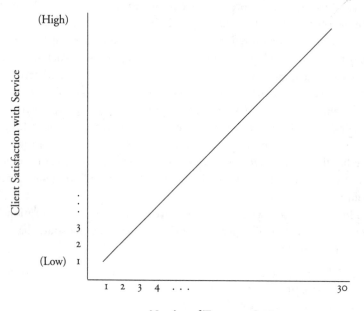

Number of Treatment Sessions

FIGURE 2.3   Positive Correlation

of a second variable. That would be premature, since we still are dealing with only the second of the three conditions required to demonstrate a causal relationship between two variables.

In the television-watching example, a strong correlation would exist if there were a clear pattern showing that children who spend more time watching television behave more aggressively than do children who spend less time watching television. There may be some exceptions, but a correlation must show a definite pattern along these lines. Correlations between variables can be strong, moderate, weak, or nonexistent.

Social workers should be able to recognize three major kinds of correlations: positive, inverse, and curvilinear. A *positive correlation* shows an *increase* in the value or magnitude of one variable associated with an *increase* in the value or magnitude of a second variable, or a *decrease* in the value or magnitude of one variable associated with a *decrease* in the value or magnitude of a second variable.

Suppose the clinical director at Mt. Washington finds evidence of a positive correlation between the number of treatment sessions and clients' satisfaction with the services they received from the agency. This would mean that those

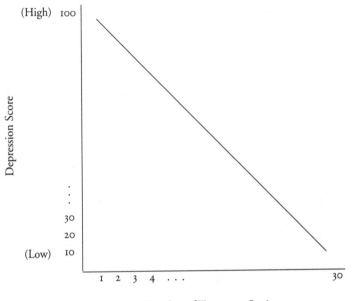

FIGURE 2.4   Inverse Correlation

clients who attended more counseling sessions tended to be more satisfied with the services and those clients who attended fewer counseling sessions tended to be less satisfied with the services. This is a good example of a positive correlation (see figure 2.3).

In contrast, an *inverse correlation* would show an *increase* in the value or magnitude of one variable associated with a *decrease* in the value or magnitude of a second variable (or vice versa: a *decrease* in the value or magnitude of one variable is associated with an *increase* in the value or magnitude of a second variable). For example, Mt. Washington's clinical director would have evidence of an inverse correlation if she found that those clients who attended more counseling sessions tended to have lower depression scores on a standardized instrument and that those clients who attended fewer counseling sessions tended to have higher depression scores (see figure 2.4).

A *curvilinear relationship* is quite different. Positive and inverse correlations have what researchers call a *linear* relationship between the two variables. That is, as the value or magnitude of one variable increases (or decreases), the value of the other variable increases (or decreases). The higher the value of one vari-

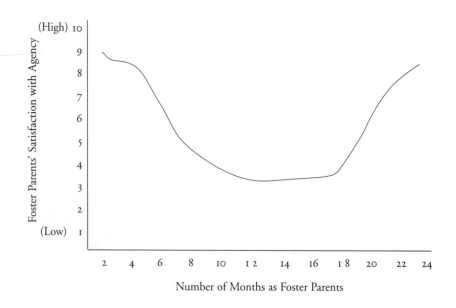

FIGURE 2.5   Curvilinear Relationship

able is, the higher (or lower, in the case of an inverse relationship) the value of the other variable will be, with no or relatively few exceptions. When you graph various pairs of scores—that is, the pair of scores that each client, family, or whatever would have on the two variables—the points form a line or a pattern that looks like a line, hence the name *line*ar.

Curvilinear relationships show a very different pattern. Instead of the pattern of points looking like a line, they look like a curve. What this means, for instance, is that lower scores on one variable may be associated with both higher and lower scores on the other variable. Or lower scores on one variable may be associated with moderately high scores and also very high scores on the other variable. Different curvilinear relationships produce different kinds of curves.

Let's consider a couple of examples to illustrate this. Suppose that as part of Mt. Washington's study of foster parent retention, the staff decided to examine the relationship between the number of months that foster parents participated in the program and their satisfaction with the agency. One of the agency's social workers wondered whether these two variables had an inverse relationship, that as the number of months or years in the program increased, the foster parents' satisfaction with the agency decreased—a linear relationship. To the staff's surprise, the relationship turned out to be curvilinear. That is, foster parents tended to be more positive about Mt. Washington's administration of the foster care program both early in their involvement (during the first six months or so) and after they had been with the program for quite some time (more than eighteen months). During the middle period (between six and eighteen months), however, foster parents were more likely to be dissatisfied. This sort of pattern produces a curve that resembles a horseshoe (see figure 2.5).

How can we explain this? One possibility is that many foster parents' satisfaction with the agency declined over time and that those who were unhappy dropped out but that those who were able to resolve their concerns or who felt positively about the program all along and stayed in it (and thus were in the program long enough to be able to comment on their attitudes after eighteen months of participation) were likely to respond favorably to questions about the agency's administration of the program. If this is what happened, the result would be a curvilinear relationship, with shorter and longer periods of participation correlated with more positive perceptions of the agency's performance.

Let's say that the social worker in this example also wanted to explore the relationship between the foster parents' ages and the length of their participation in the program. He wondered whether younger foster parents had more energy for dealing with challenging foster children and hence were less likely to drop out of the program. If this were the case, we would have a linear correlation (as age increases, the likelihood of dropping out of the program increases). To explore this correlation, the social worker looked at the association between the foster parents' age at the time they entered the program (in the case of couples who served as foster parents, the average of the two ages was used) and the length of time they stayed in the program. The sample of cases included all those foster parents who entered the program exactly ten years ago. The social worker used this time interval to have an adequate follow-up period.

The data suggest an interesting curvilinear pattern (see figure 2.6): between the ages of 25 and 35 it looks like a positive linear correlation but begins to change at age 38. Between the ages of 36 and 45 there does not appear to be much correlation at all, as indicated by the flat line in this interval. That is, between the ages of 38 and 45, the length of time in the program stays about the same (approximately three years). After age 45, however, there is a decline in the curve, indicating that those foster parents who began in the program during their middle-age years or later tended to drop out rather quickly. It's hard to know, of course, the reason for this pattern. There are all kinds of possibilities related to the age gap between children in foster care and foster parents, the amount of physical energy required to care for children in foster care, and so on. In any case, understanding that the relationship between these two variables is curvilinear—at least at this one agency—gives the staff lots to think about. This information can feed discussion about the reasons for this pattern and the pattern's implications for the agency's approach to foster parent recruitment, training, and retention.

These are only two examples of curvilinear relationships. As you might imagine, some curvilinear relationships resemble horseshoes (they can be right-side up, upside down, or sideways), and some look like an S (they can be forward, backward, or sideways). Some of the curves are obvious and some are subtle. Put simply, any relationship that is not linear, or nearly linear, is curvilinear, at least to some degree.

As I said earlier, correlation is an essential ingredient or necessary condition in causal relationships. This, too, should be obvious. How could we say that there is a causal connection between children's television watching and their aggressive behavior if there was not a clear correlation between these two variables? If some children who watch a lot of television behave aggressively but other children who watch a lot of children do not behave aggressively, one or more factors must account for the aggressive behavior; television watching by itself could not be the principal cause, since some children who watch a lot of television do not behave aggressively. Therefore, correlation is a necessary but not a sufficient condition of a causal relationship between two variables. And as I also said earlier, many things (or variables) in the world are correlated but not causally related (like the example of the drum beating and the sunrise).

The third condition of causality is, without question, the most complicated and difficult to satisfy. Here we must be able to show that all other factors or possible causes have been ruled out. That's quite a challenge, particularly in social work, as we may be dealing with zillions of possible causes of the outcomes we observe in clients' behavior or emotional status, community well-being, agency stability, and so on.

We often refer to these possible other causes as *extraneous factors*, and we have already encountered some of them. Remember the confusion concerning the possible causal relationship between children's television watching and their aggressive behavior? One possible extraneous factor in that example is what researchers sometimes call *contemporaneous events*. Contemporaneous events are all those other things that might be going on at the same time as the

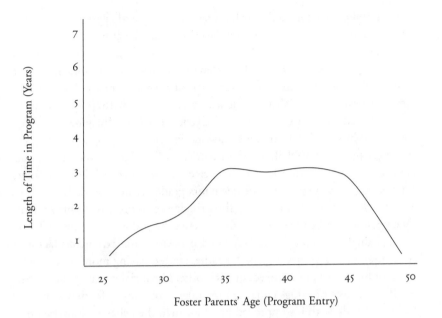

FIGURE 2.6 Curvilinear Relationship

intervention, or presumed cause, whether they are events that occur in the clients' lives, in the agencies that serve the clients, or in the communities where they live. In the television-watching example, contemporaneous events could include the fact that children who watch a lot of television may also have parents who do not pay a great deal of attention to them, do not arrange for their children to participate in other structured activities, and so on. Thus the contemporaneous effects of parenting style may have something to do with the children's aggressive behavior, apart from whatever effects television watching by itself might have.

Another extraneous factor is known as *historical events*, or the characteristics or attributes that clients, organizations, communities, and so on already possess before an intervention or some other allegedly causal factor is introduced. For example, children who watch a great deal of television may have already been raised in a certain fashion that contributes to their aggressive behavior. That is, there may be a correlation between these children's past upbringing and their present television-watching habits. If the children's upbringing can explain their aggressive behavior and their television-watching habits are only an incidental by-product of their parenting, we can conclude that the real causal connection is between parenting and aggressive behavior. The television watching may not be the critical causal factor.

In many instances, we need to be concerned about an extraneous factor that researchers call *maturation*, which is often present when social workers explore an intervention's effect on clients over a period of time. Suppose that you were the caseworker at Mt. Washington who was working with Toby E. and his teacher to reduce Toby's problematic behavior in school. Imagine that when you and Toby's teacher started a behavioral intervention program, she began to collect information daily on the frequency of his "acting-out" behaviors. Let's say the intervention lasted for twelve weeks. Based on the data Toby's teacher collected, his acting-out behaviors gradually decreased. Is it safe to assume that the intervention was the principal cause of this improvement? One possibility, of course, is that there were other things going on in Toby's life that might account for his improved behavior—the extraneous factor of contemporaneous events. Maybe his father started having more contact with Toby, or his nutrition improved, or his mother's financial picture got a lot better. If these sorts of things enhanced the quality of Toby's life, they may have had more to do with his improved behavior than the behavioral intervention did.

Events in Toby's past—historical events—might also have contributed to his improved behavior. Perhaps he received some treatment from another social worker earlier in the year, and his improved behavior in the classroom was a delayed effect of this past intervention.

Another possibility is that Toby simply matured or "grew up" during the behavioral intervention introduced by Toby's teacher. That is, if maturation were a factor, we would conclude that his behavior would have improved anyway, even without the behavioral intervention.

Maturation is often an extraneous factor in social work. Since social workers often are interested in changing people's lives, there is always the possibility that whatever change they discern is—at least in part—a result of maturation, as opposed to intervention. Changes in such things as clients' feelings of self-esteem, attitudes toward illegal drug use, criminal behavior, and parenting skills may be due to the mere passage of time and the kind of maturing that many people experience when left to their own devices.

The final category of extraneous factors—*testing*—is a bit different. Social workers evaluating the effectiveness of their interventions need to find evidence of change. If we are trying to help a Mt. Washington client feel less depressed, we might have him fill out a standardized depression scale every week during his treatment. If we are trying to increase the employment rate in the community served by Mt. Washington, we might collect weekly employment data. If we are trying to improve morale among staff members at Mt. Washington, we might have them respond periodically to a questionnaire that addresses morale-related issues. It is possible, in these instances, that some of the change we detect over time—for example, in the client's depression scores, the community's employment rate, and staff morale—may be due to the way we collected the data. Perhaps the client who was feeling depressed wanted to please his social worker and thus exaggerated his "positive" responses on the depression scale. Or while the staff at Mt. Washington were monitoring local unemployment figures, the state agency responsible for data collection changed its definition of unemployment. Changes in the definition or operationalization of a concept while data are being collected obviously can distort the picture. What may appear to be an improved employment climate in the Mt. Washington community may merely reflect changes in the middle of the data collection period in the state agency's definition of what counts as a job. Similarly, changes in the staff's morale may reflect their concern about giving negative or critical feedback to their administrators. Some staff members may worry that if they complain too much, their job will be in jeopardy. They may therefore "sugarcoat" some of their answers about their morale, leading to a false or misleading picture of what is really going on in the agency.

In summary, four major categories of extraneous factors can account for what may at first appear to be a causal relationship: contemporaneous events, historical events, maturation, and testing. One of the major challenges in social work is to try to account for, explain, or rule out the influence of these extraneous factors when exploring a causal connection between factors, especially between interventions and outcomes. In chapters 3 and 4, I will talk more about how social workers deal with extraneous factors.

An Example of Distinguishing Correlation and Causation

We need to be sure that we understand the difference between correlation and causation, as it is one of the most important points in this book. Let's take a look at another program at the Mt. Washington Family Service Agency. In this program, social workers at the agency provide services to a group of adolescents having difficulty with their parents. The group meets for three months. Most of the clients are between the ages of fourteen and sixteen and were referred to the agency by a school counselor, but some of the youths were referred by their parents.

The group, which usually numbers eight, meets weekly. The group is facilitated by a staff social worker and an MSW student intern. The primary purpose of the group is to give the youths an opportunity to talk about their relationship with their parents and to brainstorm ways of dealing with these issues. The group is also designed to raise the members' self-esteem, which is often low, and to improve their ability to resolve conflicts with their parents.

The social worker who is responsible for this group, Alan F., has decided to monitor the youths' self-esteem and the quality of their relationship with their parents while the youths participate in the counseling group. Alan F. looked through several texts to find easy-to-administer scales designed to measure self-esteem and the quality of adolescents' relationships with their parents. He finally settled on two that could be administered in about eight minutes (Alan F. did not want to irritate any of the youths with time-consuming data collection instruments).

Alan F. administered the "self-esteem" and "quality of relationship" scales to the youths at the beginning of their participation in the group and again after six weeks and twelve weeks. After compiling the results, Alan F. detected a clear pattern. The average self-esteem score for the group increased substantially between the first and twelfth weeks, indicating an impressive improvement in the youths' self-esteem. In addition, the scores on the quality-of-relationship scale also rose, although not quite as dramatically as the self-esteem scores.

Alan F. was delighted and eager to share the impressive results with his colleagues and supervisor. This is just the sort of information he had been hoping for to demonstrate the value of the group.

What do you think of Alan F.'s enthusiasm? Is it safe for him to assume that the intervention—the adolescent support group—is what caused the improved scores? We would certainly hope that the intervention is what led to the improved scores. After all, that's what social workers aim for. But we need to take a closer look at how well Alan F.'s analysis of the information satisfies the conditions we just reviewed concerning evidence of a causal relationship between an intervention and outcome.

The first condition, remember, is that the intervention must precede the outcome in time. This condition is not difficult to meet in this case, as the intervention did occur before the final self-esteem and quality-of-relationship scores were obtained.

The second condition is that there must be evidence of a correlation between the two variables. This condition also seems to be satisfied, in that the change in the youths' scores coincided with the intervention. We can't yet say that there is a causal relationship between the variables, but at least we have evidence of a correlation.

Now comes that demanding, and often confounding, third condition: ruling out or accounting for the influence of extraneous factors. Here we seem to have a problem. One possibility is that other events, activities, or circumstances took place in the youths' lives at the same time as they were in the support group and that these other phenomena influenced the youths' self-esteem apart from the intervention itself. The self-esteem of some of the youths may have improved because of other treatment programs they were in at other social service agencies or because of success at school, not because of the Mt. Washington support group. The quality of the youths' relationships with their parents may have improved because of changes in their parents' behavior following marriage counseling or because of other important events in their parents' lives (for example, substance abuse treatment or a new job). Thus, the extraneous factor of contemporaneous events may have something to do with the changes in the youths' scores.

The extraneous factor of testing could also be important. Some of the youths may have guessed that Alan F. was evaluating the effectiveness of the support group, and when they read the questions on the two scales at the beginning of the intervention, they may have figured out what Alan F. was striving for. Hence, when the same instruments were administered some weeks later, some of them may have exaggerated their responses to please Alan F. or for some other reason (perhaps to place themselves in a better light for self-esteem purposes). Thus, increases in the youths' scores may have been a result of the measurement or testing, as opposed to the intervention itself.

The extraneous factor of maturation could also be important. This intervention dealt with a client group—adolescents—who are experiencing many changes in their lives. Social workers know quite well that adolescence is a period when many developmental changes take place. It certainly is possible that some of the changes in the youths' scores were a result of these "normal" developmental changes or maturation, as opposed to the intervention.

In light of these various possibilities, can we really say that the adolescent support group was the sole cause of the youths' improved scores? Unfortunately, no. I say unfortunately because it would be nice to be able to attribute these positive results to the social worker's diligent efforts. As much as we might want to conclude this, however, we simply don't have the evidence to back up such a claim. The research design in this case—following one group of clients over a period of time—simply isn't adequate if we want to make claims about the causal effectiveness of a social work intervention. This is frustrating, especially when we realize how common this scenario is in social work. It is important, therefore, for social workers to understand the limitations of this kind of design and to avoid making conclusions about the causal effectiveness of social service interventions when data are not available to support them.

3

DESIGNING SOCIAL WORK RESEARCH AND EVALUATION

Now that you understand the various ways that research and evaluation skills can be applied to social work, we are ready to discuss actually doing so. A research and evaluation design is similar to a detailed road map showing how to get from point A (the initial research or evaluation question) to point B (the acquisition of information or data that enables social workers to answer this question). These designs contain the directions and elements needed to carry out the research and evaluation.

In this chapter we review a number of concepts related to the research and evaluation designs that social workers use for exploratory, descriptive, and explanatory/evaluative research and evaluation. We focus on basic research and evaluation design issues related to both direct practice with individual clients, families, and groups and indirect practice regarding agency administration, community organizing, advocacy, social welfare policy, and other "social change" activities. In subsequent chapters we examine a number of finer-grained details related to research and evaluation methodology, for example, sampling, measurement, data collection, and data analysis. Throughout the discussion I use examples from the Mt. Washington Family Service Agency.

Which of the various research and evaluation designs social workers choose to use depends on the particular kind of research and evaluation they are interested in. A design appropriate for an explanatory/evaluative project is different from one suitable for a descriptive project. For example, in chapter 2, I described an exploratory project in which a Mt. Washington social worker wanted to know whether her clients with eating disorder problems also might have problems with self-esteem. Her plan was to ask her clients a few simple questions about their self-esteem and then ask each one to complete a simple, standardized self-esteem scale.

This use of research skills calls for a straightforward design. The social worker collects information or data at only one time—like a snapshot of her clients' self-esteem issues. She doesn't plan to evaluate the effectiveness of her intervention or to monitor her clients' status over time. This isn't very complicated, is it?

But now consider one of the other examples presented in chapter 2, in which a Mt. Washington social worker was interested in comparing the effectiveness of the agency's one-on-one and group-counseling approaches to substance abuse treatment (specifically, cocaine abuse). Recall that the agency had begun using a group-treatment approach, in part because of budget shortfalls and because several Mt. Washington social workers actually preferred a group-treatment approach in their work with substance abusers.

Clearly, this kind of situation poses a different, more complicated challenge. It wouldn't be enough for the social worker to simply take a one-time "snapshot" of the clients' status. What help would that be if staff members were interested in the effectiveness of these two intervention approaches *over time?* At the very least they would have to collect data at two times—one before and one after the intervention—to determine whether the change in the participants' substance abuse patterns differed. This situation thus calls for a somewhat more complicated research design.

Let's start by looking at research and evaluation designs that are useful in direct practice with individual clients, couples, groups, and families. In general, two kinds of social work research and evaluation designs are appropriate for direct practice: those that focus on individual clients, one case at a time, and those that focus on groups of clients. I use the term *client* broadly, to include individual people, couples, groups, and families.

Most social work research and evaluation that focus on one case at a time are concerned with individual people, because most social workers are engaged in direct practice with individual clients. Research designs that concentrate on individual cases have several different names: single-system designs, single-case designs, and $N = 1$ designs (the letter N is commonly used to symbolize the size of a research or evaluation study's sample; thus designs involving one case are often referred to as $N = 1$ designs). I prefer the term *single-case design* because I think it is the clearest and most informative of the various terms, and it is the one I use throughout this book.

The second kind of social work research and evaluation design is suitable for projects in which information is gathered about groups of clients, whether they are individuals, families, or groups. These are called *group designs*.

As we have already seen, both single-case and group designs may be appropriate when social workers are interested in gathering information about some aspect of direct practice. Hence we need to learn about both.

SINGLE-CASE RESEARCH AND EVALUATION DESIGNS

Under what circumstances would a social worker use a single-case design? The first instance is when a social worker wants to *monitor* a client's progress in some way. This circumstance is roughly comparable to what I referred to earlier as descriptive projects.

Consider a Mt. Washington social worker who is counseling a twenty-nine-year-old woman, Ms. L., who has been battered by her husband on a number of occasions. Ms. L. was referred to the family services unit of Mt. Washington by the local police department after Ms. L.'s most recent call to the police for help.

A social worker at Mt. Washington, Cleo S., talked with Ms. L. at length, and the two of them decided that Ms. L. should move into the battered women's shelter operated by the agency and that Ms. L. should receive counseling services from Cleo S.

The main goals of the counseling sessions were to help Ms. L. explore issues related to her dependency on her husband and her chronic feelings of low self-esteem. Based on prevailing views among domestic violence specialists and extensive research evidence concerning the dynamics of domestic abuse, Cleo S. used an empowerment approach to help Ms. L.

One of the things Cleo S. wanted to do was to monitor regularly Ms. L.'s feelings about herself, because she suspected that Ms. L.'s self-esteem and self-confidence needed to improve in order for her to avoid being victimized by her husband in the future. One way for Cleo S. to do this would simply be to ask Ms. L. regularly how she was feeling about herself. This may be useful qualitative information. But Cleo S. could also gather this information in a consistent, structured manner—and in a way that was not time-consuming, intrusive, or complicated.

Later I describe some simple qualitative and quantitative measurement tools that can be used to monitor or keep track of some aspect of a client's life. For now, let's just say that a social worker in Cleo S.'s position could use one of these easy-to-use tools to monitor Ms. L.'s self-esteem and self-confidence. For example, Cleo S. might have Ms. L. answer one question once each week concerning how she was feeling about herself. The question (statement, really) might be "Today, I feel _____ about myself." The response choices might

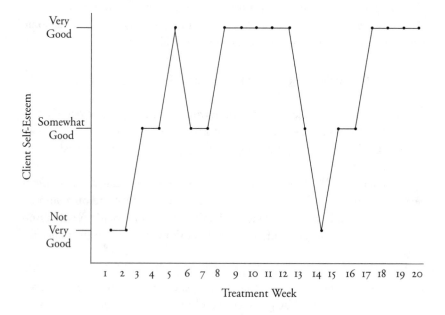

FIGURE 3.1   Graph for Client Monitoring

be (1) very good, (2) somewhat good, or (3) not very good. Of course, there are other ways to ask the question and many different responses and scales one could use. More about that later. In the meantime, let's consider how Cleo S. might keep track of Ms. L.'s weekly responses. She could construct a simple graph or chart, with each date across the bottom (known as the *horizontal axis*) and the responses along the left-hand side (known as the *vertical axis*). She could then place a dot on the chart each week, corresponding to Ms. L.'s response to the question about how she was feeling about herself. As we can see in figure 3.1, Ms. L.'s feelings of self-esteem began to improve somewhat during the third week of counseling and then leveled off between the eighth and twelfth week. Her self-esteem scores fell somewhat during weeks 13 and 14 and then began to improve again.

What is the value of this kind of monitoring? First, it can give both the social worker and the client a general sense of the client's progress. This is always useful. Second, such monitoring can offer clues to what might be going on in a client's life. Substantial changes in the curve on the chart might indicate a significant change in the client's circumstances.

The visual display also can help both the social worker and client focus on relevant issues. For example, Cleo S. and Ms. L. might find it useful to pay attention to what was going on in Ms. L.'s life during the time surrounding weeks 13 and 14 that might account for the decline in Ms. L.'s feelings about herself. Thus, the graphic display can alert practitioners and clients to important clinical issues. In this sense, single-case monitoring and data collection is a key clinical tool (another illustration that research activities can be an integral part of practice).

The third way that such monitoring can be useful is helping social workers and practitioners think about possible causes of changes in clients' status or circumstances. After looking at the overall improvement in Ms. L.'s scores, it may be tempting to conclude that the counseling, in general, has been effective. But having mastered the concepts related to causation that were presented in chapter 2, we now know that it would be a mistake for us to assume that the overall improvement in Ms. L.'s self-esteem scores was necessarily the result of Cleo S.'s counseling. We might believe that Cleo S. is an incredibly talented clinical social worker whose skill is the likely cause of Ms. L.'s improvement. However, we should now be at a point when red flags automatically appear when someone asserts this kind of causal connection.

First, did the intervention precede the outcome in time? That's easy. Of course it did. The graph shows Ms. L.'s responses after she began receiving counseling from Cleo S. Second, is there evidence of a correlation between the possible independent variable (the intervention) and the dependent variable (the self-esteem scores)? Yes, there is. It isn't a perfectly linear correlation, since the line connecting the dots does curve some, but it is a good illustration of a mildly curvilinear relationship between the two variables. The relationship seems strong enough to conclude that there is evidence of a correlation.

Not surprisingly, we run into some trouble with the third condition required for a causal relationship between two variables: accounting for or explaining the influence of extraneous factors. What are the possibilities? One is that other events or circumstances in Ms. L.'s life had a positive impact on her self-esteem, apart from Cleo S.'s clinical intervention. Perhaps Cleo S.'s intervention did the trick, but there may have been other causes (that is, the influence of contemporaneous events). Maybe after she left her husband, Ms. L. started to spend more time with good, supportive friends, and this contact improved her self-esteem. Perhaps Ms. L. was enrolled at the same time in a job-training program, and her stellar performance gave a significant boost to her self-esteem. Or Ms. L. may have been taking an antidepressant medication that lifted her self-esteem.

Another possibility is that the way Cleo S. collected the self-esteem data affected Ms. L.'s scores. Perhaps Cleo S. subtly communicated to Ms. L. that she was interested in how much her self-esteem scores improved over time. Ms. L. may have felt some pressure to "score well" in order to please her social worker. Maybe Ms. L. held Cleo S. in such high regard that Ms. L. did not want to do anything to disappoint Cleo S., so a possible result is that Ms. L.'s self-esteem scores are somewhat inflated and do not accurately reflect her actual feelings.

Given the research design used in this case, we can only speculate about the actual impact of these phenomena. But we do know that it would be a mistake to maintain that Cleo S.'s clinical intervention was the sole cause of Ms. L.'s improved self-esteem scores. We must be sure to qualify these kinds of claims and to think carefully about other plausible explanations.

This problem brings us to the second set of circumstances in which social workers might want to use a single-case design: when evaluating the effectiveness of social work interventions. It should be clear by now that if we want to claim the effectiveness of social work interventions—a causal relationship— we need to use research designs that take into account other explanations for whatever change we document. Shortly I will offer an overview of the research and evaluation designs commonly used for this purpose.

THE BASIC ELEMENTS OF SINGLE-CASE DESIGNS

Before we describe some popular single-case designs, let's look at the other essential ingredients. As you have probably realized by now, single-case designs require the identification of *relevant variables* that are *measurable* (these concepts, and many others included in this section, also are applicable to discussions of group designs). We have already stressed that social workers must identify variables that are germane or appropriate to their intervention goals. We don't want to waste time on variables that are irrelevant or too abstract to be helpful. If a social worker is trying to help a client reduce his cocaine use, he shouldn't waste his time organizing a single-case design around a variable like "intrafamilial synergism"—whatever that is.

Similarly, if Cleo S. and Ms. L. decide to spend a lot of time on Ms. L.'s self-esteem, they shouldn't organize a single-case design around measuring Ms. L.'s authoritarian personality. Maybe there is a relevant clinical issue involving authoritarian personalities and self-esteem, but I think it's safe to say that this kind of variable should not be the heart of a single-case design in a case of this sort.

It also is important that the variables we choose to focus on are measurable.

Cleo S. may want to speculate about Ms. L.'s "phobic tendencies," but unless she can measure this concept, it won't be helpful for her to incorporate it into a single-case design. How can she monitor changes in Ms. L.'s phobic tendencies if she has no valid or reliable way to measure them? Remember, we must consider both qualitative and quantitative measures—both are legitimate, as we'll see in chapter 6.

Many single-case designs focus on specific behaviors that clients wish to change. For example, a client with a serious eating disorder might focus very narrowly—and appropriately—on changes in the number of calories she consumes each day. A client who is concerned about his ability to manage his child's problematic behavior might focus on the number of times he yells at his child each day. A client who has problems with incontinence might track the number of "accidents" each day. This kind of data collection can be helpful to both clients and social workers trying to change these behaviors.

Not all single-case designs focus on behaviors. Some single-case designs for individual clients focus on changes in attitudes, feelings, and knowledge. Consider, for example, the case of Tammy N., a seventeen-year-old client at Mt. Washington. Tammy was referred to Mt. Washington by her school guidance counselor. According to the guidance counselor, for several weeks Tammy has seemed very "blue" and distracted. Tammy told the guidance counselor that she was feeling "very troubled" but didn't feel comfortable talking about her problem to anyone at the school. Tammy did, however, agree to talk to a counselor at Mt. Washington.

Tammy told her Mt. Washington social worker, Anne C., that she has been "living with a secret" for a long time and that the secret "is beginning to eat me up inside." After casual discussion with Anne C., Tammy told her that she had been "feeling attracted to girls instead of boys" and was confused about what this meant. Tammy said that she felt "different from other kids" and that people were beginning to make fun of her. Tammy told Anne C. that things had been so bad that on a few occasions she had even thought about killing herself.

Anne C. completed a standard suicide assessment and concluded that Tammy N. was not in any imminent danger. After talking with several colleagues and Mt. Washington's consulting psychiatrist, Anne C. arranged to meet weekly with Tammy for counseling. Each week, Anne C. had Tammy answer a few simple questions about how she was feeling about herself, how her acquaintances were treating her, and her suicidal thoughts. Few of the questions pertained to behaviors; rather, they concerned Tammy's feelings, thoughts, and perceptions.

Vertical Axis

Horizontal Axis

FIGURE 3.2   Basic Graph for Single-Case Design

Here's another example. Mark G., one of Mt. Washington's clinical social workers, was counseling a married couple who reported that they were having a significant amount of conflict with their nineteen-year-old son. The son was living with his parents, and according to the parents, for months there had been "enormous conflict between us." The parents stated that their son's behavior had been defiant, hostile, and uncooperative and that they were feeling frustrated and angry.

Mark G. spent a lot of time during the counseling sessions exploring the conflict between the parents and their son. Mark G. also worked with the parents to develop various strategies that might help them deal with their son and smooth out their relationship with him. As part of the intervention, Mark G. had the parents indicate each week how they were feeling about their son. He gave them a sentence to complete: "Today my feelings toward my son are _____." The response categories were (1) very positive, (2) somewhat positive, and (3) not very positive. The parents were also encouraged to add their own qualitative comments in narrative form. Mark G. used their

responses to monitor their relationship with their son and to begin their counseling sessions each week. He usually asked the parents to elaborate briefly on
their response and then used their comments to guide the counseling session.

Social workers often find it helpful to graph the quantitative information
or data they collect from clients as part of a single-case design. Usually the
graphs consist of a horizontal axis and a vertical axis, each used for a different
variable. The term *horizontal axis* is just a fancy name for a straight line that
runs across from left to right (see figure 3.2). Almost always, the horizontal axis
is used to mark intervals along some kind of time frame, with the beginning
time on the left and the ending time on the right. The time frame might be
hours, days, weeks, months, years, and so on. As you might imagine, a social
worker simply uses whatever time frame makes sense given the clinical situation and intervention goals. For instance, a clinical intervention for a client
engaging in self-mutilation might be assessed hour by hour. In contrast, a clinical intervention for a client feeling depressed might be assessed week by week.

The *vertical axis* is nothing more than a straight line that runs up and down
and begins at the leftmost point of the horizontal axis. The vertical and horizontal axes intersect in the lower left-hand corner (see figure 3.2).

Many different variables can be plotted on the vertical axis, such as clients'
behaviors, feelings, attitudes, knowledge, or whatever we happen to be measuring. The units of measurement and the size of the intervals depend on what
we are interested in and what would be meaningful. If we were interested in
the number of calories a client consumes each day, the vertical axis would mark
calorie intervals, perhaps in increments of 50 or 100. If we were interested in
clients' feelings of self-esteem, we might use a scale of 1 to 10, with 1 reflecting
low self-esteem and 10 reflecting high self-esteem; thus the vertical axis would
be divided into ten segments. If we were interested in the number of argu-
ments a married couple had each day, the vertical axis might simply be a frequency count from 1 to 8 or so (let's hope the upper limit for this scale doesn't
need to be that high).

The intervals on the two axes must be exactly the right size—not too large
and not too small. If the intervals are too large, clinically significant differences
might be missed or camouflaged. For example, if each category on the vertical
axis marks an additional 100 calories, a 70-calorie increase in a client's intake
would not show up clearly, even though it might be clinically relevant. Hence,
it is important to choose categories that are small enough to reveal clinically
significant differences among scores.

At the same time, you don't want intervals that are too small. For instance,
if each interval on the vertical axis represented only one calorie, the vertical

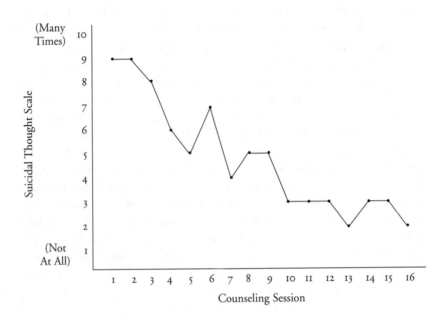

FIGURE 3.3   Case Example of Client Monitoring

axis would be so high that you would need an extension ladder to see the top of it. Somewhat larger intervals are more relevant to the clinical goals and much easier to manage.

Now let's put the vertical and horizontal axes together and see what we've got. Figure 3.3 shows the data concerning the case of Tammy N., the young woman who was struggling to deal with sexual orientation issues. Recall that during each counseling session, Tammy's social worker, Anne C., collected data concerning Tammy's feelings about herself, suicidal thoughts, and so on.

One of the sentences that Anne C. asked Tammy to complete each week was "This week I thought about killing myself. . . . " Tammy was asked to circle a number on a 10-point scale, with 1 indicating "Not at all" and 10 indicating "Many times." As you can see in figure 3.3, the horizontal axis contains 16 points, corresponding to sixteen consecutive counseling sessions (approximately four months). The vertical axis has 10 points, corresponding to the 10-point scale Tammy used regarding the frequency with which she thought about committing suicide. The graph shows that Tammy's thoughts about committing suicide generally decreased during the sixteen counseling sessions, although the pattern showed some fluctuation.

An Overview of Single-Case Designs

Now we are ready to look at several popular single-case designs. The first thing we need to do is agree on notation. Over the years, various conventions regarding single-case designs have evolved. Several letters of the alphabet are used to symbolize different components of single-case designs. The letter B is used to symbolize an intervention such as counseling, medication, a client's vocational training program, or the use of behavioral techniques. The letters C and D are used for changes in the initial intervention. For example, if the initial intervention (B) used cognitive therapy techniques with a client manifesting symptoms of depression, the letter C might stand for the addition of psychotropic medication during the fifth week of treatment or the withdrawal of the cognitive therapy and the introduction of group therapy. The letter D might refer to the combination of cognitive therapy techniques, psychotropic medication, and group therapy introduced during the tenth week of treatment. The letter A symbolizes the *baseline period*, the period during which no treatment or intervention occurs. This alphabetical overview may seem rather abstract at this point, but it should become much clearer after we discuss some examples.

The B Design

The simplest single-case design, known as the *B design*, is used mainly to monitor clients rather than to evaluate the effectiveness of an intervention. The use of the letter B by itself indicates that we simply want to monitor changes in the client's status during the time a particular intervention is used. There is no baseline period (A) and no variations in the intervention introduced later on (C, D, etc.).

Let's illustrate this by going back to the example of Ms. L. and her social worker at Mt. Washington, Cleo S. In this case, Ms. L. was receiving counseling from Cleo S. on domestic violence issues, and she had moved into an emergency shelter operated by the Mt. Washington staff.

Let's suppose that one of the issues that Ms. L. wanted to focus on in counseling was her lack of self-confidence. In Ms. L.'s opinion, a big reason that she had tolerated her husband's beatings over the years is that she lacked self-confidence and the means to live independently. As a result, Ms. L. and Cleo S. spent a lot of time during their counseling sessions exploring ways to boost Ms. L.'s self-confidence. Cleo S. helped Ms. L. identify her strengths and used cognitive therapy techniques to raise Ms. L.'s self-confidence. This was the basic intervention approach (indicated by the letter B).

Cleo S. was interested in monitoring the level of Ms. L.'s self-confidence

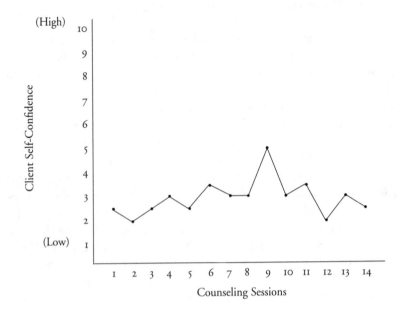

FIGURE 3.4   B Design

over time. At the beginning of each counseling session, Cleo S. had Ms. L. indicate the extent of her self-confidence on a 10-point scale, with a score of 1 indicating very low self-confidence and 10 indicating very high self-confidence. This was a simple way for both Ms. L. and Cleo S. to keep track of changes in Ms. L.'s perception of her self-confidence (figure 3.4). At the beginning of each counseling session, Cleo S. also gave Ms. L. an opportunity to give, in her own words, her own qualitative assessment of her self-confidence.

A fairly simple B design also is appropriate in the case of Toby and his mother, Ms. E. Remember that Toby's schoolteacher complained about his behavior in the classroom and was feeling rather desperate for some help in managing him. As the Mt. Washington social worker in this case, in your capacity as a consultant to the school, you helped the teacher learn a number of behavior management techniques that are often effective with children diagnosed with attention deficit disorder (you know this, of course, because you took some time to review the literature summarizing the research on and evaluation of the effectiveness of these intervention approaches).

After consulting with the teacher, the two of you agree that it would be helpful to concentrate initially on Toby's tendency to get up from his desk and walk around the classroom when the students are supposed to be seated at their desks and working on an assignment. Each class day includes a 45-minute period when students are expected to sit at their desks to complete these assignments. You teach Toby's teacher the basic principles of positive reinforcement and extinction. Your hope is that by consistently using positive reinforcers, Toby will be more inclined to remain in his seat and complete his work.

Both you and Toby's teacher think that it would be useful to monitor his behavior for at least four weeks. To collect the data, you devise a chart on which the teacher can keep track of Toby's behavior. Down the left-hand side of the chart are the dates on which the teacher will be monitoring Toby's behavior. Next to each date is a space for her to write in the number of times during the 45-minute period that Toby gets out of his seat and walks around without permission. The paper also provides space for her to add her own qualitative or narrative description and assessment of Toby's behavior.

After the four weeks are up, you plot the quantitative results on the chart. On the horizontal axis you write the number of each class session (or the date). On the vertical axis you mark various frequencies, ranging from a low of 0 to a high of 10 (this range of frequencies is sufficient, since Toby never got out of his seat more than ten times during any 45-minute period). As you can see in figure 3.5, Toby's behavior fluctuated quite a bit, although the general trend was in a favorable direction.

At this point, of course, you would not be able to assume much about the effectiveness of the intervention. One problem is the ambiguous results. The second problem (which I probably don't even have to point out, now that you understand the concept) is that many other factors could account for any change in Toby's behavior (the extraneous factors we talked about earlier). The teacher's narrative comments and qualitative assessment, along with qualitative information obtained from Toby's mom, could help explain the changes. Something going on at home or in the community might have something to do with the changes in Toby's behavior. Or maybe Toby was placed on medication, or his dosage was changed, during the data collection period, and this had some influence on his behavior, apart from the teacher's skillful intervention.

What should be clear immediately is that the B design does not provide any way to *control* for the various extraneous factors that can account for changes in a client's status over time. Although B designs are not helpful in instances when we want to *evaluate* the effectiveness of an intervention and rule out plausible alternative explanations for the results, these designs are useful if our

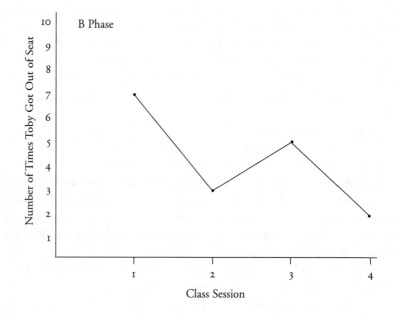

FIGURE 3.5   B Design

goal is simply to *monitor* or *describe* changes in a client's status (consistent with the goals of descriptive research and evaluation). Sometimes all we want to know is how a client is doing, period. Even though it might be nice to pinpoint the causes of changes in a client's status over time, it may not always be a priority.

The AB Design

Without much more effort than the B design requires, social workers can often acquire considerably more information than a B design produces. The trick is to build in a brief data collection period before the intervention begins. This period is called the *baseline period*, denoted by the letter A. Hence, an AB design is one in which a baseline data collection period, the A phase, is followed by an intervention period, the B phase. (Wouldn't you think that whoever invented this notation would have used the letter B to indicate the *base-line* phase rather than the intervention phase?)

In what way can this design be more helpful than the B design? Although neither the B nor the AB design conclusively rules out or explains the influence of extraneous factors, the AB design does provide more information about the contrast between a client's status before an intervention and during it. As a result, social workers can at least answer the question, "Did the client's status improve between the period before the intervention and the intervention period?" The answer is important, even though the AB design does not enable a social worker to discover exactly why a client's status changed. For this, we need a different, and more complicated, design.

For Toby and his teacher, for example, you may decide to delay the implementation of the behavioral intervention by one week in order to gather baseline data. Although Toby's teacher was eager to start the intervention, the two of you believe that it would be helpful to have the baseline data for comparison purposes. As Toby's teacher said, with some resignation, "I've been dealing with this behavior all year. What's another week?"

It turns out that having the baseline information is helpful. During the week before the start of the behavioral intervention (the A phase), Toby was getting out of his seat about seven times each day (the range was from five to ten). Although there was some fluctuation during the intervention, or B, phase—which lasted for two weeks—there was noticeable improvement (figure 3.6). Toby's teacher admitted that even though things were far from perfect, she did sense a difference in the right direction, and seeing the graph helped convince her that something useful was happening. Although neither of you could say definitively that the intervention was indeed the cause of the change in Toby's behavior, you were encouraged enough by the single-case design data that you decided to stick with the intervention plan for at least two more weeks before reassessing the situation.

THE VALIDITY OF RESEARCH AND EVALUATION DESIGNS

Neither the B nor the AB design will be helpful if the goal is to evaluate the effectiveness of a particular intervention. Sometimes a particular intervention is expensive or stressful for the client (or social worker), so it is important to know whether it is doing any good. When this is the situation, we need a research and evaluation design that can rule out extraneous factors and provide evidence of a *causal relationship*, if any, between an intervention and the outcome.

This brings us right back to the ideas we discussed earlier concerning the evidence that social workers need to demonstrate a causal relationship between two variables or, more specifically, between an independent variable (the intervention) and the dependent variable (the outcome). Here we go again. What were those extraneous factors? By now, you should be able to list the four broad

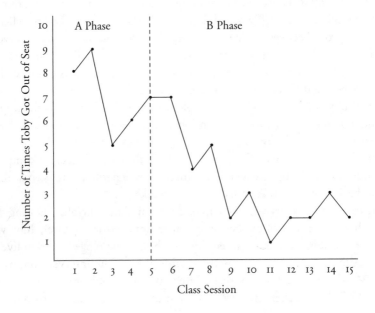

FIGURE 3.6   AB Design

categories (at least that's my hope): historical factors, contemporaneous factors, maturation, and testing or measurement.

But how can social workers rule out the influence of extraneous factors so
as to attribute change in a client's status to the intervention itself? To answer
this question, we need to take a close look at a key concept: *control*. The concept of control in research and evaluation has to do with incorporating certain
features into a research and evaluation design to enable a social worker to rule
out extraneous factors. Another way to say this is that certain research and
evaluation designs have features allowing social workers to *control for* the
effects of extraneous factors, to rule out plausible alternative explanations of
the results obtained, and hence to attribute any changes in a client's status to
the intervention itself. Although this approach isn't foolproof, it works pretty
well.

Internal Validity of Research and Evaluation Designs

What I am talking about here is what researchers call the concept of *design
validity*. A valid design—a design with *internal validity*—is one that enables
you to rule out the influence of extraneous factors and plausible alternative

explanations. Thus the B design and the AB design are not valid if your purpose is to evaluate the effectiveness of an intervention (although these two designs are valid if your purpose is to monitor and describe changes in a client's status).

What are the characteristics of a design with high internal validity? Actually, I described them briefly in chapter 2. Internal validity enables a social worker who is assessing some kind of cause–effect relationship (often the effect of an intervention or an outcome) to conclude that the independent variable (the intervention, say), rather than extraneous factors, was the cause of change in the dependent variable (the outcome). Research and evaluation designs with *high* internal validity contain controls for extraneous factors and permit the social worker to rule out plausible alternative explanations for observed changes; whatever change is observed can then be attributed to the independent variable or intervention. Conversely, research and evaluation designs with *low* internal validity do not contain adequate controls for extraneous factors; changes in the dependent variable or outcome can therefore be due to causes other than the independent variable.

Now let's talk about the kinds of extraneous factors that research and evaluation designs need to rule out and that threaten a project's internal validity. In 1963, two scholars by the name of Campbell and Stanley published a very influential monograph (*Experimental and Quasi-Experimental Designs for Research*) outlining various threats to internal validity. Campbell and Stanley's list has stood the test of time quite well and is generally regarded as the "classic" statement on the subject. I have already touched on several of the threats. The following is a more detailed list.

History.   I noted earlier that circumstances or events from a client's past can account for change that occurs after the introduction of a social work intervention. For example, if Toby had been in counseling before his enrollment in his current school, the effects of this earlier counseling might have begun to take hold at the time his teacher started to use the behavioral intervention.

Or suppose a Mt. Washington social worker is counseling a hospitalized client with an eating disorder. The data the social worker collected concerning the client's calorie consumption suggest that the intervention is having a negative effect, that the client's food intake has actually dropped since the intervention began. But conflicts with her parents at the time of the client's hospitalization triggered her memories of being sexually abused—and subsequently hospitalized—when she was eight years old. These memories are quite traumatic and interfere with the Mt. Washington social worker's ability to work with her client. Thus it is not the counseling that led to the decline in the client's food consumption but the client's recollection of trauma earlier in her life.

Another way to think about the effects of history is to identify any circumstances or events occurring at the same time as the intervention that might account for changes in the dependent variable (sometimes called *contemporaneous events*). As I said earlier, when social workers evaluate the effectiveness of an intervention, contemporaneous events are often the most common extraneous factor.

The passage of time or maturation.   Another common extraneous factor is the passage of time, or what researchers often call *maturation*, which simply means that many people change over time for reasons that have nothing to do with any kind of professional intervention in their lives. A juvenile offender who participates in a counseling program at Mt. Washington may commit fewer delinquent offenses following the intervention, but much, or even all, of this change could be due to the youngster's "growing up." Similarly, a client who is being treated for symptoms of depression may improve as a result of the mere passage of time.

The same could be true for Toby, a young boy who is certainly experiencing significant developmental changes in his life. Despite his teacher's behavioral intervention, it is quite possible that the passage of time and Toby's maturation are responsible for whatever behavior changes he displays.

Evaluation and testing.   All of us have been evaluated at some point in our lives. We have taken exams in school and been observed by employers. For most of us (perhaps all of us), the very fact that we are being observed has some effect on our behavior and performance, assuming that we are aware that the observation is taking place. Anxiety connected with taking an exam or knowing that someone is standing in the back of a room monitoring our work can have a detrimental effect on or interfere with our performance.

The same phenomenon can occur in social work research and evaluation; it is sometimes known as *reaction* or *reactivity*. Clients who are completing an instrument assessing their attitude toward domestic violence may realize that some aspect of their future may be influenced by their responses (what kind of counseling services they will receive or when they will be discharged from a residential program). Likewise, clients who are asked to answer questions about their feelings or attitudes after the social work intervention may be influenced by their familiarity with the questions if the same questions were also asked before the intervention. In Toby's case, the social worker's presence in the back of the classroom might have influenced his behavior if he felt that he was being "watched."

Clients who are not aware that they are being observed (sometimes called *unobtrusive measurement*) are not influenced by this phenomenon. For unobtrusive measurement, a social worker may use a one-way mirror to record some aspect of a client's behavior, or the client simply may not notice the observer. This kind of measurement may raise complicated ethical questions about whether clients should always be informed when they are to be observed. As we'll discuss later, ethical and methodological considerations sometimes conflict.

Instrumentation. Evaluation and testing can cause problems if the measurement instrument itself is flawed. Questions may be worded poorly or biased, or the instrument may be administered improperly. For example, an instrument designed to assess the attitudes of people of color toward the Mt. Washington Family Service Agency might include items that are culturally insensitive and that bias the responses. A particular depression scale being used at the agency might be scored improperly. In Toby's case, the instrument used to record his classroom-based behaviors may have been designed in a way that caused errors or inconsistencies in the teacher's summary of her observations.

Selection bias. As we will see shortly, in many instances, social workers want to compare two or more groups of clients. Perhaps the Mt. Washington staff want to compare the effectiveness of two different treatment approaches, say the relative merits of group and individual counseling for clients with substance abuse problems. This is fine if the two groups are similar with respect to such traits as the severity of their substance abuse problems, treatment histories, age and gender distribution, the kinds of substances they are abusing, and their ethnicity. But suppose the persons receiving individual counseling have more severe substance abuse histories than do those receiving group counseling. This difference could explain results indicating that the clients who received individual counseling had more relapses, on the average, than did those who received group counseling.

Sample mortality. Fortunately, sample mortality does not refer to deaths among people in a social worker's research or evaluation project.

Despite the awkward, and rather ominous, wording, *sample mortality* is an important concept regarding the fact that in many research and evaluation projects, some people who initially participate as part of the sample drop out over time. This attrition can occur for any number of reasons. Clients move, lose interest in the project, or become overwhelmed with other problems that prevent their continued participation (of course, death is one possible reason for attrition). Because it is common, sample attrition is something a social worker should be prepared to deal with.

Apart from doing whatever they can to minimize attrition in their sample, social workers need to understand the effect that sample mortality can have on the results. It is another one of those extraneous factors that can lead to flawed conclusions about the cause-and-effect relationship between an intervention and its outcome.

Let's go back to the comparison between the effectiveness of the group-counseling and the individual-counseling approaches used with Mt. Washington clients with substance abuse problems. Assume that the final results of the project suggest that the group-counseling approach is superior; that is, clients who received group counseling had fewer relapses than did those who received individual counseling.

Now suppose that sixty people began in the "individual-counseling" group and sixty people began in the "group-counseling" group. By the end of the project, twelve of the people who started in the group-counseling group had dropped out, and twenty of the people in the individual-counseling group had dropped out. This translates into a 20 percent attrition rate in the group-counseling group and a 33 percent attrition rate in the individual-counseling group.

What effect might these attrition rates have on the results? Maybe those people who completed the counseling program had better support systems, were in better physical or emotional condition, or were more motivated than were those who dropped out of the program. We wouldn't know this for sure, of course, without comparing the characteristics of those who completed the counseling with those who did not. Nonetheless, it seems reasonable to speculate that there may be differences between those who completed the counseling and those who did not and that the different attrition rates for the group-counseling and individual-counseling groups (20 percent and 33 percent, respectively) might explain much, or at least some, of the difference between the relapse rates of the two intervention groups. Since the group-counseling group had a smaller attrition rate (sample mortality), it may have had a higher proportion of clients who were less likely to relapse, regardless of which intervention they received. This could occur if, for example, the "higher-functioning" clients were assigned to group counseling and the "lower-functioning" clients were assigned to individual counseling.

Contamination between individuals or groups. As I mentioned before, social workers often want to compare clients who are receiving different interventions. In this situation, we must make sure that the interventions really do differ as much as we think they do. Suppose, for example, that the Mt. Washington social worker who provides individual counseling to clients with substance abuse problems occasionally brings her clients together in a group to discuss various treatment-related issues (for example, coping strategies, dealing with denial). In a sense, this would "contaminate" any comparison between the individual-counseling and the group-counseling groups, since the clients receiving individual counseling would also be occasionally exposed to group counseling. This may make clinical sense, but it would create problems if the goal were to compare the individual- and group-counseling approaches. Instead, the social worker would be comparing the "individual-with-occasional-group-counseling" approach with the "group-counseling" approach. Although this isn't necessarily a problem—particularly if it makes clinical sense—social workers must know what they are, in fact, comparing, so that they do not mislead anyone with their results.

This sort of contamination could also occur with a single-case design comparing two clients, in which one received an intervention and the other did not. If one client who received an intervention has extensive contact with a second client who has not yet received the intervention, the second client's behavior (or feelings, attitudes, etc.) may be influenced by the first client's. (We will see how this can occur when we talk about using multiple-baseline designs.)

Statistical regression. Statistical regression is another concept with a clumsy name. It is used in research and evaluation projects dealing with clients who are, in some way, extreme. For example, clients may be extremely violent, depressed, self-destructive, or undernourished.

We know that over time, many people who are in some kind of dire circumstances are likely to show some improvement, regardless of their exposure to any intervention. Why? Because they already are at the far end of the spectrum with respect to the severity of their circumstances (sometimes known as the *floor effect* because these people can't go any lower). If they experience any change at all, it can be in only one direction, and that is up.

Likewise, the same logic applies to instances in which clients are in extremely good shape to begin with. There may be only one direction in which they can move, if their status changes at all, and that's toward some degree of deterioration (sometimes known as the *ceiling effect*).

This phenomenon is called *statistical regression*. In the statistics field, *regression toward the mean* (or *average*) means that over time, people tend to change in a way that moves them closer to the average for all people, regardless of the presence or absence of an intervention.

Suppose Toby's teacher began collecting data on his behavior on an unusually bad day (for Toby). Toby's "score" on this first day would be extreme, and so Toby's behavior would likely show some improvement over time, whether or not he was exposed to an intervention. It may be that a skillfully applied intervention would also have an effect, but the phenomenon of statistical regression could also account, at least in part, for his improvement.

As a group, these various extraneous factors—history, maturation, evaluation and testing, instrumentation, selection bias, sample mortality, contamination between individuals or groups, and statistical regression—constitute threats to internal validity. As we will see, there are a number of ways to eliminate or greatly reduce these threats.

External Validity of Research and Evaluation Designs

Next we shall look at another type of validity: external validity. It is a topic that will come up again later when we discuss the subject of sampling, but we shall describe it briefly now.

External validity is the extent to which the results of a research or evaluation project can be generalized to other settings (for example, client groups, agencies, communities). A project must possess certain characteristics for the results to be generalizable. First, the people or cases (agencies, communities, etc.) in the project—the sample—must be representative of the larger group of people or cases to which the social worker wants to generalize the results. If the sample is biased or skewed in some way, the results cannot be generalized to other people, settings, and so on. This could lead to terrible results.

For instance, suppose that a Mt. Washington social worker is developing a counseling program for gay and lesbian adults who are struggling with their sexual orientation. To plan the program, the social worker reviews previously published literature on the subject. One of the journal articles describes the results of a needs assessment conducted with a sample of gay and lesbian adolescents living in a rural community. This may be a fine and important study, but how applicable are the results to the proposed program at Mt. Washington? The study's results may be generalizable in a number of ways to similar programs elsewhere in the country for gay and lesbian adolescents in rural communities, but shouldn't the social worker question the generalizability of the results to a population of gay and lesbian *adults* in an *urban* community?

Let's also look at the external validity of a different kind of situation. The results of a single-case design involving Toby may produce useful information about the intervention introduced by his teacher, but how generalizable are these results? It usually is difficult to generalize the results of single-case designs, given the uniqueness and idiosyncratic circumstances of an individual client.

In addition to problems with the representativeness of a study's sample, external validity is threatened by many of the same factors that threaten the internal validity of a research or evaluation project. That is, if a particular project's results are questionable because of the influence of extraneous factors such as historical or contemporaneous events, maturation, instrumentation, and statistical regression, a social worker could hardly generalize the results to other clients, settings, or circumstances, right?

Another way to describe the relationship between internal and external validity is to say that for a project to have high external validity, it must also have high internal validity. Internal validity is an essential ingredient of external validity, although high external validity includes other ingredients as well (for example, a representative sample). To use more formal language, we can say that internal validity is a necessary, but not a sufficient, component of external validity. Internal validity is essential to high external validity, but it is not enough by itself.

Now let's return to single-case designs to see where they stand with respect to their internal validity. Clearly, the B design has low internal validity, since changes in a client's status could be due to various phenomena. The B design also has low external validity, since one client cannot be a truly representative sample of anything. That doesn't mean the B design is useless; the data it yields may be useful for monitoring purposes. But if we want to explore the effectiveness of an intervention and cause–effect relationships, the B design can't take us very far because of its low internal validity.

The AB design enhances the internal validity somewhat, but not a great deal. Although the addition of baseline data is useful, it still doesn't allow us to rule out the possible influence of all the extraneous factors that could account for changes in the client. What we need are research and evaluation designs that give us more assurance of their internal validity.

The ABAB Design

One of the most common ways to enhance the validity of a single-case evaluation is to use an ABAB design. For reasons that should be clearer in a moment, the ABAB design is also referred to as a *reversal design*. Like the AB design, the ABAB design begins with a baseline period during which data on the duration, frequency, or intensity of the target problem are collected before introducing the intervention. The purpose here is the same as the purpose of the baseline or A phase in the AB design—to permit a social worker to contrast the client's status during the intervention with his or her status before the intervention.

The ABAB design, however, introduces an additional twist to enable a social worker to begin to speculate, with a reasonable degree of confidence, about the likelihood that the intervention was, in fact, the *cause* of the change in the client's status. Remember that with the AB design, it is difficult to assert that change in a client's status from the A (baseline) phase to the B (intervention) phase is a direct result of the intervention. There usually are too many extraneous factors to rule out that could account for this change.

So how does the ABAB design allow a social worker to explore a possible *causal* connection between an intervention and outcome? In short, in the ABAB design, and various other single-case designs, *the client is used as his or her own control.* In the ABAB design, the intervention is withdrawn (or "reversed") after a reasonable period of time (the second A phase), to see whether the original behavior, feelings, attitudes, or whatever return. One would think that if the intervention were making a difference, its withdrawal after some time should also make a difference and that this would be reflected during the second A phase of the design. Then, after a reasonable period of time, the intervention is reintroduced to see whether there is again a change in the client's status. If we find a noticeable pattern in which the client's status changes for the better during the intervention or B phase, as compared with the baseline or A phase, we would have reason to believe that the intervention was having an effect. Extraneous factors may account for the changes in the client's status. This is always something to consider. But the nature of the ABAB or reversal design is such that it would be a remarkable coincidence if the change in the client's status happened to be correlated in this way with one or more extraneous factors or events in the client's life. That is, the ABAB design offers us a higher degree of internal validity than does the B or AB design.

Suppose that Toby's teacher initially collected baseline data—both quantitative and qualitative—on Toby's ability to stay in his seat for one week and then introduced the behavioral intervention and collected the appropriate data during the next two weeks (at this point, this would look like an AB design). Then, after the two weeks of intervention, Toby's teacher withdrew the intervention for one week to see whether Toby's behavior deteriorated (the second baseline or A phase). This would be followed by the intervention again (the second intervention or B phase). The graph of the reversal design looks essentially like two AB designs placed side to side (figure 3.7).

But an ABAB design isn't always possible. In many situations, the social worker, the client, or someone else who has regular contact with a client (for example, a teacher or parent) can't tolerate the thought that the client's undesirable status (whether behavior, feelings, or attitudes) might return during the second baseline period. Toby's teacher might fear that possibility, since she has found Toby's behavior so difficult to cope with. In other situations, however, social workers, clients, and those who have regular contact with clients are so eager for an intervention to work, and to know that it's the intervention and not something else that is making the difference, that they are willing to reverse the design and risk whatever might happen during the second baseline phase.

The second possible problem is that the ABAB design may not be useful when the changes brought about by an intervention are likely to endure for some time, during the period when the intervention is withdrawn. Some social work interventions are effective at bringing about short-term or temporary changes; others are more likely to have lasting effects. If we're dealing with the latter, an ABAB design would not be able to provide the evidence we want concerning the effectiveness of the intervention. That is, it would be hard to distinguish between the effectiveness of the intervention and the extraneous factors.

Suppose that a Mt. Washington social worker was working with a client with a history of depression. It is possible that an effective intervention would have some lasting effects that would continue through a second baseline phase, but an ABAB design wouldn't be able to demonstrate this kind of effectiveness.

The third possible problem—and the most compelling one, in my view— is an ethical one. You can easily imagine various situations in which it would be unethical to withdraw an intervention that might be doing some good, particularly in instances in which a client or someone else could be seriously harmed. One example is a client in a psychiatric facility who mutilates himself by gouging his skin with his fingernails so severely that scarring and serious infections often result. Suppose the introduction of an intervention was at least *correlated* with change in a favorable direction (less mutilation). Wouldn't it be unconscionable to withdraw the intervention and run the risk that the health-threatening behavior might return? In this sort of case, the social worker might never know whether the intervention was the sole cause of the favorable change, but that's a disadvantage he might have to tolerate in light of the ethical concerns. (We will explore these issues in greater depth in chapter 4.)

Variations of the ABAB Design

Sometimes a social worker cannot collect baseline data before introducing an intervention, but it would be unconscionable and unethical to postpone the intervention. We could hardly condone deliberately delaying an intervention

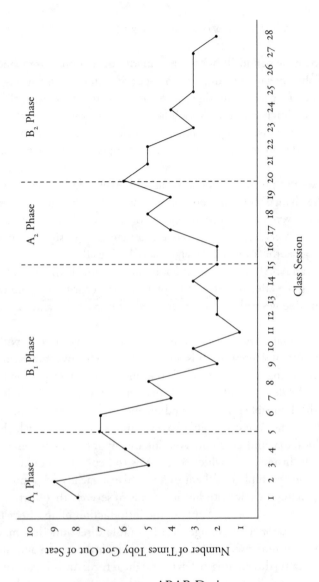

FIGURE 3.7   ABAB Design

when, for example, clients are engaged in harmful or life-threatening behaviors. But in some situations, a client's status stabilizes in a way that makes it possible to withdraw an intervention for a period of time to see whether the client's status will change. Obviously we would not want to do this if something very serious could happen to the client or a third party as a result.

In Toby's case, his teacher might be impatient and would not want to wait a week before introducing a behavioral intervention. Let's assume the intervention is at least correlated with some positive change. After this respite, the teacher might be feeling somewhat more patient and tolerant and therefore might agree to remove the intervention for a week to see whether Toby's inappropriate behaviors return. Perhaps the teacher can understand the importance of knowing whether the intervention, as opposed to other extraneous factors, accounts for Toby's behavior change. In this case, we would have an intervention phase followed immediately by a baseline period and then another intervention phase—hence the BAB notation. Although this design does not provide as much information concerning the possible impact of the intervention as does the ABAB design, it is stronger than the simple AB design.

Another possibility that is useful in some situations is known as the BCBC design. This design can be used in instances when it seems unwise or unethical to withdraw an intervention entirely and revert to a baseline period and when it makes sense to compare two different intervention approaches. The letter C, like the letter B, denotes an intervention; the C indicates that an intervention different from the B intervention was also used in the case.

As the social worker in Toby's case, you have two different interventions in mind. They differ with respect to the kind of reinforcer used when Toby stays in his seat (one reinforcer offers the use of the classroom computer, which Toby loves to work on, and the other earns points that can be traded for toys that Toby enjoys playing with). You think both may be effective and so want to compare them.

A disadvantage of the BCBC design is that you can't say anything about the impact of an intervention compared with no intervention. But this design does permit you to compare the relative effectiveness of two (or more) interventions.

Now that we have reviewed the AB, ABAB, BAB, and BCBC designs, you probably think that features of these designs can be mixed and matched to form what are called *multiple-component designs*. Indeed, in some situations, it might make sense to use an ABCBC design, for example, when it is possible to collect some baseline data, it is not possible to withdraw an intervention, and you want to compare the relative effectiveness of two interventions. Or in another situation, it may not be possible to collect baseline data initially, you want to compare two different interventions, a brief baseline period is feasible and ethical, and you want to combine the two interventions for a period of time. This design would be "spelled" BCA(BC). Social workers simply need to know the basic or component parts of the various single-case designs and use their imagination and practice wisdom to construct the most suitable design.

Multiple-Baseline Designs

Multiple-baseline designs are helpful when a social worker cannot withdraw an intervention (for practical or ethical reasons) and wants to explore the impact of an intervention on several different clients or target outcomes (for example, different behaviors or feelings manifested by one client) or in several different settings.

Comparisons across outcomes. Suppose that Toby's teacher is concerned about three different behaviors involving Toby's tendency to (1) get out of his seat when he should be seated, (2) fail to complete assigned tasks (for example, reading and arithmetic assignments), and (3) talk to other students while the teacher is talking to the class. The teacher and social worker agree to apply, over time, the intervention to all three behaviors.

This is an instance in which a multiple-baseline design can be used to assess the effectiveness of an intervention. The logic of this design is straightforward. Instead of introducing an intervention and then withdrawing it at some point (as happens in a reversal design), the introduction of the intervention for each of the three target behaviors is staggered, with each intervention phase preceded by a baseline period.

Let's see what this would look like. For example, we decide to focus first on Toby's tendency to get out of his seat when he's not supposed to. We collect baseline information on this behavior for a week before starting the behavioral intervention *with respect to this one behavior.* That is, Toby's teacher records quantitative and qualitative data on Toby's seat-abandoning behaviors for one week and then applies the behavioral principles of positive reinforcement to *only* this one behavior. At the same time, Toby's teacher collects baseline data on two other behaviors (Toby's ability to complete assigned tasks and avoid talking to other students while the teacher is talking to the class). After the intervention has been applied to the first behavior (getting out of his seat) for a reasonable length of time (one week, perhaps), the behavioral intervention (stars on a chart that Toby can cash in for an item on his menu of rewards, such as five extra minutes at recess or a nifty pencil eraser) is introduced with respect to the second behavior (Toby's failure to complete assigned tasks) *and* is continued with respect to the first behavior (the seat-abandoning behavior). While the behavioral intervention is being applied to these two behaviors simultaneously, Toby's teacher continues to collect baseline data on the third behavior (talking to other students while the teacher is talking to the class). After another week, Toby's teacher introduces the behavioral intervention with respect to the third behavior.

The rationale here is that the staggered introduction of the intervention allows the social worker to determine the effectiveness of the intervention without withdrawing it. If the baseline data show little or no improvement in the three behaviors during the baseline periods and there is evidence of improvement in the three behaviors when the intervention is applied to each of them, the evidence is strong that the intervention is the principal cause of the positive change. This is the pattern we see in figure 3.8, in which the graph displays the quantitative results of the multiple-baseline design used to address Toby's three problematic behaviors. It certainly is possible that extraneous factors have something to do with the behavior change (for example, some sort of contemporaneous event), but wouldn't it be amazing if extraneous factors, and not the intervention, were responsible for the significant shift in behavior at three different times that happened to coincide with the time the intervention was introduced? I think we can agree that such a coincidence is unlikely, although it is technically possible.

Comparisons across settings.   Multiple-baseline designs can also be used to assess the effectiveness of an intervention introduced in different *settings* with one client. It is conceivable, for example, that Toby's mother also reported that Toby was misbehaving inappropriately at home and in his after-school recreation program, as well as in school.

It might be too ambitious to introduce the behavioral intervention in all three settings simultaneously. Also, a multiple-baseline design would help all the parties involved decide whether the intervention was having an effect on Toby's behavior.

This is how it would work. If Toby's mother seems the most desperate for some change in Toby's behavior at home—because of the amount of time she spends with her son—all the people in the case might decide that it would be best to start with Toby's behavior at home. Initially, the social worker would work with Toby's mother, his teacher, and the coordinator of Toby's after-school program to arrange for them to collect baseline data on Toby's behavior (for example, Toby's complying with his mom's daily instructions to clean his room). After a reasonable baseline period, the social worker would train

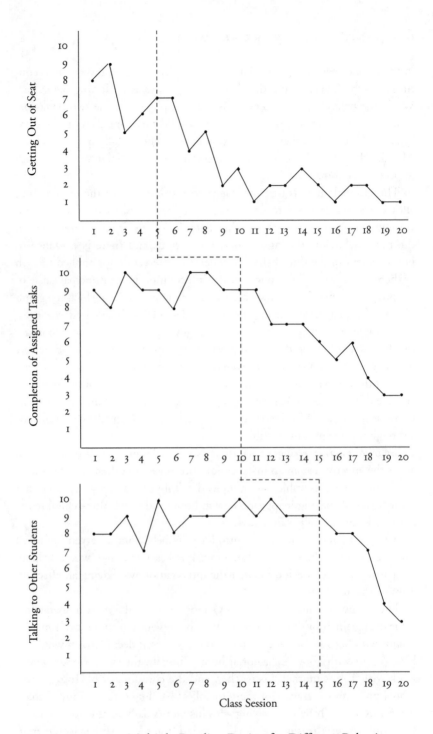

FIGURE 3.8   Multiple-Baseline Design for Different Behaviors

Toby's mother in the proper use of behavioral principles. While Toby's mother implemented the intervention at home, Toby's teacher and the coordinator of his after-school program would continue to collect baseline data. After two weeks had passed, Toby's teacher would implement the same intervention on the same behavior at school (following instructions) while Toby's mother continued to implement the intervention and the coordinator of Toby's after-school program continued to collect baseline data. After another week, the coordinator of Toby's after-school program would implement the same intervention on the same behavior in that setting.

Ideally, the graph of the quantitative data for each setting would indicate improvement in Toby's behavior after the intervention was implemented, and this improvement would be corroborated by qualitative reports from the adults in each of the settings. If this occurred (and wouldn't it be nice if our interventions always worked so nicely?), there would be strong evidence of the intervention's effectiveness (figure 3.9). Of course, the intervention might be successful in only one or two of the three settings. This might happen if one of the parties (Toby's mother, teacher, or after-school program coordinator) did not implement the intervention properly or for some other reason having to do with unique circumstances in one or two of the settings. The multiple-baseline design graph should help the parties pinpoint possible problems with the implementation and lead to constructive discussion about what might have occurred and possible remedies.

Comparisons across clients. A third way that multiple-baseline designs can be used is to compare the effectiveness of an intervention used with two or more clients receiving help for a similar problem. In Toby's class, according to Toby's teacher, two other children, Sarah and David, also display behavioral problems. Like Toby, they have difficulty staying in their seat when the teacher is talking to the class.

We can imagine that Toby's teacher would be very interested in using an intervention to address all three children's behavior. One possibility would be to use a multiple-baseline design to assess the effectiveness of this approach. First, the teacher would collect baseline data on all three children's behavior, say for ten school days. At that point, the teacher would introduce the behavioral intervention with Toby only, while continuing to collect baseline data on Sarah and David. After ten more school days, the teacher would introduce the intervention with Sarah, continue the intervention with Toby, and continue the collection of baseline data on David. Finally, after an additional ten days, the teacher would introduce the intervention with David while continuing the intervention with Toby and Sarah.

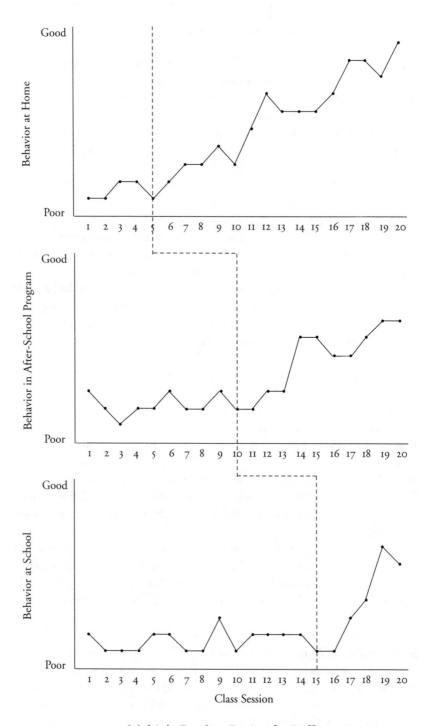

FIGURE 3.9   Multiple-Baseline Design for Different Settings

The quantitative results suggest that the intervention had a positive effect on Toby and Sarah and a moderately positive effect on David (figure 3.10). These changes in the children's behavior may have been a function of extraneous factors, but here too it would be a remarkable coincidence if extraneous factors, and not the intervention, were the principal cause of this positive change.

Social workers need to be careful when they use multiple-baseline designs to assess the effectiveness of an intervention with two or more clients receiving help for a similar problem. If these clients interact with each other in a significant way, the interaction itself, rather than the intervention, may produce the change (one client's change may influence another client).

GROUP RESEARCH AND EVALUATION DESIGNS

Single-case designs can be useful in direct practice with individuals, families, and groups. But in many situations, social workers need to take a broader look at issues. By broader I mean research and evaluation projects that draw on information from larger samples. In chapter 2, I talked about a wide range of exploratory, descriptive, and evaluative/explanatory projects that depended on information collected from groups of people, case records, and so on.

As with single-case designs, many different designs can be used to collect information from larger samples. Which design social workers decide to use depends on many factors, including the project's goals (exploration, description, and/or evaluation/explanation), what is feasible in regard to budget and time, logistical constraints (for example, a social worker's access to clients or agency records), and ethical considerations. Not surprisingly, different group designs have different strengths and limitations, particularly with respect to their internal and external validity.

Preexperimental Designs

In general, group designs are divided into two groups: preexperimental and experimental designs. *Preexperimental designs* offer virtually no control over threats to internal and external validity. They are typically used for exploratory projects in which social workers aren't trying to say anything conclusively about the effectiveness of an intervention or another cause–effect relationship. A good example of this kind of design is the one-shot case study design.

One-shot case-study design.   Think of all of the situations in social work when we want to find out how a group of clients are doing. Social workers participating in residential treatment programs for clients with mental illness, for

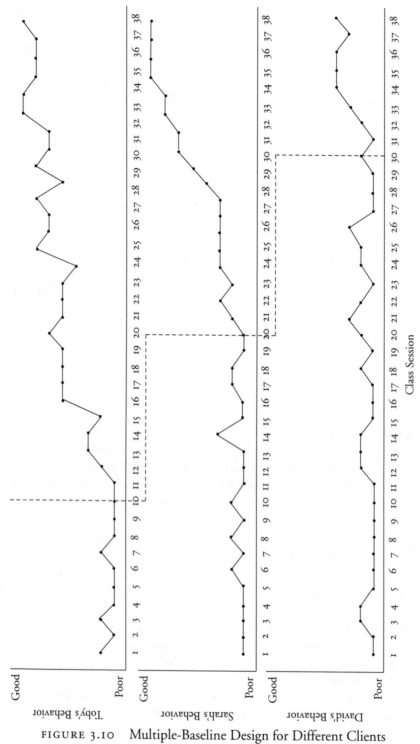

FIGURE 3.10   Multiple-Baseline Design for Different Clients

example, want to know about their clients' status at some point in time.

The Mt. Washington social worker in charge of the agency's substance abuse treatment program wants to measure the clients' substance abuse rates at the end of the treatment, to see how they are doing. This quantitative data could be supplemented by qualitative reports by the clients and other important people in their lives. This is a good example of the one-shot case study design. The notation used for this design is

$$X \ O$$

where the X indicates an intervention and the O indicates an observation. (I'm sure you see how similar the X is to the B in single-case designs.) With the one-shot case study design, we simply make one observation at the conclusion of an intervention. This is better than nothing but somewhat limited if we are interested in the intervention's effectiveness. Furthermore, this design doesn't control for the large number of extraneous factors that could influence the outcome.

In addition, this design doesn't show whether there was any change in the group's status compared with that in the period immediately preceding the intervention. Despite these limitations, the one-shot case study design at least gives social workers basic descriptive information about their clients' status following an intervention, and we shouldn't minimize the value of that.

One-group pre-test–post-test design. We could remedy this part of the problem by making another observation before the observation, so that we would have something with which to compare the post-treatment substance abuse rates. This design is known as a *one-group pre-test–post-test design* and is denoted by

$$O_1 \ X \ O_2$$

The symbol O_1 refers to the measurement before the intervention, or what is sometimes called the *pre-test* or *Time-1 measurement*. The O_2 symbol refers to the measurement following the intervention and is often called the *post-test* or *Time-2 measurement*. (Designs that entail a long-term follow-up of clients require multiple observations after the intervention. These are called *longitudinal designs*. We would need several O's after the X to indicate multiple observations.)

This design still wouldn't rule out the extraneous factors and plausible alternative explanations of any change in the group's status after the intervention

(low internal validity). Hence if we documented improvement in the participants' substance abuse rates and the quality of their lives, based on the clients'
self-reports, we would not be able to assume that the intervention actually
caused the favorable outcome. Even though the intervention might well have
brought about the change, we can't assume this. If we return to the criteria
(presented earlier) necessary to demonstrate a causal relationship between an
intervention and an outcome, we will see that only two are satisfied. We thus
can say that the intervention preceded the outcome—the Time-2 measure—
in time. And we can demonstrate that there is a correlation between the intervention and outcome. What we don't have, unfortunately, is a way to rule out
plausible alternative explanations and extraneous factors.

Post-test-only design—nonequivalent groups.   In social work, practitioners
often introduce an intervention and then decide they want to compare the
group's status after the intervention with another group of clients not exposed
to the intervention. Let's suppose that a group of Mt. Washington clients with
substance abuse problems participated in the treatment program sponsored by
the agency. After the intervention, the program's director decided to compare
the results with the substance abuse rates of a group of people on the waiting
list to enter Mt. Washington's substance abuse treatment program. Because of
budget and staffing constraints, Mt. Washington has had to keep a waiting list
of people who have applied to enter the agency's substance abuse program.
Ordinarily, the waiting list has about twenty-five names on it.

This comparison may be useful, but social workers need to know its limitations. The post-test-only design—nonequivalent groups is symbolized this
way:

$$X \ O$$
$$\overline{}$$
$$O$$

The main problem is that when comparing groups like this, we have no way
of knowing whether the initial differences between the groups account for the
differences in outcome, if there are any. The people on the waiting list may be
different from those who actually received the intervention, with respect to
such factors as substance abuse histories, ethnic or cultural backgrounds, age,
financial resources, social support, or motivation to change. These differences
could account for any differences in outcome.

Given these limitations, which are sometimes unavoidable, what's a social
worker to do?

EXPERIMENTAL DESIGNS

Social workers sometimes can use a research and evaluation design that rules out plausible alternative explanations and controls for common extraneous factors (high internal validity). The logic here is much the same as the logic for single-case research and evaluation designs. With single-case designs, we need to introduce controls to rule out plausible alternative explanations. We usually use the client as his or her own control, by using either a reversal design or some kind of multiple-baseline design.

With group designs, we typically use a second group as a control (as we'll see shortly, sometimes there are more than two groups). The traditional features of experimental designs are the random assignment of individuals to an experimental and control group, the introduction of an intervention to an experimental group and the withholding of the intervention from the control group, the administration of pre-tests and post-tests, and the comparison of results for the experimental and control groups. The best-known example of this approach is the *classical experimental design.*

Classical experimental design.   The classical experimental design solves two problems. First, it provides a mechanism to compare one group of "subjects" (individual clients, families, etc.) who received an intervention (the "experimental" group) with a second group of subjects who did not (the "control" group). Without this comparison, it would be difficult to know whether the intervention caused a change different from the change that would have occurred anyway.

Second, the classical experimental design usually ensures equivalence between the experimental and control groups. Remember that earlier I pointed out that when social workers compare the outcomes of two groups of clients that aren't similar to begin with, it creates a problem. Any differences between the groups, whether they were exposed to two different interventions or whether one was an experimental group and one was a control group, could be due to differences between the groups *before* the intervention. The classical experimental design usually resolves this problem by randomly assigning people to the two groups. You can do this by assigning every other name on a list of clients to the experimental group and putting the remainder in the control group, or use some other random assignment mechanism (for example, a table of random numbers—which I will explain in chapter 5—or something as simple and straightforward as coin flips).

This concept of random assignment is important. Sometimes social workers are skeptical that random assignment actually works. They have difficulty

believing that random assignment actually produces groups of clients that are comparable or equivalent with respect to variables such as age, gender, ethnicity, and clinical symptoms. But if social workers make the random assignment properly with a large enough sample, it usually works, allowing for a relatively small margin of error.

The classical experimental design (also known as the *pre-test–post-test, control-group design*) is diagrammed as

$$R \; O_1 \; X \; O_2$$
$$R \; O_1 \quad \; O_2$$

The R denotes random assignment, and the other symbols should be familiar to you by now.

With our case example, the Mt. Washington social worker would, if feasible, randomly assign those clients who have applied for the substance abuse treatment program to either an experimental group or a control group. Although we need to think carefully about the ethical issues (which we will, shortly), in principle it is possible to place the control group clients on a waiting list and then offer them services when the evaluation of the program's effectiveness is complete. The clients could be randomly assigned by selecting every other name, flipping a coin, or using a table of random numbers.

But in many instances, social workers cannot randomly assign clients to experimental and control groups, because of logistical or ethical restrictions. A compromise is to match clients instead. It isn't an ideal solution, but it's a reasonable, and fairly common, alternative when random assignment isn't feasible.

With matching, the social worker identifies characteristics or variables on which the groups differ before an intervention is introduced that could account for differences in outcome between the groups. In our case example, the clients might be matched on characteristics such as age, ethnicity, gender, and substance abuse and treatment history (both of which would need to be operationally defined). Clients would be matched on these characteristics one by one, with matched pairs split between the groups to enhance the likelihood that the groups were comparable. Although this process can be difficult and time-consuming, matching can be an effective way to rule out plausible alternative explanations due to initial differences between the experimental and control groups. Of course, we can match only when we have the necessary information before the introduction of an intervention.

It may have dawned on you that there can be a problem with the classical experimental design. In some cases, although certainly not all, clients' exposure to the pre-test, whatever it assesses, can affect both the experimental group's and the control group's responses to the post-test. That is, clients' behaviors, attitudes, opinions, and feelings can be affected not only by the intervention but also by their familiarity with the project's measurement instruments. The pre-test may alert clients to the social worker's goals and anticipated outcomes, and this can be a biasing factor.

Getting rid of the pre-test might solve that problem (that would be a post-test-only-control-group design), but it would create another one. Without a pre-test, we wouldn't know for sure whether the random assignment worked and whether the two groups were indeed comparable, and we wouldn't be able to assess changes in clients' status between the Time-1 and Time-2 measures.

A clever way around this problem—although one that, practically speaking, is often difficult to implement—is the *Solomon four-group design* (a former student of mine once asked whether this design was invented by King Solomon. Nope.)

Solomon four-group design. The Solomon four-group design essentially combines the best features of the pre-test–post-test control-group design and the post-test-only control design while eliminating their limitations. It requires us to use four groups (a practical problem in many situations). Clients are randomly assigned to the groups. Two of the groups receive a pre-test, but only one of them is exposed to the intervention. A third group is exposed to the intervention but does not receive a pre-test. The fourth group receives only the post-test. The other three groups also receive a post-test.

The advantage of this design is that it enables social workers to compare the experimental group that received the pre-test with the experimental group that did not and to compare the control group that received the pre-test with the control group that did not, to see whether the pre-test itself influenced the post-test scores. In addition, the control-group feature allows social workers to rule out the influence of extraneous factors. The Solomon four-group design is diagrammed as follows:

$$R \ O_1 \ X \ O_2$$
$$R \ O_1 \quad \ O_2$$
$$R \quad \ X \ O_2$$
$$R \quad \quad O_2$$

QUASI-EXPERIMENTAL DESIGNS

Because of a variety of practical constraints—political, ethical, or logistical—social workers cannot always randomly assign clients to experimental and control groups. For example, the staff may feel uncomfortable withholding an intervention from some clients, or clients may have already been assigned to treatment groups once a social worker decides to conduct an evaluation. In these instances, the best that social workers can do is approximate experimental designs with what are called *quasi-experimental designs*. These designs don't offer the high internal validity that experimental designs do, but they sometimes offer more control of extraneous factors than do preexperimental designs. That is, with respect to internal validity, quasi-experimental designs fall somewhere between preexperimental designs and experimental designs.

Nonequivalent control-groups design. Suppose the Mt. Washington social worker in charge of the agency's substance abuse treatment program is running one treatment group that meets on Tuesday evenings and another that meets on Thursday afternoons. The social worker wants to see whether the participants' relapse rates can be reduced if their group treatment is combined with weekly individual counseling sessions. One possibility is to add individual-counseling sessions to the Tuesday group and to withhold these counseling sessions from the Thursday group. In a sense, the Thursday group would be a control group. This design might make sense if the social worker has reason to believe that the groups do not differ with respect to key variables such as age, ethnicity, gender, and substance abuse and treatment history. Actually, the social worker can probably compare the characteristics of the two groups by examining data in the case records. If the two groups seem reasonably similar—even though they were not randomly assigned—they can be compared. The internal validity of this design is not perfect, but it's better than that of a design that doesn't include a control group (actually, *comparison group* is a more accurate term when random assignment isn't possible). This design is diagrammed as

$$O_1 \ X \ O_2$$
$$O_1 \quad\ O_2$$

You'll notice that this diagram looks almost the same as the one for the classical experimental design. The only difference is that the R's indicating a random assignment of clients to the experimental and control groups are missing. Otherwise, the diagrams are the same. The experimental and comparison groups are measured before the intervention regarding their alcohol consumption (O_1); the experimental group is offered the intervention (the individual-counseling sessions, denoted by the X); and both groups are measured after the experimental group receives the intervention (O_2).

Comparison-group post-test-only design.   Sometimes it isn't feasible to obtain a pre-test or Time-1 measure if the social worker is concerned that the pre-test measure might bias the post-test measure, the Time-1 measure would be too intrusive, or the persons in the project simply aren't available to be measured. This is hardly a desirable situation, but it happens, and we wouldn't want to assume too much based on a comparison of the two groups' results. They may have been quite different to begin with, and the intervention may not have been the primary cause of any differences between the groups. Nonetheless, it still may be useful to know whether there are any differences between the groups following the intervention. This design is diagrammed as

$$X \ O$$
$$O$$

Time-series designs.   Thus far we have looked at situations in which social workers assess clients' status just before and just after an intervention. This kind of snapshot often makes sense.

But in certain circumstances, social workers must follow or monitor clients over an extended period of time. Many of the problems for which clients seek help may not be resolved right away or may warrant monitoring for quite a long time. In these instances, time-series designs are suitable because they include quantitative and/or qualitative assessments or measures at several different times.

The most straightforward design is a *simple interrupted time-series design*. It does not have a control group, which is the principal reason it is considered a quasi-experimental design rather than an experimental design. Let's suppose that one group of Mt. Washington clients was participating in group-counseling sessions to address their problems with alcohol abuse. The group met twice each week, and at each meeting the participants were asked to record the number of alcoholic drinks they had consumed each day since the last meeting. (We will assume that the participants reported honestly.) After five weeks of the group sessions, each participant also began individual counseling once each week. The social worker in charge of the program continued to collect quantitative data on the participants' alcohol consumption for another five weeks, along with the participants' qualitative self-reports about their status. The social worker is interested in knowing whether the pattern changed after the individual-counseling sessions were introduced. The graph in figure 3.11 shows that the participants' average alcohol consumption declined somewhat after the group sessions were supplemented with individual-counseling sessions. Although significant changes in the pattern after the intervention cannot be attributed entirely to the intervention, because of the possibility of uncontrolled extraneous variables, the time-series data can be very suggestive. This simple interrupted time-series design is diagrammed as

$$O_1 \; O_2 \; O_3 \; O_4 \; O_5 \; X \; O_6 \; O_7 \; O_8 \; O_9 \; O_{10}$$

In principle, it also is possible to strengthen the simple interrupted time-series design by adding a comparison group. If we could randomly assign individuals to the two groups, we would have a form of experimental design. More commonly, however, social workers have to use a nonequivalent comparison group and to take into account the possible influence of initial differences between the groups. This is known as a *multiple time-series design* and is diagrammed as

$$O_1 \; O_2 \; O_3 \; O_4 \; O_5 \; X \; O_6 \; O_7 \; O_8 \; O_9 \; O_{10}$$
$$O_1 \; O_2 \; O_3 \; O_4 \; O_5 \quad\; O_6 \; O_7 \; O_8 \; O_9 \; O_{10}$$

These are the quasi-experimental designs that social workers are most likely to encounter.

This is hardly an exhaustive overview, however; there are many other possibilities. As with the single-case designs we reviewed, there are all kinds of

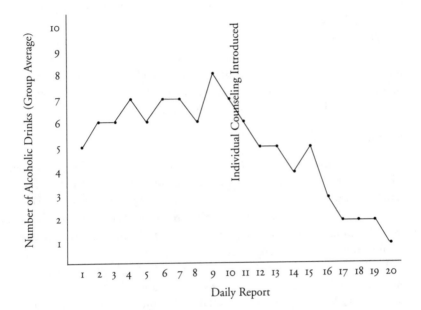

FIGURE 3.11   Simple Interrupted Time-Series Design

ways to modify the basic designs and adapt them to one's unique circumstances. The same goes for quasi-experimental designs. There is nothing sacred, for instance, about five measures before and five measures after an intervention. A different frequency may make more sense in a particular situation. It's fine to play around with different designs. The important thing is for practitioners to understand the strengths and limitations of various designs, particularly with respect to their internal validity.

Now that we've reviewed various research and evaluation designs related to direct practice, let's look at designs that can be used in indirect practice.

RESEARCH AND EVALUATION DESIGNS: INDIRECT PRACTICE

Most of the group research and evaluation designs appropriate to social work with individuals, families, couples, and groups are also suitable, depending on the circumstances, for indirect practice involving agency administration, community organizing, advocacy, social welfare policy, and other "social change" activities. Often social workers need to draw on their research and evaluation skills to conduct needs assessments or community surveys, evaluate programs, analyze policies, and so on.

Which research and evaluation designs are best depend on the social worker's goal. Those that are suitable for exploratory projects may not be useful for descriptive projects. Designs that work well for descriptive projects may be inadequate to evaluate a social service program. Let's turn next to the designs useful in these different circumstances.

Exploratory Projects

We said in chapter 2 that social workers usually carry out exploratory projects when they are at a beginning stage of research or evaluation. Practitioners may have a preliminary idea that they want to investigate, or they may need certain information related to their work. Exploratory projects usually gather small or modest amounts of information from a relatively small sample of clients, records, practitioners, or administrators.

Earlier I described several situations at the Mt. Washington Family Service Agency in which exploratory projects would be appropriate. One of the examples was Mt. Washington's family life education program and the lack of attendance by local ethnic minorities and people of color. As a first step, the director of the agency's family life education program wanted to obtain information from a relatively small number of these residents concerning their perceptions of the agency's program. But the program director may not have enough time or resources to conduct a large-scale survey at this point.

Given his goals, what kind of design would be best? He could conduct interviews with a few community residents who are willing to share their views about Mt. Washington's role in the community and its programs. Although it may be useful for the program director to chat informally with the residents, it may be more productive to use a structured or semistructured interview guide that includes a number of carefully worded questions. Using such an instrument would have a couple of advantages. First, it would help the program director focus the interviews so that they do not meander from topic to topic in a conversational free-for-all. Second, an interview instrument would provide some consistency from conversation to conversation, to ensure that each community resident had an opportunity to comment on the same topics. (At some point, of course, we should talk about how to select, or sample, the community residents who would participate in the interviews. This will come up in chapter 5, when we discuss sampling.)

I am sure you've noticed that there is nothing unusual about this design. There are no pre-tests or post-tests, no control groups, and so on. None of this is necessary, given the purpose we have in mind here: a program director at a social service agency who wants to gather some preliminary information from a relatively small group of people who may have something to say about the agency's programs. Perhaps this beginning inquiry will lead to a larger collection of data, perhaps not. Wherever it leads, the information gathered from this kind of exploratory project can be useful.

One of the other examples we discussed in chapter 2 was an important social policy issue that seemed to be affecting a number of social service agencies. The associate director for administration at Mt. Washington, Nancy C., has been concerned about the amount of stipend that the state child welfare agency provides to foster parents. In Nancy C.'s experience, some foster parents drop out of the program because of the stipend's small size.

To address this problem, Nancy C. decided to contact other family service agencies in the state that have contracts with the child welfare agency, to determine whether they also are having similar difficulties. Nancy C. thought that if she found evidence that all or many of the agencies had similar difficulties, the agencies might organize to lobby for a larger stipend.

As a first step, Nancy C. compiled a list of executive directors of the family service agencies that had contracts with the state's child welfare agency to provide foster care services. She then wrote a list of questions concerning the directors' experiences with their foster care programs, the stipend, and so on. Specifically, her questions concern the number of foster care cases the agency typically handles, feedback or complaints that agency administrators have received from foster parents about the stipend, and directors' views of whether foster parents leave the program because of the stipend's size.

Here, too, we don't need a complicated design. Because we aren't trying to evaluate the foster care program, we don't need long-term follow-up or data collection, a control group, and so on. Instead, we need only gather exploratory information at one time to help clarify a difficult issue. This project could, in principle, lead to a more ambitious project, but it doesn't need to. This exploratory project may be sufficient, particularly if it produces information that helps family service agency administrators advocate for a change in the state's child welfare agency's stipend policy.

Descriptive Projects

Descriptive projects pose a different kind of challenge. Let's go back to the example of the concern among Mt. Washington staff about the lack of clients who are ethnic minorities or people of color. In addition to conducting the exploratory project interviewing community residents, the agency's staff gath-

ered basic descriptive information about community residents in the surrounding geographical area who are ethnic minorities or people of color. This
kind of information can be useful to staff who are developing outreach efforts
to these members of the local community. What ethnic and cultural groups are
represented in the community? How many persons are in each group? What
are their demographic characteristics (for example, age, gender, family status)?
What are their income and education levels? How have these patterns changed
over time?

To gather this information, the Mt. Washington staff need a solid research
design to ensure collecting comprehensive information about the community
residents' characteristics.

As the first step in this design, the Mt. Washington staff decide exactly what
information they think they need for a complete picture of the community
residents' characteristics. The staff might sit around a table in the agency and
brainstorm categories of information, such as those used earlier. Obviously,
they should collect only information that is likely to be useful and relevant to
their efforts to strengthen services to community residents who are ethnic
minorities and people of color. Why waste precious time gathering superflu-
ous facts and details?

Next, staff members must determine where all this information would
come from. Most likely, they would get information from many sources. Some
might be readily available from public and private agencies in the area. Often,
state, county, or municipal governments have planning departments (the
name may vary) that routinely collect or collate data on communities' demographic, economic, and social characteristics. In addition, private agencies
often gather this kind of information for planning purposes or to use in grant
applications. Examples are local United Way agencies, foundations, and neighborhood social service centers. It may not take much more than a couple of
telephone calls to find reports summarizing some of the information that Mt.
Washington staff are looking for.

But perhaps no agency has exactly what the Mt. Washington staff want. If
this is the case, they must figure out a way to get it.

Unfortunately, this kind of data collection can be time-consuming and
expensive. It may require a fairly labor intensive effort to generate a sample of
community residents (more about that in chapter 5), interview them, and
summarize the data. It takes time, people, and—surprise—money. Ideally, Mt.
Washington would have some funds in its budget to carry out this task or to
hire an outside consultant to do it. The expense would be justified if this information enabled the agency to enhance the delivery of its services to commu-

nity residents who are ethnic minorities or people of color. The information might also be used in a grant application to a foundation or some other source for funds to develop outreach services for this population.

Here, too, we don't have to have a complicated design. Once again, we do not even need to think about such phenomena as causal relationships, independent and dependent variables, experimental and control groups, and longitudinal data collection. None of that is relevant. All we're talking about here is a design that would enable a one-time collection of descriptive data that would help Mt. Washington strengthen the delivery of its services to ethnic minorities and people of color.

Mt. Washington's staff would face a similar challenge if they wanted to carry out the descriptive project presented in chapter 2 concerning social welfare policy issues related to affordable housing in the community. Earlier I mentioned that one of the ongoing problems in the Mt. Washington area is the lack of affordable housing for low- and moderate-income people. One of Mt. Washington's staff, Andrew R., serves on an interagency task force that has been meeting for several months to devise a strategy for the state's housing finance agency and the governor's policy office to make the area's housing more affordable. The interagency task force includes representatives from several nonprofit community development and housing agencies, agencies serving homeless people, and the United Way.

The task force's goal is to lobby for larger subsidies for first-time low- and moderate-income home buyers and renters. The task force members know they face an uphill battle because of constraints in the state's budget and federal limits on money that the state can raise through issuing bonds. Nonetheless, they are encouraged by the successes of their counterparts in two nearby states and are eager to lobby for increased funding.

Andrew R. agreed to spearhead the task force's documentation of the need for more affordable housing. Here's the design he came up with. First, he met with task force members and employees of the state housing finance agency to make up a list of key indicators of the local affordable housing problem. In research jargon, Andrew R. identified the relevant concepts and operationalized them. He decided he needed data on such phenomena as the percentage of potential low- and moderate-income home buyers who do not meet the standard income guidelines to qualify for a mortgage; the percentage of renters who are spending an inordinate amount of their income on rent; the numbers of people who have been displaced from their apartments because they cannot pay the rent increases; the number of rental units for low- and moderate-income residents that have disappeared from the market owing to abandonment, deterioration, arson, or conversion to condominiums; and the increase in home prices and rents during the past two years, particularly compared with the increases in wages in the local economy. Andrew R.'s goal is to obtain information that paints a compelling portrait of the local affordable housing crisis and that will help address an important social welfare policy issue.

As with the earlier example of collecting descriptive information related to the characteristics of ethnic minorities and people of color in the Mt. Washington area, this project requires descriptive information from various sources. Some of this information may be easy to obtain. For example, the state housing finance agency may have a planning unit that routinely gathers and analyzes data on changes in housing prices and rents in different communities. This is the kind of basic information that a state housing agency needs to stay on top of local housing conditions throughout the state.

Some of this information may not be so easy to obtain. For example, where would Andrew R. and his colleagues find data on the number of people who have been displaced from their apartments because of deteriorated conditions, conversion to condominiums, or rent increases? This is not the sort of information that any agency would necessarily gather routinely. If it seems important to have, Andrew R. may need to design a project that would sample residents and interview them about their recent housing history, including the number of times they have moved and why. This information may be enormously useful, but here, too, collecting it may be expensive and time-consuming. At some point, members of the task force must decide whether to make the investment.

Explanatory/Evaluative Projects

Now we come to what are typically more complex research and evaluation designs. In chapter 2, I described an explanatory/evaluative design for a program at Mt. Washington to provide transitional housing to a group of single mothers and their children. The women selected to participate in this program have been on public assistance for at least three years and are trying to move off public assistance and into private-sector jobs. The program's clients will participate in both educational and vocational programs and counseling during the time they spend in their subsidized housing unit. The program will also provide child care during the mothers' education, training, and counseling.

To evaluate the effectiveness of this transitional housing program, Mt. Washington staff will monitor the clients' progress over time. It would be helpful to know, for example, the percentage of women in the program who are able to find jobs within three months following their completion of the program, the percentage of these women who remain employed for different periods of time following the program's completion (say, for three, six, nine, and twelve months), the wages paid to the women, the various costs and benefits of being employed as opposed to being on public assistance (for instance, the net gain or loss in income and assets, health care coverage, child care), and the women's subjective reports of the impact of the program on their quality of life.

To determine the program's impact, the Mt. Washington staff must rule out other factors that could explain changes in the women's circumstances following their completion of the program. As we know from our earlier discussion of the concepts of control and extraneous variables, the research and evaluation design used in this case would have to be able to rule out various plausible alternative explanations (such as the effects of maturation, the measurement procedures, and other contemporaneous events). How should the staff do this?

Ideally, the Mt. Washington staff should be able to compare the various outcomes for women participating in the transitional housing program with a comparable group of women who are not participating in this program. This is possible if many more women are eligible for the program than the program can accommodate. That is, there simply may not be enough funds or room to serve all the women who meet the program's admission criteria.

If this is the case, those women who are eligible for the transitional housing program can be randomly assigned to either the program or a control group that will receive the services ordinarily provided to this client population. Let's say that fifty women are randomly assigned to each group.

Each mother assigned to the transitional housing program agrees to participate in the program for two years. According to the program's design, at the end of the two-year program, the mothers should be in a position to obtain private-sector employment and unsubsidized housing. The women in the control group will receive the services ordinarily provided to women in their circumstances (public assistance, subsidized health care, and so on).

Now let's fast-forward the tape and assume that of the fifty women who enrolled in the transitional housing program, thirty-six completed it. Fourteen mothers either dropped out of the program on their own or were asked to leave because they did not comply with one or more program rules or requirements.

The study design calls for Mt. Washington's staff to collect data on the program participants' and control-group members' employment status, income, and assets and to conduct follow-up interviews with all control-group members and program participants, including those who did and did not complete the program. Some of the data are collected before the start of the transitional housing program (for example, income and asset data, attitudes toward work) and then are collected again at different times during and after the end of the program. Following the program's completion, the research staff obtain detailed information about the participants' status (for example, employment, income, housing situation) and their perceptions of the program's strengths and limitations.

Once the data have been collected, staff members compare the experiences and status of the program and the control groups. Any differences between the two groups with respect to some or all the outcome measures can be attributed to the program. That is, the research and evaluation design enables the Mt. Washington staff to control for extraneous factors and rule out plausible alternative explanations of any differences found between the program and the control groups.

Let's look at another example of a research and evaluation design related to indirect practice, in this case the national social policy problem of teenage pregnancy. For a number of years, there has been significant national concern about this problem. One can find volumes of data documenting the often tragic consequences of teenage pregnancy, including inadequate prenatal care, low birth weight, developmental problems in children born to teenage mothers, poverty, and increased health, social service, and welfare costs.

Let's suppose that the U.S. Department of Health and Human Services (DHHS) announces a large-scale research and demonstration program to address teenage pregnancy. The DHHS issues a "request for proposal" (typically called an RFP) inviting public and private agencies throughout the United States to apply for a $3.5 million grant. The general guidelines call for the implementation and assessment of an intervention model designed to reduce teenage pregnancy rates. Applicants are required to submit a detailed proposal describing the intervention model they would use in various sites throughout the United States and the evaluation plan they would use to assess the intervention's effectiveness. The proposals are to draw on the best available empirical research concerning interventions designed to reduce teenage pregnancy.

Eight agencies submit proposals. Most of the applicants are private nonprofit child welfare agencies with offices in Washington, D.C., or throughout the United States. The interventions described in the various proposals vary considerably. Several combine school-based preventive education and counseling. Others emphasize broader-based public education campaigns and the distribution of contraceptives.

The proposal selected by the DHHS contains several components, including school-based education, a media campaign, and a plan to educate parents about ways to prevent teenage pregnancy. The agency that is awarded the grant has its headquarters in Chicago and branch offices in seven other states.

According to the agency's proposal, the intervention will be carried out in twelve sites around the country—large, medium, and small urban centers and several rural areas. A senior staff member of the Chicago-based child welfare agency will serve as the principal investigator and recruit cooperating child welfare or family service agencies in the twelve intervention sites. Each cooperating agency will receive a portion of the grant funds to implement the intervention locally and to participate in the evaluation.

After seeing a program announcement in a professional journal, the director of the Mt. Washington Family Services Agency applies to participate in the national program. The agency director agrees to assign three staff members to work on the program full time. These staff members have considerable experience working with pregnant and parenting teenagers and had training in social work research and evaluation as part of their master's degree in social work.

The evaluation design identifies "experimental" and "control" neighborhoods in each program site. Using extensive measures, the communities are to be matched on such variables as income distribution, poverty rates, family size, racial and ethnic composition, education levels, unemployment rates, infant mortality rates, and teenage pregnancy rates. Those communities in the experimental group will receive the carefully designed intervention, but those communities in the control group will not. The intervention will take place during one academic year.

Before the intervention, a sample of local residents—both adults and teenagers—will be interviewed concerning a variety of issues, including attitudes toward teenage pregnancy, contraception, premarital sexual activity, sexually transmitted diseases, and future educational and vocational plans. These interviews will be conducted again immediately following completion of the intervention and also one year later. In addition, the various evaluation teams will collect data on the communities' teenage pregnancy rates one year, two years, and three years after the intervention.

This is an ambitious and sophisticated design. Clearly, the overall intent is to assess the effectiveness of the intervention model and, to the extent possible, to rule out extraneous factors that might account for differences between those communities that are exposed to the intervention and those communities that are not. Although this design has some limitations (for instance, it may be difficult to come up with a "perfect" match for every community in the national program), it can do a reasonably good job of controlling for and ruling out plausible alternative explanations.

4

ETHICAL ISSUES IN SOCIAL WORK RESEARCH AND EVALUATION

What's your reaction to the following circumstances:

A clinical social worker at the Mt. Washington Family Service Agency wants her supervisor to observe her work with a family and offer feedback concerning her listening skills (specifically, the social worker's ability to respond empathetically to the clients' comments). The supervisor agrees to observe the social worker and family through a one-way mirror and to record data on the social worker's listening skills, using a structured data collection instrument. The social worker does not want to tell the family that someone will be observing them through the one-way mirror, because she thinks that knowing this would make her clients feel uncomfortable and self-conscious. Would it be acceptable to allow the supervisor to observe the family through the one-way mirror without telling them?

The psychiatrist who consults with Mt. Washington's mobile treatment team—which provides support services to people with chronic mental illness—has approached the staff about participating in a new drug study to evaluate the effectiveness of an experimental antipsychotic medication. The medication may help people who have severe delusions and hallucinations. The study's design calls for Mt. Washington's clients to be randomly assigned to an experimental group, which would receive the new medication, and to a control group, which would receive the agency's usual services. One of the possible side effects of the new medication is violent behavior, although this has occurred only rarely in the clinical research trials conducted thus far. Should the Mt. Washington staff agree to participate in the study?

To monitor the quality of Mt. Washington's services, an agency administrator decides to pose incognito as an agency client, sit in the agency's waiting room several times during a one-week period, and chat informally with some of the agency's actual clients about their experiences as clients. The administrator does not plan to disclose his true identity, believing that this is the best way to obtain candid feedback about the agency's services. Is this sort of deception acceptable?

A clinical social worker at Mt. Washington wants to interview a sample of agency clients about their experiences as childhood sexual assault victims. The social worker plans to use the data as part of her doctoral dissertation, in which she is exploring the relationship between childhood sexual abuse and subsequent substance abuse. The social worker is concerned, however, about the possible harmful psychological effects of encouraging clients to think and talk about painful childhood experiences. How should the social worker handle this situation?

One of the things social workers know well is that they must be more than proficient practitioners who can implement complex interventions. They must also practice ethically. Since the earliest days of its history, the social work profession has recognized the importance of ethical standards in practice.

The same is true of social workers' research and evaluation. It is not enough for social workers to understand and be able to implement various research and evaluation methodologies. Sure, it's important for social workers to grasp the technical information and skills discussed in this book, related to, for example, research and evaluation designs, sampling, measurement, data collection, and data analysis. But all this is meaningless if social workers disregard the wide range of ethical issues in research and evaluation. The violation of clients' rights and the abandonment of ethical principles concerning research and evaluation are no more tolerable than are the ethical violations and misconduct that occur in direct practice with individuals, families, couples, and groups or in indirect practice involving community organizing, social policy, agency administration, and social action.

THE EMERGENCE OF ETHICAL ISSUES IN RESEARCH AND EVALUATION

In recent years, members of all professions, including social work, have developed a much keener interest in ethical issues. For a variety of reasons, professionals as diverse as engineers, nurses, lawyers, accountants, journalists, military officers, police, physicians, psychologists, dentists, and social workers have begun to pay closer attention to ethical issues affecting their practice. Journalists need to understand how to resolve conflicts between citizens' privacy rights and the public's "right to know." Nurses need to know how to handle situations in which a physician has issued orders that, in a nurse's judgment, would be unethical to carry out. Accountants must know how to handle situations in which a client appears to be submitting a fraudulent tax return to conceal illegal activity.

Why are professionals so interested in ethical issues these days? After all, it's not as if ethical issues haven't always been around. There's no denying that every profession has faced complicated ethical issues ever since they opened their doors for business. Why, then, has this relatively recent surge of interest affected the ways in which research and evaluation are carried out in the professions, as well as the ways in which professionals carry out other aspects of their work?

There are several reasons. One is the introduction of complicated and controversial technology—much of it related to health care—which has led to vigorous ethical debate. Examples are the ethical controversy surrounding the transplantation of animal organs into human beings, the use of artificial organs to keep people alive, genetic engineering, and the use of psychotropic drugs to change people's personalities and behavior. In addition, the widespread use of computer technology has generated troubling ethical issues, mostly related to privacy.

Professionals' interest in ethical issues also has been stimulated by the widespread media attention to a number of scandals involving public figures and officials. It wouldn't take long for every one of us to recite the names of nationally known and local people whose misdeeds have been splashed across television screens and newspapers' front pages. I'm not just talking about politicians. These lists also would include physicians, lawyers, clergy, police, and—gulp—social workers (the good news is that the subjects of these stories constitute a very small percentage of professionals, most of whom usually behave quite ethically). One result of this disconcerting publicity is that professionals are now paying much more attention to ethical issues.

Professionals' interest in ethical issues is also partly a legacy of the 1960s, when the nation's awareness was changed forever by the introduction of legislation and public policy concerning such phenomena as hospital and psychiatric patients' rights, prisoners' rights, welfare rights, and civil rights in general. The intense debate dramatically changed the ways that professionals and other citizens think about ethical issues, professionals' ethical obligations, and clients' rights.

Like people, professions also mature, and the professions' escalating interest in ethics is also a function of the passage of time and increased opportunity for practitioners to understand how ethical issues are embedded in their work and why they are an inescapable feature of their professional life.

We must also recognize, however, that ethical issues related to research and evaluation have their own—and sometimes grisly—history (Levine 1991). Perhaps the pivotal event was the trial of the Nazi doctors at Nuremberg in 1945. These legal proceedings documented and publicized in unprecedented fashion the harm that can be caused by unethical research, in this instance, for the benefit of the Third Reich military. The inhumane experiments conducted with unconsenting prisoners showcased the pain and suffering that research can inflict. Out of this horror, fortunately, came the Nuremberg Code and other international codes of ethics written to protect research participants. These seminal documents helped lead to standards in research requiring that subjects' participation be both voluntary and informed and that they be protected from unjustifiable risk.

Two other significant events stemmed from notoriously unethical and highly publicized medical studies. The Tuskegee syphilis study, a forty-year project begun in 1932 by the U.S. Public Health Service, was designed to study the natural history of untreated syphilis. The study's sample was made up of poor black men from Alabama who were told that they had "bad blood" and that research procedures such as spinal taps would be provided as "free" treatment. These men were not given what was then the standard treatment for syphilis, or penicillin when it became available later during the study. The men in the sample were not informed of the research design and its risks to them based on the study's methodology. Many of them died, but the study's unethical features did not come to light until 1972.

The second noteworthy study—the Willowbrook study—also investigated the natural history of an untreated disease, in this case infectious hepatitis. In this study, a group of children diagnosed with mental retardation, who lived at the Willowbrook State Hospital in Staten Island, New York, were deliberately infected with hepatitis. The study's purpose was to study the history of the disease when left untreated and later to assess the effects of gamma globulin as a therapeutic intervention. This study generated a variety of concerns, chief among them the deliberate infection of the children and the attempts to convince their parents to enroll them in the study in exchange for admission to the hospital (which was short of space).

Public policy and regulations designed to prevent such abuses were introduced in 1966, when U.S. Surgeon General William Stewart issued a U.S.

Public Health Service directive on human experimentation. This document announced that the U.S. Public Health Service would not fund research unless the institution receiving the grant spelled out the procedures in place to ensure the subjects' informed consent, the use of appropriate and ethical research procedures, an adequate review of the risks and medical benefits of the study, and the general protection of the research subjects' rights.

Since the mid-1960s, the federal government has developed a detailed list of regulations. Most of the ethical principles underlying the current regulations and standards are contained in the Belmont Report, prepared by the National Commission for the Protection of Human Subjects of Biomedical and Behavioral Research (National Commission 1978).

ETHICAL ISSUES IN SOCIAL WORK EVALUATION AND RESEARCH

Social workers do not face exactly the same ethical issues encountered by medical and health care researchers, as social workers do not administer medication or study organically based diseases. Nonetheless, social workers do face potentially problematic ethical issues when they use their research and evaluation skills to explore, monitor, and assess their work.

The ethical issues that social workers encounter fall into three categories: issues that arise (1) when social workers begin or embark on research and evaluation activities, (2) while the research and evaluation are actually being carried out, and (3) at the conclusion of the research and evaluation, when the results are in.

Getting Started: Initiating the Research and Evaluation

Informed consent. Perhaps the most important lesson learned from the infamous practices of the Nazi doctors and the abuses carried out during the Tuskegee and Willowbrook experiments is that people recruited to participate in research and evaluation cannot be exploited. They must be *informed* about the purposes, methods, and risks associated with the research, and they must voluntarily *consent* to participate in it. The key concept here is *informed consent.*

The concept of informed consent as it's used in social work may be so familiar to you that you may think it's been around forever. Not so. Certainly, the concept has been around for quite some time, but its formal application to research and evaluation is relatively recent.

The historical roots of informed consent have been traced to Plato, who in *The Laws* compares the Greek slave-physician who gives orders "in the brusque fashion of a dictator" with the free physician who "takes the patient and his family into confidence . . . [and] does not give prescriptions until he has won the patient's support" (President's Commission 1982:5). The medieval French surgeon Henri de Mondeville also highlighted the need to obtain the patient's consent and confidence, although he also urged his colleagues to "compel the obedience of his patients" by selectively slanting the information provided to them (President's Commission 1982).

The first major legal ruling in the United States on informed consent was in the 1914 landmark case of *Schloendorff v. Society of New York Hospital*, in which Justice Benjamin Cardozo stated his oft-cited opinion concerning individuals' right to consent: "Every human being of adult years and sound mind has a right to determine what shall be done with his own body" (President's Commission 1982:28–29). To do otherwise, Cardozo believed, was to commit an assault on the person.

The other major red-letter event in modern history was the 1957 case of *Salgo v. Leland Stanford Jr. University Board of Trustees*, in which the term *informed consent* was actually introduced. The plaintiff in this case, who became a paraplegic following a diagnostic procedure for a circulatory problem, alleged that his physician had failed to disclose properly ahead of time important information concerning the risks associated with the procedure (President's Commission 1982).

The concept of informed consent clearly is relevant to social work practice with respect to the disclosure of confidential information, the use of various intervention techniques, and audio- or videotaping. Informed consent is also necessary for social work research and evaluation. According to the National Association of Social Workers (NASW) Code of Ethics (standard 5.02[e]),

> Social workers engaged in evaluation or research should obtain voluntary and written informed consent from participants, when appropriate, without any implied or actual deprivation or penalty for refusal to participate; without undue inducement to participate; and with due regard for participants' well being, privacy and dignity. Informed consent should include information about the nature, extent, and duration of the participation requested and disclosure of the risks and benefits of participation in the research.

Over the years, various court decisions, regulations established by government and private-sector agencies, and scholarly inquiry have combined to produce a list of core ingredients that ought to be included in informed consent procedures pertaining to research and evaluation.

1. Not using coercion.   People cannot be coerced to participate in research and evaluation. Social workers must present their proposal for research and evaluation in a way that does not make clients feel pressured to accept. Such a proposal can be tricky, particularly in light of the unique relationship between social workers and their clients. Many research projects have no prior formal, or even informal, relationship between the researchers and their subjects. Social work, however, is typically a different story. In many instances, although certainly not in all, social workers use research and evaluation tools with their own clients or with people who are seeking their services. Although some research and evaluation do not involve clients (for example, when a social worker surveys a sample of community residents about their perception of an agency's mission), many of the activities discussed in this book do involve actual or potential clients who are current, recent, or possible recipients of services.

You can probably imagine how complicated this can get. Suppose a Mt. Washington Family Service Agency social worker invites a client who is receiving counseling services to record data for a single-case design. Will that client feel free to refuse? Understandably, some clients, perhaps most, will feel some pressure—whether or not it is deliberately imposed—to comply with the social worker's request, because they want to be helpful, appreciate the relevance and value of the data collection, or are worried that their receipt of services may be affected or jeopardized if they refuse to participate or that their refusing to participate may alienate the social worker.

Accordingly, social workers who approach clients or other people about participating in research and evaluation should avoid saying or doing anything that is coercive or that clients might interpret as coercive. Clients should not be "talked into" or otherwise seduced or pressured into participating in research and evaluation that might not be in their best interest (for example, promises of services or money inducements in exchange for their participation).

2. Ascertaining competence.   Social workers who invite clients and others to participate in research and evaluation must be sure that they are mentally competent to provide consent. Individuals asked to consent to evaluation and research must be able to understand the project's purpose, possible benefits, risks, and so on. Persons who are not competent or whose competence is uncertain should not be asked for their consent. Either they should be excluded from research and evaluation that require formal consent, or their consent should be obtained from their legal representative.

Although professionals agree that only competent persons are capable of giving informed consent, there is some disagreement about how that competence should be defined. According to Applebaum and Roth (President's

Commission 1982), practitioners should consider individuals' ability to make choices, comprehend factual issues, manipulate information rationally, and appreciate their current circumstances. Olin and Olin believe there ought to be a single standard for determining competency, based on people's ability to retain information, but Owens argues that practitioners should merely assess individuals' ability to "test reality" (President's Commission 1982). In contrast, the President's Commission for the Study of Ethical Problems in Medicine and Biomedical and Behavioral Research (1982) asserted in its oft-cited report that competence should be determined by a person's possession of a set of values and goals, ability to communicate and understand information, and ability to reason and deliberate.

Although there is some debate about the criteria that should be used to determine competence, there is general agreement that incompetence should not be presumed for any particular client group, such as children, the elderly, the mentally ill, or the mentally retarded, except for people who are unconscious. Rather, individuals in some categories—such as children or severely retarded adults—should be considered to have a *greater probability* of incompetence.

When potential participants in social workers' evaluation or research are not competent to give informed consent, social workers must obtain consent from someone who is legally authorized to provide it. In addition, the fact that individuals may not be competent to give informed consent to their participation in evaluation or research doesn't mean that social workers shouldn't explain to them the project's purposes, methods, and so on. That is, when feasible, even incompetent individuals should be given information and asked for their cooperation, even if their informed consent must be obtained from another party. As the NASW Code of Ethics (standard 5.02[f]) states, "When evaluation or research participants are incapable of giving informed consent, social workers should provide an appropriate explanation to the participants, obtain the participant's assent to the extent they are able, and obtain written consent from an appropriate proxy."

Obtaining consent to use children in research or evaluation projects can be difficult. Children usually do not have the legal authority to consent to participate in research projects. Social workers ordinarily obtain consent from the children's parents or legal guardians, although it often makes sense to include the children, especially older children, in the decision-making process.

Social workers may encounter circumstances in which it is not clear who a particular child's legal guardian is, perhaps because records are inaccurate or missing. In these instances, social workers should probably obtain consent from all those who might be the child's guardian. Although this can be burdensome and redundant, it's better to be safe than sorry. Similar ambiguity can surround situations in which social workers need to obtain consent from a legal guardian for an elderly or mentally disabled person whose competence is uncertain.

   3. Waiving informed consent.   Not all research and evaluation activities require formal consent. Some, even many, of these activities require only *implied* consent.

   Some examples may help. Let's suppose a Mt. Washington Family Service Agency social worker and the agency's psychiatrist are evaluating the effectiveness of two different treatments of clinical depression: group counseling with a new psychotropic drug and group counseling without medication. Eligible clients will be randomly assigned to the two groups. Each client in the project will complete a standardized depression inventory every eight weeks, beginning with the commencement of treatment.

   This is an example of an evaluation project requiring formal informed consent procedures. Participants have the right to know the social worker's and the psychiatrist's general aims, possible benefits, and possible risks. It would be unconscionable to carry out this sort of project without the participants' consent.

   In contrast, consider a Mt. Washington social worker who wants to interview a cross section of community residents concerning their impressions of Mt. Washington's services and mission. Certainly such a project would incorporate many of the research and evaluation skills addressed in this book, related to design, measurement, sampling, and data analysis. But does this mean that the social worker must obtain formal informed consent from every community resident who agrees to be interviewed? No. Instead, it is sufficient for the social worker, and anyone else who conducts the interviews, to explain the purpose of the project to potential respondents, the uses to which the results might be put, and any other relevant information (keeping in mind that the interviewers need to be careful not to say anything that would bias people's responses). If community residents agree to spend some time with the interviewers answering questions after the interviewers have invited them to do so, it's safe to say that the community residents have offered their consent. This is a good example of *implied consent.*

   The same phenomenon occurs with many single-case designs. If a Mt. Washington social worker wants to use research and evaluation skills and tools to monitor a client's progress (say, having a client with an eating disorder keep track of the number of calories she consumes daily), it may not be necessary for the social worker to go through formal informed consent procedures. A clear explanation of the social worker's approach and rationale should be enough, assuming that the social worker and client have agreed on the target problems to be addressed, goals, intervention methods, and length of service.

I want to avoid conveying the impression that every research and evaluation project is big and complicated and always requires social workers to use formal informed consent procedures. Rather, in real life, many, if not most, social work research and evaluation warrant only *implied* consent, because practitioners often use research and evaluation as part of their practice—to enhance the delivery of services or to explore community, organizational, or social policy issues—not for research per se.

Of course, social workers must be scrupulous when they rely on implied consent or decide to waive informed consent procedures. Implied consent may not be a problem when social workers gather data from case records. But waiving formal consent procedures is more complicated when it's used to authorize gathering data by, for example, observing clients' behavior in a residential program through a one-way mirror. In such instances, social workers need to be certain that the research methods have been scrutinized by colleagues, including an appropriate institutional review board. Waiving informed consent procedures should not be taken lightly. As the NASW Code of Ethics (standard 5.02[g]) states,

> Social workers should never design or conduct evaluation or research that does not use consent procedures, such as certain forms of naturalistic observation and archival research, unless rigorous and responsible review of the research has found it to be justified because of its prospective scientific yield, educational, or applied value and unless equally effective alternative procedures that do not involve waiver of consent are not feasible.

4. Obtaining participants' consent to specific procedures or actions. When informed consent is warranted, social workers should be sure to explain clearly to potential participants the purpose of the research and evaluation, possible benefits and costs, and alternatives or other options that the participants may want to consider. Broadly worded and vague explanations are not sufficient.

In addition, the language and terminology on consent forms must be clear and understandable, and those persons asked for consent should be given ample opportunity to ask for clarification (see figure 4.1 for a sample informed consent form). Social workers should avoid using complex and technical jargon. The specific wording on consent forms varies according to the particular research and evaluation project. Similar information should be contained in a cover letter inviting individuals to participate in the project.

You are invited to participate in a research/evaluation project being conducted by the Mt. Washington Family Service Agency. This project involves (briefly describe the nature of the project). I am a (social worker, student, etc.) at the Mt. Washington Family Service Agency. (If you are a student, explain how the research project relates to your degree program.) The purpose of this project is to (describe purpose and possible value of the project). You are being invited to participate in this project because (state reason).

This project will involve (describe the specific procedures that will be followed; the reasons; the timetable or schedule for the various procedures; possible risks, inconveniences, and benefits; alternative procedures or options that the participant might find appealing or useful; and any standard treatment that would be withheld).

Any information obtained from you or about you in connection with this project will remain confidential and will be disclosed only with your permission, as permitted or required by law. (Describe plans, if any, to release information to third parties, the purpose for the disclosure, the nature of the information to be released, and the circumstances under which it would be released).

You are not under any obligation to participate in this project, and your decision will not affect your future relationship with the Mt. Washington Family Service Agency. Furthermore, if you decide to participate, you may stop at any time without penalty or prejudice. (For projects using mailed surveys or questionnaires, you may want to include the following or a similar statement: "Your completion and return of the enclosed survey/questionnaire will indicate your willingness to participate in this project and your consent to have the information used as described above.")

Please contact (insert names and telephone numbers of all appropriate contact persons) if you have any questions about this project or your participation in it.

Your signature below indicates that you have read the information provided on this form, it has been explained to you, you have been offered a copy of this form to keep, you have been given an opportunity to ask questions about this form, your questions have been answered, and you agree to participate in this project.

_____   _____
Signature   Date

_____   _____
Signature of Parent or Legal Guardian (if necessary)   Date

_____   _____
Signature of Child (when appropriate)   Date

_____   _____
Signature of Witness   Date

_____   _____
Signature of Project Director/Investigator   Date

FIGURE 4.1 Sample Consent Form

Special care should be taken with persons who do not have a good command of English; social workers should be aware that some people who speak English reasonably well (expressive language skill) may not be as good at understanding it (receptive language skill). In such instances, social workers should use an interpreter. In addition, they should be certain that persons with auditory or visual impairments are given the assistance they need to provide informed consent.

Explaining to potential participants the purpose of the research or evaluation may seem straightforward—and it usually is. But in some circumstances, social workers may be reluctant to say too much about the research or evaluation to avoid biasing the results. Suppose, for example, that a Mt. Washington Family Service Agency social worker is evaluating the effectiveness of a behavioral intervention designed to reduce symptoms of clinical depression. The social worker decides to use an ABAB design, which calls for temporarily withdrawing the intervention after it has been implemented for a time. If the social worker spells out in detail how the design works, the client's self-report of symptoms may be shaped by the explanation itself. That is, the social worker's explanation may influence the client's self-report (something like a self-fulfilling prophecy), thus generating misleading results.

Of course, withholding information about a design's purpose violates the very principle behind the concept of informed consent. Nonetheless, many researchers argue that withholding some information is justifiable when it is necessary to avoid jeopardizing the validity of the project's results. Otherwise, in many research and evaluation projects it would be difficult to obtain useful results. If social workers believe that it is necessary to withhold some information to potential participants in order to preserve the project's integrity, they should have their position and reasons reviewed carefully and critically by an independent committee (discussed in detail later).

5. Having the right to refuse or withdraw consent.   One of the key principles of informed consent is that people have the right to make informed decisions to refuse or withdraw their consent. Their refusal to give their consent or to withdraw it may be based on their concern about such things as the amount of time their participation would require, psychological or confidentiality risks, or their lack of interest in the topic. According to the NASW Code of Ethics (standard 5.02[h]), "Social workers should inform participants of their right to withdraw from evaluation and research at any time without penalty."

Social workers should keep in mind that simply having someone sign a consent form is not sufficient. Informed consent is a process that includes the deliberate, systematic disclosure of information and an opportunity for individuals to discuss and ask questions about the research or evaluation. As part of the process, social workers should be sensitive to clients' cultural and ethnic differences regarding the meaning of such concepts as self-determination, autonomy, and consent. For example, Hahn notes that "the individualism central in the doctrine of informed consent is absent in the tradition of Vietnamese thought. Self is not cultivated, but subjugated to cosmic orders. Information, direct communication, and decision may be regarded as arrogant" (President's Commission 1982:55–56). In contrast, Harwood notes that mainland Puerto Rican Latinos expect to be engaged in the therapeutic process and have a strong desire for information, conveyed without condescension (President's Commission 1982:56). Thus social workers need to be aware of the ways in which cultural and ethnic differences may affect the informed consent process.

Institutional review. One of the most useful innovations in the history of research and evaluation was the invention of *institutional review boards (IRBs)*, a formal mechanism to enhance the likelihood that research and evaluation are conducted ethically. IRBs, sometimes known as *human subjects protection committees*, became popular in the 1970s as a result of the national attention to ethical issues in research and evaluation. Now all organizations and agencies that receive federal funds for research are required to have an IRB review the ethical aspects of proposals for research involving human subjects. Prior approval of the IRB is required for the study or project to be carried out. Before approving a proposal, it is not unusual for an IRB to ask for additional information and details or to request certain changes in a study's research design.

Assume that Mt. Washington Family Service Agency receives federal funding for a substance abuse treatment programs and, therefore, is required to create an IRB to review research proposals involving human subjects. Let's say that the staff want to conduct research to compare the effectiveness of group- and individual-counseling approaches. Eligible clients would be randomly assigned to the two intervention groups. But the agency's IRB might insist that the explanation of the study that the staff plan to give to eligible clients is not detailed enough and that more information be added about other treatment options. As the NASW Code of Ethics states, "Social workers engaged in evaluation or research should carefully consider possible consequences and should follow guidelines developed for the protection of evaluation and research participants. Appropriate institutional review boards should be consulted" (standard 5.02[d]), and "Social workers engaged in evaluation or research should protect participants from unwarranted physical or mental distress, harm, danger, or deprivation" (standard 5.02[j]).

Not every research and evaluation activity proposed in social service agencies or academic settings requires a full-fledged IRB review. Typical exemptions are for research and evaluation activities that are a routine requirement of an educational or academic program, analyze secondary (existing) data in a way that preserves confidentiality, depend on interviews or surveys, are part of federal demonstration projects, or entail observation of public behavior. Also, many social workers use research tools to collect data for practice purposes, not for research purposes. Many research and evaluation activities that are part of social work *practice* do not fall under the purview of IRBs, whose primary responsibility is to assess the ethical aspects of formal research studies. Social workers should review government guidelines and their own agency's guidelines concerning which research and evaluation activities require formal review by an IRB.

The Actual Project

Research designs. A number of ethical issues can come up while social workers are actually carrying out the research and evaluation projects. Perhaps the most prominent has to do with the research designs, particularly the ways in which social workers attempt to control for extraneous factors in projects designed to evaluate causal connections between interventions and outcomes. In single-case designs, for example, social workers who use some form of a reversal design (ABAB or some variation of this design) have to consider the ethical implications of (1) delaying the start of an intervention and (2) withdrawing an intervention once it has been in place for some time. Certainly in some instances, social workers would be reluctant to delay an intervention because the client's presenting problem is so severe. Suppose, for instance, that a Mt. Washington Family Service Agency social worker was providing clinical services to a twenty-one-year-old woman who was clinically depressed and suicidal. Understandably, the social worker would not want to withhold an intervention for any length of time to evaluate its effectiveness. Emergency and other compelling circumstances require immediate intervention. In addition, if a suicidal client's condition improves significantly during the time an intervention is in place, the social worker would be reluctant to withdraw it to obtain additional evaluative data. Social workers are likely to have a similar reaction in any instance when clients face life-and-death issues or are engaged in behaviors that threaten themselves or others.

But most clients don't face such dire circumstances. Rather, most clients receive services for problems that don't involve life-and-death issues or serious threats to themselves or others. Examples are clients who are working on self-esteem or relationship issues that are upsetting but not overwhelming. Consequently, in many cases, neither the clients' nor others' well-being would be seriously threatened were an intervention to be delayed or withdrawn to collect data.

You may be wondering why anyone in his or her right mind would want to take any risk in these situations. Why would social workers delay the introduction of an intervention or withdraw it after it has been in place for some time just so they can collect data for research or evaluation purposes? If that thought ran through your mind, welcome to a club with a large membership!

Let me take this opportunity to remind you of something I stated earlier— a point that is key to this book and my approach to research and evaluation. Remember that most of what we are reviewing in this book is information that teaches social workers practical skills that they can use in their job. My goal is not to train sophisticated researchers who gather data for "scientific" and "theoretical" purposes. Although these are noble enterprises, they aren't part of my agenda. Rather, I am focusing on research and evaluation tools that are part of practice and that social workers have an *ethical obligation* to use to ensure that they are accomplishing what they intend to accomplish and are not wasting their or their clients' time. In fact, in my view, we social workers would be ethically remiss if we did not systematically and deliberately attempt to assess the nature, quality, and effectiveness of what we do as social workers. Having said this, I also admit that sometimes it would be unethical to delay the introduction of an intervention or to withdraw it once it has been implemented. As with all professional practice, good judgment is required to balance these trade-offs.

Similar issues arise with respect to using control groups in group designs. Recall the classic pre-test, post-test control-group design, in which individuals in an "experimental" group receive some kind of intervention and those in the control group do not. Imagine a case in which a social worker directs a treatment unit that provides services to a group of children who frequently engage in serious self-harming behaviors, for example, banging their heads against a wall or stabbing themselves with sharp objects. Left unsupervised, these children are likely to injure themselves seriously. Then this social worker recently learned of a behavioral intervention designed to reduce these self-destructive behaviors. You can understand why she might have some misgivings about withholding the intervention to half the children in her program who would be assigned to a control group. In her view, the behaviors are so threatening that a promising intervention should not be withheld from any eligible child, and the evaluation of the effectiveness of the intervention would have to take second place to the children's needs.

This is a difficult—and commonly encountered—dilemma. You may already be familiar with it because of reports you have read or heard about, in which people with particular health care problems are recruited into research "protocols" in which they have a fifty–fifty chance of being assigned to the experimental group that will receive the new medication or treatment. This arrangement places very ill and sometimes desperate people in a difficult position. They must risk the possibility that they will be assigned to the control, or "no treatment," group in order to have a 50 percent chance of gaining access to the experimental medication or treatment. Scientists argue, however, that controlled experiments of this sort are absolutely necessary to determine the efficacy and safety of untested, albeit promising, treatment options. No one has been able to improve on the logic of the control-group design as a way to rule out extraneous factors that could influence results. On one hand, then, it may seem unethical to withhold a promising medication or intervention from someone who might benefit from it. On the other hand, one could argue that it would be equally or less ethical to make available to the general public a medication or treatment whose effectiveness is unknown and that could, in fact, be harmful. This is a difficult and frustrating trade-off that scientists and professionals have learned to live with—or at least have become resigned to.

Whether using a control group in a social work research or evaluation project is ethical is always a matter of judgment. Some cases are clearer than others, and IRBs can help make a judgment, particularly when the IRB members have been trained to think through the ramifications of these issues.

A practical compromise that social workers sometimes use is to compare the effectiveness of two (or more) interventions rather than to withhold an intervention completely from the people in the control group. For example, the Mt. Washington staff might compare the effectiveness of both group and individual counseling with substance abusers. This may seem more ethical, or at least easier to live with, than a design withholding intervention entirely for a period of time. The disadvantage of this design is that it allows the staff to determine only whether there are differences between two (or more) interventions. It doesn't allow them to determine whether a particular intervention is better than no intervention.

In one set of circumstances, a control group can be used without introducing lots of complicated ethical issues. Many social service programs have waiting lists, or at least have more people asking for service than the programs can provide, because of funding or space constraints. Although this is unfortunate—social workers would certainly prefer to be able to offer services to all those who need them—these circumstances sometimes create a "natural" control group with which one can compare those people who do receive services. Ideally, the people in the control group are given services immediately or shortly after their participation in the control group. Granted, many people can't wait for services; the problems they face simply are too compelling. This is not always the case, however.

Deception. Most social work research and evaluation projects are relatively straightforward and are not deceptive. Projects such as needs assessments, client satisfaction surveys, and retrospective analyses of service utilization patterns usually don't need to "fool" or mislead anyone.

In some instances, however, social workers may feel that some form of deception is necessary, whether mild or substantial, to achieve their research or evaluation goals. This isn't the malicious sort of deception seen in some notorious research projects, in which research subjects were exploited to suit the researchers' ignoble purposes. Rather, this deception is relatively benign. That's not to say that every instance of deception sponsored by social workers is justifiable; reasonable people can and do disagree about the legitimacy of various forms of deception in social work research and evaluation.

Let's review some examples. At one extreme, we have instances in which social workers may withhold relatively innocuous information so as not to jeopardize the validity of their research. Suppose a Mt. Washington Family Service Agency administrator, Sue K., had been receiving complaints from a number of clients about the rude behavior of several staff members. Ms. K. therefore decided to conduct a client satisfaction survey to explore the problem. She developed a questionnaire that included a variety of questions about clients' satisfaction with agency services, staff, facilities, and so on. Ms. K. decided to use this opportunity also to obtain clients' opinions about a variety of issues rather than to focus exclusively on their perceptions of staff members' behavior, even though this was Ms. K.'s primary concern.

Ms. K. selected several staff members—not those in service delivery—to administer the questionnaire to a sample of clients at the time they terminated their services. If Ms. K. were to be completely candid, she would have her staff explain to the clients that the agency was concerned about complaints concerning the behavior of some staff members and that the agency was surveying clients to obtain more information.

But does this make sense? First, telling this to clients could very well bias their responses. Indeed, such an explanation might encourage some of them to be more critical or "negative" than they would be otherwise. The reverse is possible, too. Some clients, particularly those who were pleased with the services they received, might feel protective of the agency and its staff and, consequently, might give excessively positive feedback. In addition, sharing with clients the fact that administrators had received negative feedback about some staff members' behavior would be inappropriate professionally. It is important for administrators to maintain proper boundaries in their relationships with clients. Ordinarily, clients should not be privy to internal controversies or personnel issues, since this could be confusing to them, undermine their confidence in the agency, and, ultimately, interfere with the help they are seeking. Administrators and staff, of course, have a professional responsibility to investigate and respond to these issues, but they should not involve clients in them.

Hence there are good reasons for Ms. K. not to tell the clients being interviewed about the actual or primary reason for the survey. It would be better for her to instruct the interviewers to explain that the agency is gathering information from a group of clients as part of its ongoing effort to monitor the quality of the services it delivers. One could argue that this is a form of deception, and I suppose it is. In my view, however, it is a relatively harmless and justifiable form of deception.

In another case, Marcia R., one of Mt. Washington's caseworkers, was providing counseling services to an eleven-year-old boy, Ned, who was referred by his school principal because he seemed to be depressed. Ned's teacher said that he usually was listless, was uninterested in schoolwork, and had difficulty making friends. Ned's mother recently died from a drug overdose, and his father is in prison.

Marcia R. met with Ned's foster parents and schoolteacher, and together they formulated an intervention plan. They agreed that Marcia R. would provide individual counseling to Ned and family counseling to Ned's foster parents. Marcia R. would also refer Ned for a psychiatric consultation to see whether medication might relieve his symptoms of depression.

The consulting psychiatrist prescribed psychotropic medication for Ned's depression. She recommended that Ned's foster parents administer the medication for three months, withdraw the medication for three weeks, resume the medication for six weeks, and then withdraw the medication for three weeks. Essentially this is a BABA design. During the evaluation period, Marcia R. would ask Ned to complete a simple instrument each week that measures depression, and she also would have Ned's foster parents fill out a similar form assessing Ned's depression. The psychiatrist's plan was to use Ned as his own control and analyze the data to determine whether the medication was having a significant effect on his symptoms.

This design would require a modest amount of deception to study the medication's effectiveness. The treatment team would not tell Ned everything about the treatment plan and the reason for alternating periods with and without medication. Their reasoning was that Ned's behavior and responses to questions about his depression might be shaped by his knowledge of what the treatment team was trying to do by withdrawing the medication for periods of time

Does this sort of deception trouble you? Does it seem unreasonable or unethical? My own feeling is that this kind of deception is justifiable. Although deception in any form troubles and worries me, I can see why some modest, yet fairly benign, deception may be necessary if social workers are to fulfill their ethical obligation to monitor and evaluate their practice.

Sometimes, however, the nature and extent of the deception do seem unethical. Assume that a Mt. Washington administrator, Joanne A., wanted to determine how efficiently the clinical staff spend their time with clients. Let's say that financial pressures have led Joanne A. to become concerned about the number of clinical staff the agency employs, given the number of clients the agency serves. Joanne A. suspects that two full-time staff could be laid off and the agency could still meet the demand for its services as long as the remaining staff worked efficiently.

To test her suspicions about the staff members' efficiency and to gather data to help her determine who the most and least efficient staff are, Joanne A. decides to eavesdrop on a sample of clinical sessions by hiding tape recorders in various clinicians' offices. Joanne A. hopes to discover how focused and "on task" clinicians are, as opposed to spending significant amounts of unfocused time with clients.

Did your blood begin to boil as you read this description? Doesn't this kind of deception seem blatantly unethical and abhorrent—a form of spying? That is certainly my reaction. It begins to smack of the unconscionable deception carried out in the name of science during the Tuskegee and Willowbrook scandals.

To be sure, thoughtful, reasonable people can disagree about how ethical the procedures in a given research or evaluation project are. Take the example I mentioned earlier in which Mt. Washington staff wanted to compare the effectiveness of individual- and group-counseling approaches to substance abuse treatment. How candid and forthcoming should the staff be with prospective clients concerning this project's nature and aims? I can imagine some social workers arguing that the agency's staff must be open and completely honest about the project's purposes, that prospective clients should be told that the agency is comparing the effectiveness of these two approaches, and that with their permission, prospective clients will be randomly assigned to one of the two groups. Others, however, may argue that this degree of candor will affect the clients' participation and behavior (including, perhaps, the way they answer questions administered as part of the evaluation) and that prospective clients should be given a less detailed, more ambiguous explanation of the project's methods and purposes. Prospective clients might be told, for example, that the agency was looking at different ways of helping people with substance abuse problems and that prospective clients would be assigned to one of two options available at the agency. Of course, prospective clients would be allowed to refuse to consent to such an arrangement. Those who wanted more detailed information might be excluded from the study, although they certainly wouldn't be deprived of service as a result.

What's your reaction to this approach? Does this kind of vagueness trouble you, or does it seem reasonable? Does the omission of certain details seem unethical, or does it seem to be an acceptable compromise? Given that reasonable people can have differing opinions in such situations, it's good that many agencies now have institutional review boards (IRBs) to help review research and evaluation proposals that contain questionable or controversial features.

Confidentiality.   The concept of confidentiality is central to social work. Social workers know that confidentiality is absolutely necessary, especially to promote client's trust in clinical work. Nonclinical social workers also know how important confidentiality is. For example, administrators frequently must keep sensitive personnel matters confidential, and community organizers often need to keep secret the information shared with them during their work.

Confidentiality also is relevant to social work research and evaluation, for several reasons. Perhaps the most obvious has to do with social workers' need to protect the confidentiality of data, in whatever form they are obtained. Data documenting clients' behaviors, feelings, attitudes, psychiatric status, and other personal details must be kept secret in order to respect clients' rights to privacy and to avoid undermining the general public's trust in researchers and evaluators. You can just imagine how public perception would be affected if word were to get out that social workers were sloppy or careless about protecting the confidentiality of their research and evaluation results. As the NASW Code of Ethics (standard 5.02[l]) states,

> Social workers engaged in evaluation or research should ensure the anonymity or confidentiality of participants and of the data obtained from them. Social workers should inform participants of any limits of confiden-

tiality, the measures that will be taken to ensure confidentiality, and when any records containing research data will be destroyed.

There are virtually no exceptions to social workers' obligation to keep research and evaluation data confidential. Notice, however, that I said *virtually*. Suppose a Mt. Washington staff member, Mark G., is interviewing clients at the termination of their service to gather information about their satisfaction. Ordinarily, anything clients say in such an interview should be kept confidential, for people who believe that their responses may not be kept confidential are far less likely to be candid. What should Mark G. do, however, if a client expresses great dissatisfaction with the agency's services, particularly with his own social worker, and, during the interview, talks about how he wants to harm the social worker (let's say the client and his wife received marriage counseling from the social worker, and in the client's opinion, the social worker was far more sympathetic to the client's spouse than to him)? Assuming that Mark G. believes the threat to be genuine and likely to be carried out in the near future, it's hard to imagine anyone arguing that he, who was not the client's service provider, should keep quiet about the threat.

Social work has norms that permit the disclosure of confidential information in exceptional situations. Social workers agree that certain compelling circumstances—such as when a client has abused a child or threatened to harm a third party—justify the disclosure of confidential information. Although there is some risk that such occasional breaches of confidentiality may undermine clients' trust in their social workers, social workers generally agree that such limits must be placed on confidentiality to protect third parties from serious harm. There is a trade-off, to be sure, but it seems to be a reasonable one. The NASW Code of Ethics (standard 1.07[c]) states, in fact, that

> social workers should protect the confidentiality of all information obtained in the course of professional service, except for compelling professional reasons. The general expectation that social workers will keep information confidential does not apply when disclosure is necessary to prevent serious, foreseeable, and imminent harm to a client or other identifiable person or when laws or regulations require disclosure without the client's consent. In all instances, social workers should disclose the least amount of confidential information necessary to achieve the desired purpose; only information that is directly relevant to the purpose for which the disclosure is made should be revealed.

Should confidential information shared by clients or other persons participating in research or evaluation be handled differently from confidential information obtained in clinical relationships? Is there any reason to believe that confidential information obtained during research or evaluation is more sacred or sacrosanct? Although I would argue that social workers need to be vigilant in their efforts to maintain the confidentiality of information obtained as part of their research and evaluation, I would also argue that exceptions permitting disclosure to third parties should match those now widely accepted in social work practice more generally.

Hence it is important to tell participants in research and evaluation what the limits to confidentiality are. They should be told as early in the relationship as possible what information will and will not be treated as confidential and the circumstances requiring the social worker to disclose confidential information even without the client's (or other participant's) permission. This approach is identical to that commonly followed in clinical social work practice and endorsed by the NASW Code of Ethics (standard 1.07[e]):

> Social workers should discuss with clients and other interested parties the nature of confidentiality and limitations of clients' right to confidentiality. Social workers should review with clients circumstances where confidential information may be requested and where disclosure of confidential information may be legally required. This discussion should occur as soon as possible in the social worker–client relationship and as needed throughout the course of the relationship.

Exactly what sort of information might social workers obtain as part of research or evaluation that might lead them to conclude that it must be disclosed? Keeping in mind that such circumstances are rare indeed, one possibility, as just mentioned, is that during an interview a client (or some other respondent) who believes that his comments are confidential reveals that he plans to injure a third party or has abused a child. Another possibility is that someone makes a similar kind of comment on a self-administered, written questionnaire.

Social workers should be aware of the widely imposed guidelines governing the disclosure of confidential information. Every state, for example, has mandatory reporting laws that typically require social workers to disclose confidential information when they know or even suspect that a client has abused or neglected a child (many states also have similar statutes pertaining to the abuse and neglect of old people).

In addition, some states have "duty to protect" laws that require social workers and others to take steps—which may include disclosing confidential information—when a client has threatened to harm a third party. Also, several prominent court decisions holding that social workers whose clients threaten third parties have a duty to protect those third parties may create the same expectation, even in those states that have not enacted "duty to protect" statutes (Reamer 1994, 1995a, 1995b).

Privacy. In addition to confidentiality, social workers also need to be concerned about people's privacy. On the surface, it may seem that confidentiality and privacy are the same. But they are not, although they certainly are related. In sum, in most circumstances people have a right to their privacy, to not be pressured or coerced into revealing details about their lives—their thoughts, feelings, personal histories—to others. People should be able to tell others what they want to tell them, period. In clinical social work, it's a given that clients must grant permission to social workers to disclose personal details about their lives and that the therapeutic conditions should enable clients to share what they want to share, but clients should not be pressured to share what they do not want to share or are not ready to share. Confidentiality, in contrast, concerns the social worker's duty to not disclose private information to third parties. The NASW Code of Ethics (standard 1.07[a]) acknowledges this important distinction: "Social workers should respect clients' right to privacy. Social workers should not solicit private information from clients unless it is essential to providing services or conduting social work evaluation or research. Once private information is shared, standards of confidentiality apply." The code (standard 5.02[k]) also states, "Social workers engaged in the evaluation of services should discuss collected information only for professional purposes and only with people professionally concerned with this information."

Some social work research and evaluation, though certainly not all, explore the private domains of people's lives. Social workers may interview or survey clients or others about such intimate matters as their history of sexual abuse, domestic violence, suicidal thoughts, sexual activity, criminal behavior, infidelity, and substance abuse. Measurement tools used to monitor the effectiveness of psychotherapy may explore clients' most private or intimate thoughts about themselves, self-esteem issues, and personal relationships. Clearly, social workers must respect people's wish or need for, and right to, privacy. Research and evaluation must be designed to be sensitive to privacy and allow participants not to reveal or explore what they do not want to reveal or explore.

Social workers must also recognize that attention to and exploration of sensitive topics and issues sometimes dredge up unpleasant or painful feelings or memories. That is, the research and evaluation themselves may lead to stress and emotional trauma, and social workers need to factor this possibility into their decision to go ahead with their research and evaluation agenda. In addition, social workers have an ethical obligation to be familiar with supportive services that clients and others may need to resolve issues that surface during research or evaluation. The NASW Code of Ethics (standard 5.02[i]) states, "Social workers should take appropriate steps to ensure that participants in evaluation and research have access to appropriate supportive services."

Conflicts of interest.   Social workers in evaluation or research also need to keep in mind the potential for conflicts of interest, particularly when their evaluation or research "subjects" or "respondents" are also their professional clients. In these situations, social workers should make certain that they are not exploiting their clients for evaluation or research purposes or involving them in evaluation or research activities that aren't in their clients' best interests.

For example, let's say a Mt. Washington clinical social worker is counseling a client, Mr. N., who has been diagnosed with depression. At the same time, the social worker is enrolled in a social work doctoral program and is taking a course that requires the social worker/student to carry out a single-case design. The social worker decides to use Mr. N.'s case for his school project. The research design requires collecting data for a period of eight weeks.

With Mr. N.'s permission, the social worker gathers data every week concerning Mr. N.'s progress during treatment. But in the counseling session in week 5, Mr. N. announces that he's "feeling much better" and doesn't need more counseling. Although the social worker is pleased to hear about Mr. N.'s progress, he's privately distressed that his school project involving the single-case design is falling apart before his eyes. Would it be ethical for the social worker to talk Mr. N. into continuing his counseling, perhaps by citing additional clinical issues that Mr. N. ought to address? Of course not. In this instance, the social worker has a conflict of interests that must be resolved in the client's favor. This may be frustrating for the social worker, but he has no choice.

Social workers in evaluation or research also should be concerned about what are known as *dual* or *multiple relationships*. In general, a dual or multiple relationship is one in which a social worker relates to clients in more than one relationship, whether professional, business, or social. Examples are a social worker whose clinical client also babysits for the social worker's children, a clinical social worker who invests money in a current client's business, a social worker who gives a client a service in exchange for the client's painting her house, and a social worker who develops a sexual relationship with a client.

What kinds of dual or multiple relationships can be formed with social workers in evaluation or research? First, social workers must avoid entering into any professional, social, or business relationships with evaluation or research "subjects" or "respondents" when there is a risk of exploitation or potential harm to the individuals involved. For example, a social worker in

evaluation or research shouldn't develop an intimate relationship or a business partnership with a person the social worker is studying as part of a longitudinal study of the treatment of depression or addictions if there is any risk of exploitation or harm to that person. As the NASW Code of Ethics (standard 5.02[o]) states, "Social workers engaged in evaluation or research should be alert to and avoid conflicts of interest and dual relationships with participants, should inform participants when a real or potential conflict of interest arises, and should take steps to resolve the issue in a manner that makes participants' interests primary."

Handling Research and Evaluation Results

You might be tempted to think that the ethical issues disappear once the research results are in. Not so! In fact, some of the most complicated ethical issues I have encountered emerge at this final stage of the process. I have already touched on the issue of confidentiality. Social workers need to be exceedingly careful to protect the confidentiality of research and evaluation results. As the NASW Code of Ethics (standard 5.02[m]) states, "Social workers who report evaluation and research results should protect participants' confidentiality by omitting identifying information unless proper consent has been obtained authorizing disclosure." But there are other issues too.

Reporting results accurately.   Reporting results accurately goes without say-ing, no? Fortunately, social workers nearly always report research and evalua-tion results accurately. Unfortunately, however, sometimes they exaggerate the results to support a position or point of view they endorse, or distort the results to undermine an opposing position or point of view. Research and eval-uation results are sometimes altered (or "fudged" or "cooked") to make a good impression on funding sources, insurance companies, or government agen-cies. But in short, inaccurately reporting research and evaluation results is fraudulent. Social workers who manipulate results in this way are playing with fire and behaving unethically. According to the NASW Code of Ethics (stan-dard 5.02[n]), "Social workers should report evaluation and research findings accurately. They should not fabricate or falsify results and should take steps to correct any errors later found in published data using standard publication methods."

Disclosing results to participants.   Deciding whether to disclose results to research and evaluation participants might seem like an odd issue to raise. After all, who would argue that the results should be withheld from the very people who provided the data?

The fact is, however, that in some circumstances, social workers are tempted to withhold some or all results from clients or others participating in research or evaluation. One instance occurs when social workers' research or evaluation reveals information that, in the social workers' judgment, would be hurtful or harmful if they shared it with the research or evaluation projects' participants. If a Mt. Washington social worker administers to a client an instrument that measures clinical depression and shortly thereafter the client becomes suicidal, the social worker may hesitate to disclose "negative" test results, at least at that particular moment, because of the client's acute vulner-ability. Whether such information should be given to the client—who, by the way, asked for the results—is, in part, a clinical judgment, but it is also an eth-ical judgment in which the social worker must balance the client's "right to know" with the social worker's obligation to protect the client from harm. If the social worker believes that disclosing the results of the depression instru-ment would exacerbate the client's clinical condition, is it ethical for the social worker to refuse to disclose or to postpone disclosing the results?

Conversely, suppose a Mt. Washington social worker is studying the preva-lence of HIV infection and AIDS in the surrounding community. The state health department is administering HIV blood tests to a sample of commu-nity residents, and a Mt. Washington social worker is working in conjunction with the health department to provide services to those who are anxious about the test results. One of the community residents who has agreed to be tested told the social worker and health department nurse that he does not want to know the results of the test. What should the social worker do if the test results are positive? Does she have an ethical obligation to give this information to the community resident so that he can get appropriate treatment, counseling, education, and supportive services (which may prevent further spread of the virus to others), or should the social worker respect this man's right to not know the results, even though his ignorance could lead to the subsequent infection of others if the man engages in high-risk behaviors?

Unfortunately, there are no simple answers to these questions, which have generated significant controversy in the social work and health care communities. The good news, however, is that social workers and others have a much greater awareness of and sensitivity to such questions and now have access to forums (for example, agency-based ethics committees, institutional review boards, ethics consultants) that can help social workers think through these issues.

Giving credit for research and evaluation.   Once the research and evaluation results are in, social workers must decide how to disseminate them. In chapter 12 we'll discuss in detail the various available options, including conference and agency presentations, research and evaluation reports for circulation inside and outside the sponsoring agencies, and formal publication in academic and professional journals. In many instances, data collected by individual practitioners are for their own use only, so discussions of dissemination aren't necessary.

Social workers should always be conscientious when crediting those helping with the research or evaluation. Those who directly participated in the work should be acknowledged in a manner consistent with their level of contribution. In projects with a research or evaluation staff, it is customary to list first the project director's name (sometimes known as the "principal investigator") in any formal reports or publications, followed by the names of other staff who were directly involved in the project. When staff contribute different amounts of effort, their names are usually listed in order from the highest to the lowest levels of effort. Staff who contributed equally are usually listed in alphabetical order.

This seems pretty straightforward, and it usually is. Sometimes, however, ethical issues arise. Occasionally, for example, someone who was minimally involved in a project attempts to take undue credit, or a project director assigns credit based on friendship or "politics" rather than genuine effort. Social workers must be aware of these occasional ethical breaches and skillful in their efforts to deal with them. As the NASW Code of Ethics states, "Social workers should take responsibility and credit, including authorship credit, only for work they have actually performed and to which they have contributed" (standard 4.08[a]), and "Social workers should honestly acknowledge the work of and the contributions made by others" (standard 4.08[b]). Any social worker who has ever worked with a group of people or been in an organization (and that includes all of us, I trust) knows how complicated these politically charged situations can be.

In addition, when preparing research or evaluation reports or publications, social workers should make sure to acknowledge the sources on which they have relied throughout the project. In the first section of the report or publication, for instance, social workers should cite the literature (both published and unpublished) and other sources, such as personal interviews, that influenced or shaped the ideas discussed in the project. Similarly, in the methodology section, social workers should cite the literature or other sources that they used when developing data collection instruments, such as questionnaires, interviews, surveys, and assessment tools.

SAMPLING

Except when they're conducting single-case designs, social workers in research and evaluation projects gather information from groups of people (or a group of records about people). Program evaluations, for example, often assess the status or progress of a group of clients. Client satisfaction surveys look at a group of clients following the delivery of services. Needs assessments often ask a group of people (for instance, community residents or agency staff) about their perceptions of problems or issues that warrant attention.

Sometimes social workers want to gather information from the entire group of people with whom they are dealing—what's known in research jargon as the *population*. For example, a Mt. Washington Family Service Agency social worker who wants to gather client-satisfaction information from the eight clients participating in a battered women's counseling and support group could certainly question all eight clients. Similarly, a Mt. Washington administrator who wants to obtain information from the agency's six division directors concerning their training needs could certainly survey all six persons.

In many instances, however, social workers choose to gather information, or data, from a subset or *sample* of the group, usually for one of two reasons. First, sometimes it is too expensive or time-consuming to gather data from every single person or from every single record. You can probably imagine the various costs of gathering data. Because the interviewers and clerical staff must be paid, the more hours they spend collecting data, the higher their bill will be. Practically speaking, social workers and their agencies may not be able to afford the staff time and funds required to collect information from every individual or record.

The second reason is that apart from the expense, in many instances—

although, as we shall see, not all—there is virtually nothing to be gained by collecting information from every person or record in the target population. That is, a carefully drawn sample of people or records can provide almost exactly the same information that one would obtain from examining every member of the entire group. Why waste the time and effort?

Social workers who rely on samples to reflect population characteristics should be aware of different sampling procedures and their advantages and disadvantages. Different circumstances call for different sampling methods. For example, a Mt. Washington social worker who wants to sample a single client's reports of her feelings of depression throughout the day would approach the task differently than would a social worker who wants to interview a sample of gay or lesbian adolescents in the community about their social service and mental health needs.

The samples that social workers typically use fall into two categories: probability and nonprobability. Briefly, *probability samples* are those in which every person (or record or event) in the original group, or population, has a known chance (or probability) of being selected for the sample. Because of the way that probability samples are drawn, social workers can claim that the sample is representative of the population.

This is not the case with nonprobability samples. With a *nonprobability sample*, social workers don't know how representative or biased the sample is of the population from which it was drawn. This can be a problem because one usually can't generalize the results obtained from a nonprobability sample to the broader population of clients, community residents, and so on. But as we'll see shortly, sometimes only a nonprobability sample is possible or makes sense.

PROBABILITY SAMPLES

When social workers use samples, they usually want to be able to generalize the results to the population from which the sample was drawn. A study whose results can be generalized elsewhere has high *external validity*. If Mt. Washington staff can't afford to survey all clients who received services last year but can afford to survey 30 percent of them, it would be nice if the results obtained from the 30 percent could be generalized to the entire group of clients who received services. Similarly, if a clinical social worker at Mt. Washington wants to gather data on a particular client's classroom behavior in order to help the child and his teacher resolve his behavioral problems but can't afford to observe the child all day long for several days, she would like to be able to generalize the results she obtains from a sample of classroom observations.

To generalize in this way, social workers must use probability samples. If every "element" in the population (person, record, event, etc.) has a known chance of being included in the sample and if the sample is of sufficient size, social workers can generalize sample results to the population from which it was drawn.

Let's review the most commonly used probability samples.

Simple Random Sampling

Suppose a Mt. Washington administrator, Janet P., is concerned about the effect of managed care on the quality of clinical services provided to families. One of the things that Janet P. would like to know is whether over time the number of clinical hours spent with families has fallen. This is part of a larger assessment by the Mt. Washington staff of the effects of managed care, which also includes a survey of clients' opinions about how well the clinical services have met their needs.

Janet P. wants to look at changes during the past five years in the number of clinical hours spent with clients in the agency's family-counseling unit. Janet P. and her staff do not have nearly enough time to record the number of clinical hours spent with every family that received services during the past five years. Such a massive data collection effort would also be expensive. As an alternative, Janet P. could use simple random sampling.

Simple random sampling is, well, simple, at least in principle. One begins with the population, in this case all the families that received counseling services from the Mt. Washington Family Service Agency during the past five years and whose cases have been closed. The total is 655. Some of these families received services only briefly (one or two sessions), whereas others received services for a long period of time (more than a year). This is the study population, or *sampling frame.*

The next step is selecting the sample size. I'll have more to say about this topic later—it can get a bit complicated—but for sake of this example, we'll choose a sample size of 250. Janet P. decided that it would make sense to select 50 cases from each of the five years (for a total of 250 cases).

How should Janet P. select the 50 cases from each of the five years? (The average number of total cases in each of the five years was 131.) Let's brainstorm the possibilities (you might want to do this yourself before reading on). One possibility would be for Janet P. to write each of the 655 names or case numbers on slips of paper, put the slips of paper in a box, close her eyes, shake the box, and then randomly select 250 slips. This method likely would generate a good, representative, simple random sample (about a 38 percent sample; that is, 250 divided by 655 equals 38.2 percent).

Although this approach is fine, it's a little cumbersome and time-consuming (you'd also have to keep your eyes closed for a long time in order to select 250 slips). Another possibility would be to use a *table of random numbers*, which is, well, just a bunch of numbers—page after page of them. Many statistics textbooks contain tables of random numbers in an appendix that are used by practitioners, researchers, or anyone else who needs to select a sample randomly. Here's what a portion of such a table looks like:

37583	40583	72085	03967	74083
58265	07351	65093	76209	85710
10937	27696	03875	63017	38250
20739	18239	82406	73426	95217
82409	58924	62413	79365	18450
95621	48673	09274	87753	46452
62881	94710	37607	35266	85137

FIGURE 5.1. Excerpt from a Table of Random Numbers

This display isn't very exciting, is it? How do you use such a table? First, you assign a unique number to every person, record, or whatever that's eligible to be in the sample. Our example has 655 possibilities. The first case is 001, the second 002, and so on, all the way up to 655. (An alternative is to use part of the case identification number assigned when a family began to receive services from Mt. Washington. Presumably, every family has a unique case ID number.) Obviously, the numbers to be selected from the table of random numbers should correspond to the number of digits in the population size. That is, a population of 655 requires the selection of three-digit numbers; a population of 1248 requires the selection of four-digit numbers. Now notice that each of the numbers in figure 5.1 has five digits. So which three do you use? It doesn't really matter as long as you're consistent. You can use the first three, the last three, the middle three, or whatever.

To start the actual selection of numbers, you pick a spot on one of the random number pages randomly (surprising, huh?). You can do this by closing your eyes (this time only briefly) and pointing or by using some other method (for instance, say your age is thirty-two. You could pick the third page and the second column.). Then you decide whether you'll go down the rows, up the rows, to the left, or to the right (you could even go diagonally, but I suspect this would make you rather dizzy). You also must decide how many digits you need. If you're drawing the sample from numbers of three digits—such as a three-digit case identification number—you'll need to use groups of three digits. If you're drawing the sample from numbers with five digits, you'll need to use groups of five digits.

If you come across a number that's outside your range, you simply ignore it (for example, if you come across 732 and there are only 655 people in your population). You also ignore any number that you've already selected (that's not likely to happen very often). You just keep going until you've reached the total you need for your sample.

Now here's a different kind of simple random sampling, one for a single client. Consider the case at Mt. Washington involving Ms. E. and her son Toby. Toby was having behavioral problems at school, and the agency's clinical social worker, Ms. E., Toby, and Toby's teacher all devised an intervention plan.

Before settling on a sensible plan, however, the social worker wanted to gather some baseline information about Toby's behavior. The social worker couldn't afford to spend hours and hours in the classroom recording Toby's appropriate and inappropriate behaviors, but she could spend a few hours doing so.

The social worker decided to use simple random sampling to pick the times when she would observe Toby's behavior. She knew that she should observe Toby at different times of the day and on different days of the week. Can you figure out why? Toby's behavior tends to deteriorate throughout the day as he becomes more tired; he also tends to struggle more toward the end of the week than at the beginning, when he is somewhat more rested. To obtain a cross section of observations, Toby's social worker decided to randomly select six different times during a one-week period: midmorning and late afternoon on Monday, early morning and midafternoon on Wednesday, and late morning and early afternoon on Friday. The social worker then spent one-half hour in the classroom at each of these times observing Toby's behavior (later we'll explain how to record these observations).

Systematic Random Sampling

Sometimes you can use a somewhat different approach. Let's say you have 200 case records and want to select a sample of 50. One possibility is to line them up (in a file drawer, for example) and pick every fourth record (4 x 50 = 200). It's usually best to start this process by picking the first case randomly. As long as the cases are lined up randomly (that is, there's no systematic bias built into the order in which they appear), the results of systematic random sampling are usually the same as with simple random sampling.

Here's a slightly different application of systematic random sampling for a single client. One of the Mt. Washington clinical social workers, Maria D., was working with a young man, Wally A., who sought services because he was feeling very depressed. Wally A. had been hospitalized a year earlier with symptoms of depression. Early in their work together, Maria D. suggested that Wally A. record each day the degree of his depression. Wally agreed to record how he was feeling when he woke up in the morning, at lunchtime, and at bedtime. Maria D. explained that the two of them might find it useful to keep track of Wally A.'s feelings over time. She devised a simple item and had it printed on sheets of paper for Wally A. to use. The item read:

> Today I feel (1) very depressed, (2) somewhat depressed, (3) a little depressed, (4) not at all depressed.

Every two weeks, Maria D. and Wally A. looked at the data Wally A. recorded. They talked about the pattern and different events and circumstances that seemed to be correlated with significant changes in Wally A.'s moods. After working together for six months, Maria D. suggested that she and Wally A. look at the entire pattern of self-report data. Since Wally A. had recorded his level of depression every day, he had 183 data points. Because this seemed rather cumbersome to plot, Maria D. decided to sample the data and cut her task in half by plotting the data from every other day—a form of systematic random sampling.

Stratified Random Sampling

There is one other type of random sampling we need to talk about: *stratified random sampling*. Social workers use stratified random sampling to gather data on important subgroups in a population when simple random sampling may not produce enough people (or case records, etc.) in each of the various subgroups.

This is a fairly abstract idea, so an example might help. Let's say the executive director of Mt. Washington wants to conduct a comprehensive client satisfaction survey. The survey would be designed to gather data from clients whose cases closed in the last nine months, on issues related to the perceived quality of services and staff, accessibility of services, agency fees, agency location, and so on.

In the past nine months, the agency closed approximately 400 cases. Given the expense of locating and interviewing this many people, the Mt. Washington staff decided to sample 150 clients (a 37.5 percent sample).

One of the survey's goals is to see whether there are significant differences among specific subgroups in the client population. In addition to comparing

clients enrolled in different agency programs, the staff are particularly interested in comparing responses from clients of color with all other clients served
by the agency. These data are important because of the agency's concern about
the relatively few people of color who use the agency. The staff's hope is that
data from clients of color might provide useful information to help staff members map out a strategy to recruit more clients of color from the local community. In the past nine months, 10 percent of Mt. Washington's clients whose
cases were closed were people of color ($N = 40$).

This means the staff have a problem. If they use simple random sampling
procedures, they will probably end up with only 15 people of color (10 percent
of the sample of 150). That's hardly enough to make a meaningful analysis of
trends or patterns in the data or comparisons with responses of clients who are
not people of color.

So what do you do in a situation like this? You use *stratified random sampling*, by dividing the population into the different subgroups important to the
analysis, known as *strata* (hence the name, stratified random sampling). In this
case we would have two strata, clients of color (40 out of 400) and clients not
of color (360 out of 400). Let's say that the staff decide to interview at least 30
clients of color in order to gather meaningful data and also to interview 120
clients not of color (remember, the agency's budget will permit the staff to
interview about 150 former clients). Staff members will then randomly select
30 of the 40 former clients of color (a 75 percent sample) and 120 clients of the
360 clients not of color (a 33.3 percent sample).

The advantage of this approach is that it produces a large enough sample of
clients of color to enable a meaningful analysis (although it would be even better if all the clients of color could have been interviewed). But there's also a disadvantage.

If one of the project's goals is to generalize the sample's responses to the
agency's entire recent clientele—which is usually what one has in mind when
drawing a random sample—the disproportionate sampling of the two groups
(clients of and not of color) will prevent that. The reason is that the final sample does not reflect the population from which it was drawn; clients of color
would be overrepresented. Instead of having 15 clients of color in the sample
(consistent with the 10 percent of clients in the population who are people of
color), there would be 30 clients of color (20 percent of the sample). That is,
clients of color would be overrepresented in the sample by a factor of 2. This
disproportionate weighting would skew the results unless the responses of
clients of color were distributed exactly like the responses of clients not of color
(something we cannot assume).

Is there a way around this problem? Ideally, we would like to take advantage of the opportunity that stratified random sampling creates to examine data for subgroups that would be too small if simple random sampling were used and, simultaneously, to take advantage of the opportunity that simple random sampling offers to generalize the results to the population from which it was drawn.

Well, there is a way out of this methodological pickle. It's also not very complicated. All you need to do is weight the data to reflect the subgroups' actual representation in the population. So, if clients of color actually make up 10 percent of the population of clients but 20 percent of the final sample, the group's data are weighted to reflect this. In this scenario, we have to adjust the unweighted sample of clients of color by a factor of one-half to compensate for the fact that the stratified random sampling doubled their representation (doubling the value of the responses of clients not of color would accomplish the same thing). This is called *disproportionate stratified sampling*.

The other circumstances in which social workers might use stratified random sampling are when they are dealing with a fairly diverse population and want to minimize the sampling error and increase the likelihood that the final sample will be truly representative. Suppose the Mt. Washington staff want to be sure that the final sample of clients includes a proportionate number of people from four of the agency's various programs (substance abuse treatment, foster care, family counseling, and elderly services). That is, staff members want an accurate cross section; in this instance they may not be concerned about comparing data across the groups. To ensure an accurate representation of the agency's programs, the staff could list the cases according to each program and then randomly select from these lists. If the agency staff want a final sample of 100 from the population of 400 (a 25 percent sample), they could select 25 percent of each program's list. This is called *proportionate stratified sampling*. It is particularly useful when one is dealing with a heterogeneous population and is concerned about capturing all the diversity with a simple random sample. Proportionate stratified sampling is less compelling when one's sample is relatively homogeneous.

Cluster Sampling

Random sampling, whether simple or stratified, requires some kind of list or known group from which names, cases, and the like can be drawn. In some instances, however, social workers want to sample randomly but do not have a list from which to work. Consider the project I mentioned in chapter 2, in which a Mt. Washington social worker, Andrew R., was serving on a task force to address the lack of affordable housing in the community. The task force's principal goal was to gather data on the extent of the local affordable housing problem to support a proposal it planned to submit to the state housing finance agency.

The task force's plan was to survey a random sample of households in the Mt. Washington community to determine the percentage of their gross monthly income they were spending on housing. The task force believed that a large proportion of community residents were spending far above the widely accepted norm of 28 to 30 percent of monthly income for housing.

A major problem, however, was that they had no master list of community residents from which to sample. An alternative is what is known as *cluster sampling*—an ambitious, but rather reliable, approach. The first step is to list all the community's blocks and to select randomly from that list. Suppose there are 450 blocks (or clusters) in the Mt. Washington community. The task force might decide to randomly sample 100 of those blocks (about a 22 percent sample).

The second step is to sample households from these 100 blocks. There are 3700 known housing units in the 100 blocks, many of them apartments. The staff decide to survey a random sample of 370 of the addresses (a 10 percent sample of the sample). A particularly ambitious survey might include a third step, in which the individual to be interviewed from each of these households is sampled (for example, a female head of household in one address, then a male head of household in the next). Social workers may also need extra steps to adjust for significant differences in the "size" of each cluster. (For example, some city blocks are more densely populated than others, and this would affect the likelihood of any one household's being selected for the sample. As with stratified random sampling, an adjustment can be made to reflect these differences in cluster size. This is known as *probability-proportionate-to-size sampling*.)

Cluster sampling provides a useful, although cumbersome, alternative when other forms of random sampling aren't possible, especially when no master list is available. A trade-off, however, is that the various sampling stages increase the possibility of sampling error. There may not be a good way around this problem. At each step in the process, one simply has to do whatever is possible to minimize the likelihood of sampling error.

NONPROBABILITY SAMPLES

Often social workers need to sample but are unable to generate a probability sample. One common reason is that there is no "master list" from which to

sample, using a lottery, a table of random numbers, or any other randomization procedure. Suppose that social workers at Mt. Washington want to interview a sample of gay and lesbian community residents concerning their mental health needs, to design services for them. How would the social workers develop their sample? Certainly they can't expect to sample randomly from a list of all gay and lesbian people in the agency's catchment area.

Another reason that probability samples may not be feasible is that they can be very time-consuming—and hence expensive—to generate. Think of all the people and time it would take to create a probability sample using cluster-sampling techniques. A cluster sample may be appealing, but it may also be unrealistic in light of an agency's budget, personnel, time constraints, and other resources.

What are the alternatives? Nonprobability samples. In short, a *nonprobability sample* is one in which not every element in the population (people, case records, or what have you) has a known chance of being selected for the final sample. I know this sounds like a pretty abstract definition, but this is the way that probability and nonprobability samples are distinguished. As I noted earlier, a *probability sample* is one in which every element in the population does have a known chance of being selected for the final sample.

Now that I have presented the formal definition, let me try to explain it more simply. When social workers deal with probability samples, they know (usually precisely) the number of people (or whatever) in the population. They also know how many people will be selected for the final sample. It is easy to figure out the likelihood that each member of the population will be selected for the final sample; one simply divides the number of people to be selected for the final sample by the number of people in the population and converts that fraction to a percentage. Thus if the population is 750 and the final sample will contain 150 people, we know that each member of the population has a 20 percent (or one out of five) chance of being selected.

But we wouldn't know this if the Mt. Washington staff were trying to identify a sample of gay and lesbian community residents; that is, although we would know the size of the sample to be interviewed, we wouldn't know the size of the population from which the sample would be drawn. This lack of information, in turn, would affect our ability to know how representative the sample is of the population from which it was drawn, that is, the survey's external validity.

How, then, might such a sample be selected? One possibility would be to identify local gay and lesbian support and advocacy groups that may have members living in the Mt. Washington community. Of course, for privacy reasons, such groups would not be able to hand over lists of such individuals, but group officials or leaders might be willing to publicize the survey among their members living in the Mt. Washington neighborhood and encourage them to contact the agency to participate in the survey. When several gay and lesbian community residents willing to participate in the survey are identified, the Mt. Washington staff could ask them to contact other gays and lesbians who might be willing to participate. This can be an effective approach to generating a nonprobability sample. Although it is impossible to know how representative the final sample is—thus limiting the survey's external validity—the Mt. Washington staff nonetheless would have an opportunity to gather important information from key sources.

In social work, four major types of nonprobability samples are useful: convenience or availability samples, snowball samples, purposive samples, and quota samples.

Convenience, Availability, or Accidental Sampling

In the example we just discussed, the Mt. Washington staff may need to use relatively informal means to locate gays and lesbians living in the agency's catchment area. Since they don't have a master list, staff members may have to rely on "word of mouth" to generate a reasonable sample of people to survey. If the final sample includes gay and lesbian people who heard about the survey, either from local gay and lesbian support or advocacy groups or through some other means, the Mt. Washington staff would be basing their survey on a *convenience, availability, or accidental sample*.

Here's another example. Suppose that the Mt. Washington staff want to know how often children in the community are exposed to lead. Staff members are aware of widespread concern about lead poisoning among children as a result of their exposure to lead paint, lead particles in yard dirt, water that has a high lead content because it flows through old pipes, and other sources. Social workers at Mt. Washington are worried that children's exposure to lead may cause, or exacerbate, brain damage, behavioral or learning problems, and developmental difficulties.

To combat this problem, a Mt. Washington administrator, Jeanne R., would like to form an advocacy group to raise public awareness, to work with local landlords to rehabilitate deteriorated housing that poses special lead-related hazards, and to lobby the city council and state legislature for more stringent housing regulations. As a starting point, Ms. R. decides to survey a group of local residents considered to be at risk for lead poisoning, to find out their perception of the magnitude of the problem, what needs to be done to address the problem, and their willingness to participate in a lead-poisoning advocacy group.

Here, too, the Mt. Washington staff face a practical problem: no master list of community residents with lead-poisoning problems. Of course, some families already have been identified by public health officials as being at risk. Their children may have been screened by pediatricians and found to have lead poisoning, and they may have been referred to a local hospital for treatment. But because of (understandable and appropriate) confidentiality constraints, the Mt. Washington staff may not be able to obtain such a list (unless, for example, they conduct the study in conjunction with the local health department).

How, then, might the staff collect a sample? One possibility would be to talk to local pediatricians and hospital staff treating lead poisoning, explain the survey's purpose and the agency's goal (to form an advocacy group), and ask them to ask families with whom they have worked to contact Ms. R. for permission to share their names with the staff. This, too, would be a convenience, availability, or accidental sample. Mt. Washington's staff members wouldn't be able to generalize the survey's results to all families in the Mt. Washington area who have experienced, or are at risk of experiencing, lead poisoning (low external validity), but the survey might yield valuable information and might identify a number of people who would be willing to become active in a lead-poisoning advocacy group sponsored by the Mt. Washington Family Service Agency.

Snowball Sampling

It is not unusual for convenience or availability sampling to be combined with snowball sampling. In *snowball sampling*, persons who have been identified for a study's sample are asked to name other persons who meet the study's eligibility criteria. This approach is useful when potential participants are hard to identify and locate.

We can see that Mt. Washington staff might want to rely on snowball sampling to identify gay and lesbian community residents or families who have had a problem with lead poisoning. As with all nonprobability samples, it's impossible to know how representative the sample is.

Social workers need to be especially concerned about confidentiality when they use snowball samples in regard to sensitive issues or topics. That is, people may feel violated if survey participants give their names to social work researchers or evaluators who have asked them to suggest others who meet the study's eligibility criteria. An accepted way to avoid this problem is to ask survey participants to think about others who may be suitable participants and to have the participants ask those persons for permission to be contacted by the researchers or evaluators (or the social workers could give the respondents copies of a letter that they could in turn give to potential respondents, asking the latter to contact the researcher). This may seem rather cumbersome, and it is. But it's a necessary hurdle when social workers are concerned, as they ought to be, about people's privacy.

Last year, for example, one of my social work colleagues wanted to survey gays and lesbians who had been victims of domestic violence. This is an important topic and one that has not received much attention. My colleague decided to gather data on the incidence and nature of the problem, with the goal of educating and raising the awareness of mental health professionals.

Obviously, my colleague could not generate a random or representative sample from a master list. A probability sample was out of the question. Instead, he had to begin with a convenience or availability sample, which included six acquaintances in the community who had revealed their victimization to him. My colleague interviewed these persons and then, using a snowball-sampling technique, asked them to identify other gays and lesbians who had revealed their victimization. For ethical reasons, it would not have been appropriate for my colleague simply to have asked the initial respondents for the names and telephone numbers of other known victims. This would have been an egregious violation of these individuals' privacy rights. Instead, my colleague asked the initial six respondents to try to locate other victims of gay or lesbian domestic violence and to ask them for permission to be contacted by the social worker. This extra step may have reduced the size of the available sample but seems to have been the only reasonable way to identify a sample whose privacy must be respected.

Quota Sampling

In the discussion of probability samples, I referred to situations in which social workers want to compare groups of people and in which, as a result, it may be important to use a stratified random sample. Remember that this kind of sample is useful when one needs sufficient numbers of people in different categories (such as ethnic groups or groups of clients exposed to different interventions).

As you might imagine, sometimes social workers want to make these kinds of comparisons but can't sample randomly, again usually because no master list is available. Consider Mt. Washington staff's interest in surveying ethnic minorities and people of color in the surrounding community, concerning their perception of Mt. Washington's services and mission. The Mt. Washington staff may want to compare the responses of several groups, including African Americans, Southeast Asians (Cambodian, Laotian, Hmong, and Vietnamese), Mexican Americans, and other Latinos.

Since they have no master list from which to select, the staff may want to use a *quota sample* (a nonprobability version of a stratified sample). They might begin by determining a reasonable total sample size (let's say 120) and obtaining census data on the percentage of each of the ethnic groups in the local community. Using these percentages, it would be easy to figure out how many people in the final sample should be from each ethnic or racial group (if

African Americans comprise 27 percent of the local community, then 27 percent of the final sample—or 32 people—should be African American). Then using some combination of convenience- and snowball-sampling techniques, the Mt. Washington staff would identify community residents for the sample, adding members of each ethnic group until each "quota" was reached.

Despite all this effort, however, they still would not be able to assume that the sample was representative. Nonetheless, quota sampling can be a valuable approach when comparing information gathered from different groups.

Purposive Sampling

Social workers often want to gather information from a select group of people. For example, if a Mt. Washington administrator wants to know why ethnic minorities and people of color in the local community are not using the agency's services, she might begin by identifying a few important, influential leaders who may have special insights to offer. She might enlist the informal help of her colleagues in compiling a list of these local leaders. The administrator then might ask these leaders whether they would be willing to participate in an in-depth interview concerning their impressions of community residents' attitudes toward Mt. Washington. Sometimes such individuals are referred to as *key informants* because of their unique and valuable knowledge about the topic of interest. They are invited to participate with a particular *purpose* in mind (hence the name of this type of sample, *purposive sample*).

Another example of purposive sampling comes from the research project I described earlier, concerning the stipends paid to foster parents. In this example, a Mt. Washington administrator decided to contact a number of colleagues in other social service agencies to determine whether they, too, were having difficulty retaining foster parents because of the size of the stipend paid to them by the state child welfare agency. To gain a broad perspective, this administrator might choose a sample of colleagues from a range of agencies, including both public and private agencies, agencies of different sizes and geographic locations, agencies serving different ethnic groups, and agencies varying in the range of programs and services they offer. Again, even though a purposive sample may limit one's ability to generalize the results obtained, it can be a source of rich, detailed information.

There's no magical formula to use when selecting a purposive sample. Rather, social workers simply need to know what they are trying to do and the advantages and disadvantages of all their sources of relevant information. Beyond that, all they need to do is find respondents who are willing to participate in the data collection.

SAMPLING ERROR

One of the biggest challenges in sampling is to reduce the likelihood of *sampling error*—error that results when one's sample does not accurately reflect the population from which it was drawn. Particularly with probability samples—when we would like to be able to claim that the sample is representative and that the research or evaluation project's results can be generalized from the sample to the population from which it was drawn—we need to be confident that the sampling error is minimal.

Let's look more closely at this concept of sampling error. Suppose, as in one of the examples I presented earlier, a Mt. Washington administrator, Janet P., wants to examine a sample of case records from the last five years from the agency's family-counseling program. She decides to use a sample of 250 cases from the total of 655 available cases (a 38 percent sample). If Janet P. performs this task carefully (using a table of random numbers or some other acceptable form of lottery), chances are that her sample will accurately resemble the population of cases. That is, if you were to compare the sample and the population of cases on variables such as average age, level of education, income, presenting problems, and length of service, the pairs of figures would probably be very close.

Notice, however, that I said the *chances are* that Janet P.'s sample data and the population data would be similar. Even with the most conscientious and careful sampling efforts, there's a chance of some error. The more careful we are, the less chance there will be for error. (You know how newspapers and television news broadcasts often report the results of surveys with statements like "In a recent *New York Times*/ABC News survey, more than half a sample of adults from throughout the United States opposed planned federal cutbacks in welfare benefits; about one-third favored proposed cuts. The survey has a margin of error of plus or minus three percentage points." What they're talking about is sampling error. That is, the actual percentages in the population from which the sample was drawn could be three percentage points higher or lower than those reported by the sample.)

Let me illustrate this idea of sampling error with a simple example. Suppose you are working as a social worker in a shelter for battered women. You want to compare the average length of the residents' stay during the past year with the average length of their stay five years ago. Five years ago the shelter was a relatively small program, so you don't need to sample from that year, when only 48 women resided at the shelter. However, since then the program has grown; during the past year 212 women lived at the shelter and its satellite facility. Instead of searching through all 212 records, you decide to sample 50 of them. Each resident's file has a unique four-digit case number, so you use a table of random numbers to select 50 cases. Now suppose that during the past year, the *actual* average length of stay for the population (the 212 cases) was 3.7 months. What do you think the result will be for the random sample of 50 cases? We can't know for sure, of course, but we can be reasonably confident that the sample's result will be around 3.7 months, although perhaps not exactly. The reason that we can be reasonably confident is that you are sampling carefully using truly random procedures. This usually produces a satisfactory result, particularly when sampling nearly one-fourth of the population (as we will see shortly, in many circumstances a small sample can be a relatively "unstable," or imprecise, estimate of a population). Let's say the sample's result for the average length of stay is 3.6 months. That's not too bad and not very misleading, even though it's not entirely accurate. The discrepancy between 3.6 and 3.7 is the sampling error.

A practical problem, however, is that we usually don't know the population statistic (or, to use statisticians' terminology, the population *parameter*) for which the sample statistic is an estimate (the term *parameter* usually refers to a population, and the term *statistic* refers to a sample). It's usually too time-consuming or cumbersome to calculate the population parameter, which is why we use samples in the first place.

Instead, we can use a widely accepted method to *estimate* the degree of sampling error. To make this point, I need to ask you to use your imagination. Pretend that we selected one sample of 50 from the population of 212 cases, just as we did before. The result we got was 3.6 months. Now imagine that you started over and selected a second sample of 50 (perhaps including some of the same cases as in the first sample, which can happen using random-sampling techniques). Let's say the result for this second sample was 3.9 months. Then we started yet again and selected a third sample of 50, and the result was 3.8.

Imagine that we had a slow day (better make that a *real* slow day), with few distractions, and we repeated this procedure 100 times. What do you think the result would be? As you might have guessed, we would end up with some sample estimates below the population parameter of 3.7, some exactly 3.7 or extremely close to it, and some above 3.7. We might end up with a few that are quite a bit below or above 3.7 (statisticians call these *outliers*), but most would be in the general vicinity of 3.7. What I'm describing here is a well-documented and rather remarkable phenomenon, almost like a law of nature. It's known as *probability theory*. According to probability theory—whose validity

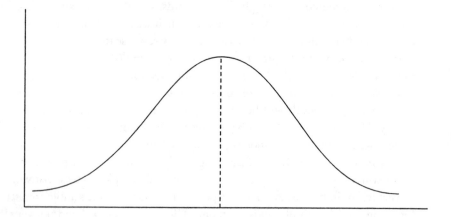

FIGURE 5.2   The Normal Curve

has been demonstrated time and time again—the results of repeated samples drawn randomly from a population will form a predictable pattern called a *normal curve* (figure 5.2). Perhaps you've heard of this (it's commonly referred to as a *bell-shaped curve*).

One of the best illustrations of this phenomenon I've ever seen was in the Chicago Museum of Science and Industry. I visited this exhibit a number of times when I was attending social work school. (The museum was fairly close to my apartment. Occasionally, when I ran out of laundry or housework to do, I'd go to the museum.) The exhibit consisted of a large wall display with rows and columns of evenly spaced pegs that were perpendicular to and protruding from the wall; a pane of glass was in front of the pegs. I don't recall exactly how many rows and columns of pegs there were, but let's say it was around ten rows and ten columns.

At the base of the display was a very large collection of what seemed like hollow balls, sort of like Ping-Pong balls (more than a hundred, I would say). A little mechanism would transport one ball at a time to the top and middle of the pegs and release it. The ball would hit the peg directly beneath it and then bounce randomly from one peg to another before it settled to the bottom. The process was repeated until all the balls had been released and had piled up on top of one another (they were contained by the pane of glass in front of the pegs). Then the balls were released to the bottom of the display, and the whole process would start again.

Guess what shape the balls formed when all of them were piled up? A nor-

mal, or bell-shaped, curve. Every time. I watched that series of random events
I don't know how many times during my years in Chicago (seven years, including a number after graduate school), and it never failed. Probability and randomness are amazing phenomena. Some things in life are indeed predictable.
Although we cannot predict the path and ultimate location of any particular
ball, we can predict the overall result or pattern. (Think why this might be
analogous to what social workers can predict about clients on their caseloads.
It may be hard to know exactly how a particular client will end up, but one
may have had enough experience with such clients to be able to predict an
overall pattern.)

Now let's think about this curve, because it's an important concept. If we
were drawing repeated samples of 50 from 212 cases in a shelter for battered
women, would we want this curve to be narrow or broad (or, if you prefer,
skinny or fat)? I hope you answered narrow (or skinny). Why? If we were actually to perform this task, we would want our sampling procedures to be so
good that nearly all the estimates were very close to the actual population parameter. This would result in a narrow bell curve, although the chances are
(there's that probability language again) that there would be a few outliers at
what statisticians call the *tails* of the distribution. Another way of putting this
is that any one sample's result is likely to be a good estimate of the population
and that there is relatively little sampling error. This is significant because in
real life we usually select only one sample. We don't bother with this business
of repeated samples.

In contrast, what would we conclude if the bell curve were quite broad?
This would indicate a great deal of sampling error. Hence if we actually needed
to rely on just one sample, we couldn't be very confident that the one we ended
up with was a good estimate of the population.

At this point, I hope you're wondering what factors influence whether the
bell curve is narrow or broad. (I can't imagine that you were thinking about
anything else.) This is an excellent question, and it brings us to a discussion of
sample size and what statisticians call *confidence intervals*.

Sample Size

One of the questions I am asked most often by students and practicing social
workers who are planning to conduct some kind of research or evaluation project is, "How big does my sample need to be?" This is a perfectly reasonable
question, but the answer, unfortunately, isn't so simple.

Basically, there are two ways to determine a sample's size: what I will call the
"quick-and-dirty" way and the "scientific" way. For many situations in social

work, the quick-and-dirty approach is just fine. In some instances, however, social workers need to determine a sample's size more scientifically. As you may have guessed, this takes more time and is more cumbersome.

The easiest way to describe the quick-and-dirty approach is to say that you sample as many people (or case records or whatever) as you need to and can afford to. Generally speaking, the larger the sample is, the better it will be. This may not seem like very helpful advice, but that's pretty much all there is to it. For example, if a Mt. Washington social worker plans to interview community leaders who are likely to know something about their community residents' perceptions of the agency, a sample of ten or twelve may seem "about right" for an exploratory study of this sort, large enough to get a superficial sense of people's opinions. If the social worker wants more detailed information from a sample of former foster parents concerning their reasons for terminating their service, a larger sample, perhaps in the vicinity of fifty, may be large enough to capture the variety of respondents' opinions. If a social worker wants to compare the relative effectiveness of individual and group counseling for clients being treated for substance abuse problems, it might be a good idea to have at least twenty clients in each group, to minimize the likelihood that "outliers" will unduly influence the results. There's no magic to this. One simply consults with colleagues who know something about analyzing data, considers the amount of time one has, takes into account budgetary considerations, and makes a reasonable guess as to an appropriate sample size.

This is in contrast to a more scientific approach, which is usually used for relatively large, ambitious research and evaluation projects. Samples of a certain size may be necessary to perform certain statistical analyses (you can learn about these requirements and statistical procedures in a data analysis course). For example, a widely accepted guideline is that the statistical procedure called *multiple regression* requires ten cases for each variable studied. Some people contend that a survey that will lead to fairly sophisticated data analysis should cover at least 100 people. Another common guideline is that a sample should be at least one-tenth the size of the population, although there are many exceptions to this. Also, careful determination of the sample size can be important when the implications of one's findings are potentially profound or the findings are likely to have a major impact.

Details of the scientific approach to determining sample size are beyond the scope of this book. Suffice it to say that very few social workers ever need to use this approach. It involves some reasonably complex statistical calculations based on the size of the population from which one is sampling and an estimate of the degree of variation in that population (regarding whatever one is measuring). To make these calculations, one must be familiar with some pretty complicated statistical concepts, such as confidence intervals and standard error. (For those of you with some intestinal fortitude when it comes to fairly complex statistical concepts, here's a brief introduction: A *confidence interval* is a statistical device enabling one to estimate the accuracy or representativeness of a sample. It is calculated by determining something called the *standard error*. The standard error is an estimate of the variation that one would see if, as we discussed, repeated samples were taken from the population being studied. The standard error is calculated by using a formula that takes into account how much variation or diversity there is in the population—remember, the more diversity the population has, the bigger the sample will need to be to capture it accurately—and the size of the sample that one is actually using. Ideally, of course, we want the standard error—which reflects the degree of sampling error—to be as small as possible. Using these formulas, we can say things like "Results based on this sample will be accurate 99 times out of 100, plus or minus 3 points." You would need to consult a statistics book for more detailed information on these calculations, but this overview should give you some sense of the concepts involved. Aren't you glad you asked?)

Perhaps the most important point to make about sample size is that it is not necessarily based on the size of the population from which one plans to sample. That may sound odd. On the surface, it may seem that the larger the population is, the larger the sample will need to be to represent it accurately. But that's not always true. What is more important than the size of the population is the degree of variation within it. That is, the more diversity within a population—for example, with respect to such traits as age, race, ethnicity, socioeconomic status, family status, education, social problems, and mental health status—the larger the sample will need to be to "capture" or adequately represent this variation. The less heterogeneity, or the more homogeneity, there is in the population, the smaller the sample will need to be. Another way to say this is that the greater the likelihood of sampling error is, because of diversity within the population, the larger the sample will need to be.

Here's an extreme illustration. Suppose you wanted to conduct a survey of adolescent girls' attitudes toward illegal drug use. The population from which you plan to draw your sample is a county in your state that is almost entirely Mormon and includes families in which the majority of the parents have attended college and, for those parents who work outside the home, are employed in white-collar occupations. Contrast that situation with a similar survey for which the population from which you plan to draw the sample is

Brooklyn, New York. Wouldn't you need fewer people to capture the variation in the first example than in the second?

Here's another startling fact—one that surprises a lot of social workers. How many people would you need in a random sample of adult Americans to produce a good representation of opinion about, say, the next presidential election or some controversial social issue (for example, assisted suicide or the death penalty)? Because of the millions and millions of adult Americans, you might think you would need a very large sample. Not true. With careful sampling procedures, you would need a sample of only about 1100. (Take a close look at newspaper summaries of national polls conducted by major television networks, newspapers, and polling organizations. You'll see that most of the national samples have somewhere around 1000 or 1100 people, with fairly modest margins of error—about plus or minus three percentage points.) Actually, you would need about the same-size sample to represent the state of California or Pennsylvania, because states like these contain populations that are about as diverse—with respect to age, gender, ethnicity, socioeconomic status, and so on—as the U.S. population. Again, what really matters more than the size of the population is the degree of diversity or variation within it.

MEASUREMENT ISSUES

Now that we have some sense of how to design research and evaluation projects and generate samples, we can turn to the business of actually collecting the information itself—usually known as *data*. Before we discuss specific data collection tools and procedures (in chapters 7, 8, and 9), we should review some of the core concepts related to measurement.

The first question is, What is measurement? In social work, *measurement* is the assessment of something related to our work as clinicians, community organizers and advocates, administrators, or policy analysts. Sometimes we measure precisely and deliberately, for example, when we administer diagnostic instruments to assess clients' clinical depression, self-esteem, suicide risk, or anxiety level or gather data as part of a single-case evaluation. Consider the Mt. Washington social worker's attempt to help a local schoolteacher learn behavior management principles that might be useful with Toby, the young boy we discussed earlier. As part of the intervention, the social worker decided to collect some baseline data concerning Toby's behavioral problems, which included getting out of his seat when he was supposed to be seated, fooling around at his desk when he was supposed to be completing a learning task assigned by the teacher, and talking with other children when the teacher was talking to the class.

Other formal attempts to measure are carefully designed needs assessments and program evaluations. For example, for the Mt. Washington staff to conduct a needs assessment of problems faced by community residents, they would have to develop an interview form or questionnaire to measure different phenomena, such as the types of problems people face, the extent of those problems, the type of help people feel they need, and where people are inclined to seek help. Similarly, if the Mt. Washington staff want to evaluate the effectiveness of a substance abuse treatment group, they need a tool to measure successful outcome.

Sometimes social workers measure things informally. An administrator at Mt. Washington who is concerned about employee morale might chat casually with senior staff about the issue. This kind of data collection may not be a formal use of interviews or questionnaires, but it is measurement nonetheless; the administrator is gathering information (data) to help her do her work. Similarly, a clinical social worker at Mt. Washington also is measuring when she has an informal chat with a new client about the client's various problems and prior attempts to obtain help for them. The results of this kind of measurement may not be summarized with numbers and statistics, but this informal effort does indeed produce data.

Some measurement efforts produce quantitative data, and others produce qualitative data. Briefly, *quantitative data* consist of information summarized by numbers. For example, when we say that Toby inappropriately got out of his seat four times during a 30-minute observation period, we have quantified the data (frequency = 4). When we say that a client has a depression score of 35, based on his answers to a formal depression scale, we have quantified the data. When we say that 71 percent of Mt. Washington's clients report being satisfied with the services they received from the agency, we have quantified the data.

In contrast, *qualitative data* are information summarized with words rather than numbers. For example, if a Mt. Washington administrator talks with a number of senior staff and find from their comments a pattern of morale problems among line staff, we are dealing with qualitative data. If an agency clinician writes a process recording of a family-counseling session she conducted and shares it with her clinical supervisor, she has produced qualitative data. If a Mt. Washington social worker in community organizing attends a meeting of neighborhood residents to plan a strategy to lobby for more police protection, she can observe the proceedings and obtain qualitative data concerning interpersonal relationships and group dynamics among the community leaders.

Neither quantitative data nor qualitative data are necessarily superior. Some social workers think that data that can be presented in the form of numbers—quantitative data—are necessarily better than data presented in the form of words—qualitative data. I don't agree. In my experience, social workers should use the data most appropriate to a particular set of circumstances. Sometimes, depending on the phenomena being measured, the amount of time and resources available for data collection, and one's audience, quantitative data seem more suitable. For instance, if the Mt. Washington staff want to present data to a state legislative subcommittee to support their claim that the community has a serious shortage of affordable housing, the chances are that carefully compiled numbers, graphs, charts, and so on will have more impact than will qualitative data alone. However, in this situation, reports of qualitative data collected from homeless persons and families fruitlessly seeking scarce affordable housing or at risk of eviction—perhaps in the form of anecdotes gathered from various community residents—can have a powerful effect.

I've seen this happen myself. For eight years I was a commissioner of a state housing and mortgage finance agency. All states have such an agency, which is typically created by the state legislature to help provide affordable housing to low- and moderate-income people. Using a variety of mechanisms—such as bond financing, tax credits, housing vouchers, mortgage credit certificates, reverse equity annuities, and state subsidies—these agencies offer rental assistance, below-market mortgage loans, and rehabilitation loans and grants to individuals, families, and organizations. I can remember many board (and other) meetings at which housing advocates would make formal presentations with fancy charts, graphs, and tables that displayed the extent of people's housing problems and the likely impact of various programs designed to address them.

This kind of quantitative data can be compelling. But the data that often had an even more powerful impact were qualitative, such as reports from homeless people or testimonies from low-income families about their dire circumstances and difficulties. Time after time, I saw administrators, legislators, newspaper reporters, and agency board members profoundly influenced by such qualitative data in ways that sometimes can't be matched by thirty-page summaries of quantitative data with accompanying charts, tables, graphs, and fancy statistical displays. The quantitative data may be essential, but they may not have the power of qualitative data or "sing" the way qualitative data can. Often, it's not a matter of social workers choosing between quantitative and qualitative data but of knowing how to use both to produce the most informative and persuasive picture.

The debate over the value of qualitative and quantitative data is one reflection of the changes in social workers' thinking about measurement. For decades—in fact for most of social work's relatively young life—social workers followed the lead of social and physical scientists, who believed that the only form of measurement that counted was "objective," "value free," and "neutral." This point of view, often referred to as *positivism*, shaped much of the research and evaluation in social work. (Positivism is a philosophical term that refers to a school of thought that emerged in the late eighteenth and early nineteenth century with philosophers David Hume and Auguste Comte.)

Beginning especially in the early 1980s, many social workers began to question the underlying assumptions of positivism and to offer alternative perspectives. According to its critics, the basic principles on which positivism is based are naive and do not reflect real life. There is no way, for example, that a social worker conducting a research or evaluation project can be completely objective, value free, or neutral. Every human being is susceptible to bias, and it is virtually impossible to remove the influence of one's subjective experience from a research or evaluation project. The influence of one's values and subjective opinions may not always be obvious, but it is there. Social workers' values may, for example, subtly influence the way a question in an interview is worded, the way a respondent answers a question, or the way qualitative data are interpreted.

Social workers now agree that to measure adequately, they must obtain data from various sources, recognizing that each source is accompanied by biases and subjective impressions. That is, it's doubtful that we will ever know what "truth" is or whether there is any objective reality out there. Instead, we must seek the most comprehensive information possible from as many sources as possible, with the hope that by comparing and contrasting various perspectives, we will understand what we are studying. Thus, if a Mt. Washington social worker is interested in a client's feelings of depression, he may decide to administer a standardized depression scale or inventory, interview the client himself about his feelings of depression, interview family members and friends who can offer insights into the client (with the client's permission, of course), and use the social worker's impressions to construct a comprehensive picture of the client's mental health—and to report the results in the form of qualitative and quantitative data. Similarly, a Mt. Washington social worker interested in why so few people of color in the community use the agency's services might gather quantitative and qualitative data from community leaders and a sample of community residents using a formal interview guide, qualitative data obtained from informal discussions with various community groups, and quantitative and qualitative data obtained from interviews with members of local organizations like church groups and social clubs.

This approach is often called *triangulation*, a concept borrowed from navigation. In triangulation, one gathers and analyzes information from various perspectives (angles) before proceeding. This helps social workers consider and account for possible biases in the different points of view.

Triangulation can differ depending on the different data sources, measurement tools, and data analysis techniques used. Thus as I mentioned earlier, a social worker might consider data collected from clients, family members, and other professionals before reaching conclusions about a client's situation. This information might be gathered using different measurement tools, including formal interviews or questionnaires, diagnostic instruments, informal discussion, and observation (both quantitative and qualitative measures). Finally, the data might be analyzed using various techniques, such as statistical analysis, content analysis, and process recordings (discussed in more detail later).

Whatever source of data we rely on and whatever tools and data analysis techniques we use, as social workers, we must master validity and reliability, standard concepts in the research and evaluation world.

VALIDITY

Didn't we already deal with validity when we discussed research and evaluation designs and our ability to generalize results obtained from samples? In fact, in chapter 3, I talked about what is required for a research and evaluation design to be valid. This type of validity is relevant to explanatory or evaluative designs, in which we need to control for extraneous factors (such as maturation, contemporaneous and historical events, and measurement) that might account for changes in the dependent or outcome variables, instead of or in addition to the intervention (or independent variable). Using control groups and random assignment enhances our ability to control for such extraneous variables. In chapter 5, I described validity with respect to our ability to generalize results obtained from probability or nonprobability samples (external validity).

These types of validity—which have to do with the validity of research and evaluation designs and sample data—are different from the types of validity I describe in this chapter, which have to do with the validity of measures and of the data themselves.

In sum, validity related to measurement pertains to how well the data we collect—whatever the source—actually reflect the phenomena we are trying to measure. When we measure something—like clients' feelings, social workers' morale, or service utilization patterns—we want the results to be "accurate," in the sense that they do not create a distorted picture of what we are measuring. If the results are flawed (for instance, if interview questions are worded poorly or respondents falsify their answers or exaggerate their opinions), we would be foolish to make much of the results or report them with confidence.

Suppose that a Mt. Washington social work supervisor decided to survey a sample of clients who participated in a treatment group for people arrested for domestic violence. The survey is designed to gather self-report data from clients about their acts of aggression before, during, and after the intervention. All the clients were required by the local county's criminal court to participate in the treatment group as a condition of probation. The supervisor wants to use the data for two purposes: to monitor each client's progress and to support her application to the county court for additional funding for the program.

Let's say the supervisor did not have much training in research and evaluation, and so she did not carefully word the questions about acts of aggression. As a result, many clients were confused about the supervisor's definition of this concept (later, when I explain how to construct questions, I will show how this can happen). Consequently, many clients' responses did not accurately reflect the number of aggressive acts they actually had committed. This inaccuracy threatened the data's validity, in that the supervisor did not measure what she hoped to measure.

To understand validity, we must look at several different aspects of the concept that are relevant to measurement: content or face validity, predictive validity, concurrent validity, construct validity, and the validity of self-report data.

Face and Content Validity

The terms *face* and *content validity* are often used synonymously, but they do have some important differences. Put simply, a measurement tool (an interview instrument, a questionnaire, or a standardized recording form) has face validity when its items provide, on the surface, a good indication of what we're trying to measure. For example, to measure housing affordability, asking Mt. Washington clients what percentage of their monthly income they spend on rent would have face validity. Similarly, asking the agency's clients to comment on the quality of the services they received as an indicator of client satisfaction would have face validity. That is, "on the face of it," the measure makes sense.

Conversely, content validity is the result when a measuring instrument's items accurately reflect the concepts that the social worker wants to measure.

Let's return to the example in which the Mt. Washington supervisor, Marcia R., wants to gather data on clients participating in the domestic violence intervention program. One of her goals is to keep track of clients' acts of aggression before, during, and after the program. To collect these data, she needs a measure of "aggressive act" that has both content and face validity.

Suppose Marcia R. asks each client to answer the following question at the end of every week: "How many times during the past week did you treat your spouse/partner aggressively?" Do you find any problems with that question?

One is that Marcia R. hasn't precisely defined *aggressively*. It's quite possible—and quite likely in my experience—that clients will define this term differently; hence their responses will include apples and oranges, so to speak (or at least different kinds of apples). Some clients may assume that *aggressively* means hitting, and others may think it includes pushing, name calling, or swearing.

Instead, Marcia R. decides to ask two different questions: "How many times during the past week did you physically strike or hit your spouse/partner?" and "How many times during the past week did you push or shove your spouse/partner?" Would this take care of the problem? No, it would not. If I saw these questions in a research or evaluation report, I would have to conclude that the social worker's measurement lacked content and face validity.

Here's the crux of the problem: For questions like these to have content and face validity, they must incorporate *all the relevant aspects of the concept being measured*. For instance, anyone who has worked in the domestic violence field knows that aggression takes various forms, not all of which are physical. If the questions address only physical aggression and ignore verbal aggression such as yelling, screaming, berating, and harassing, they will fail to address all relevant aspects of the concept of aggression, and so the measure will lack face and content validity. To achieve content and face validity, therefore, Marcia R. must add items that address both physical and verbal aggression.

Let's look at another example, that of Toby, whose teacher complained that his behavior in the classroom was difficult to manage. One of the social worker's goals in this case is to help Toby's teacher learn behavior management techniques. To monitor and evaluate the effectiveness of this approach, the social worker will collect data on Toby's "acting-out" behavior.

Assume the social worker collects data on only the frequency with which Toby gets out of his seat when he is supposed to be working on an assigned task. Does this measure have either content or face validity? I don't think it does, because getting out of his seat is only one aspect of the behavioral problems that Toby's teacher mentioned. Other behaviors are talking to other children and not looking at the teacher when she is talking to the class. Omitting these indicators of Toby's behavioral difficulties threatens the measures' content and face validity.

How do we strengthen content and face validity? There's no precise formula or series of steps to follow. In most cases, we simply have to use what is typically called *common sense* (which, unfortunately, is sometimes not so common). One standard way to enhance content and face validity is to conduct a comprehensive literature review of the concept we want to measure, to ensure that we are aware of all its relevant components or dimensions. For example, a comprehensive literature review of substance abuse would reveal that it includes more than alcohol abuse, that it also includes the abuse of substances such as heroin, cocaine, amphetamines, and barbiturates. A comprehensive review of attention deficit hyperactivity problems among children would identify a range of behaviors, such as impulsivity and distractibility, that often must be considered when designing and evaluating an intervention.

Another way to enhance content or face validity is to talk to colleagues and experts who know a great deal about the concept you are studying, about the best way to measure the phenomenon. This can take time, but it's a great way to test your own thinking and make sure you aren't missing an important aspect of the concept. (Later I'll talk about why, to enhance its content and face validity, it's useful to share a draft of an interview or questionnaire with knowledgeable colleagues and experts.)

Predictive Validity

Alvan K. is the social worker at Mt. Washington directing the agency's program for men charged with domestic violence and ordered by the county's criminal court to participate in the program as a condition of probation. Alvan K.'s staff does not have to accept every court referral. The agency's agreement with the court is that Mt. Washington staff can interview individuals referred by the court's probation staff and decide which ones to accept.

Part of Alvan K.'s job is to interview each referral for the domestic violence program. He asks each man a series of questions to determine such things as the candidate's willingness to acknowledge and take responsibility for his behavior, his level of denial and motivation to change, and his history of abusive behavior. When Alvan K. has collected the data, he shares the results with his clinical staff who, together, decide whether to accept the referral.

This is a common routine. Many social work programs—including those for people with substance abuse problems, criminal offenders, sexually abused adolescents, or people with physical or mental disabilities—administer some kind of assessment or screening tool to determine whether the program is suitable for that person. (Schools and departments of social work also perform a similar procedure when their faculty review admission applications.)

Clearly, when social workers collect data for these purposes, they are assuming that the variables or indicators are good predictors of the desired outcome. Alvan K. presumably believes that his questions provide important information correlated with the likelihood that the men who participate in his domestic violence program will attend the sessions, participate meaningfully, and benefit from the counseling. Other social workers assume that assessment or screening data are highly correlated with who will benefit from counseling services, residential treatment programs, and so on.

How often do we stop to think about the evidence on which these assumptions are based? How confident are we that the data we collect when we assess or screen candidates for service are, in fact, highly correlated with whatever dependent or outcome variable concerns us? What would happen if we were to discover that the assessment criteria that social workers use to determine admission are not good predictors of outcome? What if it turns out that the information that Alvan K. collects is not correlated with measures such as client attendance, level of participation in counseling, and subsequent incidents of domestic violence? It means that lots of admission decisions would have been based on an incorrect belief that the assessment criteria can forecast or predict who is likely to succeed in the program and who is not. That's a pretty sobering thought, particularly in light of the widespread use of these kinds of assessment and screening procedures in social service programs.

What I am talking about here is the concept of predictive validity, which is one type of *criterion validity*. *Predictive validity* indicates the extent to which an instrument or a set of items (like interview or screening questions) is correlated with another measure. In social work, this often takes the form of correlations between assessment tools and outcome measures, as in the example of Alvan K. and the program for men who batter. Assessment and screening criteria with high criterion or predictive validity are good and accurate predictors of outcome. That is, we can say with confidence that people who answer questions in certain ways or who have certain characteristics (for example, age, number of prior offenses, previous treatment history) are, or are not, good candidates for admission. Assessment and screening criteria with low predictive validity are poor or inaccurate predictors of outcome. That is, people who answer questions similarly or who have similar characteristics will have different outcomes. Or people who give different answers to questions or who have different characteristics will have similar outcomes. If it turns out, for example, that Alvan K.'s screening questions have low predictive validity, it wouldn't make sense to base admission decisions on them (although these data may serve some other useful purpose, such as giving the staff basic background information about their clients).

Concurrent Validity

Occasionally you may come across references to the concept of *concurrent validity*, the second type of criterion validity we will discuss. Concurrent validity is often mentioned in discussions of instrument development. For example, a social worker may be developing a rapid-assessment, easy-to-use instrument that can be administered in clinical settings to evaluate people's propensity to engage in domestic violence or substance abusers' risk of relapse. The goal may be to construct an instrument that can be administered easily and quickly, or one that takes less time to administer than others used in a particular setting. As part of the instrument development process, the social worker and her colleagues may correlate their results with clinicians' assessments of how their clients are functioning or with the results of other well-known, commonly used, and widely accepted instruments, to determine whether the new instrument provides similar results in less time. An instrument with *high concurrent validity* is one that correlates well with other measures; an instrument with *low concurrent validity* does not correlate well with other measures. Thus if a shorter and less time-consuming instrument has high concurrent validity, we can use it with confidence.

Construct Validity

Social workers in research and evaluation seldom use construct validity, a rather abstract concept that is more valuable to social workers in theory development. I mention it only because you may come across the term in your reading and should know what it means.

In short, *construct validity* refers to the extent to which a measurement instrument actually measures a theoretical construct. A *theoretical construct* is an idea or a concept that cannot be measured directly but must be measured indirectly. For example, we can't "see" or "hear" clinical depression, but we nonetheless rely on indirect measures of clinical depression, including people's reports of their moods, daily activities, and behaviors. A measurement instrument that adequately captures such a construct is said to have *high construct validity*. (Other examples of constructs are family dysfunction, self-esteem, ego strength, formal organization, and distressed community.)

Validity of Data

Earlier I stated that social workers who collect data should be able to assume that the data are accurate, that they actually reflect what we think they reflect. Another way to say this is that we don't want our data to be filled with errors.

Let's think about possible sources of error. If Alvan K. gathers some of his data about potential clients from criminal court records—such as their age, race, marital status, and prior criminal offenses—it is possible that the data will contain some errors. These things happen, particularly when we rely on

human beings to collect and record information. For instance, whoever collected the information for the court's records might have misunderstood what
someone said, written it down incorrectly, or punched the wrong button when
entering the data into the computer. This is one type of error. We don't like it,
but we've learned to live with it, at least to some extent.

Another type of error is faulty memory. Alvan K. may ask potential clients
to indicate the number of prior arrests for domestic violence or the number of
treatment programs they have previously participated in. Someone might say
"three" when he really meant "four," and the problem could be one of faulty
memory.

Of course, in some instances people provide false information deliberately,
for several reasons. One is that people who agree to answer social workers'
research or evaluation questions may worry that they will be punished or
penalized if they answer honestly. For example, the people that Alvan K. interviews may be concerned that they will not be admitted to Mt. Washington's
program if they are candid about the severity of their criminal histories. Since
these individuals want to avoid a prison sentence and want to be able to participate in Mt. Washington's domestic violence program as a condition of probation, they may have an incentive to minimize their problems. (Of course,
Alvan K. may be looking for just the opposite, that is, an honest admission of
the severity of one's problems. What matters, however, is the price that the
respondent believes he will pay for being honest.)

In many other situations, clients may be tempted to be less than truthful in
response to research and evaluation questions. For example, at the conclusion
of the intervention program, Alvan K. uses a standardized instrument to assess
each participant's risk of further engaging in domestic violence. Many of the
clients seem to develop a close, meaningful relationship with Alvan K. In addition to not wanting to "look bad," some clients may give unrealistically positive answers to Alvan K.'s questions, in part to avoid disappointing him. His
clients know that Alvan K. is committed to changing their behaviors and attitudes, and some may bend over backward to make him believe that his efforts
have been successful. That is, in addition to giving "positive" responses for self-
interested reasons (to obtain a favorable report to the court and avoid prison),
some clients may bias their answers to avoid disappointing Alvan K.

Two important, and often related, phenomena are at work in these situations. One is called *socially desirable responses*, and the other is called *evaluation
apprehension*. People give socially desirable responses to questions in order to
cast them in an unrealistically positive light (Crowne 1959; Crowne and
Marlowe 1964; Edwards 1957), because they want to protect or preserve their

self-image or because they want to be viewed favorably by others. This phenomenon occurs in research and evaluation in general, but it is a special challenge in social work settings, in which clients may feel, understandably, that honesty may have a steep price. Clients need things that social workers control, such as admission to programs, services, stipends, referrals, and positive recommendations related to discharge.

Considerable empirical evidence suggests that the social desirability phenomenon actually exists. If we extrapolate cautiously, a fascinating series of experiments conducted in social psychologists' laboratories point to the kind of effect the social desirability phenomenon may have on responses obtained from social work clients. In these experiments, researchers distinguished between so-called high-need-for-approval and low-need-for-approval people; they hypothesized that the high-need-for-approval people would be, for instance, more inclined to conform to group pressure, take less risk, and be less willing to criticize others than would low-need-for-approval people. For example, Crowne and Marlowe (1964) hypothesized that people scoring high on the Marlowe–Crowne Social Desirability Scale, indicating a high need for approval, would be more willing to suppress their own views of an obviously boring task they performed than would low-need-for-approval people. They gave their research subjects a task devised by Festinger and Carlsmith (1959) that requires subjects to pack and unpack spools of thread for a lengthy period of time. In response to a short questionnaire following the experiment, the group reporting a high need for approval expressed more favorable attitudes toward the menial task than did the low-need-for-approval subjects.

An experiment conducted by Strickland and Crowne (1962) examined the relationship between conformity as a result of group pressure and research subjects' level of need for approval. The researchers predicted that high-need-for-approval subjects would be more willing than low-need-for-approval subjects to violate a personal norm, conviction, or strongly reinforced habit in order to receive a favorable evaluation on an experimental task. Strickland and Crowne gave their subjects a task similar to that developed by Asch (1956), in which the subjects' own perceptions clearly contradicted the reported perceptions of a "confederate" majority in a group setting (the term *confederate* refers to participants in a research study who have been informed of the study's hidden agenda and have agreed to help the researchers deceive the actual subjects). In this study the subjects listened to a tape recording of a series of easily counted "knocks" and were instructed to state the number of knocks heard. The knocks were immediately followed by the deliberately inaccurate responses of several confederates, so that the subject would be faced with what psychologists call *dissonance*, conflicting beliefs or pieces of information. The researchers' hypothesis that the high-need-for-approval subjects would conform more often to the confederates' inaccurate reports was confirmed.

In a study of research subjects' need for approval and willingness to take risks (Crowne and Marlowe 1964), the subjects participated in a dart-throwing contest in which the subject's score was raised when he or she chose to move farther away from the target. The researchers predicted that the high-need-for-approval subjects would be more cautious and would take less risk in their choice of distance from the target. The data again supported the prediction.

Finally, in a study of the relationship between subjects' level of need for approval and willingness to criticize others, Conn and Crowne (1964) created a situation in which subjects were led to believe that they would receive a certain amount of money if they cooperated with an experimental confederate in a simple task (choosing one of two knobs on a board) or a lesser amount if they acted independently. After the subject and the confederate agreed on their intentions to cooperate—so as to maximize their profits—the confederate reneged on his promise, a strategy introduced in order to anger the subject. Conn and Crowne predicted that the high-need-for-approval subjects would be less willing than the low-need-for-approval subjects to express their hostility. Indeed, the high-need-for-approval subjects were found to be more euphoric in their postexperiment interaction with the confederates than were the low-need-for-approval subjects. The high-need-for-approval subjects also rated the confederates less negatively on an adjective scale administered after the experiment.

It seems clear that research subjects' need for approval can influence their attitudes, opinions, and behavior in research laboratories. Those subjects with a high need for approval tend to give more socially desirable responses. It seems reasonable to conclude that in social work agencies, clients' responses to research and evaluation questions may be affected similarly, perhaps even more so because of the agencies' control over clients' lives.

The following are examples of the social desirability phenomenon in social work: A client in Mt. Washington's substance abuse treatment program who is in denial about the extent of his problem may either intentionally or unintentionally exaggerate the progress he is making, to preserve his self-image and be viewed favorably by others. A client who is reluctantly participating in Mt. Washington's marriage-counseling program, perhaps because of pressure from a spouse, may minimize his emotional distress in order to appear "healthy."

The social desirability phenomenon is related to the phenomenon of *evaluation apprehension*, which refers to the anxiety that people often feel when they know they are being evaluated (Rosenberg 1965, 1969; Sigall, Aronson, and Van Hoose 1970; Thomas et al. 1974; Weber and Cook 1972). Evaluation apprehension is normal and can lead people to behave in ways they might not otherwise.

Here, too, we have a great deal of empirical evidence about the nature and impact of evaluation apprehension. Rosenberg (1969) first confirmed the influence of evaluation apprehension in a short series of simply designed studies. In the first, two groups of research subjects were asked to rate a group of pictures of strangers and to indicate the extent to which they liked or disliked the pictures. The first group of subjects was told that previous research had discovered that mature people tend to like the pictures, and the second group was told the opposite. The subjects' evaluation apprehension was aroused by the risk of being labeled *immature*, whereas a control group had no apprehension-arousing instructions read to them. The results clearly showed the significant impact of evaluation apprehension.

A second study mirrored the picture-rating experiment in design, but the experimental task was different. Subjects were asked to complete as many addition problems as possible from a thick booklet of simple arithmetic problems. One experimental group was told that mature people had been found to be highly efficient at the task; the second experimental group was told the opposite. The effect of evaluation apprehension was again clear.

In a third study, subjects were asked to tap on a key with their right and left index fingers for six 10-second intervals, half with the left index finger and half with the right. Ordinarily the index finger of the dominant hand yields more taps. After an initial arousal of evaluation apprehension by asking the subjects if they had completed a personality inventory and general abilities test administered earlier, the experimental group was led to believe that previous research indicated that people with high intelligence produce equal numbers of taps with both their dominant and nondominant finger. The difference reported between the experimental group and a control group that received only a description of the task to be performed (that is, no evaluation apprehension was intentionally aroused) clearly demonstrated that apprehensive subjects were more likely to bias their responses in cued directions.

In social work settings, evaluation apprehension, just like socially desirable responses, can be a special problem because of social workers' control over their clients' lives. In fact, Rosenberg (1969) found that one of the variables that most affected evaluation apprehension was the researcher's "gatekeeper" power over the subject (in addition to such variables as the subject's personality profile and need for approval, the ambiguity of the research task, and the importance of the research task to the subject). Thus we might expect that clients who are asked research questions or who know they are being evaluated may be concerned about the impact of their answers or behavior on their being allowed to receive services or remain in a program. For example, the men interviewed by Alvan K. for participation in his domestic violence program may feel they are being evaluated (which, in fact, they are), and this may lead them to bias their responses in ways they believe will enhance their chances of being accepted and avoiding prison.

One other threat to the validity of data pertains to what is called *hypothesis expectation* or *experimenter expectancy*. These terms refer to the occasional tendency for researchers or evaluators to communicate, often unintentionally, in subtle or not-so-subtle ways what they expect research subjects and respondents to say or do. That is, if Alvan K. strongly suspects that a particular man he is interviewing poses a serious risk of domestic violence, he may communicate that subtly in a way that influences the man's responses. (Alvan K. doesn't have a formal hypothesis, and he's not an experimenter. The terms *hypothesis expectation* and *experimenter expectancy* are used mainly in formal hypothesis testing and experimental research, but the ideas certainly pertain to the kind of research and evaluation conducted by social workers.)

The empirical evidence concerning the nature and influence of experimenter expectancy is quite fascinating. Of the many studies demonstrating this phenomenon, here are a few examples: In one study (Larrabee and Kleinsasser 1967, cited in Rosenthal 1969), experimenters gave the Wechsler Intelligence Scale for Children (WISC) to a group of sixth graders. Each child was tested by two different experimenters, one administering the even-numbered items and the other administering the odd-numbered items. For each child, one of the experimenters was told that the child had above-average intelligence, and the other experimenter was told that the child had below-average intelligence. When the child's experimenter was led to expect above-average performance, the average total IQ score was 7.5 points higher than when the child's experimenter expected below-average performance.

In another experiment (Rosenthal and Fode 1963), a group of experimenters showed a series of ten photographs of people's faces to each of the subjects. The subject was to rate the perceived degree of success or failure shown in the face of each person in the photos. The rating scale was from -10 to +10, with -10 meaning extreme failure and +10 meaning extreme success. The ten photos had been selected so that on the average, they were rated as neither successful nor unsuccessful; that is, the group of photos would have an average numerical score of 0.

The experimenters were given identical instructions for administering the experiment and standardized instructions to read to their subjects. They were told that they should not alter the wording of the instructions and that the study's principal goal was to see whether the experimenters could replicate results from other similar studies that were "well established." Half the experimenters were told that the "well-established" finding they were to try to replicate was that their subjects would rate the photos as being of successful people (positive scores), and half the experimenters were told that their subjects would rate the photos as being of unsuccessful people (negative scores). The results clearly showed that those experimenters expecting higher photo ratings obtained higher ratings than did those experimenters expecting lower ratings.

Our final example is a famous study conducted outside a laboratory setting (Rosenthal and Jacobson 1968). In this study, all the children in an urban elementary school were given a nonverbal test of intelligence at the beginning of the school year (eighteen classrooms, three for each of grades 1 through 6). The test was disguised as one that would predict when children would "bloom" intellectually. Approximately 20 percent of the children in each classroom were chosen for the study's experimental group; the other children formed a control group. Each teacher was given the names of certain children from her class and was told that they had achieved scores indicating that they would show remarkable gains in intellectual competence during the next eight months of school. Eight months later, at the end of the school year, the children in the experimental group and the children in the control group were retested with the same IQ test. The children in the experimental group gained, on average, two points more than did the children in the control group on the "verbal" subtest, seven points more than did the children in the control group on the "reasoning" subtest, and four points more than did the children in the control group in total IQ.

In addition, at the end of the school year of this study, all the participating teachers were asked to comment on their students' classroom behavior. The teachers noticeably tended to describe those students from whom intellectual growth was expected as having a significantly better chance of being successful in the future and as being significantly more interesting, curious, happy, appealing, adjusted, and affectionate.

Thus considerable evidence suggests that experimenters who expect that research subjects will behave, respond, or perform in a certain manner may communicate these expectations in a way that shapes the subjects' behavior, responses, and performance. And the experimenters' expectations may also affect how they interpret and record the subjects' behavior, responses, and performance. Whatever the case, experimenters' expectations can make a big difference. It's not much of a stretch to imagine that social workers' expectations may have a similar impact on their clients when they collect information from or about them.

RELIABILITY

Validity pertains to the accuracy of information that social workers collect from people and thus is very different from the concept of reliability. Reliability has less to do with accuracy and more to do with consistency. As we shall see, inconsistency in data collection often creates significant problems for social workers.

Data can be reliable without being valid. Here's a simpleminded example from common life circumstances. Let's say my seven-year-old child complains that she's sick. She tells me that her head, left ear, and tummy hurt and that her throat is scratchy. I feel her forehead with my hand, and it seems warm (I'd love to know how this form of measurement got started). I go to the medicine cabinet and pull out the thermometer, place it under my daughter's tongue, and after several minutes, the thermometer shows a reading of 98.4 degrees. This is puzzling to me, since my daughter's forehead felt warm to the touch. So I decide to take her temperature again, and again the thermometer registers 98.4 degrees—a consistent reading.

At that point I decide to call my daughter's pediatrician. The office nurse says to bring my daughter to the office in one hour to be examined. Just before we leave for the pediatrician's office, I take my daughter's temperature again, and again it registers 98.4 degrees. Ten minutes later we arrive at the pediatrician's office, at which point the nurse uses this fancy, battery-powered gadget to take my daughter's temperature. It registers 100.1 degrees.

What's going on here? It's possible, of course, that during the car ride my daughter's temperature went up, although I don't think that's what happened. Instead, I think that our thermometer at home may have been faulty or that I used it improperly (maybe it wasn't fully underneath my daughter's tongue). Although it's possible that my thermometer was accurate and the pediatrician's was not, I think it's more likely that mine was not accurate, given the more sophisticated instrument used in the doctor's office.

This example is a useful illustration of the differences and relationship between validity and reliability. Assuming my thermometer was inaccurate, it was not a valid measurement instrument. That is, it did not measure what I wanted it to measure. It was, however, reliable. This may sound odd, but it's true. That is, if reliability is consistency, the thermometer was very reliable. On three separate and closely timed occasions, the temperature registered 98.4 degrees. Thus a measuring instrument can be reliable without being valid, and this is a problem.

Ideally, social workers collect data that are both valid and reliable. That is, the data are accurate, and the measuring instrument produces the same result time and time again (assuming the status of whatever is being measured did not change during the process). Clearly, however, data can be reliable without being valid, as in the example of measuring my daughter's fever. But the reverse is not true. Data cannot be valid unless they are also reliable. If data are unreliable, they cannot be valid. Hence reliability is a necessary, but not a sufficient, condition for validity.

We next will discuss several major types of reliability: test–retest, equivalence, alternate forms, and split-half.

Test–Retest Reliability

Although I didn't use the term, my efforts to confirm my daughter's 98.4 degree temperature is an example of *test–retest reliability*. That is, I used the same measuring instrument repeatedly to see whether the results would be consistent—and they were. The instrument was reliable but not valid.

Often test–retest reliability is assessed when measuring instruments are developed, to ensure that consistent results are obtained in repeated administrations. For example, when professionals develop instruments to measure personality traits, depression, eating disorders, or intelligence, they usually assess them for test–retest reliability and report the results when they market the instrument (these results are generally reported in the form of a correlation coefficient, which I will explain later). Obviously, we should have more confidence in instruments that have high test–retest reliability than in those with low test–retest reliability. Instruments that yield different results in repeated administration, when the status of whatever was measured did not change, have problems. The wording of the questionnaire may be ambiguous; the measurement criteria may be vague; or other flaws may produce results that aren't reliable.

Formal attempts to assess test–retest reliability are rare in social work. Most social workers don't develop instruments and thus don't attempt to assess this kind of reliability. It is an important concept for social workers to understand, however, particularly when they read material on the reliability of standardized instruments they are considering using in their practice.

Equivalence

Another way to think about reliability has to do with the consistency of results obtained by (1) different measuring instruments, sometimes called *interinstrument reliability*, and (2) different observers using the same instrument, sometimes called *interobserver* or *interrater reliability*. For example, my daughter's temperature was taken by several different measuring instruments. The crudest measuring instrument was the palm of my hand, which suggested to me that she perhaps was feverish. However, the thermometer from our medicine cabinet, presumably a more sophisticated measuring device, showed no evidence of a fever. In contrast, the pediatrician's thermometer, which was the most sophisticated (and expensive), indicated that my daughter did have a fever. All three instruments purported to measure the same thing, but there was a reliability problem, or a problem of equivalence.

This kind of problem also can, and does, arise in social work settings. I may use several different measuring instruments to assess clients' depression or aggressiveness or to determine the extent of homelessness in a community. If the results of the different instruments are not consistent, I have a reliability problem.

Problems of equivalence can also arise with respect to a single measuring instrument administered or used by different people. Let's go back to the example of Toby, the little boy who was having behavioral difficulties in school. The social worker wanted to spend some time observing Toby's behavior before intervening. She decided to sit in the back of Toby's classroom for brief periods of time and record the frequency of specific behaviors, including the times Toby got out of his seat without permission, spoke without being called on, and did not complete assigned tasks.

Given Mt. Washington's limited resources, the social worker couldn't afford to ask a colleague to sit with her during the observation periods so that they could compare notes. Rather, the social worker had to rely on only her own observations. But assume that the social worker had arranged for a colleague to accompany her and, using the same data collection form, record the frequency of Toby's appropriate and inappropriate behaviors. Ideally, the two colleagues' data would be similar—another form of equivalence or high reliability. But what if their results differed significantly? What if there were lots of discrepancies between the frequencies they reported? If this happened, they'd have a serious reliability problem, perhaps indicating that the criteria being used were not clear or specific enough. Such results would affect their confidence in the data's reliability.

Parallel Forms

Occasionally, social workers develop instruments. For example, social workers may be part of a clinical research team in a psychiatric program that, in addition to providing clinical services, may be developing clinical measurement tools to be used in this and other settings. With this method, which is sometimes called *alternate forms reliability*, social workers develop a second form of the instrument, perhaps one that is shorter, to measure the same phenomenon (marital satisfaction, for example). Both instruments are administered to the program's clients, and their results are compared (the technical term is *correlated*). If the results are highly correlated, there is evidence of instrument reliability.

Split-Half Reliability

Split-half reliability is a fairly common method for assessing reliability when developing or using a measurement instrument. The goal here is to determine the extent to which an instrument has "homogeneity" or "internal consistency." In simpler language, split-half reliability is a way to see whether people's responses to some items in an instrument are correlated with their responses to other items in the same instrument. If there is such a correlation—which is what we hope for—we can say that the instrument has high internal consistency or reliability.

Let's assume the Mt. Washington social workers have a grant from a federal agency to implement and evaluate a new approach to treating clinical depression. As part of the treatment program, the social workers want to use a new instrument designed to measure clinical depression. It's fairly easy to use a computer program to divide the instrument's items into two halves and correlate the respective halves' subscores; this is almost as if the clients were responding to two different instruments. The computer program can then repeat this process a number of times using different items to make up the two halves for each correlation. The computer then calculates a statistic that averages all these correlations, and that's the indicator we use to assess an instrument's internal consistency (just in case you wanted to know, the name of this statistic is *coefficient alpha*).

SYSTEMATIC AND RANDOM ERROR

By now you've probably figured out that to minimize error, social workers try to enhance validity and reliability in their research and evaluation projects.

Errors are as unappealing to social workers as they are to baseball players when they play defense.

There are two kinds of error that social workers should attend to: systematic and random, which have very different implications for practice.

Systematic error occurs when inaccuracies (whether they are the result of mistakes in records, faulty memory, exaggeration, underestimation, or whatever) tend to be in one particular direction. For example, if the people that Alvan K. interviews for admission into his program typically underreport the number of times they have been arrested or have abused alcohol, this is systematic error. Or if at the end of the program, many clients tend to exaggerate the program's helpfulness—perhaps because of the phenomena of socially desirable responses and evaluation apprehension—the data contain systematic error. Systematic error doesn't require that every piece of data be biased or inaccurate or that all the inaccurate data be biased or inaccurate in the same direction. Rather, there has to be a significant *tendency* or a *pattern* for errors to occur in one direction.

Clearly, data that contain systematic error can't be used with confidence. It's true that some systematic error is worse than others, but it's nearly always problematic. A computer-programming error that inadvertently adds several months to each client's age may not be very serious (unless, of course, services are automatically terminated when clients reach a certain age), but systematic error that grossly underestimates clients' problems or inflates their progress would be very troublesome.

In contrast, random error—some of which is inevitable in many research and evaluation projects—tends to be a less serious problem. That's not to say that random error isn't a problem—all error is a problem to some degree—but that it's generally less so.

Random error occurs in unpredictable ways and for a variety of reasons, again including such things as recording errors and faulty memory. By definition, random error doesn't occur in a pattern or in any particular direction, such as consistent under- or overreporting. For example, if occasional mistakes are made when recording clients' ages or their scores on a standardized assessment instrument, they are unfortunate, but if they are truly random, the net aggregate results may not be very different than they would have been if all the data had been recorded accurately. Because random error shows no discernible pattern, some of the mistakes result in "scores" that are too high and some that are too low. In the end, the randomness results in errors that cancel each other out. In this sense, social workers usually don't have to worry too much about random error. Certainly social workers should do everything they can to minimize or eliminate all error, including random error (for example, by carefully training data entry personnel), but a minor degree of random error is often tolerable.

Let me give you a simpleminded example to illustrate the differences between systematic and random error. During one week, Alvan K. interviewed six men who applied for admission to his domestic violence program. One of the questions that Alvan K. asked each applicant was, "How many times during the last month did you physically strike your wife/partner with your hand(s)?" Figure 6.1 shows the hypothetical results under three headings: accurate results, systematic error, and random error. The accurate results are self-explanatory. The systematic error reflects the men's tendency to underreport the number of times they had struck their spouse or partner. The random error reflects a mix of accurate results, some underestimates and some overestimates.

Applicant	Accurate Results	Systematic Error	Random Error
A	4	2	3
B	3	1	3
C	5	3	6
D	1	0	0
E	4	3	4
F	2	0	3
Total	19	9	19
Average	3.2	1.5	3.2

FIGURE 6.1 Number of Times Struck Spouse/Partner

From this example, we can see why systematic error, in this instance in the form of underreporting, creates a serious problem. If Alvan K. relies on that result, he will grossly underestimate the seriousness of the clients' problem. He will then conclude that the average number of incidents for the group is 1.5 when, in fact, the actual figure is more than twice that (3.2). However, if the data are subject only to random error, as a result of faulty memory or other factors, the net result will be the same as that produced by accurate data (an average of 3.2 incidents). Although this is a simplistic example, it helps demonstrate why researchers and evaluators tend to be less concerned about random error than systematic error.

One of the possible sources of error that social workers need to be particularly concerned about is *cultural bias*, which can produce both systematic and random error, although systematic error is more likely.

Cultural bias can result from (1) the *methods* that social workers use to collect data (for example, direct observation, interviews, self-administered questionnaires), (2) the ways in which social workers *interact* with people when they collect data from them, and (3) the *topics and issues* that social workers address when they collect data.

I will discuss these issues in more detail in chapters 7, 8, and 9. Suffice it to say, however, that the methods social workers use to collect data, the way they interact with clients and others from whom they collect data, and the topics and issues social workers address in the data collection can affect the validity and reliability of the information. That is, members of some cultural and ethnic groups may not feel comfortable responding to detailed questions about their personal lives and may, as a result, answer interview questions vaguely or less than candidly to preserve their privacy as much as possible. Some people—again because of cultural or ethnic norms—may feel uncomfortable when social workers make direct eye contact with them or address them by their first name during an interview, and this may affect their responses. Furthermore, certain topics or issues may be taboo for members of certain cultural or ethnic groups to discuss. If social workers are unaware of or naive about this, they may end up obtaining data whose validity is highly suspect (not to mention violating people's cultural integrity in the process).

DATA COLLECTION: STANDARDIZED INSTRUMENTS

Once social workers have decided on the questions or issues they want to address, determined the design they want to use and the sample from which they want to collect information, and addressed relevant issues of validity and reliability, they must think about how they want to collect the information, that is, what data collection method they want to use. There are lots of options, and each must be carefully considered.

First let's think about why social workers collect information. In my experience, the majority of social workers' data collection efforts fall under one of five headings: clinical assessment, clinical monitoring, clinical evaluation, needs assessments, and program evaluation. Despite some exceptions, these categories capture the lion's share of the reasons that social workers collect data. Let's look at each of these and speculate about the kinds of data collection that would be useful.

Clinical assessment. Clinical social workers—those who deliver services directly to individuals, couples, families, and groups—often need to conduct some kind of assessment, usually at the point of intake or the beginning of service. At the Mt. Washington Family Service Agency, clinical social workers often encounter clients who should be assessed for such phenomena as suicide risk, depression, marital conflict, self-esteem, and other clinical issues. The information obtained from the assessment can help social workers determine whether an individual (or couple or family) needs assistance and the level, amount, and type that may be helpful. For example, a client who receives a high score on a "risk of suicide" assessment instrument may be given immediate assistance, one-on-one counseling, and frequent appointments. In contrast, a client who receives a moderate score on an instrument that assesses clinical depression may be invited to join an agency-sponsored support group that meets twice a month. Furthermore, if the agency has limited resources, an individual who receives a very low score on the instrument that assesses clinical depression may be referred elsewhere for assistance.

Clinical monitoring.   Once clients begin receiving services, social workers often need to keep track of their progress. Thus Mt. Washington clinical social workers who provide counseling services to people with substance abuse problems may regularly gather data from clients to monitor their substance use and other relevant aspects of their lives (for example, mental health symptoms). Mt. Washington clinical social workers who counsel couples with marital or partner difficulties may periodically gather data to monitor the status of the couple's relationship. This information can help social workers decide whether to continue with or modify their intervention plan.

Clinical evaluation.   In addition, social workers who provide clinical services may want or need to evaluate the effectiveness of their interventions, perhaps using one or more of the single-case designs I described earlier. To do so, social workers would need to collect data, typically over a period of time, and attempt to control for the various extraneous factors that might have influenced the outcome measure.

Needs assessments.   One of the most common reasons that social workers collect data is to assess the extent to which their clients' needs have not been met and ought to be addressed. At Mt. Washington, for instance, social workers have been interested in collecting data to determine the extent of community residents' problems with affordable housing and whether the social service needs of people of color and ethnic minorities who live in the community are being met.

Program evaluation.   Social workers often need to collect data to evaluate the effectiveness of an entire social service program. At Mt. Washington, for example, social workers need to evaluate the relative effectiveness of individual and group counseling for clients with substance abuse problems.

Not surprisingly, different data collection goals (clinical assessment, clinical monitoring, clinical evaluation, needs assessment, and program evaluation) rely on different data collection techniques. The basic choice is between using existing instruments (generally known as *standardized instruments*) and creating new ones for some specific use. Instruments can be self-administered questionnaires or surveys, in-person or telephone interviews, complex or simple clinical assessment tools, and recording guides used in what is called structured observation.

In this chapter, I describe existing or standardized instruments, used mostly

for clinical purposes, and in chapter 8, I explain how social workers can create their own instruments for use in interviews, questionnaires, surveys, and structured observation.

TYPES OF STANDARDIZED INSTRUMENTS

Hundreds of standardized instruments are available to social workers. In general, standardized instruments were developed with considerable attention to issues of validity and reliability, administration procedures, development of norms to help interpret results, and scoring. By definition, standardized instruments contain items that are administered in the same way in virtually all situations.

Most standardized instruments are used for clinical purposes, to assess, monitor, and evaluate clients' status. They address an enormously wide range of problems that come to the attention of social workers. Standardized instruments fall into one of two general categories: (1) fairly long and sometimes complex instruments used primarily for assessment or diagnostic purposes (for example, the Minnesota Multiphasic Personality Inventory, or MMPI), and (2) relatively short instruments that can be administered simply and rapidly.

Fischer and Corcoran (1994) reviewed the various *rapid assessment instruments (RAIs)* that social workers can use in their work with clients. RAIs are short instruments completed by clients and other people in the clients' lives (for example, spouses, partners, and schoolteachers). They usually take less than fifteen minutes to complete and are written in simple, easy-to-understand language. RAIs are easy to score and don't require any specialized, sophisticated knowledge of testing procedures (Levitt and Reid 1981). They were created for the following problem areas (Fischer and Corcoran 1994):

1. Abuse (for example, Non-Physical Abuse of Partner Scale, Partner Abuse Scale: Non-Physical, Partner Abuse Scale: Physical, Physical Abuse of Partner Scale).

2. Anger and hostility (for example, Aggression Inventory, Aggression Questionnaire, Argumentativeness Scale).

3. Anxiety and fear (for example, Clinical Anxiety Scale, Fear-of Intimacy Scale, Self-Rating Anxiety Scale, Social Avoidance and Distress Scale, Stressful Situations Scale).

4. Assertiveness (for example, Assertion Inventory, Assertiveness Scale for Adolescents, Bakker-Assertiveness-Aggressiveness Inventory, Personal Assertion Analysis).

5. Beliefs (for example, Ascription of Responsibility Scale, Beliefs Associated with Childhood Sexual Abuse, Family Beliefs Inventory, Rational Behavior Inventory, Self-Righteousness Scale).

6. Children's behaviors/problems (for example, Behavior Rating Index for Children, Childhood Personality Scale, Children's Beliefs About Parental Divorce Scale, Eyberg Child Behavior Inventory, Peer and Self-Rating Scale, Self-Control Rating Scale).

7. Death concerns (for example, Concern About Death-Dying and Coping Checklists, Death Depression Scale, Templer Death Anxiety Scale).

8. Depression and grief (for example, Brief Depression Rating Scale, Brief Screen for Depression, Depression Self-Rating Scale, Generalized Contentment Scale, Hopelessness Scale for Children, Perinatal Grief Scale, Self-Rating Depression Scale).

9. Eating problems (for example, Compulsive Eating Scale, Concern over Weight and Dieting Scale, Dieting Beliefs Scale, Eating Attitudes Test, Goldfarb Fear of Fat Scale).

10. Family functioning (for example, Family Adaptability and Cohesion Evaluation Scale, Family Awareness Scale, Family Crisis Oriented Personal Evaluation Scales, Family Functioning Scale, Family Responsibility Index, Family Sense of Coherence and Family Adaptation Scales, Index of Brother and Sister Relations, Index of Family Relations, Kansas Family Life Satisfaction Scale, Self-Report Family Instrument).

11. Geriatric (for example, Attitude Toward the Provision of Long-Term Care, Caregiver Strain Scale, Caregiver's Burden Scale, Geriatric Depression Scale, Memory and Behavior Problems Checklist).

12. Guilt (for example, Perceived Guilt Index—State, Perceived Guilt Index—Trait).

13. Health issues (for example, Adult Health Concerns Questionnaire, Hospital Fears Rating Scale, Illness Attitude Scale, McGill Pain Questionnaire, Patient Reactions Assessment, West Haven–Yale Multidimensional Pain Inventory).

14. Identity (for example, Ego Identity Scale, Separation–Individuation Process Inventory).

15. Interpersonal behavior (for example, Argumentativeness Scale, Conflict Tactics Scale, Index of Attitudes Toward Homosexuals, Index of Peer Relations, Liking People Scale, Revised Martin–Larsen Approval Motivation).

16. Locus of control (for example, Belief in Personal Control Scale, Family Empowerment Scale, Generalized Expectancy for Success Scale, Miller Marital Locus of Control Scale, Multidimensional Locus of Control Scale, Nowicki–Strickland Locus of Control Scale, Parental Locus of Control Scale).

17. Loneliness (for example, Children's Loneliness Questionnaire, Loneliness Rating Scale, Revised UCLA Loneliness Scale).

18. Love (for example, Intimacy Scale, Love Attitudes Scale, Parental Nurturance Scale, Revised Kinship Scale).

19. Marital/couple relationship (for example, Beier–Sternberg Discord Questionnaire, Competitiveness Scale, Dual Employed Coping Scales, Dual-Career Family Scale, Index of Marital Satisfaction, Kansas Marital Conflict Scale, Kansas Marital Satisfaction Scale, Life Distress

Inventory, Locke–Wallace Marital Adjustment Test, Marital Happiness Scale, Relationship Assessment Scale).

20. Mood (for example, Mood Survey, Mood Thermometers, Semantic Differential Mood Scale).

21. Obsessive–compulsive (for example, Compulsiveness Inventory, Maudsley Obsessional–Compulsive Inventory, Obsessive–Compulsive Scale, Severity of Symptoms Scale).

22. Parent–child relationship (for example, Adult–Adolescent Parenting Inventory, Child's Attitude Toward Father and Mother Scales, Kansas Parental Satisfaction Scale, Parent–Child Relationship Survey, Parental Authority Questionnaire, Parental Bonding Instrument, Parental Nurturance Scale).

23. Perfectionism (for example, Frost Multidimensional Perfectionism Scale).

24. Phobias (for example, Agoraphobic Cognitions Questionnaire, Fear of AIDS Scale, Fear Questionnaire, Fear Survey Schedule-II, Homophobia Scale, Panic Attack Cognitions Questionnaire, Panic Attack Symptoms Questionnaire).

25. Problem solving (for example, Problem Solving Inventory, Social Problem-Solving Inventory, Values Conflict Resolution Assessment).

26. Procrastination (for example, Procrastination Assessment Scale Students, Procrastination Scale).

27. Psychopathology (general) and psychiatric symptoms (for example, Auditory Hallucinations Questionnaire, Dissociative Experiences Scale, Emotional Assessment Scale, Questionnaire of Experiences of Dissociation, Symptom Questionnaire, Symptoms Checklist).

28. Rape (for example, Rape Aftermath Symptom Test, Sexual Assault Symptom Scale).

29. Satisfaction with life (for example, Life Satisfaction Index-Z, Satisfaction with Life Scale).

30. Self-concept and self-esteem (for example, Behavioral Self-Concept Scale, Ego Identity Scale, Hare Self-Esteem Scale, Index of Self Esteem, Self-Concept Scale for Children, Self-Esteem Rating Scale).

31. Self-control (for example, Children's Perceived Self-Control Scale, Impulsivity Scale, Peer and Self-Rating Scale).

32. Sexuality (for example, Hendrick Sexual Attitude Scale, Index of Sexual Satisfaction, Sexual Attitude Scale, Sexual Behavior Inventory—Female, Sexual Behavior Inventory—Male, Survey of Heterosexual Interactions).

33. Social functioning (for example, Mood-Related Pleasant Events Schedule, Social Adjustment Scale—Self-Report).

34. Social support (for example, Multidimensional Scale of Perceived Social Support, Multidimensional Support Scale, Network Orientation Scale, Perceived Social Support—Family Scale, Perceived Social Support—Friend Scale, Social Support Appraisals Scale, Social Support Behaviors Scale, Young Adult Social Support Inventory).

35. Stress (for example, Adolescent Coping Orientation for Problem Experiences, Adolescent–Family Inventory of Life Events and Changes, Family Hardiness Scale, Family Inventory of Life Events and Changes, Hardiness Scale, Index of Clinical Stress, Life Events Questionnaire, Self-Control Schedule, Young Adult Family Inventory of Life Events and Changes).

36. Suicide (for example, Hopelessness Scale for Children, Multi Attitude Suicide Tendency Scale, Reasons for Living Inventory).

37. Treatment satisfaction (for example, Client Satisfaction Questionnaire, Reid–Gunlach Social Service Satisfaction Scale, Session Evaluation Questionnaire, Working Alliance Inventory).

38. Substance abuse (for example, Alcohol Beliefs Scale, Beck Co-Dependence Assessment Scale, Co-Dependency Inventory, Index of Alcohol Involvement, McMullin Addiction Thought Scale, Michigan Alcoholism Screening Test, Spouse Enabling Inventory, Spouse Sobriety Influence Inventory).

The format and scoring of RAIs vary considerably. Although all are relatively short compared with many other standardized instruments, their lengths do differ. Let's look at a couple of examples.

A Mt. Washington social worker, Maria D., received a referral from a local school about a fourteen-year-old student, Jeff G., who, according to the school principal, seems both depressed and unusually hostile. Jeff G. also is having considerable difficulty with several classes, although for years teachers described Jeff as a "model student."

Jeff G.'s mother accompanies Jeff to his first appointment with Maria D. During Jeff G.'s meeting with Maria D., he talks at length, and with intense feeling, about his father. According to Jeff G., his father was not around much and, when he was around, often physically abused both Jeff and his mother. Jeff told Maria D. that his father seemed to have an alcohol problem.

Maria D. decided to spend some time talking with Jeff G. about his father, to give him an opportunity to explore his feelings about this significant relationship. To start, Maria D. decided to have Jeff complete the Child's Attitude Toward Father instrument (CAF). This instrument contains twenty-five items, such as "My father gets on my nerves," "I wish I had a different father," "I like being with my father," and "I can really depend on my father." Children are asked to rate each item on a 7-point scale, ranging from "None of the time" to "All of the time."

The CAF was developed using 1072 ethnically diverse students from the seventh through the twelfth grade. The instrument is scored in several steps. The first is to reverse the scoring of the "positively worded" items (for example, "I feel proud of my father" and "I really like my father") to match the scoring of the "negatively worded" items (for example, "My father is too demanding," and "I feel angry toward my father"). The second step is to sum all the answers (again, each item is worth from 1 to 7 points), subtract the number of completed items, multiply the total by 100, and divide this result by the number of items the child completed (ideally, all twenty-five items) times 6. The result will fall somewhere between 0 and 100, with the higher scores indicating a greater or more serious problem. The third step is to see whether the final result is above or below two different cutoff scores. For this scale, a score above 30 indicates a "clinically significant problem," and a score above 70 indicates "severe stress with a clear possibility that some type of violence could be considered or used to deal with problems" (Fischer and Corcoran 1994:431; Hudson 1982).

After meeting with Jeff G., Maria D. talks with Jeff's mother, Alma G. Alma G. also talks about her husband and his violence, alcohol problems, and various strains in their marriage. Alma G agrees that it would also be useful for her to meet several times with Maria D., particularly to talk about how to handle her husband's drinking problem.

To begin her work with Alma G., Maria D. asks her to complete a very different kind of standardized instrument, the Spouse Enabling Inventory (SEI), developed by Thomas, Yoshioka, and Ager (1994), whose purpose is to assess spouse behaviors that enable the use of alcohol by one marital partner.

The SEI is a 47-item instrument that asks people to rate the frequency with which they engage in various behaviors that can "enable" a spouse's use of alcohol. According to the instructions for respondents,

> This checklist is intended to provide us with information about aspects of your behavior as it relates to your marital partner's drinking. The behaviors in the list below are among those that many spouses engage in. Please indicate how often you have engaged in each of these behaviors in the past six months by circling your response for each question. This is not a test, so there are no right or wrong answers.

The SEI has five response categories, ranging from "Always" to "Never." Here are some examples of the items: "Told amusing stories about others who

As it Involves the Drinker in the Last Six Months, How Often Have you:	Always	Frequently	Occasionally	Rarely	Never
1. Told amusing stories about others who drank a lot	1	2	3	4	5
2. Spoken admiringly of the ability of others to hold their drink	1	2	3	4	5
3. Had the drinker's car repaired after an alcohol-related accident	1	2	3	4	5
4. Paid fines for drunk driving offenses	1	2	3	4	5
5. Bailed the drinker out of jail because of a drink-related offense	1	2	3	4	5
6. Returned beer bottles and/or collected and washed glasses used for drinking by the drinker	1	2	3	4	5
7. Suggested that the drinker attend activities where alcohol was to be served	1	2	3	4	5
8. Invited friends over to drink	1	2	3	4	5
9. Gone to bars with the drinker	1	2	3	4	5
10. Bought alcohol and kept it in the home	1	2	3	4	5
11. Served alcohol with meals or snacks	1	2	3	4	5
12. Helped the drinker find his/her things lost while drunk	1	2	3	4	5
13. Provided the drinker with clean clothes after he/she soiled them due to use of alcohol	1	2	3	4	5
14. Gone to drinking parties with the drinker	1	2	3	4	5
15. Arranged parties where alcohol was served and which were attended by the drinker	1	2	3	4	5
16. Made hangover remedies	1	2	3	4	5
17. Cleaned up alcohol-related messes (e.g., spilled drinks, vomit, urine)	1	2	3	4	5
18. Tended to the drinker's alcohol-related injuries	1	2	3	4	5
19. Put the drinker to bed when he/she has been drinking	1	2	3	4	5
20. Avoided social contact with friends to cover up the drinking	1	2	3	4	5
21. Avoided relationships with neighbors and others who might drop in, to cover up the drinking	1	2	3	4	5
22. Avoided social contact with the extended family to cover up the drinking	1	2	3	4	5
23. Encouraged children to be silent about the drinking	1	2	3	4	5
24. Called the drinker's place of employment	1	2	3	4	5

As it Involves the Drinker in the Last Six Months, How Often Have You:	Always	Frequently	Occasionally	Rarely	Never
to say he/she was sick when he/she could not or would not go to work because of the drinking					
25. Taken responsibility for awakening the drinker the morning after a night of drinking so that he/she would not be late for work	1	2	3	4	5
26. Canceled appointments and social engagements for the drinker because of his/her drinking	1	2	3	4	5
27. Made excuses for the drinker's behavior when he/she was drunk or had been drinking	1	2	3	4	5
28. Taken responsibility for keeping his/her drinks cold (e.g., beer, wine, mixers)	1	2	3	4	5
29. Spoken admiringly of the drinker's ability to hold his/her drink	1	2	3	4	5
30. Bought devices especially for the drinker such as shot glasses, bottle openers, drinking glasses	1	2	3	4	5
31. Said the drinker behaved better when drinking (e.g., is easier to get along with)	1	2	3	4	5
32. Offered drinks to the drinker	1	2	3	4	5
33. Given him/her something to eat when he/she got drunk to reduce the effects of the drinking	1	2	3	4	5
34. Explained, justified, or made excuses to the drinker for the drinker's drinking	1	2	3	4	5
35. Explained, justified, or made excuses to others for the drinker's drinking	1	2	3	4	5
36. Reassured the drinker that his/her inappropriate and/or embarrassing behavior when under the influence of alcohol was not all that bad	1	2	3	4	5
37. Comforted the drinker about his/her feelings of guilt about drinking	1	2	3	4	5
38. Said to the drinker or others that the amount of alcohol drunk was less than actually was drunk	1	2	3	4	5
39. Softened or covered up the obvious signs of alcohol abuse (e.g., blackouts, tremors, puffy face, bloodshot eyes, hangovers)	1	2	3	4	5

As it Involves the Drinker in the Last Six Months, How Often Have You:	Always	Frequently	Occasionally	Rarely	Never
40. Minimized the seriousness of the drinking (e.g., ignored it, said it was not a problem, said the drinker could control it when he /she could not)	1	2	3	4	5
41. Minimized the consequences of drinking	1	2	3	4	5
42. Concealed his /her drinking from others	1	2	3	4	5
43. Cut down on household expenses (e.g., groceries) to provide drinking money for the drinker	1	2	3	4	5
44. Given the drinker money for drinking	1	2	3	4	5
45. Consumed alcoholic beverages with the drinker	1	2	3	4	5
46. Told the drinker it was OK with you that he /she drank	1	2	3	4	5
47. Suggested to the drinker that he /she have a drink	1	2	3	4	5

Source: Copyright (c) by Edwin J. Thomas, Marianne R. Yoshioka, Richard Ager, and the Regents of the University of Michigan. Reprinted with their permission.

FIGURE 7.1 Spouse Enabling Inventory (SEI)

drank a lot," "Invited friends over to drink," "Served alcohol with meals or snacks," "Suggested that the drinker attend activities where alcohol was to be served," "Spoken admiringly of the drinker's ability to hold his/her drink," and "Softened or covered up the obvious signs of alcohol abuse (for example, blackouts, tremors, puffy face, bloodshot eyes, hangovers" (figure 7.1).

The SEI was based on a sample of spouses of known alcohol abusers who did not seem motivated to stop drinking or enter treatment. Most of the persons in the sample were white, educated, middle-class females. The instrument is scored by adding up each item's response and dividing the total by the number of items. Lower scores indicate a more severe problem of "enabling."

As I mentioned earlier, standardized scales come in all kinds of shapes and sizes. The following are the most common formats that social workers encounter.

Semantic Differential

The *semantic differential scale* presents respondents with two words at opposite ends of the spectrum, such as happy–sad, calm–anxious, and strict–

lenient (the semantic differential scale is also sometimes referred to as the *bipolar rating scale*, because it uses two "poles"). Ordinarily, respondents are given a scale consisting of a number of points (seven is a common number) and asked to circle the point on the scale that corresponds most closely to their feelings, thoughts, or status. For example, if Maria D. asked Jeff G. to rate his feelings about his father, she might have used the following semantic differential scale:

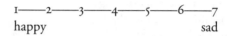

happy   sad

Self-Anchored and Graphic Rating Scales

In some ways, self-anchored and graphic rating scales are similar to the semantic differential scale. That is, a respondent selects the point on a scale that corresponds to his or her feelings, thoughts, or status. The main difference is that the rating scale has one or more anchor points throughout the scale, not just anchor points at each "pole." For example, if Maria D. asked Alma G. to complete the Self-Report Family Instrument (SFI), an instrument designed to measure how well families function, she would give Alma G. items such as "We all have a say in family plans," "There is confusion in our family because there is no leader," "It's okay to fight and yell in our family," and "We argue a lot and never solve problems" and ask her to use the following rating scale for each:

Yes	*Some*	*No*
Fits our family very well	Fits our family some	Does not fit our family
1 2	3	4 5

A graphic rating scale may also be laid out vertically. For instance, Maria D. might ask Jeff G. to place a check mark next to the number that corresponds to his feelings about his father:

100 —— I love my father a lot
90 ——
80 ——
70 ——
60 ——
50 —— I have mixed feelings about my father
40 ——

30 ——
20 ——
10 ——
0 —— I feel like I hate my father

Likert Scale

The *Likert scale* is one of the most commonly used response formats. It offers respondents several choices that are rank ordered by intensity. For instance, Maria D. could ask Alma D. to indicate the extent to which she agrees or disagrees with the following statement: "I have confidence that my husband will seek help for his drinking problem." The response categories could be

1. Strongly agree
2. Agree
3. Disagree
4. Strongly disagree

Social workers often encounter variations of the Likert scale in which respondents are asked to select from a list of options that are rank ordered by intensity. If Maria D. asks Jeff G. to indicate the likelihood that his relationship with his father will improve, the response categories might be

1. Very likely
2. Somewhat likely
3. Not very likely

Or Maria D. might ask Alma G. to indicate the frequency with which she and her husband argue, using these response categories:

1. All of the time
2. Most of the time
3. Some of the time
4. Rarely
5. Never

If an instrument contains many items using the same scale, responses can be added in order to calculate a total or average score. For example, a scale with ten items, each using a 5-point scale (say, "All of the time" = 1 and "Never" = 5, as in the preceding example), can produce a maximum total score of 50 (10 x 5) and a minimum score of 10 (10 x 1). You can easily obtain an average by dividing the total by the number of items answered. Although the scoring for some instruments is a bit more complicated, many instruments use this straightforward approach.

SELECTING A STANDARDIZED INSTRUMENT

Given the hundreds of standardized instruments available, how do social workers choose the most suitable ones? I think the best way is to ask three questions:

1. *What am I trying to measure?* The best place to begin is to determine exactly what you want to measure. Let's say at some point in her work with Jeff G., Maria D. wants to assess his symptoms of depression. Clearly, she should try to find an instrument whose principal purpose is to measure clinical depression. She would not want instruments that focus on, say, anxiety symptoms or self-esteem. Jeff G. may indeed have some noteworthy anxiety symptoms and self-esteem issues, but if Maria D. wants to measure those symptoms, she should look for instruments designed for that purpose.

2. *Where will I find various measurement instruments to choose from?* For most of social work's history, practitioners could find relatively few standardized instruments, particularly rapid assessment instruments, that they could use with clients. Now, however, social workers have better luck. The first place they should look is the publishers that market instruments. Publishers usually have catalogs describing the different standardized instruments designed for different settings, problems, and clients. Such publishers include the Behavior Science Press, Institute for Personality and Ability Testing, Inc., Psychodiagnostic Test Co., Psychological Assessment and Services, Inc., Psychological Services, Inc., and WALMYR Publishing Co. A good reference librarian at an academic library should be able to help you locate these sources.

The second place to look is books that reprint instruments. Among the best known are *Behavior Analysis Forms for Clinical Intervention* (Cautela 1990), *Measures for Clinical Practice* (Fischer and Corcoran 1994), *The Clinical Measurement Package* (Hudson 1982), and *Family Assessment: Inventories for Research and Practice* (McCubbin and Thompson 1991).

In addition, many books describe various instruments in their discussions of various measurement issues. Examples are *Psychological Testing* (Anastasi 1997), *Adult Assessment: A Sourcebook of Tests and Measures of Human Behavior* (Andrulis 1977), *Measures for Psychological Assessment: A Guide to 3,000 Original Sources and Their Application* (Chun, Cobb, and French 1975), *Assessing Mental Health Treatment Outcome Measurement Techniques* (Ciarlo et al. 1986), *The Tenth Mental Measurements Yearbook* (Conoley and Kramer 1990), *Handbook of Measurements for Marriage and Family Therapy* (Fredman and Sherman 1987), *Family Assessment: A Guide to Methods and Measures* (Grotevant and Carlson 1989), *Dictionary of Behavioral Assessment Techniques*

(Hersen and Bellack 1988), *Family Assessment: Tools for Understanding and Intervention* (Holman 1983), *Handbook of Clinical Assessment of Children and Adolescents* (Kestenbaum and Williams 1988), *Tests: A Comprehensive Reference* (Maddox 1997), *Measuring Health: A Guide to Rating Scales and Questionnaires* (McDowell and Newell 1996), *Advances in Psychological Assessment* (McReynolds 1984), *Outcomes Measurement in the Human Services* (Mullen and Magnabosco 1997), and *Handbook of Family Measurement Techniques* (Touliatos, Perlmutter, and Straus 1990).

3. *How do I decide which of these instruments is the best for my circumstances?* There are four issues to consider. First, is there evidence that the standardized instrument has acceptable validity and reliability? As I stated earlier, social workers should always determine the adequacy of an instrument's content, face, criterion, and construct validity. The instrument's items should provide a representative cross section of relevant content (for example, depression, self-esteem, anxiety), and the items should "make sense" in light of what you want to measure. In some instances, predictive or concurrent validity may be important.

In addition, you should look at the data on the instrument's reliability. Usually, two kinds of information about an instrument's reliability are reported: internal consistency and test–retest. The measure of *internal consistency*—what's called *coefficient alpha*—is basically an average of all the correlation coefficients obtained when correlating different halves of an instrument. The term *correlation coefficient*, which I'll explain in more detail later, refers to a number between −1and +1 and indicates the strength of the relationship between two sets of scores. If two halves of an instrument are strongly related, the correlation coefficient will be in the vicinity of +1. The coefficient alpha is easily obtained with a computer. The computer repeatedly divides an instrument's items in half, correlates each pair of halves, and then averages all the correlation coefficients to produce the coefficient alpha. The higher the coefficient is, the greater the internal consistency will be.

With *test–retest reliability*, you simply correlate the scores obtained at one time with the scores obtained at another time. Here, too, the higher the coefficient is, the greater the reliability will be. A widely accepted standard is that a coefficient needs to be at least .80 for an instrument to be considered reliable.

Second, how easy will it be to administer and score the instrument? You need to think about how long the instrument will take to complete (whether it's to be completed by the client, a "significant other," or you) and how easy or difficult it is to score and interpret the results. Time may decide whether or not you should use a particular instrument.

Third, when you expect the client or someone else to complete an instrument, you must take into account the respondent's literacy and ethnicity. Respondents must be able to read and understand the instrument, and they must be able to record their responses. If they cannot, you will have to arrange for assistance. For example, if English is not a respondent's first language, he or she may need a translator or interpreter.

You also should consider whether the wording of items and the concepts addressed in the instrument will mean something other than what is intended, because of the respondent's ethnicity or culture. Some instruments contain concepts that exist in one culture but not another or that are more important to one culture than another. Also, as we'll see in the next chapter, you must be careful that the items in an instrument are not worded in a way that may be misinterpreted by or offensive to members of certain ethnic or cultural groups.

ADMINISTERING A RAPID ASSESSMENT INSTRUMENT

Journalists learn during their training to answer the following questions related to a story: who, what, when, where, and how? We just covered the what, that is, what social workers should keep in mind when selecting an appropriate instrument. Now we need to talk about what they should do once they have chosen an instrument: Who should administer and complete it? When should the instrument be administered? Where should the instrument be administered? How should the instrument be administered and the results interpreted?

Who should administer and complete the instrument? Remember that my emphasis in this book is on the use of research and evaluation tools by practitioners. I am primarily interested in describing the ways in which real practitioners—clinical social workers, community organizers, administrators, planners, and so on—can use research and evaluation concepts and skills. Accordingly, in most instances the kinds of instruments I review are administered by the social workers and are completed by clients or other people involved in clients' lives (spouses, partners, children, and schoolteachers, for instance). Sometimes, but not often, it may make sense to have another professional administer the instrument.

Although the social worker should usually oversee the administration of an instrument, several different people, depending on the circumstances, may be asked to complete the instrument. In most instances, it will be the clients themselves, particularly when a social worker is trying to measure such things as a client's depression, loneliness, anxiety, marital relationship, self-esteem, or substance abuse. Of course, when social workers ask clients to complete an instrument, they must be aware of the possibility of socially desirable responses, evaluation apprehension, and the other ways in which the social worker's relationship with the client can influence the client's responses.

Sometimes a social worker may want to ask a third party to complete an instrument regarding a client. For example, the Mt. Washington social worker concerned about Toby's behavior at school might ask his teacher and his mother to complete the Behavior Rating Index for Children (BRIC), a thirteen-item instrument designed to be completed by people in a child's life. This simple scale asks them to estimate the frequency with which a child engages in behaviors such as hitting, pushing, or hurting someone, losing his or her temper, getting very upset, hiding his or her thoughts from other people, and quitting a job or task without completing it. The items are answered using a 5-point Likert scale ranging from rarely or never (1) to most or all the time (5).

In some instances, the social workers themselves may complete an instrument. This information may be useful to only the social workers, particularly if it's compared with data provided on the same instrument by clients and others in a client's life.

When should the instrument be administered? Different circumstances require different schedules. A Mt. Washington social worker who is providing counseling services to a severely depressed client may want to administer a depression scale weekly to monitor how daily events seem to affect the client's mood and to use that information to help the client change her daily routine. The social worker who is working with Toby and his teacher may want to administer a behavior-rating scale once each month to keep track of Toby's progress and to help determine whether the intervention plan needs to be changed. Maria D., who is helping Jeff G. with his relationship with his father, may want to use a rapid assessment instrument once early in the relationship and only sporadically thereafter to monitor Jeff G.'s feelings and the need to address them in counseling. A Mt. Washington social worker who wants to screen men for possible participation in a group for men who batter may use an assessment instrument only once to help him decide whether to admit applicants. In sum, standardized instruments should be used as often as it makes sense to use them. I realize that this is a vague guideline, but it's hard to be more precise. You don't want to overdo it and overwhelm a client with data collection tasks that lose their clinical relevance or underdo it and miss opportunities to track the client's progress.

Where should the instrument be administered? Clients often complete the instruments, particularly rapid assessment instruments, in the social worker's office. In these instances, the clients should be given some privacy. Sometimes, however, the respondents complete the instrument elsewhere, for example, at home. For instance, if Maria D. asks Jeff G.'s mother to complete an instrument regarding her son's behavior, it may make sense for her to take the form home and bring it back the next session. If the Mt. Washington social worker asks Toby's teacher to complete an instrument concerning Toby's behavior, the teacher may want to complete it either at school or at home.

The most important consideration is for the instrument to be completed in a setting that is not likely to produce undue bias. If a respondent is likely to be more thoughtful and relaxed completing a self-rating scale at home, for example, it may make sense to encourage that. On the other hand, if a social worker wants immediate feedback from a client, the client should complete the instrument in the social worker's office.

How should the instrument be administered and the results interpreted?
Social workers must be careful to explain an instrument's purpose and instructions clearly and simply. Respondents shouldn't have to guess at the instrument's purpose and format. They also should be given ample time to complete the instrument, so as to minimize their stress and maximize the usefulness of the information. Social workers should also explain the possible benefits and potential risks of completing an instrument (for example, increased anxiety), any relevant information concerning the confidentiality of results, and the respondents' right to refuse to complete the instrument (notice that these are similar to the earlier guidelines for informed consent procedures).

Social workers should encourage respondents to answer the questions honestly and use their clinical skills to explain why it is necessary for them to be frank and accurate. In addition, social workers should be careful to avoid saying anything or behaving in ways that might influence the respondents' answers (for example, in a way that might encourage socially desirable responses).

Social workers should always remember that the relationship skills important to clinical work are equally important when asking clients to complete research and evaluation instruments. Respondents may be anxious or uncertain about the instrument's purpose or how the results will be used, so social workers should anticipate these reactions and know how to respond to them.

In some instances, the social worker may want to score the instrument right after it is completed (for example, if a client completes the instrument in a social worker's office). In this way, clients can receive immediate feedback, and the instrument's results can become a useful intervention tool; the social worker and client can discuss the reasons for the client's scores and how this information can be used to guide intervention. Clients are often fascinated by graphic displays of their progress, so they could be made a point of departure for discussion during a clinical session. In other instances, it may make more sense to score the instrument at a later time, particularly if scoring it immediately would be distracting. Finally, more and more instruments can easily be scored easily by computer (see Hudson 1992, for example).

The results of a rapid assessment instrument should be interpreted carefully. Many instruments are accompanied by information about the meaning of different results. For example, an instrument's instructions might say that a score above 30 is clinically significant and a score above 70 indicates a severe problem. Social workers should be particularly careful to find out on what kind of sample or samples the instrument was originally tested and from which its norms were developed.

The norms for a standardized instrument are established by administering the instrument to a sample (preferably a large one) with known demographic and other characteristics. For instance, if an instrument's norms are based on a sample of white women from the Midwest between the ages of 20 and 55, it's probably a bad idea to use the published norms when interpreting the results obtained from a 75-year-old Portuguese man who recently immigrated to the United States and lives in New York City.

8

DATA COLLECTION: INSTRUMENT DEVELOPMENT

Wouldn't it be nice if there were a huge, comprehensive catalog of standard-ized instruments from which social workers could choose whenever they needed to collect data? Unfortunately, social workers often must create their own data collection instruments, usually because none exists that is appropri-ate to the task.

Certainly in many circumstances, social workers can use existing standard-ized instruments. Social workers who want to measure phenomena such as anxiety, depression, self-esteem, parent–child relationships, and severity of substance abuse can often find an acceptable instrument. But what about some of the situations encountered by Mt. Washington social workers? If they want to interview ethnic minorities and people of color living in their community about their perceptions of the agency and problems they face in their daily lives, they will need to construct an instrument tailored to the unique cir-cumstances of Mt. Washington's mission, services, and surrounding commu-nity. It's hard to imagine how a standardized instrument could do that. If Mt. Washington's associate director for administration wants to collect data from other family service administrators in the area concerning whether the state's small foster care stipend leads to attrition among foster parents, she will have to design an instrument designed for that specific purpose. The same would be true if a Mt. Washington clinician wants to measure a therapy group's sat-isfaction with how the group met several specific goals agreed to by group members. Also, if the Mt. Washington staff want to survey recently terminated clients about their satisfaction with services, they will probably need to design an instrument that addresses various aspects of the agency's programs; these questions might then be added to questions in a standardized client satisfaction instrument (examples are the Client Satisfaction Questionnaire and the Reid–Gundlach Social Service Satisfaction Scale).

In general, social workers need to design their own instruments in three sets of circumstances.

1. Social workers who provide clinical services may not be able to find a suitable instrument to measure an important aspect of their intervention. Also, the completion of a lengthy instrument is often not necessary. Instead, one, two, or three simple items designed by the social worker may be enough. Finally, subjecting clients to a lengthy or cumbersome questionnaire can be therapeutically counterproductive.

For example, in Maria D.'s work with Jeff G., the boy having difficulty in school and in his relationship with his father, she spent some time helping Jeff identify recreational activities he enjoys and that he might do with his father. Ms. D.'s goal was to find activities that Jeff can engage in with his father in order to strengthen their relationship. Once she has identified the activities, she can develop a couple of simple items that ask Jeff to rate how pleasant or unpleasant it is to spend time with his father in these activities. Such items, tailored to Jeff's circumstances, most likely won't be found in a standardized instrument.

2. Clinical social workers sometimes need to observe clients and record information, or data, about them. For instance, the Mt. Washington social worker who works with Toby, the little boy who has difficulty with his classroom behavior, wants to gather some "baseline" information before implementing the intervention designed to increase the frequency of Toby's appropriate behavior. Because there may not be a suitable existing instrument for Toby's particular behavioral difficulties, the social worker may have to create a recording guide for the specific behaviors that the social worker, the schoolteacher, Toby's mom, and Toby want to address.

3. Social workers often need to develop instruments to conduct needs assessments and program evaluations. Needs assessments and program evaluations are usually performed in one of two ways, both of which typically require the development of a nonstandardized instrument: (1) a survey instrument or questionnaire that is either mailed to respondents or completed by them in an agency and (2) a structured instrument that is used to conduct personal interviews. In most cases, a standardized instrument won't do. Most needs assessments and program evaluations explore issues unique to specific programs and local circumstances and so require a special instrument. For example, if Alvan K. wants to administer an instrument to participants in his domestic violence counseling program as part of an assessment of the inter-

vention's effectiveness, he will need questions or items that focus on that program's particular goals. If a Mt. Washington administrator wants to conduct a needs assessment to determine whether the agency should develop services for gay and lesbian youths in the surrounding community, she will have to create an instrument for that specific purpose.

I want to concentrate on two types of instruments that social workers often have to create themselves: (1) relatively simple instruments used in clinical work with individuals, couples, families, and groups and (2) survey/interview instruments and questionnaires used in needs assessments and program evaluations.

INSTRUMENTS FOR CLINICAL USE

Clinical social workers use various kinds of data collection instruments. Again, although some of them are standardized, many need to be created specially. In general, social workers create two kinds of instruments when providing clinical services: "paper-and-pencil" instruments and structured recording guides. *Paper-and-pencil instruments* are completed by clients to assess or monitor their state or evaluate their progress (for example, with respect to mood, anxiety symptoms, or suicidal thoughts). Such instruments range from those that consist of a single item to those that are fairly long. Social workers use structured recording guides to observe clients for a period of time and to record what they see and/or hear.

Paper-and-Pencil Instruments

As I mentioned in my discussion of standardized instruments, clinical social workers often need to assess or monitor a client's status or evaluate a client's progress. If no suitable standardized instrument is available, they should consider creating a measurement tool themselves. This may seem like an intimidating task, but it's not, at least not when we're talking about fairly simple, straightforward measurement tools. I don't have in mind long, complex, psychometrically sophisticated measurement tools (the term *psychometric* refers to tools that measure psychological phenomena). Rather, I'm picturing tools like the following.

1. Alvan K. wants to ask each participant in his domestic violence treatment group to indicate each week how much he felt like hitting his partner or spouse during the past week. He gives each client a piece of paper on which the following statement is written: "There were times during this past week when I really felt like hitting my partner/spouse." The clients were asked to circle one of the following response categories: Strongly agree, Agree, Disagree, Strongly disagree.

Alvan K. didn't have to know a great deal about instrument construction to design this measurement tool. All he needed to know were some basic principles related to item wording and response categories (to be discussed in more detail shortly).

2. Ivy M., a Mt. Washington clinical social worker who is working with a fourteen-year-old girl who has had difficulty leaving her home and spending time in the community because of anxiety symptoms, wants her client to rate her level of anxiety herself on a scale during each session. Instead of spending hours searching for a standardized instrument, Ivy M. invented, using a semantic differential format, one simple item for her client to complete. The client was to circle the most appropriate number on each of three scales to complete the following sentence: "When I thought about leaving my house today, I felt _____."

nervous	1	2	3	4	5	6	calm
happy	1	2	3	4	5	6	sad
confident	1	2	3	4	5	6	scared

3. Mark G., a Mt. Washington social worker who works with men with alcohol problems, is treating a twenty-seven-year-old client, Bruce P. Mr. P. recently sought help for a long-standing problem with alcohol which, according to Mr. P., "has gotten me in all kinds of trouble with the police, women, you name it."

As part of the intervention, Mark G. asked Mr. P. to carry around with him at all times a piece of paper and a pen and to write down the times, places, and circumstances when he feels an urge to drink. Mark G.'s goal is to help Mr. P. identify the circumstances in his life that sometimes trigger his drinking.

Although many of these paper-and-pencil instruments are rather simple, social workers should also be familiar with a number of time-honored techniques and "tricks of the trade" when creating their own measurement instruments. I will discuss these in conjunction with constructing questionnaires and surveys.

Structured Recording Guides

When social workers want to record systematically their observations of clients' (or someone else's) behavior, what kind of instrument is appropriate and can be easily created?

There is no single, widely used format for structured recording guides. These, too, come in all shapes and sizes and are used for various purposes. For example, structured recording may be useful in residential programs for children with psychiatric problems, when the staff want to keep close tabs on changes in their behavior. Staff members may want to record precisely how often a particular child engages in self-mutilating behaviors. Also, as I mentioned earlier, school social workers may want to use structured recording guides to assess and monitor children's classroom behavior.

Structured observation usually focuses on one or more of four aspects of behavior:

1. Presence/absence: whether or not a behavior occurred
2. Frequency: how many times a behavior occurred
3. Duration: how long the episode or incident lasted
4. Intensity: how severe the episode or incident was

Let's see how a social worker would use a structured recording guide in the case of Toby, the little boy who was referred to Mt. Washington by school personnel because of his behavioral difficulties in the classroom.

The social worker in this case, Mary A., wants to collect some baseline information on Toby's behavior before implementing an intervention strategy. In addition to the customary biopsychosocial assessment data, Ms. A. decides to spend some time actually observing Toby in his classroom. Ms. A. arranges with Toby's teacher three specific, mutually convenient times. To enhance the validity of the observations, Ms. A. decides to observe Toby for an hour on three different days of the week (Monday, Wednesday, and Friday) and at three different times of the day (9:00 A.M. on Wednesday, 11:00 A.M. Friday, and 1:30 P.M. on Monday). Although this varied schedule doesn't guarantee that Ms. A. will observe a representative cross section of Toby's behavior, it does increase the likelihood. His behavioral difficulties may be correlated with certain days of the week (perhaps Toby gets more tired and irritable as the week progresses) and with certain times (Toby may be more difficult to manage toward the end of the day, when he is apt to be more tired).

Ms. A. decides to record four pieces of information during each of her observational periods: the presence or absence of behavioral difficulties, the frequency with which Toby's behavioral difficulties occur, the duration of these episodes, and their intensity or severity. To do this, Ms. A. needs to define "behavioral difficulties" exactly (ideally, she would consult Toby's teacher about this definition). In this instance, Ms. A. defines behavioral difficulties as those incidents in which Toby (1) speaks out in class without first being called on by the teacher, (2) talks to or attempts to engage other children when he is supposed to be working on some activity alone (for example, reading, writing, arts and crafts), and (3) behaves aggressively toward the teacher or another child in the class (for example, by pushing or hitting a child or screaming at the teacher).

To record this information, Ms. A. develops a fairly simple form, or structured recording guide. It contains space to record several pieces of information. At the top of each piece of paper is a space to record the date and time of the observation (the beginning and ending times). Below this is a space to record information about each "episode" in which Toby displays behavioral difficulties that meet the criteria outlined by Ms. A. For each episode, there is a space to record (1) the time when the episode began and ended, (2) behaviorally specific details of the episode (that is, a description of the specific behaviors Toby displayed, how other children reacted, the teacher's response, and any other relevant information about the incident), and (3) the severity of the episode. To record the severity, Ms. A. devised a simple rating scale, where 1 means "not at all severe" and 10 means "extremely severe" (figure 8.1).

Now let's consider a different kind of example. Another Mt. Washington social worker, Peggy P., is currently enrolled in an MSW program and is completing her field placement at a nearby residential program for adults with some form of mental retardation. Most of the program's residents have been diagnosed with moderate or severe mental retardation.

For some time, the staff have been working on a particular resident's communication skills. The resident, Barry J., tends to be mute much of the time. Staff members are interested in helping Barry improve his ability to communicate with others, that is, his ability to ask people questions, make requests, and respond to people's questions and comments.

Peggy P. has learned a lot from her supervisor about techniques that can be used to help people such as Barry J. As part of her intervention plan, she decides to gather some baseline information on Barry J.'s communication skills and then record similar information once each week for twelve weeks (the length of the intervention). The specific information that Peggy P. wants to collect is (1) the frequency with which Barry J. responds verbally to other people's comments and questions, (2) the frequency with which he initiates conversation with others with comments or questions, and (3) the length of time these interactions last.

To record this information, Peggy P. develops a simple structured recording guide to be completed for each observation. Her plan is to observe Barry J. for forty-five minutes on five different days and at five different times (again, varying the observation times and days enhances the likelihood that Peggy P. will see a cross section of behaviors). For each observation Peggy P. plans to record the date, the beginning and ending times of the observation, the beginning

BEHAVIOR RATING FORM

Client's name _____

Date of observation _____

Time observation began _____

Time observation ended _____

Episode 1

   A. Time episode began _____

   Time episode ended _____

   B. Description of episode (include description of the specific behaviors, how other children reacted, the teacher's response, and any other relevant circumstances surrounding the incident):

   C. Severity rating (circle most appropriate number)

Not at all severe   1   2   3   4   5   6   7   8   9   10   Extremely severe

FIGURE 8.1 Behavior Rating Form

and ending times of any instance when Barry J. initiates or responds to others' communications, a description of the dialogue, and the appropriateness of Barry J.'s communication skills (where 1 = very appropriate, 2 = somewhat appropriate, and 3 = not very appropriate). The appropriateness of Barry J.'s communication skills is defined by the extent to which Barry J. responds directly to the other person's comments and questions (very appropriate) or responds with a non sequitur (not at all appropriate) (figure 8.2).

There's no precise formula that social workers can (or should) use to devise their own structured recording guides. Although some standardized structured recording guides exist, in most instances social workers will want to devise their own that directly address the information they need. What's important is that social workers know what they want to measure and why and that they are familiar with the basic methodological principles related to data collection.

Social workers who record their observations of clients' behaviors should be especially concerned about reliability, that is, how accurate their observations

STRUCTURED RECORDING GUIDE

Client's name _____

Date of observation _____

Time observation began _____

Time observation ended _____

Communication episode 1

    A. Time communication began _____

    B. Time communication ended _____

    C. Communication (check one):
    ——— Initiated by Barry J.
    ——— Initiated by someone else
      (specify:_____)

    D. Description of conversation (include details of the topic and Barry J.'s comments and questions):

    E. Rate the appropriateness of Barry J.'s communication skills:

    ——— Very appropriate

    ——— Somewhat appropriate

    ——— Not very appropriate

FIGURE 8.2 Structured Recording Guide

are. Ideally, social workers should compare their observations with those by a second person. This is the best way to assess the accuracy of one's observations. But a second observer often isn't available. In those instances, social workers must be careful to record their observations as accurately as possible.

There are several ways to assess reliability when a second observer is available, depending on whether one is measuring the frequency or the duration of the behavior. First let's think about instances when social workers want to measure the frequency of a behavior. In Toby's case, a social worker, Ms. A., observed Toby in his classroom for one hour on several different days. During that hour, Ms. A. might have had a colleague also observe Toby in order to check the reliability of Ms. A's observations. Let's say that during the hour, Ms. A. observed four instances when Toby acted out and Ms. A.'s colleague observed three instances. To calculate the reliability of these observations, we divide the larger number of observed behaviors (in this case, 4) into the smaller number of observed behaviors (3), which produces .75, or 75 percent reliability.

Ms. A. and her colleague could also check the reliability of their observation of the duration of Toby's behavioral disruption in much the same way. If Ms. A. wrote down that the first incident of the hour lasted 8 minutes and Ms. A.'s colleague noted that the incident lasted 9.5 minutes, the reliability would be 8 divided by 9.5 or .84, or 84 percent.

Yet another possibility is for Ms. A. and her colleague to divide the hour into intervals (for example, six 10-minute intervals) and place a check mark at each time interval when Toby acted out at least once during that 10-minute period. These data are summarized by calculating the percentage of intervals during which Toby acted out. For example, if there were a check mark by four of the six 10-minute intervals, Ms. A. would say that problem occurred during 67 percent of the intervals (4 divided by 6 equals 67 percent).

To check the reliability of Ms. A.'s observations, we add up the number of "agreements" and "disagreements" and then divide this total into the number of "agreements." An agreement occurs when both observers record a behavioral disruption *or* both observers conclude that there was no behavioral disruption during a particular 10-minute period. For example, if Ms. A. and her colleague agree that there was a behavioral disruption during each of two 10-minute intervals and that there was no behavioral disruption during one particular 10-minute period, the total number of agreements is three. Disagreements occur when one observer records a behavioral disruption during a particular 10-minute period but the second observer finds no behavioral disruption. Thus if the total number of agreements is 3 and the total number of disagreements is 3, the reliability is .50 or 50 percent (3 agreements divided by [3 agreements + 3 disagreements] = 3 divided by 6 = 50 percent). Reporting this percentage is a shorthand way of saying that the two observers agreed half the time about what they saw happen.

INSTRUMENTS FOR NEEDS ASSESSMENTS AND PROGRAM EVALUATIONS: SURVEYS, INTERVIEWS, AND QUESTIONNAIRES

Social workers must often design their own instruments to conduct a needs assessment or program evaluation. Although a number of standardized instruments can be useful, social workers may have to create their own, tailor-made instruments, usually because none of the standardized ones addresses exactly the issues that concern the social worker. A program that a social worker is evaluating may have some features that aren't included in a standardized instrument.

For example, Carl F., the director of Mt. Washington's substance abuse treatment program, wants to evaluate several aspects of the services that his staff provides. The substance abuse treatment program at Mt. Washington has individual-counseling, group-counseling, and support groups for clients' families and friends. The program is funded by a variety of sources, including the state's substance abuse agency, a federal grant, the local United Way, and clients' fees.

Mt. Washington's substance abuse program has not been evaluated since it started nearly ten years ago. However, two of the program's funding sources—the state substance abuse agency and the federal agency—have told Mt. Washington administrators that the program must be evaluated for Mt. Washington to continue receiving funds. Both the state and federal agencies have given Mt. Washington broad guidelines concerning the program evaluation. At a minimum, the evaluation should include both data on relapse rates for a sample of clients and data obtained from a client satisfaction survey.

Carl F. learned a great deal about research methods when he went to social work school and has decided to oversee the program evaluation himself, with the assistance of several staff members. He met with his staff to develop a plan for carrying out the program evaluation. After they discussed how to collect the relapse data (which I won't describe in detail here), the group turned their attention to the client satisfaction survey.

One member of the group suggested that they use a straightforward client satisfaction questionnaire and administer it to a sample of clients at the time they terminated services. Carl F. dug up copies of a couple of standardized client satisfaction instruments (the Client Satisfaction Questionnaire and the Reid–Gundlach Social Service Satisfaction Scale). The staff looked them over and decided that even though they included a number of useful items, they would need to create other items to address issues unique to the program. For example, the Client Satisfaction Questionnaire contains items that would be applicable to just about any social service program, such as "How would you rate the quality of service you received?" "Did you get the kind of service you wanted?" "To what extent has our program met your needs?" "In an overall, general sense, how satisfied are you with the service you received?" and "If you were to seek help again, would you come back to our program?"

Similarly, the Reid–Gundlach Social Service Satisfaction Scale also includes a number of relevant items (assessed on a 5-point scale from "strongly agree" to "strongly disagree"), such as "If I had been the social worker I would have dealt with my problems in just the same way," "I got from the agency exactly what I wanted," "The social worker took my problems very seriously," "No one should have any trouble getting some help from this agency," "Overall, the agency was very helpful to me," and "Every time I talk to my worker I feel relieved."

One problem, however, is that the Mt. Washington staff want to explore aspects of their program that aren't covered in either of these two standardized instruments. This isn't a criticism of them; it would be impossible for a standardized client satisfaction instrument to address all aspects of all social service programs. Such an instrument would necessarily have to be limited to questions relevant to just about any social service program. Thus for Carl F. and his staff to gather information from clients about some of the substance abuse program's unique features, they must create their own instrument. How should they do this?

During my career I have often needed to develop some kind of questionnaire or interview instrument. What I discovered early on is that constructing such an instrument is much harder than it may appear at first. Many people think that you pull out a piece of paper or turn on the computer and begin writing questions. As I'll explain shortly, that's usually the last step. What I've learned from my various experiences—sometimes painful ones—is that if I follow a number of steps, I will end up with a good, solid instrument. These steps may need to be varied a bit depending on one's circumstances, but for the most part I have found the following approach to be very useful.

Step 1. Identify broad categories of ideas and concepts. Many social workers rush to draft questions soon after they discover that they have to create a questionnaire or interview instrument. After all, if you need a form that has a bunch of questions on it, why not start by writing them?

Actually, this is really putting the cart before the horse. What I suggest instead is that you begin by taking out a piece of paper or, if you prefer, turning on the computer, and list the broad categories of information you want to address, without all the details. Before I share my thoughts on this with you, you may want to take a moment to figure out what you would include if you were in Carl F.'s shoes.

Here are the broad categories of information I'd probably focus on if I wanted to survey clients regarding their satisfaction with my agency's substance abuse treatment program (recognizing that I may come up with some new ideas as I proceed with the process):

Satisfaction with agency's staff
Satisfaction with agency's location

Satisfaction with agency's services
Satisfaction with agency's fees
Background information about client
Satisfaction with agency's physical facility
Satisfaction with agency's hours
Overall satisfaction with agency

Step 2. Rearrange the order of the broad categories of information into a logical sequence. At this point I'd begin thinking about what the final instrument might look like. More specifically, I'd begin thinking about the sequence of topics that the instrument will address. We don't want to ask questions in a random order; that would be too disjointed. Rather, we want to proceed in some kind of logical sequence to enhance the flow.

There's no precise way to determine the best sequencing of topics. For the most part, it is common sense. Several different sequences or orders might work well. One general piece of advice is to start out with a topic that is engaging and not too boring. Also, avoid starting out with topics that respondents might find threatening, such as questions about income, sexual abuse history, or illegal activity they have engaged in. In general (there always are exceptions), put any threatening questions near the end to avoid disrupting the data collection and introducing bias and to provide an opportunity to establish a rapport with the respondent.

Here's the order I'd use with this instrument:

1. Background information about client
2. Satisfaction with agency's hours
3. Satisfaction with agency's location
4. Satisfaction with agency's physical facility
5. Satisfaction with agency's services
6. Satisfaction with agency's fees
7. Satisfaction with agency's staff
8. Overall satisfaction with agency

Here's my reasoning. I think it would be best to begin by asking respondents for some information about themselves, as long as the information isn't too mundane or threatening. Keep in mind that much of this information probably can be found in the client's file or record. There's no need to ask for information that's easily obtained elsewhere. One reason for starting with personal questions is to engage the respondent quickly. I should add, however, that if the questions asked in this section are too threatening or boring, I'd move them toward the end of the instrument.

After these items, I'd ask the respondents to comment on several topics that are not likely to seem threatening: satisfaction with the agency's hours, satisfaction with the agency's location, and satisfaction with the agency's physical facility. Then I'd introduce questions about the agency's services, fees, and staff. Some respondents might find these topics to be somewhat more threatening than questions about the agency's hours, location, and physical facility. Questions about services, fees, and staff may require more judgmental opinions that may produce somewhat more anxiety. Therefore I'd bring up these topics toward the end. My last questions would be about the respondents' overall satisfaction with the agency; it nearly always makes sense to put this "summary" topic at the end, as a way to wrap things up.

Step 3. Decide on the main ideas and concepts you want to explore in each broad category of information identified in step 1. Once you've identified the broad categories of information, I would list, for each of them, all the specific ideas and concepts that you want to address. Again, these lists don't have to be final, but they should include nearly all that you want to ask your respondents.

How do you decide on the ideas and concepts for these lists? There are several ways. First, let's assume you already know something about the topic, whether it's client satisfaction with services, domestic violence, parent–child relationships, substance abuse treatment, or agency management. Thus what you already know should be one source.

Second, I think it's always important to locate literature on the subject to see what others have to say about it. Journal articles, books, and unpublished literature often contain important ideas and concepts that should be covered in a questionnaire or interview.

Finally, it's usually a good idea to talk with colleagues or "experts" who know something about the topic to see whether they can suggest anything you haven't thought of. (Ordinarily you'll want to avoid asking people who may end up in your sample, since this could introduce some bias into the results.)

Here's a quiz: What kinds of validity will be enhanced by using this systematic and comprehensive approach to identify key ideas and concepts? (Answer: Face and content validity. The instrument's face validity will be enhanced to the extent that the list of concepts and ideas makes intuitive sense, given the project's aims. And the instrument's content validity will be enhanced to the extent that the list of concepts and ideas reflects those encountered in the professional literature and suggested by knowledgeable colleagues. If you didn't guess the right answer, take two steps back and review the discussion in chapter 6 on face and content validity.)

Now let's talk about the concepts and ideas that might appear on the list developed by Carl F. and his staff. You may want to pause here and make up your own list before taking a look at mine. . . . OK, now here's mine:

1. Background information about client
    demographic information: age, race/ethnicity, gender, family status
    primary and secondary presenting problems
    reasons for seeking assistance at Mt. Washington
    dates of service (beginning and ending)
    specific services received at Mt. Washington
2. Satisfaction with agency's hours
    convenience of agency's hours
    preference for alternative hours
3. Satisfaction with agency's location
    usual means of transportation to agency
    convenience of agency's location
    preference for alternative location of substance abuse program
4. Satisfaction with agency's physical facility
    attractiveness of agency's physical facility
    comfort of agency's physical facility
    suggestions for improvement
5. Satisfaction with agency's services
    satisfaction with one-on-one substance abuse counseling
    satisfaction with substance abuse treatment group
    adequacy of range of services offered
    adequacy of frequency with which services are offered
    extent to which services met respondents' needs
    overall satisfaction
6. Satisfaction with agency's fees
    source of payment
    satisfaction with staff's discussion of fees
    satisfaction with staff's fee collection procedures
    affordability of fees
7. Satisfaction with agency's staff
    courteousness of staff
    helpfulness of staff
    availability of staff
    responsiveness of staff
    competence of staff
8. Overall satisfaction with agency
    general satisfaction with agency
    willingness to return in future
    willingness to recommend agency to a friend

Step 4. Rearrange the order of the concepts and ideas in each category into a logical sequence.   As with step 2, we need to think carefully about the order in which we will discuss each of the subtopics listed under the broad topics. Here, too, you should sequence the topics logically, to enhance the flow of the interview or survey. Also, it's best to put topics that are more threatening toward the end of each section.

I've rearranged the topics and placed them in an order that makes sense to me. Reasonable people can disagree about such things; I invite you to play around with an order that makes sense to you.

1. Background information about client
   demographic information: age, race/ethnicity, gender, family status [obtain from case record]
   primary and secondary presenting problems [obtain from case records]
   dates of service (beginning and ending) [obtain from case records]
   reasons for seeking assistance at Mt. Washington
   specific services received at Mt. Washington
2. Satisfaction with agency's hours
   convenience of agency's hours
   preference for alternative hours
3. Satisfaction with agency's location
   convenience of agency's location
   preference for alternative location of substance abuse program
   usual means of transportation to agency
4. Satisfaction with agency's physical facility
   attractiveness of agency's physical facility
   comfort of agency's physical facility
   suggestions for improvement
5. Satisfaction with agency's services
   adequacy of range of services offered
   adequacy of frequency with which services are offered
   satisfaction with one-on-one substance abuse counseling
   satisfaction with substance abuse treatment group
   extent to which services met respondents' needs
   overall satisfaction
6. Satisfaction with agency's fees
   source of payment
   satisfaction with staff's discussion of fees
   satisfaction with staff's collection of fees
   affordability of fees
7. Satisfaction with agency's staff
   availability of staff

> courteousness of staff
> competence of staff
> helpfulness of staff
> responsiveness of staff

8. Overall satisfaction with agency
   willingness to recommend agency to a friend
   willingness to return in future
   general satisfaction with agency

Step 5. Write questions for all the concepts and ideas that appear in step 4. It's only at this point, once we've constructed a conceptual outline, that we actually begin to write the questions. This, too, can seem deceptively easy; writing questions can be enormously challenging and difficult—and ultimately very rewarding.

As I mentioned in chapter 7, you can use lots of different styles to word questions and response categories. For example, questions may be open-ended or closed-ended. Closed-ended questions may include various response formats, such as Likert scales, semantic differentials, and self-anchored rating scales.

How do you decide which style of question-and-response format is most appropriate? In most instances, it is good judgment. Sometimes, however, you will need to think ahead about your data analysis plans. As we'll see in chapter 11, how you analyze your data depends in large part on the format you used to collect them. Responses to open-ended questions are analyzed differently than are responses to closed-ended questions. Responses to closed-ended questions that use options such as "strongly agree, agree, disagree, strongly disagree" are analyzed very differently than are questions that use options such as "yes, no, maybe." I won't go into all the technical methodological reasons for this here—I'll save that for later—but the way you ask questions and collect data often dictates what kind of data analysis you will use.

This may not seem important, but it is. Some data analysis procedures are more ambitious and sophisticated than others and, as a result, yield more useful information. Social workers who don't understand this connection at the beginning of their research and evaluation projects sometimes discover it too late. On many occasions, I've seen social workers wring their hands because they've discovered that the kinds of analyses they'd like to conduct aren't possible. These analyses might have been possible, however, if they had used different response formats to begin with.

Accordingly, one suggestion I always make is that social workers think ahead to the kinds of statements they would like to make after they have collected and analyzed the data (recognizing that specific details must await the actual results). I find it helpful, for example, to prepare an outline of the final report or paper I plan to produce. The outline lists the specific issues I would like to cover. Once I have that sketched out, I think about the kinds of data analysis procedures and techniques I will need to make those statements. At that point, I think about what response formats I will need to use to conduct those analyses.

I realize all this may sound rather abstract. It's hard for me to be more precise about these steps because I haven't yet discussed data analysis. So this brief discussion will probably make much more sense once you've read chapter 11.

Another important thing to keep in mind as you design an instrument is your respondents' cultural or ethnic background. The terminology must be clear and culturally appropriate. If your sample includes people from cultural or ethnic backgrounds that aren't familiar to you, you probably should ask thoughtful people from these groups to review a rough draft of the instrument, looking especially for terms that may confuse or offend respondents.

Also, it's important to know whether your respondents have problems with reading and writing (obviously, this pertains mostly to self-administered questionnaires or instruments that require some reading or writing ability). In addition, you need to word questions so that they can be understood by everyone in the sample.

Let's now try constructing items or questions. For this exercise, we'll focus on the section of the client satisfaction survey that addresses respondents' satisfaction with services. In step 5, I listed six possible topics:

- Adequacy of range of services offered
- Adequacy of frequency with which services are offered
- Satisfaction with one-on-one substance abuse counseling
- Satisfaction with substance abuse treatment group
- Extent to which services met respondents' needs
- Overall satisfaction

Now we can start writing the questions. One of the topics in the list is the extent to which Mt. Washington's services met the respondents' needs. I can think of several ways to formulate this question (perhaps you can think of others):

Version 1

1. Would you say that the services you received from this agency met your needs (check one)?
   ——— Very well
   ——— Somewhat well
   ——— Not very well

Version 2

1. Please indicate the extent to which you agree or disagree with the following statement: "The services I received from this agency met my needs." (check one)
—— Strongly agree
—— Agree
—— Disagree
—— Strongly disagree

Version 3

1. Please read the following statement and circle the number on the scale that best represents your opinion: The services provided by this agency

Met my   1   2   3   4   5   6   7   8   9   10   Did not meet
needs   my needs

Version 4

1. Would you say that this agency's services addressed your needs:
—— All of the time
—— Most of the time
—— Some of the time
—— Rarely
—— Never

Version 5

1. We would like to know to what extent you think this agency's services addressed your needs.
Please tell me in what ways, if any, the services you received at Mt. Washington addressed your needs. [provide space for answer]
Now please tell me in what ways, if any, the services you received at Mt. Washington did not address your needs. [provide space for answer]

Version 6

1. Would you say that the services you received at this agency addressed your needs?
—— Yes
—— No

Before reading on, I suggest that you take a few minutes to review the various versions and pick out what you think are the advantages and disadvantages of each.

Here are some of the advantages and disadvantages that I found:

The closed-ended items are generally simpler and easier to analyze than are the open-ended item (version 5). All you need to do is count up the number of responses to each of the options (there's a bit more to it, in terms of the data analysis, but the process is pretty straightforward). In contrast, with the open-ended items, someone (you, presumably) must read through every response and look for patterns. Of course, the open-ended items can yield more detailed or fine-grained data; respondents can use their own terms and offer as much information as they like. This is an obvious advantage. One disadvantage, however, is that the data analysis can be time-consuming. In addition, respondents who are asked to complete a self-administered instrument may not have the time, interest, or ability to write out their comments on open-ended items. This can significantly reduce the response rate. Furthermore, responses written on the questionnaire may be unintelligible to you. Also, when analyzing open-ended data, you must pay attention to reliability issues (see the discussion of reliability in chapter 6). Given how subjective our interpretation of responses can be, it is important to enhance reliability by having at least one other knowledgeable (and generous) person analyze the data. You will want some assurance that your classification of respondents' comments into categories is reasonable (in chapter 11, I discuss this in more depth). This, too, adds time to the process. I'm not suggesting this wouldn't be time well spent; I'm simply alerting you to the price one pays when collecting the sort of rich, valuable data that open-ended questions can produce.

What about the advantages and disadvantages of the various closed-ended items? Actually, I think versions 1 through 4 all are acceptable. Which of these you prefer is thus a matter of taste or personal preference. Version 6, however, could pose a problem. You'll notice that in versions 1 through 4, the response categories form a sort of rank-ordered scale, from most positive to least positive or from positive to negative. But in version 6 we have what statisticians call a *dichotomized variable*, which is just a fancy way of saying there are two, and only two, options. For purposes of statistical analysis, dichotomized data limit one's options. A scale of the sort you see in versions 1 through 4 permits a wider range of statistical analyses, thus providing more information about patterns in responses. I'll explain why this is so in chapter 11.

Now let's tackle another topic: clients' satisfaction with the substance abuse treatment group offered by Mt. Washington. This treatment group typically meets once each week for an hour and a half. This is an example of a topic that standardized instruments aren't likely to address. In fact, I've never found a standardized instrument that focuses specifically on clients' satisfaction with a substance abuse treatment group, although one may exist. In addition, the Mt. Washington staff may want to explore aspects of the program that are unique to this agency's approach to group treatment.

The first thing I would do for this topic is list the aspects of the substance abuse treatment program I want to ask about (excluding issues addressed elsewhere in the instrument). Here are several possibilities: general satisfaction with the substance abuse treatment group; number of people in the group; types of people in the group (for example, educational level, substance abuse history, severity and nature of current substance abuse problem); quality of leadership of the group sessions; frequency of the group sessions; length of the group sessions; and format of the group sessions (for example, topics covered, sharing of "air" time, how the weekly agenda is set). As with the other sections of the instrument, I would think carefully about the sequence of these topics; then I would begin writing the items themselves. Here's a tentative order: (1) frequency of group sessions, (2) length of group sessions, (3) format of group sessions, (4) number of people in the group, (5) types of people in the group, (6) leadership of the group sessions, and (7) general satisfaction with the treatment group. I may change the order once I look at a draft, but this is where I'll start.

The following are some sample questions and different versions of several of them. Let's start with an easy one: the length of the group sessions. Possible versions are as follows:

Version 1

1. In general, would you say that the length of the group meetings was
——— Too long
——— About right
——— Too short

Version 2

1. A. Please indicate the extent to which you agree or disagree with the following statement: "The group meetings were too long."
——— Strongly agree
——— Agree
——— Disagree
——— Strongly disagree

B. If you checked "agree" or "strongly agree," please explain why you think the meetings were too long: [provide space for answer]

Version 3

We would like to know how you feel about several aspects of your experience in the group. In general, how did you feel about the length of the group meetings? Did the length seem about right to you, too long, or too short? Please explain. [provide space for answer]

Version 1 is quite straightforward and would work just fine. Version 2 is a bit more complicated. First, the question refers only to the group meetings' being too long. Although respondents can "disagree" with the statement, this closed-ended format doesn't tell us whether the disagreement means that respondents found the group meetings to be too short or about right. Adding the open-ended component gives the respondents a chance to explain their answer, but there's no guarantee that they would. Frankly, I don't like this version. I think there's too great a chance of ending up with ambiguous information.

Version 3 also is fine, but as with all open-ended questions, more time would be required to analyze the data. In addition, we would need to be concerned about the reliability of the data recording and interpretation. On the plus side, this question would probably elicit more detailed information than version 1 would, although this would depend in part on the interviewer's ability to probe for this detail.

Now let's look at another topic from this instrument that poses more of a methodological challenge: types of people in the group. The first step is to figure out what aspects of this issue we want to know about. Here are the sorts of issues that seem relevant to me:

- The mix of clients' issues to be addressed
- The mix of clients' personalities
- Gender diversity
- Cultural and ethnic diversity
- Age diversity

Let's tackle the first one, the mix of clients' issues. I want to know whether the clients found the range of issues addressed in the group meetings to be relevant to their lives. For example, they may have brought up issues related to their marriages, relationships, children, jobs, depression, substance abuse counselors, AA meetings, or relapse-related "triggers." Some clients may have been frustrated by the diversity of issues; others may have found this mix to be interesting, stimulating, and valuable. Possible ways to approach this topic are as follows:

Version 1

1. Group members brought up a variety of issues during the meetings. In general, would you say that the topics that they brought up were (check one)
   _____ Very relevant to your life
   _____ Somewhat relevant to your life
   _____ Not very relevant to your life

Version 2

1. A. During group meetings, participants discussed a variety of issues in their lives. Please check the statement below that best describes your feeling about the issues discussed (check one):
—— I liked the variety of issues discussed during the group meetings.
—— I was frustrated by the variety of issues discussed during the group meetings.

B. Please explain your answer below. [provide space for answer]

Version 3

1. During the group meetings, participants discussed a variety of issues in their lives. Did you find this discussion useful or not? Specifically, what was (useful/not useful)? [provide space for answer]

The question in version 1 is straightforward. Although it won't generate detailed responses, it will give us a good, solid indication of clients' general feelings about the issue. Version 2 will provide somewhat more information, in that it includes an open-ended question in addition to the closed-ended one. But the closed-ended question could turn out to be a problem. You'll notice that in version 1 the response categories are in the form of a rank-ordered scale, from most to least relevant, whereas in version 2 the closed-ended response categories are dichotomized (two categories). When we get to the discussion of data analysis, you'll see that the type of scale in version 1 lends itself to far more sophisticated data analyses than does the dichotomized choice in version 2. This is another example of why it is important to have a good grasp of data analysis concepts when designing the instrument.

Version 3 once again presents the usual trade-offs encountered when one uses open-ended questions: the opportunity to gather more detailed information balanced by the burden of analyzing such qualitative data.

TIPS

Although the wording and format you use to construct questions depend mainly on your good judgment—as opposed to complicated technical considerations—you should consider the following:

- Always keep in mind your respondents' literacy skills and educational level. If the sample includes persons who may have difficulty reading or understanding complicated ideas or questions, be sure to use simple language and short sentences/questions. For example, in regard to their housing needs, if you are interviewing a group of people with little formal education, don't use terms like "subsidized housing" or "housing vouchers." Instead, use phrases like "using government money to help pay for your housing."

- Be aware that respondents may not be able to read well. Thus, if an interview requires them to read a statement, be prepared to respond tactfully to someone who has difficulty.
- In contrast, if your sample includes social service agency administrators, all of whom have graduate degrees, some respondents may be insulted if your questions are worded too simplistically. The best advice is to write questions using language appropriate to the audience. If the audience is mixed, it's best to use language and response formats that everyone can understand.
- Avoid using "negative" statements in questions (for example, statements that contain the word *not*). Here are a couple of examples: "To what extent do you think the services this agency offers are not what you need?" and "Is your experience in this group home not what you expected?" The problem is that respondents can easily overlook the word *not*, which would completely distort the question's meaning. Also, questions or statements with negatives, particularly double negatives, can be difficult to understand.
- Take into consideration your respondents' ethnicity and culture. Avoid using terms that respondents may find offensive, inappropriate, or confusing. (Also be aware that some standardized instruments may reflect a cultural bias in the language they use and the concepts they address.)
- Be sure that each item addresses one, and only one, concept. Sometimes social workers try to pack too much into one question. As a result, they may end up with questions that are hard for respondents to understand and whose answers are hard to interpret. Suppose, for example, that the Mt. Washington staff asked a sample of adolescent clients living in an agency-run group home the following question about the home's rules and regulations: "In general, would you say that the group home's rules and regulations are strict and unfair?" If a respondent answers yes, we won't know whether he is saying that the rules and regulations are strict, unfair, or both. It's possible, isn't it, that the respondent believes that the rules and regulations are strict *and* that this is fair? That is, a respondent might understand the need for strict rules and regulations that are administered fairly. Hence in this kind of situation, it is important to address these two concepts in two different questions: one about the strictness and one about the fairness of the group home's rules and regulations. Otherwise, we would have what's known as a *double-barreled question*.
- When using closed-ended questions, consider supplementing them with

open-ended items. This will enable you to take advantage of the closed-ended questions' ease of calculation and data analysis and the open-ended items' elicitation of valuable details.

- When possible and appropriate, use similar response category formats for the closed-ended questions. For example, if your instrument contains seven questions concerning clients' satisfaction with various aspects of agency services, use the same scale for each (whether it's a Likert scale ranging from very satisfied to very dissatisfied or an agree–disagree scale). Although this isn't always possible, using similar response category formats makes instruments seem less fragmented and may enable you to compute more easily an overall summary score when you analyze the data. It's easy to simplify the layout so that the items run down the left-hand side of the page and the response categories are listed across the top, from left to right.
- Be certain that the response options for closed-ended items are (1) exhaustive and (2) mutually exclusive. Obviously, the choices that respondents are given should cover all known options. For example, if the Mt. Washington staff want to ask respondents in the agency's substance abuse treatment program about their primary drug of choice when they were using it, this list should include all known options. Leaving out "cocaine" or "amphetamines," for example, would be a real problem. Similarly, if respondents are asked to describe their progress, the scale should include excellent, good, fair, and poor. If "fair" were left out, it would be a significant omission.
- You also need to avoid overlap among the response options. Consider, for example, the following response options for the question "How many alcoholic drinks do you consume in a typical week?"

———— none
———— 1–3
———— 3–5
———— 5–7
———— more than 7

- If someone usually has three or five drinks, he wouldn't know which category to check, given the overlap. This is easy to fix; simply change the numbers so they don't overlap.
- Here's a different example of response categories that aren't mutually exclusive. Suppose the instrument is designed to gather information about the kinds of programs Mt. Washington offers to adolescents with behavioral problems. One of the instrument's questions is "Please check which of the following types of programs your agency offers for this population":

_____ Outpatient counseling
_____ Family counseling
_____ Group home
_____ Halfway house

- One problem with these response categories is that family counseling is one form of outpatient counseling. Perhaps the person who drafted the instrument equated "outpatient counseling" with "individual counseling," but this isn't clear. Also, many people don't distinguish between group homes and halfway houses. The person who drafted the instrument may have had a difference in mind (for example, a halfway house may refer specifically to a facility to which the residents of a juvenile correctional facility are referred after their release, to facilitate their gradual reintegration into the community, but that probably wouldn't be clear to most respondents).
- Let's say the question asked adolescent group home residents, "Overall, how useful has your stay here been?" and the response categories were

_____ Very useful
_____ Somewhat useful
_____ Very boring

The problem here is that although the question refers to only one concept (the program's usefulness), the response options incorporate two concepts, usefulness and boredom. Instead, the response options should refer only to the concept that the question asks about: usefulness.

- Make sure that the wording of the response options in a closed-ended question is consistent with the responses people would ordinarily give. Do you see any problem with the following question in the questionnaire for adolescent group home residents: "Do you find the counselors in this program to be helpful?"

_____ Very helpful
_____ Somewhat helpful
_____ Somewhat unhelpful
_____ Not very helpful

The problem is that the wording of the response options is different from what people would ordinarily use. Most people would answer "yes," "no," or perhaps "I don't know." If we want to keep the response categories (which are fine), the question should be reworded. One possibility is "How helpful do you find the counselors in this program?"

- Here's another example. The following question appears in the instrument administered to people of color living in the Mt. Washington catchment area: "If you had a problem in your life that required mental health counseling, would you go to the Mt. Washington Family Service Agency for help?"

—— Very likely
—— Somewhat likely
—— Somewhat unlikely
—— Not likely

The response categories aren't what people would be likely to use. Again, the question invites a "yes/no" kind of response. The problem can easily be remedied by changing the question to "If you had a problem in your life that required mental health counseling, how likely is it that you would go to the Mt. Washington Family Service Agency for help?"

- In closed-ended questions that ask for an opinion, avoid including a "neutral" or "no opinion" category, because many people use this response as an "easy out" when asked for an opinion. The usual advice is to force respondents to express an opinion, particularly if the question concerns an issue about which nearly everyone is likely to have an opinion. Sometimes, however, it makes conceptual sense to have a middle category for people who feel genuinely ambivalent about an issue.
- Although it's often a good idea to follow a closed-ended item with an open-ended item (particularly when asking for an explanation or elaboration), at times the reverse order is better. Suppose the Mt. Washington staff want to know what aspects of the agency's teen-parenting program the participants find helpful and unhelpful. If the program's participants are handed a list of various aspects of the program and asked to check off those that are most and least helpful, the list may prompt responses that the clients wouldn't have given otherwise. An alternative is to ask an open-ended question first, about what aspects of the program are most helpful and least helpful. This could be followed by a closed-ended item with a comprehensive list of program features for the respondents to consider. The advantage of this approach is that clients can pick out the most salient program features without being guided by the list, which may produce a more valid reaction; this then can be followed by the clients' comments on each program feature.
- When instruments include a list of items (for example, when respondents are asked to indicate how often they have various mental health or family-related problems or how satisfied they are with various aspects of a program), consider adding an "other" category (usually known as a *residual* category) at the end of the list. The people who constructed the instrument may have omitted an item pertinent to certain respondents'

experiences. It's often a good idea to give respondents a chance to add items to the list.

- When respondents are asked questions that solicit an opinion, the question should acknowledge the range of possible options. For instance, if the Mt. Washington staff want to know whether the participants in the agency's residential substance abuse treatment program believe that they should have more privileges during evening hours, it would be a problem if the question were worded: "Do you think privileges during evening hours should be expanded?" The main problem here is that the wording is biased in favor of expanding privileges, which may influence the response. It would be better to present both options: "Do you think privileges during evening hours should be expanded, or do you think they should remain the way they are?" This question is better balanced.

- As I said earlier, the first questions in an instrument should engage respondents and not be too threatening. Ordinarily, I avoid starting off with "boring" items related to demographic details (age, ethnicity, marital status, etc.). Rather, I try to begin with questions that respondents are likely to find interesting, relevant, and not threatening. Questions likely to be perceived as threatening should come toward the end of the instrument. Examples are questions asked of participants in a substance abuse treatment program about their use of illegal drugs; questions asked of participants in a domestic violence counseling program about instances when they have abused their partner; and questions asked of agency staff about difficulties they have with their supervisors. If placed early in the instrument, such questions could upset the respondents or somehow influence their responses to subsequent items. (By the way, here's a useful tip I learned years ago: Many people are reluctant to report their income. So if that information is important to obtain, one possibility is to prepare a card with several income categories listed on it. For example, category A might be $0–$5,000, B = $5,001–$10,000, C = $10,001–$15,000, and so on. The interviewer can hand the card to the respondents and ask them simply to check the letter corresponding to the appropriate income category. This approach can help diffuse the anxiety that some respondents feel about disclosing their income. Although you will lose some information if you don't ask for specific dollar figures, this format may enhance the likelihood that respondents will answer the question at all.)

- Include a brief introduction at the beginning of the instrument explaining its purpose. This helps orient the respondents and may reduce their anxiety about the reasons for the data collection.

- When an instrument includes several sections, insert brief transition statements to alert the respondents to shifts in topics. This too may help orient them and minimize confusion.

- At the end of the instrument, ask the respondents whether they would like to make any additional comments. This gives them an opportunity to fill in any gaps and to take the lead with respect to particular points they may feel strongly about. This kind of final question also may help the respondents feel less frustrated that they didn't have a chance to add in their own ideas.
- Finally, be sure to thank the respondents for participating.

Step 6. Read through the entire instrument, and edit it as needed.   Once you have finished your first draft, read through it and edit it carefully. I usually put the draft away for a few hours, or a day or two if I have some breathing room, before I read through it again. This helps me clear my head and view the draft more objectively. When I read through it, I look closely at the sequence (of both the broad topics and the subtopics) of the questions, the wording of the items, the use of closed-ended and open-ended items, and the wording and format of response categories in the closed-ended items.

Step 7. Have thoughtful, knowledgeable colleagues review and critique your draft.   Once I have made my changes, I typically ask several colleagues to read the draft. I always am careful to ask only those colleagues who know something about the topics addressed in the instrument and are likely to be thorough and conscientious. It doesn't do me any good to enlist colleagues who will rush through the document and hand it back saying, "Looks good to me."

9

DATA COLLECTION: PROCEDURES

Thus far I have concentrated on using standardized (chapter 7) and creating (chapter 8) data collection instruments. I haven't yet talked about collecting the data.

Once social workers have chosen or created their data collection instruments, they have several choices of data collection procedures. Those who are collecting data for clinical purposes may have their clients fill out forms in the social worker's office or at home. Clinical social workers may also gather data about clients by observing them (for example, in a residential program or through a one-way mirror). Social workers who want to gather information from a group of clients, former clients, agency staff, community residents, or any other group of people may choose to interview respondents in person, give them questionnaires to complete themselves, mail questionnaires or surveys to their homes or workplaces, or interview them over the telephone. In addition, social workers may gather data from existing sources; this is known as *secondary data collection* (for example, data from agency files and government agencies, and results obtained from other research and evaluation projects).

Not surprisingly, each of these approaches has a different procedure. I've already described some of the procedures in gathering clinical data from individual clients and by observing clients directly. In this chapter I focus on the procedures followed when social workers conduct interviews (both personal interviews and telephone interviews), distribute questionnaires through the mail, use existing data, and gather qualitative data.

CONDUCTING INTERVIEWS

Conducting interviews is one of the most common forms of data collection in social work. As we have seen throughout this book, social workers often collect data in this way. Examples are interviewing staff about issues in their agency (program planning and design, employee morale, resource allocation, and so on), clients and former clients about their experience and satisfaction with agency services, colleagues in other agencies (perhaps to gather information about a public policy issue), and community residents. Once social workers have decided on a research design, drawn the sample, and chosen or created the data collection instrument, they need to keep a number of important details in mind as they begin the actual data collection.

As we review these details, it will help to discuss them as they pertain to a particular example. Assume that next year the entire Mt. Washington Family Service Agency will be going through an extensive reaccreditation process. Mt. Washington is affiliated with a national organization that accredits such family service agencies. After its initial accreditation, which Mt. Washington received six years ago, it is reaccredited every seven years.

As part of this process, members of a site-visit team, which usually includes administrators from family service agencies elsewhere in the country, examine various aspects of the agency: programs and services (range and design), staff (qualifications, education, assigned responsibilities), physical facilities (adequacy of space, physical condition, facilities for confidential storage of records), budget (accounting procedures, budget review process), board of directors (composition and functioning of board), agency records (comprehensiveness and thoroughness), program effectiveness, and so on.

In anticipation of next year's site visit, Mt. Washington's director instructs her assistant director, Alma B., to conduct a comprehensive client satisfaction survey, including several subsamples. One sample is composed of former clients who terminated after the completion of services. A second sample is former clients who terminated or left the agency before services were completed. A third sample is current clients.

Alma B. worked with two people on her staff to design the client satisfaction survey and to draw the samples. Using what they know about sampling procedures (see chapter 5), Alma B. and her staff generated a list of fifty current clients, fifty former clients who terminated from Mt. Washington following the completion of services, and fifty former clients who terminated or left the agency before services were completed. The staff would have preferred to use larger samples, but time and budget constraints got in the way (surprise).

After much discussion and after choosing staff members who would have time for this project, Alma B. decided that at the end of their next visit to the agency, the sample of current clients would be given their survey and asked to complete and mail it back to the agency within five days. Both samples of former clients would be mailed their surveys and asked to return them within five days. In addition, ten randomly selected individuals from each group would be interviewed in depth. The purpose of these interviews is to obtain more detailed information and responses than the self-administered questionnaires would yield. The personal interviews will give the staff an opportunity to probe and the respondents an opportunity to elaborate. Although staff would have preferred to conduct such in-depth interviews with all the respondents, the time and expense required are prohibitive.

PRE-TEST

In chapter 3, we encountered the term *pre-test*. In that context, it referred to research designs in which data are collected before the introduction of an intervention (the pre-test) and following the intervention (the post-test). Now we'll use the term in a second way. It's confusing that the same term means two very different things, but there's not much we can do about that.

The term *pre-test* as we use it in this chapter has to do with conducting a "dry run" or a "test drive" with an instrument before actually using it to collect data. You can probably figure out why we do this. First, it's always important to try out an instrument to see whether the sequence of questions makes sense. What seems fine when we put it on paper may seem quite different when it is pre-tested. If we're pre-testing an interview instrument, we may find that the order of the questions seems odd in one place or another and needs to be revised. In addition, whether we're pre-testing a self-administered instrument or an interview guide, we can ask respondents to offer feedback on the sequencing of questions.

Second, we need to make sure that the questions' wording makes sense. It's useful to ask respondents in a pre-test to tell us when they think questions and closed-ended response categories are unclear or confusing. Finally, we should find out during a pre-test how long it takes to complete a typical interview. Here, too, social workers are often surprised at the difference between the estimated amount of time it will take to complete an interview or instrument and the actual amount of time it takes.

It's hard to overemphasize the importance of pre-testing procedures. In almost every case, I've revised my instrument or data collection procedures as a result of the pre-test. It's not unusual for me to discover that I've overlooked something or been too pessimistic or optimistic about the time it will take to collect the data from each respondent. The feedback is invaluable.

Social workers often want to know how many people should be included in a pre-test. There's no simple answer. As with so many decisions to be made during a research or evaluation project, this generally depends on good judgment. Typically, if I plan to conduct interviews or distribute a self-administered questionnaire, I find it useful to pre-test the instrument with five to ten people. If the instrument is fairly simple and straightforward, I would probably limit the pre-test sample to five or so. If the instrument is complex, I'd use a larger number. In any case, social workers usually avoid using the pre-test participants in the final sample, since their earlier exposure to the instrument might influence their responses. The only exception to this that I can think of is the rare instance when I made no substantive changes in the instrument as a result of the pre-test. In those circumstances, it's probably all right to use the pre-test participants in the final sample (as long as their selection is consistent with the overall sampling procedure being used).

THE INTERVIEW SETTING

It's important to think carefully about the most appropriate setting for the interview. For example, if you are interviewing agency staff about ways to redesign the agency's services, you should probably conduct the interviews in the respondents' offices. In contrast, if you want to interview community residents about their attitudes toward a local agency, you should probably interview them in their own homes. For most people, their own home is the most convenient and comfortable location.

However, if you want to interview people about a sensitive, personal, or threatening topic, you may want to hold the interview away from home. Answering questions about sensitive topics in the vicinity of family members or "significant others" may be threatening and may lead to response bias (remember our discussion of socially desirable responses and evaluation apprehension?). For example, if you want to interview a sample of women about their experience with domestic violence, it's probably not a good idea to interview them at home. Their partner may arrive in the middle of the interview, and the women's answering questions on such a troubling topic in the very setting where they may have been battered could influence their responses. It would be better to hold the interview in a more neutral site, such as a social service agency.

At times you may want to interview people in an unconventional setting. Some years ago I was part of a small study by a social worker treating "high-risk" adolescents. Much of the social worker's time was spent on the street, providing counseling and information informally in the setting where the youths hung out. Over time the social worker became an accepted part of the "scene."

She wanted to interview a small sample of the youths about certain issues in their lives and their interest in getting help with these problems. In her judgment, it didn't make sense to interview these kids in their homes or in a social service agency, as that wasn't where they would feel most comfortable. Instead, the social worker invited them to join her for a quick bite at a nearby hamburger joint that the youths frequented. She had no difficulty getting them to agree to spend twenty to thirty minutes with her or to answer her questions. Indeed, the social worker's biggest challenge was getting a booth tucked away in a corner to ensure a reasonable amount of privacy.

ANONYMITY AND CONFIDENTIALITY

As in clinical social work, collecting data for research and evaluation depends on the respondents' willingness to trust that the information they share will not be revealed inappropriately or indiscriminately. It is not unusual for respondents to share personal, intimate information with social workers. Think about the kinds of topics social workers often investigate: substance abuse, marital relationships, delinquent and criminal behavior, depression, sexual dysfunction, mental illness, health problems, self-esteem, attitudes toward agency colleagues, organizational morale issues, and ethical misconduct. If respondents are to answer frankly and truthfully, they need to know that their responses will be handled properly.

In chapter 4, in my discussion of ethical issues related to research and evaluation, I mentioned the importance of anonymity and confidentiality. Anonymity is important when social workers publish or in some other way share the respondents' information. That is, the social workers must disguise the source of their information. The anonymous reporting of results means that even though individuals' responses may be reported—perhaps in a formal publication, an agency report, a classroom lecture, or a conference presentation—no identifying information is included.

The following is an example of anonymously reporting individuals' responses. The survey of clients' satisfaction with services included a question about their assessment of staff members' competence. Alma B. and her assistants found a fair amount of variation in the responses of former clients who had terminated from the agency after completing the service. Although most of them were impressed with the staff members' competence, others were quite critical.

How should Alma B. summarize these responses in her final report? On the one hand, she thinks it's important to give the report's readers, which will include agency administrators and board members, an accurate sense of the respondents' sentiments and feedback. On the other hand, she doesn't want to reveal the identity of any of the respondents because doing so would betray their trust and probably their confidence in Mt. Washington's ability to handle sensitive information responsibly.

A simple and widely accepted way to handle this kind of situation is to report the results anonymously. That is, in the final version, Alma B. can quote from the respondents' comments without attributing them to anyone. Here's an illustration of how she could do this:

The sample of former clients who left the agency after completing the service varied considerably in their assessment of the staff's competence. In answer to the question "In general, would you say your social worker at Mt. Washington was very competent, somewhat competent, or not very competent?" nearly two-thirds the respondents (68 percent) said that the staff were either "very" (24 percent) or "somewhat" (44 percent) competent. However, about one-third reported that their counselors were "not very" competent (32 percent). The following is a representative cross section of "positive" comments by respondents asked to explain their assessment of social workers' competence (the X in brackets represents the social worker's name):

"I feel like [X] saved my life. When I came here for help, I felt like I was drowning. [X] gave me the support and direction I needed." (client receiving individual counseling)

"[X] knew exactly what I needed. I really felt cared for and listened to. I never wanted the session to end." (client receiving individual counseling)

"I always felt like [X] could read my mind. He always seemed to understand what I was thinking and feeling. [X] provided the support and understanding I so desperately needed. I don't know what I would have done without him." (client receiving individual counseling)

"During the past year there were a few times when I thought I might pick up and use again. Knowing [X] was there made all the difference in the world. He was a lifesaver. [X] always seemed to know what to do so I wouldn't relapse. He deserves an award!" (client in substance abuse treatment program)

"I can't imagine what I would have done without [X]. I've been through two other programs. [X] is the first counselor who really understood where I was coming from. I remember one time, about five months ago, when I felt like giving up. My life seemed to be falling apart again. [X] spent hours with me, walking me through that crisis. Without her I probably would have killed myself or started using heroin again. I've learned so much from [X]. I'll never be able to say thank you enough." (client in substance abuse treatment program)

"I'm so much better at handling my anger now. Before I started working with [X] I didn't have a clue. [X] is really smart. He's really taught me what to do when I get upset with things at work and home. I feel like I have a new life because of [X]." (client in domestic violence program)

"There's not enough space here for me to explain how [X] has changed my life. Before I knew [X], I would fly off the handle at any little thing my wife did that ticked me off. Now I understand why I was angry so much of the time. Now I know better ways to behave when I get angry. I really feel like [X] saved my marriage. If I could promote him, I would!" (client in domestic violence program)

In contrast, the following is a representative cross section of former clients' negative comments about their social workers:

"There were several times when I thought about dropping out of counseling. When it comes right down to it, [X] didn't help me much. I felt like I was doing all the work. [X] was there physically, but I never got the feeling that he was paying much attention to me. I think he's burned out." (client receiving individual counseling)

"A lot of the time I felt like I knew more than [X]. I felt like [X] was constantly lecturing me and telling me what to do to solve my problems. I never really felt like [X] understood my problems or cared about me." (client receiving individual counseling)

"During many of our sessions, I felt like I was the social worker and [X] was the client. [X] talked a lot about his own problems. I can't believe he told me some of the things he did about his own life. Isn't that wrong? I thought I was supposed to be the one getting help. I really think this agency needs to take a close look at [X]." (client receiving individual counseling)

"I always had a funny feeling that [X] had relapsed himself. Here I was supposed to be getting counseling from [X], and he's the one who seemed to be in worse shape. I know it's good to have counselors who are in recovery themselves, but isn't it a problem when the counselor is having trouble with his own sobriety? That sure made things harder for me." (client in substance abuse treatment program)

"[X] canceled lots of our sessions. I really needed help, but I never really felt like I got it. I thought I would get in trouble with my probation officer because so many sessions got canceled. I think [X] was irresponsible, and I'm the one who's paying for it." (client in domestic violence program)

Alma B. decided to include a fairly long excerpt from the comments of one respondent who offered very detailed feedback. Notice that she presents the information anonymously.

One respondent who received individual counseling offered unusually detailed and evenhanded comments about her social worker and her experience with Mt. Washington. This middle-aged client originally sought counseling to address several issues in her marriage. She received services from Mt. Washington weekly for a period of about three months. About half the sessions included her husband. Below is an excerpt from her comments:

I came to this agency because a friend of mine recommended it. She told me she got lots of help here. Now that I'm finished with my counseling, I find that I have lots to say about it.

For the most part, I think [X] did a good job. She really seemed to care about me and often had good advice. Even though she's young, I think she is wise. I think the expression is 'mature beyond her years.' That really fits here. At first I didn't think [X] would be able to understand my marriage problems. After all, she's not married herself (at least I'm pretty sure she's not), so I thought, How could she understand what marriage problems are all about? But after a while, I realized that [X] had a good understanding of what I was going through. Also, my husband liked her and thought she was helpful. I didn't think he'd go for counseling, and I almost had to drag him into that first session. After a few times, however, my husband got into it. I think [X] deserves a lot of the credit for that. If he hadn't liked her, there's no way he would have returned.

But I also found [X] frustrating at times. Sometimes she would make comments that seemed off the wall, if you know what I mean. What I mean is, [X] would occasionally say things like 'You'll just have to learn to live with some of those little things that your husband does that annoy you. That's part of being married,' or 'Don't all marriages have these sorts of problems? What did you expect?' It didn't happen too often, but sometimes I felt like [X] didn't get it and just said things without thinking. On a few occasions I walked out of her office gritting my teeth in frustration. I guess more experience will help her.

Another thing that bothered me is that sometimes [X] would listen to me for a while and just nod her head. I used to feel that she was thinking lots of things but not telling me what she was thinking. It almost felt like a game, like she was just trying to figure me out. In a way I felt used when this happened, like [X] was studying me and judging me. I don't want to give the impression that this happened all the time. It didn't. But it happened more often than I would have liked.

As you can see, the trick is to present information in a way that protects the respondents' identity and, at the same time, gives readers a feel for their actual responses. Most of the time you can do this by describing individual respondents in very general terms, perhaps referring only to the program in which they were enrolled, their gender, their age group, and the kind of problem for which they sought help. Any information that might enable readers to identify a respondent should be omitted, of course.

Confidentiality is somewhat different. Ordinarily, confidentiality refers to social workers' obligation to not share information with third parties without their clients' explicit consent. For example, when the Mt. Washington staff interview current clients about the status of the problems for which they sought help, their responses should not be shared with their current social workers without the clients' explicit permission. Or if a current client reveals in a research or evaluation interview that in the recent past he struggled with an alcohol problem, this information should not be shared with the client's employer. Such information must remain confidential.

In general, the confidentiality guidelines that govern social workers' handling of information shared by clients in clinical contexts apply to social workers' handling of information shared by clients or respondents for research or evaluation purposes. This a well-established and important concept, one stressed in the NASW Code of Ethics. As noted in chapter 4, the code contains several relevant standards:

5.02(k) Social workers engaged in the evaluation of services should discuss collected information only for professional purposes and only with people professionally concerned with this information.

5.02(l) Social workers engaged in evaluation or research should ensure the anonymity or confidentiality of participants and of the data obtained from them. Social workers should inform participants of any limits of confidentiality, the measures that will be taken to ensure confidentiality, and when any records containing research data will be destroyed.

5.02(m) Social workers who report evaluation and research results should protect participants' confidentiality by omitting identifying information unless proper consent has been obtained authorizing disclosure.

Take time to think about the best way to approach your respondents concerning the anonymity and confidentiality of their responses. For starters, spell out clearly and specifically just how you plan to report your findings anonymously and/or protect your respondents' confidentiality. You should explain this verbally and in writing as part of the informed consent procedure.

It's possible, however, to go overboard explaining anonymity and confidentiality. A number of years ago, I helped conduct a study of juvenile offenders. The purpose of the study was to compare the effectiveness of community-based services and institutionally based services for juvenile offenders. About 500 youths who had been arrested by the police were interviewed and asked about various aspects of their lives and offenses they had committed. As you might expect, one of the things the research staff was concerned about was the respondents' willingness to be truthful. After all, we were asking youths who had been arrested about the quality of their lives and the extent of their misbehavior. Shouldn't we have expected that some of them would be uneasy about being truthful and concerned about the possible ramifications of their "confessions" once they went back to court? Although the research staff did not share any of their findings with police and court officials—except in aggregate form with no identifying information—we certainly understood why some of the kids would be worried that their responses would find their way to law enforcement officials.

To reassure the youths, we wrote out a detailed explanation of the steps the research staff were taking to ensure the confidentiality of their responses. As part of the study, however, I decided to examine the impact of the explanation about confidentiality. More specifically, I wanted to know what effect the different approaches would have on the kids' responses.

Here's how I designed this part of the study. Following the design principles we reviewed earlier (chapter 3), I randomly assigned the juvenile offenders in the sample to two groups. One group received a brief, routine explanation about the interview that did not spell out all the steps the researchers had taken to protect the confidentiality of their responses. The second group received a much more detailed explanation of the various safeguards, noting that no one would know their answers, their answers would be grouped with hundreds of others, their names would not be used, and instead a number would be used to prevent disclosing any names. The youths in this sample also received a signed statement from the study's principal investigator (that's the term used to refer to the person in charge of a study) confirming that their responses would be kept confidential.

After they were given these explanations, either the short, cursory statement or the more detailed one, the youths were asked to answer lots of questions about the frequency with which they had committed and been arrested for various behaviors, their self-esteem, their attitudes toward law abidance, and their views of the seriousness of various behaviors. At the end of the interview, the youths were also asked to fill out a separate form with eight items designed to measure the extent of their concern and apprehension about answering the interview questions. The questions measured whether they were concerned about their self-esteem, the respect of others, and the consequences of answering certain questions about their behavior and attitudes. The instrument also asked the youths to report the level of their anxiety and apprehension at the beginning and the end of the interview.

The study's findings were surprising. It turned out that the detailed explanation about confidentiality backfired somewhat, in that it increased the youths' apprehension at the beginning of the interview. But there was no significant difference between the two groups' reported anxiety and apprehension at the end of the interview, and there were no significant differences between the two groups' responses to the interview items pertaining to the offenses they had committed and been arrested for, their attitudes toward law abidance, and their views of the seriousness of various behaviors. Although the deliberate emphasis on confidentiality did not have a significant effect on the youths' responses to the main research questions, it did have a significant impact on their anxiety and apprehension at the beginning of the interview. These results suggest that social workers who are inclined to reassure respondents with detailed guarantees of confidentiality may inadvertently increase their concern and apprehension. This is not to say that social workers shouldn't talk to their respondents about confidentiality. Rather, they should be matter-of-fact in their explanations and avoid overly detailed explanations that may raise, not lower, anxiety.

Using Tape Recorders

In some instances, you should use a tape recorder, with the respondent's permission, of course. If you are conducting a lengthy interview with several open-ended questions that are likely to elicit detailed responses, it can be comforting to have a tape of the interview to ensure that you don't omit any important details from your report. Some social workers like to take detailed notes during an interview; others find that taking notes during an interview is distracting and so prefer to listen and let the tape recorder capture all the details (of course, the social worker must listen to the recording later to analyze the results—I'll discuss this more in chapter II).

Whether it makes sense to use a tape recorder also depends on the type of respondent being interviewed and the nature of the topics being addressed. Obviously (at least I hope it's obvious), if you're interviewing juvenile or criminal offenders about their illegal activity, it would be a bad idea to suggest using a tape recorder. Also, if you're interviewing agency staff about management problems in the agency, it would be unwise (to put it mildly) to tape-record the staff members' comments, because of their likely concern that their criticism would be heard by agency supervisors or administrators.

But in many instances, it does make sense to use a tape recorder. For example, my wife, who also is a social work professor, recently carried out a study of adoptive families that have contact with the children's birth parents. This study of "open adoption" was designed to explore the relationships between adoptive families and birth parents. My wife's sample contained about twenty adoptive families. She developed an interview instrument that explored a wide range of complex issues having to do with the kinds of contact between adoptive and birth families, the adoptive parents' feelings about open adoption, and their children's reactions to open adoption.

My wife was concerned about her ability to record on paper all the respondents' important comments, particularly when they were discussing compelling and emotionally complicated issues. Also, she wanted to maintain eye contact with the respondents. So she decided to ask them for permission to tape-record the interview. She explained the purpose of the tape recording and the steps she planned to take to ensure the confidentiality of the recorded information. All the respondents granted permission in writing for my wife to tape-record the interviews. Unfortunately for me and my children, now my wife has to listen to and analyze all those tapes, so for a while the kids and I have to do her chores around the house as well as our own (maybe research and evaluation aren't such a good idea after all).

The Interviewer's Dress

The interviewer's dress may seem like a trivial topic, but it's not. In our culture, the way we dress makes a statement and carries a great deal of meaning. Wearing a bathing suit at the beach is appropriate, but wearing that same bathing suit at a church or synagogue service would not be advisable.

The same is true of the way that social workers dress for interviews. Social workers who interview agency administrators and staff should be dressed professionally, wearing what the respondents typically wear for work. However, the clothes that are appropriate in a social service agency aren't appropriate if you're interviewing a group of adolescents in the local fast-food establishment. Both you and the respondents will feel more comfortable if you are dressed casually. It's important for respondents to feel comfortable so as to minimize socially desirable responses and increase the respondents' attentiveness during the interview.

There are some situations in which the appropriate style of dress isn't clear. If you're interviewing community residents in their homes about their perceptions toward the local family service agency, the appropriate dress could range from "very nice" casual clothes to somewhat understated professional dress that one would ordinarily see among staff in an agency. That one's a judgment call, I think. I don't think I would wear a coat and tie, although I might wear just a tie. As a general rule, I think it's wise to dress in a way that will put the respondents at ease and is not likely to be distracting. It's sort of like what umpires say about their role at baseball games: their main wish is that they won't be noticed.

The Interviewer's Style

Social workers can use one of three different conversational "styles" to conduct interviews: formal, informal, and a blend of the two. Sometimes it's appropriate to interview people rather formally, but at other times informality seems best. If I am interviewing a sample of senior government officials or agency executive directors, I'll probably want to take a formal approach. In contrast, if I am interviewing a sample of adolescents hanging out at a mall, I will want to be rather informal in my manner. Furthermore, if I am interviewing a sample of clinical social workers about their tasks, I may want to strike a balance between a formal and an informal style.

What do I mean by formal and informal? Beyond the issue of dress, by "formal" I mean that social workers use professional language and a somewhat impersonal and restrained manner. I know that sounds a bit vague, but I suspect all of us understand the difference between a very formal and very informal style of conversation. Formal conversation tends to be fairly unemotional and structured, whereas informal conversation is more chatty, personal, and unstructured. In addition, formal interviewing entails asking questions precisely as they are worded on the instrument, to enhance the consistency with which different interviewers pose the questions. Informal interviewing, which is often used in exploratory research and evaluation projects and with open-ended questions, sometimes, although not always, permits social workers to paraphrase questions.

Paraphrasing can be risky, however, because different interviewers may word questions differently and thus elicit different information, but variation in the wording of questions is more consequential in some instances than in others. For example, in interviews conducted with Mt. Washington clients concerning their alcohol consumption, it would be important for all interviewers to ask the question in precisely the same way ("During the past week, how many times did you drink alcohol when you were alone?" might generate a very different answer if it were paraphrased as "Recently, how many times have you had a drink by yourself?"). Even a slight variation in wording could have a significant impact on the way respondents interpret and answer the question. However, in exploratory interviews with the Mt. Washington staff concerning the potential implications of the agency's merger with another area agency, the identical wording of the questions by all interviewers may be somewhat less critical ("To what extent do you favor the merger?" and "How much do you like the idea of merging with agency X?" may be interpreted similarly).

One of the major challenges in research and evaluation interviewing is establishing rapport with respondents. In some instances, conducting interviews informally may be the best way to establish rapport; informality often puts people at ease. You can imagine how counterproductive it would be to interview that sample of adolescents formally; that would probably guarantee a low response rate and increase the likelihood of socially desirable responses. In that context, informality is much more likely to build rapport and trust, particularly given many adolescents' distrust of authority figures.

But what works in one setting or with one population may not be good for another. The sort of informality that adolescents find appealing may seem repugnant to agency executive directors, who may expect social workers to be more "professional" in their demeanor when conducting interviews. In that context, formality can be a virtue.

Not surprisingly, whether you conduct interviews formally or informally requires judgment. I find that often a blend of the two is best. Some informal exchange and small talk may be a great way to get things started and off on a good foot, whereas a more formal style may be appropriate once the actual interview begins, particularly if the topic is a relatively serious one (as most are).

I need to clarify one important point. An informal interviewing style doesn't mean that the interview is completely unstructured and freewheeling. I would never conduct an interview—no matter how formal or informal—without some degree of structure and without a clear understanding, in the form of an outline or an interview guide, of the issues and topics I want to cover. Even the most informal interview should have some structure and the sequence of questions worked out ahead of time. Although the questions may be asked in an informal manner, they should follow a conceptually sound order.

One of the things I like to do if I have to conduct an interview somewhat formally is to acknowledge the formality. For example, if I have a reasonably long interview instrument to complete and I need to follow a carefully constructed sequence of questions, I usually say something to the respondent like "Let me apologize ahead of time for the formality of this interview. I have a number of questions to ask you, and I need to ask them exactly as they are written. Thanks for bearing with me."

SKIP PATTERNS

Many interviews include what researchers call *skip patterns*. A "skip" occurs when a respondent answers a question in a certain way that permits the interviewer to skip over some of the next questions to another item. Here's an example. In the interview instrument to be administered to former Mt. Washington clients who left the agency before completing services, one question is "After leaving Mt. Washington, did you seek social services at another agency?" The response options are yes and no. If the respondent answers yes, the interviewer continues with a series of five questions concerning what other agency or agencies the respondent went to for assistance, the reasons, and the respondent's experience with services from the other agency or agencies. But if the respondent answers no, the interviewer is instructed to skip over those five questions to the next item.

The point of telling you this is to encourage you to become familiar with the skip patterns in the interview instrument you're using. You don't want to encounter one of those "skips" and then fumble around trying to figure out where to go next. That's another benefit of pre-tests; they're sort of like a dress rehearsal to help you feel comfortable with the instrument.

SCHEDULING BREAKS

It's generally a mistake to design an interview that lasts long enough to require a break in the middle. For most interviews, anything more than forty-five to fifty minutes could be a problem. (It's no coincidence that the typical clinical hour lasts about an hour. That length of time seems to work for most people when discussing important issues that require their full attention.)

Sometimes, however, interviews are necessarily long because they explore a number of complicated issues in depth. For long interviews, it's usually a good idea to anticipate when a short break might be appropriate, whether to use the restroom or simply stretch. Building in a short break may enhance respondents' willingness to complete the interview and answer each question thoroughly and thoughtfully. For example, earlier I mentioned a study my wife did in which she interviewed adoptive parents in open adoptions. Her interview addressed a wide range of complex topics pertaining to the contact between the adoptive parents and the birth parents, the adoptive parents' relationship with the birth parents, the adoptees' reactions to having contact with their birth parents, the adoptive parents' feelings about having contact with the birth parents, and so on. Many of these interviews lasted two or three hours. Fortunately, all the respondents were willing to spend that much time, in large part because of their interest in the subject. Given the length of the interview, however, it was important for my wife to build in opportunities for a short break. (Since the interviews were conducted in the respondents' homes, my wife also had to anticipate unplanned breaks required by children who scraped their knees, were in the middle of toilet training, or what have you.)

PAYING ATTENTION

One of the greatest challenges when conducting interviews is figuring out how to do three things at once: (1) pay attention to respondents when they answer a question, (2) write down their comments, and (3) anticipate the next question or series of questions. The respondents should feel that the interviewer is paying serious attention to them and that their answers matter. I suspect we've all had experiences when people have asked us a question—whether in casual social conversation or in more formal circumstances—but then don't seem interested in our answer or appear distracted. That's not only frustrating, but it also makes us less interested in continuing the conversation.

The same holds true for interview respondents, which is one reason that it may help to use a tape recorder instead of recording their answers word for word. If tape recording isn't feasible, it may be a good idea to pause and record the respondents' answers before moving on to the next question.

A common "mistake" that novice interviewers (and some experienced interviewers) make is that they are thinking about the next question to ask while the respondent is answering the current question. This often means that the interviewer isn't really paying close attention to the respondent's answer, which may irritate the respondent. It may also discourage the respondent from giving thorough and thoughtful answers. If you are very familiar with the instrument, there's really no reason to be thinking much about the next question while the respondent is talking.

Listening skills are important to every kind of interview; respondents usually want to be "heard" just as much as our clients and coworkers do.

OFFERING ASSISTANCE AND REFERRALS

Some interviews deal with very personal, intimate, and troubling issues. Mt. Washington staff members who interview clients and former clients about problems in their lives such as substance abuse, domestic violence, death, poverty, depression, and suicide may encounter respondents who unexpectedly become upset or traumatized by the interview. Respondents who thought they had "dealt with" certain issues or put certain issues "behind them" may find that the interview questions dredge up intense emotional reactions and feelings. Social work interviewers should therefore anticipate this possibility and be prepared to provide some crisis intervention.

If you conduct interviews in which such reactions are possible or likely, you also should be familiar with the appropriate referral sources. In fact, the NASW Code of Ethics states, "Social workers should take appropriate steps to ensure that participants in evaluation and research have access to appropriate supportive services" (standard 5.02[i]).

EDITING

Often it's tempting to wait a while after an interview before reading back through your notes to see whether any responses need editing or clarifying.

But it's important not to wait too long before reading through the interview to edit and check your recording of the respondents' comments. It's easy to forget exactly what a respondent said in answer to a specific question, so reconstructing a respondent's wording that you may have recorded hurriedly in shorthand may be difficult if you wait a long time. (Almost everyone uses abbreviations or shorthand at one point or another, particularly if respondents talk rapidly or throw in an afterthought that you insert quickly.)

In addition, if you conduct several interviews before reading back through them, it's easy to confuse which respondent said what. Thus even though it can be a nuisance, it's generally a good idea to read through the completed instrument as soon after the interview as possible.

ADMINISTERING MAILED QUESTIONNAIRES

Perhaps the main challenge with mailed questionnaires is to maximize the response rate, that is, the percentage of people who complete and return the instrument. One of the main disadvantages of mailed questionnaires is that the response rate can be very low. In general, you want at least a 50 percent response rate, and in many studies that can be difficult to achieve. Many people toss mailed questionnaires in the trash, put them aside to be completed "later" (and "later" never comes), or become frustrated with an instrument's length or format once they've started to complete it and then throw it away. Few things in the research and evaluation world are more painful than investing enormous amounts of time designing a survey instrument and watching a pathetic number of completed instruments trickle in. There are lots of practical things social workers can do to minimize these problems.

Physical Layout

The physical appearance of an instrument can have a significant impact on the response rate, and you can do a number of things with the physical layout to enhance the likelihood that the recipients will respond. First, try to lay out the items so they're not cluttered. I've seen instruments in which each page was so jam-packed that it took me a while to figure out how to complete them. Many respondents won't bother to take the time to figure out a complicated-looking instrument and instead will toss it out.

At the same time, you don't want to spread out the items so much that the instrument becomes too long. Some respondents get nervous when they see several pages stapled together. They may believe—sometimes wrongly—that a multipaged questionnaire will be time-consuming. There's a delicate balance between spreading the items out so they don't look cluttered and making the questionnaire so long that it scares off respondents.

Sometimes it's advisable to photocopy multipaged instruments on both sides of the paper, to make it look shorter (a little sleight of hand). Photocopying on both sides of the paper can also reduce postage costs. And this strategy also has the appealing benefit of conserving trees.

If you are concerned about an instrument's length, you can select a smaller font in your word processor or use a photocopier that reduces the print size. Of course, you don't want the final version to have such small print that you need to mail each respondent a magnifying glass along with the instrument. (Have you ever seen the compact edition of the Oxford Dictionary that comes with a magnifying glass? I'm not kidding.)

Cover Letter

Likewise, there are several things you can do with the cover letter to raise the response rate. First, it's helpful to state clearly why it's important for respondents to complete and mail back the questionnaire. Second, if possible, it's often a good idea to use real postage stamps rather than a postage meter imprint. This adds some labor, but the strategy can pay off. Can you figure out why? Some people are more likely to open an envelope with a first-class postage stamp than a "mass-stamped" envelope with a meter strip. A real stamp seems more personal to some people.

Second, mailing labels strike some people as rather impersonal. If possible, I like to handwrite people's names and addresses (unless the envelope needs to look "professional"), or if necessary, I type names and addresses right on the envelope. This may not seem like a big deal, but it can make a difference.

Third, the cover letter should specify the date by which the instrument is to be returned. This is very, very important. Although not everyone is influenced by due dates, many people are. So having a return date clearly displayed in the letter can significantly increase the response rate, and omitting a due date may mean that the envelope will be placed somewhere in the proverbial pile.

Incentives

In many research and evaluation projects, there's no need to give respondents an incentive to complete and mail back the instrument, particularly when surveying colleagues and professionals. In some instances, however, offering incentives may greatly increase the response rate.

Here's an interesting illustration of the importance of this phenomenon. A few months ago my wife and I received three similar mailings, on the same day, from the zoo in our community. Each cover letter looked the same, and all three encouraged us to become members of the zoo (never mind that we already were members). The only noteworthy difference among them was that one enclosed a nifty-looking decal we could give to our children to do heaven-knows-what with, one enclosed a certificate that we could redeem at the zoo's gift shop for a free T-shirt if we signed up as members, and the third contained just a plain old letter. One of the envelopes was addressed to me, one to my wife, and one to both of us. Clearly, the zoo staff were working from different mailing lists and didn't remove duplicated names (they probably figured it wasn't worth their while to spend staff time in that way, which I understand).

Anyway, I was curious about the three different mailings. Knowing what I do about research and evaluation, I suspected that the zoo personnel were evaluating the effectiveness of the different solicitation approaches to see whether one generated a significantly higher number of new members. I actually called the zoo's marketing director and informed her of the duplicate mailings. She laughed, apologized for the duplication, and acknowledged that the staff were, indeed, comparing the effectiveness of the three approaches. In fact, the staff person told me that the zoo had bought a number of mailing lists from various sources and then randomly assigned names to each of the three approaches. Sound like a familiar design?

Other kinds of incentives are used in mailed questionnaires. In one survey administered to former clients of an agency (similar to the one I've described concerning the Mt. Washington Family Service Agency), the principal investigator enclosed a crisp one-dollar bill in each envelope. Although many respondents probably would have completed the instrument without being offered the dollar bill and some respondents may have pocketed the dollar and not filled out the instrument, I suspect a fair number were influenced by it. I bet many of you have received surveys that contained a first-class stamp to be put on the return envelope, a pencil with which to complete the survey, or a couple of pennies. What the sponsors hope, of course, is that the enclosure will entice you to complete the survey and that you'll feel guilty pocketing the stamp or money without returning the completed survey. Do you think this works? Does it work on you?

In another survey, this one administered to community residents concerning neighborhood problems, the respondents were told in the cover letter that the agency would make a donation to a charity of the respondent's choice for each completed questionnaire (the size of the donation wasn't mentioned). Each respondent was asked to select one charity from among a list of five.

In my favorite example, brought to my attention by one of my students, respondents in a survey of women's health issues were told that the names of those who completed the questionnaire would be entered in a lottery for a cash prize. The wife of one of my students, who completed the questionnaire, won the $750 prize!

SASE

Are you familiar with the abbreviation SASE? It stands for self-addressed stamped envelope. Include one. If respondents don't have to go to the trouble of digging out a return envelope, addressing it, and contributing first-class postage, they're more likely to return the instrument. It costs extra to supply the envelopes and postage, but they can make a big difference in your response rate.

Follow-Up

Once the due date has passed, it is important to follow up with those in the sample who did not return the questionnaire. A common strategy is to send remiss respondents a postcard or letter politely reminding and encouraging them to return the instrument as soon as possible. The message should state briefly why the returned instrument is so important to the study, and it might also include a statement that if the recipient has misplaced the original, he or she should call a specific telephone number and request a replacement. In some instances, social workers may simply send all the "delinquent" recipients a second questionnaire.

What should you do if you don't know who has and hasn't returned the instrument (for example, because you deliberately omitted identifying information—names or identification numbers—from the instrument)? In this situation, social workers often send a postcard or letter to everyone in the sample. The message thanks all those who returned their instrument and asks those who haven't to return it as soon as possible. The message might remind recipients why they're receiving the postcard or letter even if they've already returned the instrument, that is, the follow-up card needs to be sent to everyone because the researcher or evaluator deliberately omitted identifying information from the instrument in order to ensure anonymity.

TELEPHONE INTERVIEWS

In some cases, social workers choose to conduct interviews over the telephone. For instance, the Mt. Washington staff may decide to use telephones to conduct a communitywide needs assessment to obtain data for a major grant application. Why, you might ask, would the agency approach the task in this way rather than conduct personal interviews or mail surveys?

There are several reasons. First, telephone surveys are often much less expensive, since you don't have to pay for the interviewers' travel time or expenses. Second, telephone surveys can usually be carried out more quickly (and you don't have to get dressed up for them). Third, there are no mailing costs, and printing costs are often lower, since interviewers may need multiple copies of the answer sheets only, not of the instrument itself. Fourth, with telephone surveys you don't have to worry about your interviewers' personal safety. Finally, interviewers are able to gather information from respondents who have difficulty with reading and/or writing.

Not surprisingly, however, there are trade-offs. First, social workers are often interested in gathering data from low-income persons, who are much less likely than the general population to have a telephone. Thus low-income people may be underrepresented or systematically excluded from telephone surveys. Second, telephone surveys often must be limited to very simple questions. Complex or detailed questions can be difficult to convey over the phone. In addition, telephone interviews don't let interviewers observe nonverbal reactions to questions. Despite these limitations, telephone surveys can be useful and efficient.

What are some of the procedures to follow in a telephone survey? If the Mt. Washington staff want to conduct a communitywide needs assessment, they would first have to design the data collection instrument. The procedures would be virtually identical to those for any interview or questionnaire, although, as I noted, telephone questions may need to be especially short and simple, and the interviewer will not be able to show the respondents any lists, charts, and the like.

Next, the Mt. Washington staff member in charge must train telephone interviewers. It's important to pay attention to things like telephone etiquette and style, voice quality, and what to do if a respondent threatens to terminate the interview or expresses anxiety about some aspect of it.

Finally, the staff must make up a list of telephone numbers and conduct the actual interviews. As I'm sure you realize, there's no such thing as a master list of telephone numbers for all Mt. Washington residents. The staff must be more creative. The telephone book won't help much, since listings aren't organized by neighborhood. In addition, an increasing number of people have unlisted telephone numbers.

The most common strategy used is a technique known as *random digit dialing*. Telephone companies ordinarily use specific three-digit prefixes in certain geographical areas or neighborhoods. For instance, the prefixes 723, 726, 727, and 729 are used exclusively in the Mt. Washington area. Tables of random numbers or computer programs can then be used to generate the last four digits. This technique is often used to produce a representative sample in a geographical area (at least of those who have telephones). Of course, a disadvantage of this approach is that you don't know who you're calling (which could be helpful if you're trying to assure respondents of their anonymity).

When the respondents agree to be interviewed, the staff ask the questions, recording the answers in writing or, when closed-ended questions are asked, merely checking the categories. Increasingly, social workers are using computer-assisted telephone interviewing, in which the questions appear directly on the interviewer's computer screen and the interviewer types in the responses. The advantage is that the data are recorded immediately. This avoids the steps—and occasional error—in transcribing the information for computer entry.

USING EXISTING DATA

Although social workers often need to use standardized instruments or design instruments to gather the original data, sometimes they may want or need to examine data gathered by someone else—that's called *secondary* (versus *original*) *data analysis*. Actually, social workers may be ecstatic when they discover that important data already exist.

You may be tempted to think that the hard part is over when you discover that data you want already exist somewhere. But that's not necessarily so. In fact, social workers must master several skills to make good, and appropriate, use of existing data.

In three main sets of circumstances, social workers can make valuable use of existing data. They may want to examine data that are (1) collected routinely by national, state, and local public and private agencies concerning various "quality of life" indicators; (2) drawn from case records in social workers' own agencies or in other agencies' records to which social workers have access; and (3) gathered by other researchers who make their "data sets" available to interested parties.

Many public agencies collect data of interest to social workers. The following are examples of federal agencies that produce data available to social workers (a good place to get an overview of available data and sources is the *Statistical Abstract of the United States*, published by the U.S. Commerce Department):

- Administration for Children, Youth, and Families: foster care, adoption, day care, and programs for children with special needs.
- Administration on Aging: the status of older Americans and programs designed to address their needs.
- Agency for International Development: poverty, social welfare needs, and relief efforts in other nations.
- Bureau of Indian Affairs: the welfare and status of Native Americans and programs designed to address their needs.
- Bureau of Justice Statistics: crime and criminal justice (for example, police, courts, correctional programs).
- Bureau of Labor Statistics: wages, consumer prices, employment patterns, and unemployment rates.
- Centers for Disease Control: the prevalence, causes, and treatment of various diseases (for example, various forms of cancer, HIV/AIDS).
- Congressional Budget Office: the federal budget and federal spending and revenue.
- Developmental Disabilities Administration: the prevalence, prevention, and treatment of such disabilities as autism, cerebral palsy, mental retardation, and seizure disorders.
- Health Care Financing Administration: national health programs and financing (for example, Medicare, Medicaid).
- National Center on Child Abuse and Neglect: the magnitude of child abuse and neglect and efforts to address these problems.
- National Center for Health Statistics Research: the quality of Americans' health, the magnitude of health-related problems, and efforts to address them.
- National Institute of Corrections: U.S. jails and prisons, sentencing patterns, probation, and parole.
- National Institute of Mental Health: various aspects of mental health and mental illness.
- National Institutes of Health: a wide range of health-related issues.
- Office of Juvenile Justice and Delinquency Prevention: juvenile offenders and programs designed to address juvenile delinquency.
- Office of Management and Budget: the federal budget and federal spending and revenue.
- U.S. Census Bureau: a wide range of topics, such as poverty and income, family status and household composition, marriage and divorce, geographical mobility, and housing conditions.
- U.S. Department of Health and Human Services: such diverse human service issues as aging, child abuse and neglect, health care (Medicare and Medicaid), and disability.
- U.S. Department of Housing and Urban Development: all aspects of

housing, including low-income housing, homelessness, mortgage sub-sidy programs, home building, and public housing.
- U.S. Department of Labor: employment and unemployment, job-training and vocational programs, working conditions and job safety (occupational safety), and employee benefits.
- Veterans Administration: the status of and problems facing veterans.

In addition, many state and local agencies also routinely collect data that social workers can access. For instance, states typically have an agency or office with a title like Division of Planning or Department of Planning, whose func-tion is to gather data on important aspects of the state's population, programs, services, and so on. This office may gather information on, for example, statewide housing and health-care needs for low-income people, schools and educational services, job creation and loss in the state's economy, infant mor-tality, or causes of death. The data's primary purpose may be to inform public agencies, legislatures, and officials whose jobs address these problems. Such data are usually made available to members of the public, including social workers.

Social workers should be aware, as well, of various municipal agencies that may have useful data. For example, social workers interested in the effective-ness of local crime prevention efforts can ask their local police department for data on arrests for a certain period of time. Social workers interested in the incidence of lead poisoning in certain neighborhoods can ask their local health department for data on reported cases. Social workers interested in how many low-income people are being evicted from the apartments for nonpayment of rent should contact their local housing office or housing court.

Social workers should also know about those private agencies and organi-zations—both national and local—that may have useful data. For example, social workers interested in changes in employment patterns in the profession can contact the National Association of Social Workers for the data that it col-lects from its members. Social workers interested in social work education can contact the Council on Social Work Education. Those interested in child wel-fare, for example, related to childhood poverty, abuse and neglect, and pro-grams for children with special needs, may contact the Child Welfare League of America or the Children's Defense Fund. Social workers interested in data on criminal justice issues or programs available for inmates released from pris-ons may contact organizations such as the National Council on Crime and Delinquency and the American Correctional Association. People interested in the elderly may obtain useful information from their local agencies on aging. The American Hospital Association may have useful data on hospital and health-related issues. In addition, it's often a good idea to contact the local

United Way agency. Many of these offices, particularly the larger ones, have access to data on a wide range of human and social service issues.

CASE ILLUSTRATIONS

Let's look now at the ways in which an agency such as the Mt. Washington Family Service Agency might use data collected by other agencies. There are many reasons that Mt. Washington's social workers may find it useful to examine data that have been collected elsewhere. Here are some illustrations:

> The state health department recently issued an "RFP" (request for proposal) inviting area agencies to apply for funds to study lead poisoning in the Mt. Washington and surrounding communities. The program's objectives are to identify children who have been poisoned by lead (lead screening), educate parents and caretakers about the risks of lead poisoning (the ways in which children's development can be affected by lead), provide temporary housing for families whose apartments are being treated for lead poisoning, and develop a strategy for working with landlords to eliminate lead from their housing units.
>
> To apply for these funds, the Mt. Washington staff need to put together a comprehensive grant application. In addition to describing how the agency would meet the program's objectives, they must include data estimating the magnitude of the problem. This means that the Mt. Washington staff will have to find existing or secondary data on area children's exposure to lead, the number of housing units with documented lead problems, and complaints filed against landlords.
>
> Not all the data that Mt. Washington staff need may exist. But some may be available. Where should staff members go to find out whether such information exists? My guess is that they should start with agencies such as the state and local (city or county) health departments and the state and local housing offices. In addition, it may be wise to contact area hospitals and neighborhood health clinics or the statewide association of hospitals and health care agencies.

* * *

Lisa C., a clinical social worker at Mt. Washington, has expertise in clinical issues of gays and lesbians. The Mt. Washington neighborhood is known to have a large gay and lesbian population. Over time, Lisa C. has worked with a number of clients who have been abused by their gay or lesbian partners or have been victims of "hate crimes" in the community. In Lisa C.'s judgment, these problems have been neglected. Although the public is generally aware of domestic violence in heterosexual couples, they have little awareness of domestic violence in gay and lesbian relationships. In addition, the public is generally unaware of hate crimes against gays and lesbians.

To remedy these issues, Lisa C. decides to apply to a prominent local foundation for funds to hire and train an outreach worker whose job would be creating a public awareness campaign in the local community, publicizing the availability of clinical services at Mt. Washington, and making contact with victims of domestic violence and hate crimes.

To submit a compelling application to the foundation, Lisa C. knows that she needs data on the magnitude of the problem. The chances are that no comprehensive data are available. But Lisa C. figures that the city's police department may have some data on hate crimes and domestic violence. Although the police reports may not specify the victims' sexual orientation, some of the information could be used to support the grant application.

* * *

Leah S., the administrator of Mt. Washington's substance abuse program, is interested in strengthening the agency's presence in neighborhood schools. Ideally, Mt. Washington would sign a contract with the local school department to provide substance abuse prevention and counseling services in the community's two grade schools, middle school, and high school.

Leah S. recently became aware of federal and state funds that the local school department can use for this very purpose. To apply for these funds, Leah S. needs to submit an application giving Mt. Washington's estimates of the extent of the substance abuse problems in each of the community's schools, the agency's plan to address the problem in each school, specific outcome measures, and plans to evaluate the effectiveness of the approach.

Where would Leah S. find information about the magnitude of the substance abuse problem in Mt. Washington's schools? Unfortunately, and typically, there may be no data pertaining specifically to the Mt. Washington area schools. If there are, it's a fortuitous, and unusual, circumstance. Rather, Leah S. may have to piece together data as best she can. Although it would be great if she could gather original data herself, she doesn't have the time or money for such an ambitious project.

If I were Leah S., I would probably go to the state and local health departments to see whether they had any data on substance abuse problems in the neighborhood schools. If these agencies don't, which is likely, I would ask whether they have data on substance abuse among similarly aged children from similar neighborhoods and socioeconomic circumstances. Although this kind of indirect measure is not ideal, it may be the best data available.

Now let's consider a different set of circumstances in which the Mt. Washington staff need to explore existing and secondary data. Because Mt. Washington is a prominent provider of services to children, it was asked to serve in an advisory capacity with the KIDS COUNT project. KIDS COUNT is a national and state-by-state project designed to assess and monitor the status of children in the United States. Every state in the nation is participating. The project is funded nationally by the Annie E. Casey Foundation, with additional support in each state provided by local sources (local foundations, for example).

Each year, local KIDS COUNT projects produce a "factbook" summarizing important statistical information about children. The goal is to provide important data to individuals and groups addressing children's needs. This information might be used for planning purposes, policy formulation, academic research, or, as in Mt. Washington's case, grant applications.

The *KIDS COUNT Factbook* is one of the best examples I have seen in the human services of the systematic use of existing and secondary data. For this discussion, therefore, I will describe the production of the Rhode Island *KIDS COUNT Factbook*.

The *KIDS COUNT Factbook* summarizes the data on twenty-three different quality-of-life indicators related to children and organizes them into five major categories: Family and Community, Economic Well-Being, Health, Safety, and Education. For example, under Family and Community, the book summarizes data concerning children in single-parent families, children in poverty, children receiving public assistance, and housing costs. Under Health, the book summarizes data concerning prenatal care, low-birth-weight infants, infant mortality, births to teens, children receiving school breakfasts, children with lead poisoning, and children without health insurance. Under Safety, the book summarizes data concerning child deaths, children referred to family court, and child abuse and neglect. Under Education, the book summarizes data on child care, children enrolled in the Head Start program, reading achievement, high school graduation rates, and teens not in school or working.

For each indicator, the KIDS COUNT staff gathered secondary or existing data from a wide range of national and local agencies and presented them in summary form (using easy-to-read tables and charts). Along with the data, the book offers a brief overview of key statistics and findings.

Many of the statistics presented in the *KIDS COUNT Factbook* were obtained from the U.S. Bureau of the Census (such as children living in single-parent families, household income, children in poverty, teens not in school or working). Other statistics were obtained from various state and local agencies, such as the Rhode Island Department of Human Services (children receiving public assistance, children without health insurance); the Rhode Island Department of Health (prenatal care, low-birth-weight infants, infant mortality, births to teens, children with lead poisoning, child and teen deaths); the Rhode Island Department of Elementary and Secondary Education (children receiving school breakfasts, reading achievement, high school graduation rate); the National Council on Crime and Delinquency, the Children's Defense Fund, and the U.S. Department of Justice (youths referred to family court); the American Bar Association Center on Children and the Law, the National Health and Education Consortium, and the Rhode Island Department of Children, Youth and Families (child abuse and neglect); the Greater Providence (Rhode Island) Chamber of Commerce (child care); and the Rhode Island Head Start Programs (children enrolled in Head Start).

As you can see, this is an impressive undertaking, a wonderful example of how existing and secondary data can be gathered and presented in a clear and organized way for use by many different people and organizations.

USING DATA FROM CASE RECORDS

Sometimes social workers have access to valuable data right under their noses—in their own case records. Some evaluation and research questions require the close examination of existing information about clients and the services provided to them. In these instances, social workers need to know how to make full use of this information.

For example, the Mt. Washington staff can use the information in their files to help them better understand the extent to which the agency has been providing services to people of color. Although staff have anecdotal information, they have never looked systematically at the data.

To remedy this, the agency's director met with Emma R., a social work graduate student completing her field placement in the agency, to work out a data collection plan. Emma R. had just finished a course on social work evaluation and research methods and was eager to apply what she had just learned (now that's the kind of enthusiasm I like).

This is how Emma R. approached the task: First, she made sure she understood exactly what questions that her supervisor, the agency director, wanted answered. The questions are (1) At present, what percentage of our clients are people of color and/or ethnic minorities? (2) How does this percentage compare with the percentage from two years ago? Four years ago? (3) What services are people of color and/or ethnic minorities receiving, which of the agency's programs are they enrolled in, and how do these data compare with similar data for the agency's other clients? (4) What percentage of clients who are people of color and/or ethnic minorities terminate services prematurely? How does this percentage compare with similar data for the agency's other clients?

Fortunately, these data are already in Mt. Washington's files. The agency's intake form includes information about race and ethnicity, so Emma R. simply needs to summarize it. In addition, each case record contains a "case closing" summary, in which workers describe the circumstances under which the services were terminated, that is, whether they were terminated as planned, the client "disappeared," or the agency terminated services prematurely for other reasons (such as the client's noncompliance with treatment or nonpayment of their bills). Emma R. must figure out how to extract this information.

The second thing Emma R. must do is decide whether to search every file from the past four years or draw a sample of files. Ideally, Mt. Washington would have this information on computer, and Emma R. would simply ask the agency's management information specialist to print out the data. Unfortunately, the agency did not begin until recently to put this information on computer, so much of it must be pulled by hand from the case files.

If Mt. Washington were a relatively small agency, it might make sense for Emma R. to review each file. For example, if the agency typically opened two or three new cases per week, she could use the "population" of cases rather than a sample. Although this would be time-consuming, it might be manageable. However, given the large number of new cases Mt. Washington opens each week (usually between ten and fifteen), Emma R. will need to sample the cases.

You may want to take a moment to think about how Emma R. should sample the case records. There will be three relevant time periods: four years ago (Time 1), two years ago (Time 2), and the past year (Time 3).

One possibility is to draw a random sample from each of the three time periods. During Time 1, the agency opened 612 new cases; during Time 2, 593 new cases; and during Time 3, 627 new cases. Emma R. figures that given the time available in her schedule, the amount of clerical help the agency can provide, and the time it will take to record the information from each case record, a sample of 150 cases from each time period is practical.

To draw these cases randomly, Emma R. simply divides the number of new cases for the relevant time period by 150 to determine the skip interval (that is, to determine what k will be if Emma R. selects one of every kth case). So for Time 1, Emma R. samples one of every four cases, or about a 25 percent sample (612 divided by 150 equals 4.08). The skip interval for the other two time periods is the same, since both 593 divided by 150 and 627 divided by 150 are fairly close to 4.

Another way to obtain a 25 percent sample would be to select those cases opened during three different months of the year (3 of 12 months also equals

25 percent). If I were sampling in this way, I would select 3 months from very different times of the year (say January, May, and October) in order to minimize the influence of seasonal bias.

My guess is that the results of these two sampling approaches would not be significantly different, but it's hard to say for sure. If I had a choice, I'd probably go with the random sampling of every fourth case, which would ensure a spread of cases opened throughout the year.

The next task would be to develop a coding sheet for each case. On the coding sheet, I would list each piece of information I wanted to record, along with the relevant categories. Then I would include the following: (1) case identification number, (2) date that case opened, (3) date that case closed, (4) race/ethnicity, (5) services received/programs enrolled in (the categories would correspond to the agency's formal list of services and programs), and (6) service termination (the categories would indicate whether services were terminated according to plan, the client "disappeared" without completing services, or services were terminated prematurely for other reasons, such as the client's noncompliance or nonpayment of bills).

Emma R. and her assistants would collect this information for each of the cases opened during the three time periods. (Emma R. should limit her data collection to cases that have closed, since one of the variables she wants to examine is the circumstances surrounding the cases' closure.) Emma R. would then collate all this information and analyze it using one of the techniques we will discuss in chapter 11.

Now let's look at a project that would require the Mt. Washington staff to gather information from another agency's records. Alvan K. received a grant from a local foundation to expand his domestic violence counseling program. All the referrals for this program come from the county probation office. The clients are men who have been arrested for domestic violence and who are considered to be good candidates for rehabilitation. In these cases, the judges have agreed to place the men on probation, with mandatory participation in the Mt. Washington program in lieu of a jail or prison sentence.

As a condition of the grant, Alvan K. had to formulate a plan to monitor the clients over time, particularly with respect to their subsequent arrest records. Because the courts had many more potential participants to refer to the Mt. Washington program than the program could accommodate, the referring judges agreed to randomly assign eligible participants, to enable a formal evaluation of the program's effectiveness. These sorts of circumstances—when random assignment is possible—are rare, so all the parties involved agreed to cooperate with the evaluation design.

The plan was for Alvan K. to examine subsequent arrest records to determine the recidivism rate, for both the program's clients and a comparison group of men who were deemed eligible for Alvan K.'s program but were not selected for it because of the randomization procedure. The comparison group would receive the sanctions or services ordinarily imposed by the court (ordinary probation, etc.). One year after the termination of services for each client, Alvan K. plans to examine police department records in the city and county where Mt. Washington is located, to gather arrest data for each man. To gather these data, Alvan K. must negotiate agreements with police officials in each of the relevant police departments. With the court's help, however, this may not be too difficult. Alvan K. can then find the arrest data for each man in the sample.

If I were doing this, I would probably search the police departments' records for arrests primarily related to domestic violence. Relevant charges include domestic assault, assault with a deadly weapon, assault and battery, and violation of a restraining or no-contact order. By reading the police reports, Alvan K. could determine whether the arrest pertained to a domestic violence incident of the sort addressed in his counseling program.

If I had the time, I might also look at arrests for other offenses. For example, one of the things we know very well is that many men committing domestic violence also have substance abuse problems, and part of Alvan K.'s program deals with substance abuse issues. Hence an individual's arrest record may show his involvement in crimes that do not entail domestic violence but are related to substance abuse problems. Examples are driving an automobile while under the influence, possession and/or sale of illegal substances, and breaking and entering (to steal goods that can be fenced for money to buy drugs).

Of course, relying exclusively on arrest records has limitations. The main problem is that police records tell us only about those instances in which the men were "caught," so to speak (assuming that they were in fact guilty). But what about all those domestic violence–related incidents never brought to the police department's attention? We know there are many. Victims may fear retribution by the perpetrator or may want to avoid getting involved further with the criminal justice system. Whatever the reason, we know that only a fraction of domestic violence incidents come to the attention of the police. As a result, police records may give us only a partial picture of the extent of the problem. However, if time and money aren't available to conduct extensive interviews with clients and their partners (which would have their own measurement problems), Alvan K. must live with these limitations. Although the information may not be ideal, it's still valuable.

Practically speaking, Alvan K. would need to develop a coding form on which for each man in his sample he would record whether the man had been arrested during the one-year follow-up period and the particular offense. A list of relevant offense categories would be worked out ahead of time so that Alvan K. or one of his assistants would simply have to check the appropriate box. Once the data were collected, Alvan K. would analyze them using some of the data analysis techniques described in chapter 11.

USING EXISTING DATA SETS

Occasionally social workers find it useful or necessary to analyze data collected by some other person or agency. This is more than simply summarizing information collected by others, as I have explained. Rather, it entails actually analyzing someone else's data set. You are more likely to have to do this in academic settings than in practice settings, although there are exceptions.

For example, as I mentioned earlier, my wife does research on adoption. She recently learned of a major survey of adoptive parents conducted by colleagues at another university. That survey included a number of questions of particular interest to her. In principle, my wife could contact those colleagues and ask them to send her a copy of the data set so that she could analyze the data to explore issues that didn't especially interest the study's principal investigators. Sometimes agencies that fund research require that the principal investigators make the data set available to other researchers after the principal investigators have had ample opportunity to analyze the data themselves. In fact, many archives house data sets that are available to social work researchers and others, related, for example, to child welfare, mental health, public health, criminal justice, poverty, housing, aging, and substance abuse. Reference librarians and staff at major research centers can be helpful if you want lists of available data sets.

METHODOLOGICAL ISSUES

Even though reporting and analyzing existing or secondary data can be useful, social workers need to be aware of some of the methodological issues and limitations.

Defining Variables

Just as when collecting original data, social workers who rely on existing data also need to define the variables precisely. If Alvan K. records arrests for "incidents of domestic violence," he needs to specify what constitutes such an incident. Should he limit himself to only an actual charge of "domestic violence," or should he include other charges that may not specify domestic violence but nonetheless involve it, such as assault and battery or violation of a restraining or no contact order?

In the project collecting data on Mt. Washington clients who are people of color and/or ethnic minorities, Emma R. needs to define precisely what she means by such terms as *person of color, ethnic minority*, and *termination of service*. Vague or ambiguous definitions can seriously compromise a project's results.

Validity and Reliability

Now we return to the subjects of validity and reliability. In Alvan K.'s case, what kind of validity does he need to be concerned about? First, Alvan K. needs to be concerned about the internal validity of his design. If he compares the recidivism rates of participants in his domestic violence program with those of men handled in more routine ways by the courts, he will need to ensure that differences in subsequent arrest rates aren't simply caused by the initial differences between the two groups. This is the same idea I discussed in chapter 3 concerning the extent to which various evaluation and research designs control for extraneous factors. If Alvan K. can actually use randomization procedures to determine which men end up in his program and which are handled in more routine ways by the courts, the chances are that he will have controlled for extraneous factors effectively. Otherwise, he would have to produce a matched sample to ensure comparability between the groups, which is not a simple task.

Alvan K. is not done with validity, however. What other types of validity are relevant? Perhaps the most important are face and content validity. Recall that face validity reflects how well a measurement measures what we think it measures (sort of a commonsense belief that the measure is appropriate to our aims) and that content validity reflects how well the indicators selected represent the range of possible indicators. So, when Alvan K. defines domestic violence and translates that definition into specific empirical indicators (such as arrests for domestic assault, assault of a spouse or partner with a deadly weapon, violation of a restraining or no-contact order), these empirical indicators must have demonstrated face and content validity. That is, these criminal charges should have some obvious connection to domestic violence and should be representative of the relevant charges.

The reliability of these data is a different matter. The aspect of reliability with which we need to be especially concerned is equivalence and interrater reliability. That is, when social workers examine existing data, they often must interpret and code or classify the information they find. Because of the subjective judgment this often entails, social workers must try to enhance the data's reliability. We need to be reasonably confident that different people examining the same data would interpret and code or classify them similarly. Alvan K. shouldn't have to be concerned about whether either he or one of his assistants examines the arrest records for a particular program participant but should have some assurance that they would interpret the data in the same way. Similarly, Emma R. shouldn't worry about which staff member codes information from case records concerning why clients' services were terminated.

The best way to enhance reliability is to construct precise empirical indicators and operational definitions so that subjective judgment is minimized. This isn't always easy, but it's the ideal. Any staff in the data collection process should be trained thoroughly to enhance consistency. During the training, they should be given a range of examples, especially "gray area" examples, to reach a consensus on how to interpret and code the information.

Another method is to have several different staff or "raters" code information from a subsample of records. The principal investigator can then evaluate the staff's coding to determine its consistency or inconsistency. This can be time-consuming, but if there are reliability problems, the principal investigator should know about them. Time invested at the front end of a project can help avoid enormous problems later on.

Sampling Records

Social workers usually associate sampling with the selection of real live people for interviews, observation, and self-administered questionnaires. The principles we reviewed in chapter 5 related to probability and nonprobability sampling also pertain to the use of existing or secondary data. For example, Alvan K. needs to understand probability sampling in order to know how to select a representative collection of case records from six years ago, four years ago, and the past year. In principle, Alvan K. could also use stratified random sampling procedures if he wanted to compare the recidivism rates for certain subgroups of clients and discovered that certain subgroups have to be oversampled to generate enough cases for analysis. In both instances, Alvan K. must know how to select case records randomly using a table of random numbers, lottery, or some other accepted technique.

Alvan K. could also use the nonprobability sampling technique known as purposive sampling. He may want to look at the case records of a handpicked sample of former clients with unique and important characteristics. For instance, Alvan K. may want to examine a small group of men in the domestic violence program who also have serious psychiatric problems. Or he may want to focus on men from a particular ethnic group whose culture is somewhat accepting of domestic violence.

Recording Data

When taking data from case records, as opposed to analyzing data already aggregated by another person or a public or private agency, it's useful to develop some kind of data-recording instrument. Often this isn't more complicated than a sheet of paper (or several sheets of paper). There's no precise format. All you have to do is figure out what you want to collect and write down the items and various response or coding categories on the form. It's particularly important that the format be clear when you rely on other people to record some of or all the data. You don't want people guessing about how to code the information or interpret the various categories.

Alvan K., for example, might construct a very simple form that includes the following information:

1. Name _____
2. Date of birth _____
3. Date that participation in program was completed _____
4. Total number of arrests during year following termination of services
   _____
5. Number of arrests for offenses involving domestic violence
   _____
6. Narrative description of each arrest involving domestic violence (description of parties in and circumstances of the incident, sequence of events)
   _____
   _____
   _____
   _____
   _____

The staff members responsible for recording this information on the form must be instructed what constitutes "offenses involving domestic violence." Alvan K. would have to provide a precise definition and give the data collection staff some practice cases to ensure consistency among them (reliability).

LIMITATIONS

Social workers should be aware of several limitations that are often, although not always, associated with the use of existing or secondary data. One potential problem is that the data aren't of uniformly high quality. Since the social worker using the data was not involved in its original collection, there's no way to know about the quality control. How well were the data collection staff trained? How much attention did the principal investigator pay to reliability? How much latitude did the staff have in interpreting the data? How much error do the data contain? Were the data recorded sloppily?

If you're using data collected by agencies such as the U.S. Census Bureau or the Department of Labor, you can be reasonably sure that the data are of high quality. Most federal agencies are very sophisticated in their collection of data and pay close attention to issues of validity and reliability. The same is true of many state, county, and city agencies, although I tend to find less methodological sophistication at these levels. In my experience, problems with poor quality data tend to be more prevalent when the data were collected by social service agencies whose staff don't have much research and evaluation expertise. Fortunately, your taking a course on research and evaluation and reading this book will help resolve that problem.

Unfortunately, social workers who rely on existing or secondary data can do little about the data's limitations. One problem is that the original data collectors may not mention—or even be aware of—these limitations, and hence those later using this information won't know about them either. Of course, if those using these data discover the limitations, they must decide whether the limitations are so great that they devalue the information or whether the limitations aren't great enough to detract from the data's overall value.

Reports that use existing or secondary data often contain a brief and candid statement about limitations, so that the readers can decide for themselves how important they are. Here's an example of a statement that appears in the KIDS COUNT report I mentioned earlier, which depends entirely on existing and secondary data obtained from public and private agencies:

> In any data collection process, there are always concerns about the accuracy and completeness of the data being collected. All data used in the 23 indicators were collected through the U.S. Bureau of the Census and through routine data collection systems operated by different agencies of the state of Rhode Island. We do not have estimates of the completeness of reporting to these systems. In all cases, we used the most reliable data currently available.

QUALITATIVE EVALUATION AND RESEARCH

In recent years, social workers have come to appreciate the ways in which qualitative evaluation and research methods can help their practice. Qualitative evaluation and research "produces descriptive data based upon spoken or written words and observable behavior" (Sherman and Reid 1994:1). In contrast, quantitative evaluation and research refer to numerical measurement (or quantification) of the phenomena of interest to social workers (for example, numerical measurement of clients' self-esteem, level of functioning, substance abuse problems, measurement of organizational functioning or community dynamics).

Social workers' interest in qualitative methods has increased for two reasons. First, social work scholars have begun exploring in more depth the ways in which qualitative methods can strengthen the profession's grasp of social problems and intervention approaches. Second, social workers have become more aware of quantitative methods' shortcomings. In particular, they have begun to appreciate that even though quantitative data—collected via various standardized and unstandardized questionnaires, surveys, and interview instruments—can provide valuable information, numerical summaries don't always capture important aspects of the phenomena being measured.

Social workers have become especially interested in understanding more about the subjective experience and interpretations of clients, colleagues, and members of the public. Over time it has become clearer to us that "objective" measurement using quantifiable means is rather illusory. Although there is certainly a place for quantification—when the things we measure are added, totaled, divided, or placed on scales, for example—there also is an important place in social work evaluation and research for qualitative methods.

For example, Alvan K. may find it useful to gather quantitative information about the men in his domestic violence program. I can understand why he would want to have the participants complete standardized instruments that would yield quantitative data pertaining to aggression, self-esteem, relationships with partners, and so on. At the same time, I can see the value of using qualitative methods to assess the men and describe their behaviors during the group meetings.

Similarly, the social worker who is spending time with Toby and his mom in an effort to improve Toby's behavior in school may want to rely to some extent on the quantifiable results of standardized instruments designed to measure children's behaviors and relationships with peers. However, this information might be supplemented in useful ways with qualitative reports or narratives of Toby's behavior during various classroom periods.

I also understand why the Mt. Washington staff may want to quantify the attitudes and opinions concerning the agency expressed by neighborhood residents who are people of color. Quantifiable information obtained from a representative sample of community residents may provide invaluable data. At the same time, it may be useful to gather qualitative data from participants in a "focus group" discussion of the issues or to observe the lifestyles of people of color and ethnic minorities in the Mt. Washington neighborhood (for example, where people tend to congregate and socialize) and how these patterns differ from those of the majority of Mt. Washington's clients. This information may offer valuable clues to how the agency might aid people of color and ethnic minorities in the area.

One major point, then, is that social workers don't need to choose between quantitative and qualitative methodology. Although sometimes it makes sense to use only one or the other method, more often than not the combined use of quantitative and qualitative methods produces the best understanding of the phenomena of interest to social workers. The two approaches can complement and supplement each other.

Qualitative evaluation and research is often associated with ethnographic methods. The term *ethnography* comes from anthropology and ordinarily refers to the study of a community or culture by immersing oneself in such settings, participating in the community's or culture's life, and observing it. Cultural anthropologists, and now some social workers, refer to these activities as *field research*.

Social workers doing ethnographic evaluation and research may have different agendas. One aim may be to find important patterns of behavior and interaction in a group of people, for example, residents in a group home, agency board members during regularly scheduled meetings, or tenants living in a low-income housing development. Or social workers may use these techniques to describe and evaluate their work with one client—an in-depth case study. Another aim may be to summarize people's views on an important issue or interpretations of a significant event, for example, the death of a client in a residential program or the sudden resignation of a number of key staff.

Ethnography, or what is sometimes called *naturalistic observation*, essentially is careful, systematic observation of people's verbal and nonverbal behaviors, styles of interaction, group norms, and understanding and interpretations of the events and circumstances surrounding them. Social workers who use this approach collect their data by recording what they see and hear. The qualitative data may include quotations from and summaries of people's interactions, behaviors, and views, or data obtained from clients or others in the form of first-person narratives (for example, a client's detailed summary of her life or a portion of it) or logs (for example, detailed descriptions of a special event or set of circumstances). The social worker may function as an outside observer or may actually participate in the life of the community, group, or organization being studied. Data may be gathered via direct observation, interviews with individuals or groups of people, or participation in focus groups formed to discuss specific issues.

What ethnographic methods do you think the Mt. Washington staff could use to gather information about the underutilization of the agency by people of color and ethnic minorities? Several occur to me. First, staff members might form focus groups of community residents to talk about their perceptions of the agency, the reasons that people of color and ethnic minorities do or don't use the agency for services, and the ways in which Mt. Washington might attract people of color and ethnic minorities. The staff could use ethnographic methods to summarize and characterize the participants' perceptions.

Second, the Mt. Washington staff could use ethnographic methods to observe behavioral patterns in the surrounding community and norms regarding social contact, specifically how social interaction and exchange is segregated. Evidence of significant segregation, if it exists, may help the staff understand why people of color and ethnic minorities avoid the agency, particularly if it is perceived by many to be a "white" agency.

Finally, ethnographic methods may be used to conduct interviews with local residents, known in ethnographic jargon as *informants*, to explore their own views and opinions concerning Mt. Washington, its mission, ways to expand its delivery of services to people of color and ethnic minorities, and, in particular, what life is like in the Mt. Washington area for a person of color or an ethnic minority. These interviews are different from formal research interviews and clinical interviews. In ethnographic interviews, the informant is regarded as the "expert" with important views to convey. The interviewer is more passive than in formal research and clinical interviews, thereby providing as much room as possible for informants to offer their opinions. Sometimes interviews with informants are relatively formal and structured, and sometimes they are relatively open-ended. In all cases, whether using formal or informal question guides, social workers using ethnographic methods should know exactly where they are going and why.

Social workers, especially clinical social workers, may also use narrative methods to gather information (Laird 1993). A *narrative* is a personal history or "story" told to a social worker by a client or some other party. Narratives, in which people describe their lives in their own terms, can be used as a therapeutic tool or as data for oral history. A Mt. Washington clinical social worker who provides family therapy might use the narrative method to encourage each member to convey his or her life story in the context of the family or to describe the "family's" story from different perspectives. This approach could also be used by a Mt. Washington social worker who is interested in developing services for gays and lesbians who are victims of domestic violence. As a prelude to developing a program, and then later as part of the program, gays and lesbians who have been battered could be given an opportunity to tell their stories and to describe their experiences from their own point of view.

As you might imagine, qualitative methods use some of the same principles as quantitative methods do, although the application may differ. It's not unusual, for example, for qualitative evaluation and research to use sampling procedures and issues. After all, as in quantitative evaluation and research, social workers conducting qualitative evaluation and research sometimes find that they have to limit the number of people, settings, or circumstances they can observe, interview, or participate in. Consequently, they may need to apply probability or nonprobability sampling procedures (purposive sampling is commonly used, in which persons, organizations, communities, or events may be handpicked because of the valuable information they are likely to yield). The choice of sampling procedure, of course, affects the generalizability of the results. For example, a Mt. Washington social worker may use purposive sampling and qualitative methods to evaluate the effectiveness of her work with a particular client who has a serious eating disorder. The data may provide a detailed picture of the client's progress, but the results may not be generalizable. In a sense, this approach would constitute a case study—a valuable case study, but a case study with limited generalizability, nonetheless.

The collection of qualitative data may be somewhat less formal than typically found in quantitative evaluation and research. Instead of using structured interview forms, checklists, and answer sheets, social workers in qualitative evaluation or research may record data using a tape recorder (with the appropriate permission obtained) or a pad of paper on which they scribble notes, observations, and quotations.

The analysis of qualitative data poses a special challenge, which we will discuss in chapter 11.

PROGRAM EVALUATION

Because social work is a profession, its practitioners tend to be more interested in research that has practical relevance than research that has more abstract goals, for example, hypothesis testing or theory development. The former type of research is often called *applied research*, and the latter is often called *basic or pure research.*

Applied research in social work usually focuses on clinical work, needs assessments, or program evaluations. In this chapter, I describe program evaluations, a topic that has grown in importance for several reasons. First, funding agencies are increasingly insisting that social service agencies document the effectiveness of services paid with grant or contract funds. Once upon a time, funding agencies—both government agencies and private foundations—expected little in the way of program evaluation. In this era of accountability, however, funding agencies want to know more and more about what's being done with their money, and that's understandable.

Second, social workers have become more knowledgeable about program evaluation tools and techniques. As a result, and apart from their accountability to outside parties, social workers have become more interested in documenting program effectiveness for their own personal knowledge and practice competence.

Third, along with their better grasp of program evaluation designs and methodology, social workers have become more interested in contributing to the professional literature and making presentations at professional conferences. As a profession we've become more dedicated to disseminating knowledge about what works and doesn't work. We're not nearly so willing as we once were to accept at face value that our efforts are useful and effective. We now recognize that our good intentions don't always produce intended outcomes.

In general, program evaluation is the application of research tools to determine how effective our efforts have been. Some program evaluations are carried out internally by the social service agencies themselves. These evaluations may be for internal use only (for example, for program-planning purposes), or the results may be prepared for submission to an outside funding or accreditation agency. Other program evaluations are conducted by outside parties. In some cases, a social service agency hires outside experts or consultants to conduct a program evaluation because the agency's staff don't have the time or technical expertise to do it. In other instances, a funding source (a government agency or a foundation, perhaps) has an independent evaluator assess a program that the funding source has supported. The funding source may choose an outside evaluator to obtain a more "objective" assessment.

In this chapter, I describe the evaluation of a Mt. Washington Family Service Agency program designed to strengthen families in which the children are at risk of being removed from the home or have been placed in foster care because of suspected abuse or neglect. The program is funded through the county department of social services. The overall goal is to enhance the likelihood that at-risk children living at home will be able to remain with their families of origin and that children living in foster care will be able to return to their families of origin or, if that's not a realistic option, to make a permanent plan for children (which may include adoption or, for older children, independent living).

According to the contract between the county and Mt. Washington, Mt. Washington is to use the funds to recruit, hire, and train social workers to provide intensive home-based services to meet the program's goals. As part of their training, staff members attend workshops on clinical interventions for work with high-risk, multiproblem families. The social workers in the program have relatively small caseloads, allowing them to spend a lot of time with the families with whom they work. In addition, the social workers are closely supervised by more experienced colleagues.

Understandably, the county officials overseeing the program, known as Families First, are interested in the program's effectiveness, and so they issued a request for proposal (RFP) inviting applications to evaluate the Families First program. County officials circulated a notice to human service research firms, colleges, and universities throughout the region and held one meeting at which they announced their expectations, funding for the evaluation, timetables, and application procedures.

Three organizations submitted proposals for the program evaluation, and staff from the county social services department reviewed the proposals. They used a checklist to assess the quality of each proposal, considering such things as the soundness and feasibility of the research design and data collection methods, the quality of the personnel involved, the timetable for the evaluation, the budget, and the reviewer's overall opinion of the proposal's quality. Each factor was assigned a certain number of points. The ratings from each of the four people on the selection team were added together, and the applicant with the highest point total was selected. In this instance, the grant was awarded to a faculty member at a local school of social work.

Now let's look at the key issues in a program evaluation.

PLANNING AN EVALUATION

To begin a program evaluation, social workers need to address four major issues.

1. *Who wants the evaluation and why?* It's important to know who wants the program evaluation and why. The case involving Mt. Washington is fairly typical: a funding agency wants to know how well its funds are being used. But not all program evaluations are this simple. For example, an influential politician may be skeptical of a particular program's effectiveness and so arranges to have it evaluated, with the aim of sabotaging or eliminating it. Although we would like to think that programs are evaluated for only noble reasons—to assess their effectiveness—some programs are evaluated for more sinister reasons or with ulterior motives.

Program evaluations also may be carried out or sponsored by people who don't have a significant investment in them. It's not unusual, for example, for the evaluation of programs funded by contracts or grants to be required. Some grants and contracts actually specify the percentage of the budget that must be spent on evaluating the program. Sometimes the officials sponsoring a program aren't interested in evaluating it. Either they're already convinced of the program's merits (or demerits) and don't care about the results of a formal evaluation, or they're skeptical of the value of formal research and evaluation. As a result, you may find them going through the motions to satisfy the contract or grant requirements, but without any interest in the quality of the evaluation.

In any case, you should find out who is requiring the program evaluation, the extent of their interest and investment in the process, and the ways in which they might use the results. This information can help you decide which people to involve in the evaluation, and in what ways, and which people to avoid. You should not be naive about the people's various agendas and motives in regard to program evaluations.

You also should identify the principal stakeholders, the people with a vested interest in the program evaluation. Typically they are agency administrators and staff. You may want to enlist their expertise concerning the program to be evaluated, as they may be a useful source of ideas about what ought to be evaluated and how the agency might cooperate in carrying out the evaluation (for example, explaining the evaluation to staff, providing access to data).

In addition, it's important that such stakeholders not be excluded from the process. What do you think the repercussions could be if you ignored or didn't pay sufficient attention to the people who cared most deeply about the program and its future? First, excluding stakeholders can lead to the results being ignored. Second, stakeholders can help you ask the right questions. Third, slighting the stakeholders could lead to their lack of cooperation and perhaps even hostility and sabotage. It's much wiser to cultivate good relationships with stakeholders, let them know you value what they have to offer, and enlist them as partners (sort of) in the program evaluation. I say "sort of" because it could be a mistake to have agency administrators and staff too involved in the process. That could make it difficult to include in your final report any constructively critical feedback and observations. Rather, it's best to include stakeholders in the planning and implementation of the evaluation in a way that doesn't reduce your objectivity and ability to provide candid feedback.

Fortunately, in Mt. Washington's case, the senior staff are quite enlightened and understand the need for independent or outside evaluation. Even though no administrator is eager for negative or critical feedback, Mt. Washington's executive director is not defensive and welcomes an "honest" evaluation in order to provide better service and use funds more effectively. But an administrator with a different personality or political agenda, focused mainly on his or her own career advancement, might handle the situation very differently. In that case, it's still important to use your engagement and collaboration skills to include the administrator in the process.

2. *What are the goals of the program evaluation?* Notice that I said the goals of the program evaluation, not the program itself. They are very different. Some program evaluations have relatively simple, straightforward goals: to determine the program's effectiveness and to obtain information about the program's operation (for example, staffing patterns, resource allocation, case assignment, supervision). Goals of this sort are sometimes known as *manifest goals*, the "official" goals announced publicly. In contrast, some program eval-

uations are designed to achieve *latent goals*, the goals pursued "beneath the surface" or "behind the scenes." Sometimes latent goals are part of some administrator's "hidden agenda" and thus aren't announced publicly. Nonetheless, latent goals can be as, if not more, influential than manifest goals.

What kinds of latent goals might we find in the evaluation of the Families First program? There might be some resentment in the county social services department that these social services were contracted out to a private agency instead of being handled in the department. Some staff may be angry that some jobs that could be under the control of the union for the county social services agency were "lost" to the private sector. Thus, one or more of the people helping select the outside evaluator may favor one of the applicants who is known to be very critical in his evaluations, hoping that his assessment will not be favorable to the Families First program.

3. *How will the results be used?* First, the results may be used only inside the agency, or internally. For example, if Mt. Washington administrators evaluate their substance abuse treatment program, they may want to learn only about which treatment approaches are most effective. This evaluation may not be required by any outside body. Rather, the agency may want it for the most noble of purposes: to learn more about the impact of their services and ways to improve them.

Second, the results may be used primarily by an outside entity. Funding bodies often insist that social service agencies collect evaluation data that the agency is not particularly interested in and would not collect otherwise. For example, a federal agency that is funding a particular program may also be funding similar programs around the nation and wants to collect large amounts of evaluation data. In chapter 9, I referred to a study in which just this sort of thing happened. Some years ago I was part of a study of juvenile offenders sponsored by the U.S. Department of Justice, which also was funding similar programs in other states. In each state, local public and private agencies collaborated to provide community-based services to juvenile offenders who otherwise would have been incarcerated in a locked facility. To receive the federal funds, the participating programs had to agree to collect large volumes of data on the services they provided and the populations they served. Some of the local program staff were not particularly interested in the data; rather, their main aim was to obtain federal funding for their program. They therefore cooperated with the data collection because it was the price they had to pay to receive the federal funds.

The third option is the instances when program evaluation results are used both internally and externally. The case we've been discussing, the evaluation of Mt. Washington's Families First program, is an example. On the one hand, the county social services department, which is funding the program, requires the evaluation and plans to use the data to monitor and assess the program's effectiveness. This seems reasonable and responsible. On the other hand, these data should be enormously useful to Mt. Washington staff, who may use the information to make changes in the program's design, intervention approach, staffing pattern, and so on.

Understanding which audiences are likely to use the data may affect the research design and data collection procedures. If the results will be used externally by other persons and organizations, you should take account of their needs and include questions and measures that will give them useful data. In addition, knowing how the information will be used may determine what kinds of data are collected and how questions are worded. You don't want to collect data in a way that is likely to undermine a program to which you are committed.

In contrast, if the program evaluation will be used internally, you should be aware that the staff may be worried about or threatened by the results. They may feel that their jobs, beliefs, or professional reputations are on the line, and this, too, may affect what concepts and issues are explored in the evaluation, how the items are worded, how the data are collected, and what sources are used.

4. *Who should design and carry out the evaluation?* This is a simple question with a complicated answer, one part of which concerns the staff's technical competence. Staff members who are responsible for carrying out and overseeing the program evaluation need to know something—actually a great deal— about research design and methodology, such as experimental and quasi-experimental designs, sampling, validity, reliability, instrument construction, data collection procedures, and data analysis. Staff members who don't know much about these areas (but who may think they do) can be nothing short of disastrous. Bad decisions made at the front end of a program evaluation—for example, related to sampling procedures or the wording or layout of items on a questionnaire—can come back to haunt the entire project. Often such mistakes can't be rectified and are fatal.

Ensuring that only competent staff with the requisite expertise evaluate a program is tricky. Because program evaluations are not always viewed as the most exciting thing to do (hard to imagine, isn't it?), some agencies assign those staff with the least experience and seniority.

In addition, it's important to think politically. If you want your staff to feel part of the program evaluation, it's usually wise to involve them in the planning stages, when design questions and overall goals are discussed. This can help engage the staff and help them feel that their knowledge and expertise are valued. If they feel snubbed and ignored, they may not go out of their way to be helpful and, in fact, may go out of their way to hinder the evaluation. As a general rule, be sure to include stakeholders in ways that recognize their knowledge and expertise and generate goodwill and support.

IDENTIFYING GOALS

Perhaps the most important step in program evaluations is identifying and clarifying goals. There are several ways to think about goals. First, social workers may be interested in information about various aspects of the program's design and the procedures used to deliver services, rather than information about actual program outcomes. Assessments that focus on program design features and procedures are *formative evaluations*.

Formative Evaluations

Formative evaluations explore what a program does, as opposed to what it accomplishes. The primary purpose of formative evaluations is to gather information that enables the staff to "stay on top of" what's going on in a program. Formative evaluation describes a program's actual operations. Sometimes I call this *temperature-taking evaluation* because the information helps social workers monitor the "health" of a program's approach.

For example, the formative evaluation of the Families First program may focus on a number of issues related to the way the program's services are delivered. Possibilities are the match between the clients' race/ethnicity and the social workers' race/ethnicity, the number and types of services the clients are receiving, length of service, cost of providing services, referral sources, and payment sources. Data from the formative evaluation may reveal, for example, a mismatch between the clients' race/ethnicity and the staff's race/ethnicity in a significant percentage of cases, which may encourage the program administrators to recruit new staff as quickly as possible. Or the formative evaluation may show that expected referral sources are not actually referring cases and that some services that administrators expected to be rather inexpensive to deliver are very costly, in part because clients are receiving more services and for longer periods of time than the staff had predicted. This information may lead staff to look more closely at the referral process and the service delivery. This emphasis on formative evaluation does not mean that measuring outcomes is not important; of course, it is. But it can be useful to supplement outcome measures, what's called a *summative evaluation*, with data from a formative evaluation.

I've just mentioned several issues that might be addressed in a formative evaluation of Mt. Washington's Families First program. There are many more. Let's pause for a moment to think about how a social worker might generate a list of issues for a formative evaluation.

My own inclination would be to go back to the steps I outlined for the construction of an interview instrument or questionnaire. The process is much the same. That is, we would begin with a list of major or broad topics, which in this case might be client characteristics, staffing patterns, the referral process, and services provided. Then we would decide on subtopics for each of these broader topics. For example, under client characteristics might be subtopics such as age, race/ethnicity, gender, family/marital status of parents/guardians, family functioning, children's behavior and mental health status, and the circumstances that led the family to be considered "high risk" or that resulted in the placement of a child or children in a foster home. Under staffing patterns might be staff-to-client ratios, staff demographic characteristics (age, gender, race/ethnicity), and staff education and training backgrounds. Under the referral process might be different referral sources, how often different sources make referrals, and the types of cases or presenting problems referred by different sources. Under services provided might be subtopics related to the range of services provided, the frequency with which services are provided and their duration, and service delivery costs.

Next, just as with instrument construction, we would "operationalize" each of these variables and settle on precise indicators of them. Some of the variables are easy to operationalize, such as the demographic characteristics, referral sources, services provided, and staff-to-client ratios. Others, however, require more creative effort. For example, measuring variables such as the children's behavior and mental health status and the circumstances that led to the families' being regarded as high risk or to the placement of children in foster care will require using standardized tools or creating measurement items specifically for this purpose.

Formative evaluations usually are designed for internal use, that is, to provide information about service delivery and program implementation to program administrators and staff or a board of directors. Of course, this kind of information also may be of interest to outside parties, such as independent evaluators or funding sources. Deciding with whom to share the results of a formative evaluation is a judgment call that requires careful thought about ethical, financial, political, and interpersonal factors.

Summative Evaluations

Now let's turn to summative evaluation, whose main purpose is to determine how well a program has achieved its objectives. Given what you know about the Families First program, what objectives do you think the staff should measure?

Here are some possibilities that occur to me: the number of high-risk families able to retain custody of their children (that is, the children are not placed in foster care), the number of children in foster care who are returned to their families of origin or placed in stable independent living arrangements, changes in family functioning and children's functioning over the course of the program (we hope for the better, of course), and the cost effectiveness of this intervention approach.

As with the measures used in the formative evaluation, some of these variables are relatively easy to measure, and others are more difficult. It's pretty easy to measure the number of high-risk families able to retain custody of their children and the number of children in foster care who are returned to their families of origin or placed in independent living arrangements. However, it may be difficult to find a valid and reliable way to measure concepts such as family functioning and children's functioning. Fortunately, a number of impressive standardized tools are available to measure these concepts. The evaluator of the Mt. Washington Families First program would need to be sure, however, that these measures are appropriate (with appropriate face and content validity, right?) and not too time-consuming for the staff. As I mentioned earlier, if the staff members collecting the data aren't committed to the process or feel burdened by it, there's a good chance that the quality of the evaluation will suffer.

A tool sometimes used in program evaluations is Goal Attainment Scaling (GAS), which has been around since the 1960s. It's a technique used with many different populations pursuing specific goals. Examples are participants in substance abuse treatment programs who want to stop using alcohol and other drugs, participants in eating disorder programs who want to increase or decrease their caloric consumption, autistic children who engage in self-destructive behaviors, nursing home residents who are trying to regain continence, and schoolteachers who are trying to help students improve their behavior.

GAS basically identifies individual goals, usually three to six behaviors that warrant serious attention and have a reasonable potential for change. Each goal is then assessed at various times and is assigned a score ranging from, for example, −2 to +2. A −2 means that the progress is much less than expected; −1, somewhat less than expected; o, what was expected; +1, somewhat more than expected; and +2, much more than expected.

GAS can be used for individual families or children to measure their progress toward specific goals. For families, specific goals may be the parents using "time-out" interventions effectively when their children behave aggressively, reducing the incidence of physical violence in the family, and increasing the amount of time family members spend in recreational activities with one another. For children, specific goals may be reducing the frequency of hitting, increasing school attendance, improving school grades, and raising self-esteem. Somewhat more sophisticated versions of GAS use more detailed and refined scales, but this is the general idea. (You also can use some data analysis techniques to measure how well clients have met their goals, but they're beyond the scope of this discussion.)

For summative evaluations, social workers should consider the research designs discussed throughout this book. For some such evaluations, single-case designs may be useful and appropriate. In the Families First program evaluation, for example, a series of single-case designs could be used to examine the impact of the home-based services provided. I can imagine using an ABAB design in my work with a single parent who is eager to learn how to manage her toddler's behavior. The intervention might include instruction in using positive reinforcers to help manage the child's behavior. The ABAB design, which alternates between baseline and intervention periods, can be a good way to measure the effectiveness of this intervention, assuming that the problematic behaviors can be tolerated during the baseline periods. If the behaviors are so threatening or inappropriate that the social worker wouldn't want to withdraw the intervention once it has started (assuming it's correlated with improved behavior), an AB design may be more appealing. Although the AB design doesn't control as well for extraneous factors, it's still a good way to gather information about changes in a client's status.

Group designs—whether experimental or quasi-experimental—are commonly used to evaluate programs. In some cases, clients are randomly assigned to experimental and control groups. In principle, this is the best way to control for extraneous factors, but it is not always feasible. In other situations, social workers may use comparison groups, each of which is exposed to a different intervention, or matched groups, in which the people in each group are matched according to key variables to control for differences between the groups. In the evaluation of the Families First program, for example, the waiting list to get into the program may be so long that there's a control group built in. Or if those on the waiting list have access to the county department of social services' traditional assistance, those clients would be part of a comparison or contrast group. Comparing clients who receive the "traditional" or "ordinary" intervention with those receiving a more innovative or "experimental" intervention is a common strategy.

Like formative evaluations, summative evaluations may be conducted for different purposes. One common objective is to give the program's administrators, staff, and board of directors "bottom line" information about whether a program is working. Clearly, Families First administrators, staff, and the program's board of directors—the program's stakeholders—are keenly interested in the extent to which the program's objectives are being met. In this instance, the summative evaluation would be designed primarily for internal use.

But there are several good reasons that summative evaluations would have an "external" audience as well. First, so-called demonstration projects are often evaluated. A demonstration project, which may be funded by a government agency or a foundation, is ordinarily designed to test or explore the effectiveness of a particular intervention model that, if the results are encouraging, might be expanded to other sites. Those funding the demonstration project may be interested in how well the model can be generalized to other settings and replicated and only secondarily interested in the program's impact on the particular site where it is first implemented.

For example, the Families First program is financed with county funds. One of the reasons that the county administrators decided to underwrite the cost of the program at Mt. Washington was to gather evidence of its effectiveness and to see whether this model, if successful, could be implemented elsewhere in the county. With demonstration projects, the funders' general strategy is to invest a modest amount of money in one or more sites for a period of time, sort of as a "trial balloon," to determine whether there is sufficient evidence to warrant replication of the model elsewhere, which of course would require additional funds (you might say that a major goal of this type of summative evaluation is to see whether a particular intervention model has external validity).

This leads to a second reason that summative evaluations may have an "external" audience. Sometimes it's too simplistic to think about the wholesale replication of an intervention model in other sites, or what I like to call *blanket generalizability*. The replication of an entire intervention model, with all its peculiar features and designs, seems to assume that the conditions in the other sites match or are similar to the conditions in the site of the original demonstration project. But how realistic is this assumption? How many other neighborhoods in the county where Mt. Washington is located are identical or even very similar to the Mt. Washington community with respect to variables such as racial/ethnic composition, socioeconomic status, unemployment and crime rates, incidence of teenage pregnancy and divorce, and people living in poverty? If the Families First model were first tried out in a larger metropolitan area, such as Baltimore, how generalizable would it be to other major urban areas, much less nonurban areas?

Accordingly, a goal of many summative evaluations is to show which of a program site's features make a difference in the outcome. Thus a comprehensive summative evaluation may use more than the bottom-line outcome measures (for example, the number of children in foster care who were reunited with their biological families or the number of foster placements of at-risk children that were prevented). In addition, the evaluators may look for patterns or isolate certain variables, or combinations of variables, that seem to tip the scales in a program's favor. For instance, a summative evaluation of a program like Families First may find that the program is particularly effective with two-parent families in which only one parent works outside the home, as compared with single-parent and two-parent families in which both parents work outside the home. This family profile may be more prevalent in some communities than in others. Or the summative evaluation may find that the program is least successful with urban families living in poverty, in which a caretaker has a serious substance abuse problem. That is, it's usually a mistake to carry out a summative evaluation assuming that "one size fits all," that, like a circus, positive outcomes in one setting mean that the model can be packed up and moved to another site, with no alteration in design, and yield similar results. Summative evaluations need to be carried out with the understanding that they may have only modest external validity.

Ambitious summative evaluations, however, take into account this phenomenon. Summative evaluations carried out on a large scale, usually with large amounts of money, typically cover several sites to explore and control for significant differences. For example, a federal demonstration project designed to evaluate the effectiveness of an intervention model to help juvenile offenders might include large, urban settings (Los Angeles, Miami, Cleveland, and Boston), medium-size urban settings (Toledo, Ohio; Gary, Indiana; Portland, Oregon), and rural areas (rural counties in southern Illinois, South Dakota, Maine, and Mississippi). This kind of variation would enable the evaluators to explore correlations between key outcome indicators and numerous other variables, such as community size, delinquency rates, urban versus rural, ethnic and racial composition, and geographical region. Although the external validity still wouldn't be perfect (to get close to perfection, we'd need to include an enormous number of program sites reflecting dozens and dozens of different types of communities), it certainly would be better.

One other reason that external audiences may be interested in summative evaluations is to test a hypothesis for theory development. Academic researchers, in particular, are often interested in using summative evaluations to test the accuracy of their hunches about the causal connection between certain independent variables, including intervention approaches and certain outcome measures. In these circumstances, researchers may not be especially concerned about a program's impact on a particular community because of their deep attachment to or interest in that community. Rather, in these situations the site in which the summative evaluation is carried out is mainly a means to an end, that is, a convenient laboratory setting in which to test out a hypothesis.

Another possible scenario is that a faculty member at the university near the Mt. Washington Family Service Agency has done research for years on various ways to help high-risk families avoid placement of their children in foster care and to help children in foster care return to their families of origin. This faculty member may have applied for and received research funds from a federal agency or a prominent foundation to test the effectiveness of a new intervention model. The model may be based on a number of hypotheses about the impact of specific treatment approaches, such as a particular type of parent education, mentoring services, and financial incentives that provide positive reinforcers for parents' consistent participation in the program. The model's components may be based directly on the literature and research evidence relevant to work with such high-risk families and children.

To conduct the research, the faculty member must find a family service agency that is willing to cooperate. The researcher could ask Mt. Washington's executive director, who might agree to participate in part because of the extra "free staff," paid for with the research project's grant money, she would receive as a result. Although this summative evaluation might produce useful information for internal use in the Mt. Washington Family Service Agency, its main audience would be external to the agency.

MEASURING COST BENEFIT AND COST EFFECTIVENESS

Cost benefit is a widely used term, for which everyone seems to have his or her own definition. That is, we seem to agree on the idea of cost benefit, but we have difficulty agreeing on the variables that enter into its calculation.

For example, social workers often claim that investing in preventive social services is wise because it's cost effective. This sort of argument is used frequently to justify programs designed to prevent such problems as juvenile delinquency, substance abuse, child abuse, domestic violence, and sexually transmitted diseases. Provide preventive services now, we argue, and avoid the costs of the problem down the road. Pay for child abuse prevention programs now and avoid having to pay for more prisons and drug abuse programs in the future. Yet although we may "know" in our gut that good-quality programs are cost effective, how can we demonstrate this empirically? How, exactly, should we calculate the savings?

Before we do that, though, we need to know the difference between cost benefit and cost effectiveness. In cost–benefit analyses, social workers assess both the costs and the benefits in monetary terms, that is, in dollars (or pesos in Spain and lira in Italy). The basic conceptual approach is clear and straightforward: all we have to do is add up the costs of providing the social services, subtract this figure from the dollar amount of the benefits associated with the services, and compare the result with the dollar costs that are likely to result if a particular social problem is not prevented. This will give us the net savings from investing in preventive social services.

In contrast, cost–effectiveness analysis focuses exclusively on the costs themselves. Such an analysis might compare the relative costs of two similar programs, calculate the cost of a program per client, or determine whether costs associated with a particular program rose or fell over time.

Let's illustrate this difference for the Families First program. We'll start with a cost–benefit analysis. The first challenge is figuring out what costs we should include when estimating the costs of the social services. Some possibilities are staff salaries and fringe benefits (health care and retirement, for example), office facilities (rent, utilities, computer equipment, ordinary office supplies, furniture), insurance (property and liability), consultation fees (psychiatric, nursing, and educational consultation), books and professional journals, and travel (local travel for casework and travel to professional conferences).

Now how do we measure the benefits of the social services provided by the Families First staff? Here are the kinds of general things I'd expect people to mention: less demand on the county social services department staff as a result of fewer child abuse and neglect investigations, less demand for foster care and adoption services, fewer delinquent offenses committed by participating children, less demand for law enforcement agencies' involvement in these families' lives, lower incidence of substance abuse among these children and their parents, fewer special education services required at the children's schools, less demand for hospitalization and emergency health care, increased employment, and less demand for public assistance by the children's parents.

Even if we could agree on the potential benefits, we would still have to decide on specific indicators or measures of each of these concepts. For example, how would you measure less demand for law enforcement agencies' involvement in these families' lives? Would you look at changes in the number of calls to 911 and estimate the cost of responding to each such call (for instance, the personnel costs, overhead, training)? Would you include the costs of probation and parole officers? What about the court system that handles a lot of these cases? How would you measure the program's impact on the demand for hospitalization and emergency health care? Would you try to estimate the decline in the sample's use of emergency rooms and hospital inpatient facilities (perhaps resulting from a lower incidence of abuse and neglect, failure to thrive, and so on) and multiply that by the cost of the average emergency room visit and inpatient hospital stay? Complicated, isn't it?

Now how would you approach measuring the costs of *not* providing the preventive services? What would happen if Families First did not exist? In principle, I suspect we would try to calculate the flip side of the list we just discussed, that is, the costs of welfare and public assistance, emergency room use and inpatient hospitalization, law enforcement involvement in the families' lives, and hiring new child welfare professionals, protective service workers, and school personnel. This process seems so complicated and unwieldy, it's hard to know where to begin.

Fortunately, some well-accepted norms and standards are used to conduct cost–benefit analyses in the human services, discussed in detail in a number of different books (a good place to start is H. M. Levin's *Cost-Effectiveness: A Primer*, 1983). Although there is still plenty of room for social workers to use their judgment and lots of areas where social workers are likely to disagree, at least we have a well-accepted general approach.

One of the main problems with cost–benefit analyses is the assumption that all costs and benefits can somehow be converted to some kind of monetary value. For example, it's one thing to make a monetary estimate of variables such as staff salaries, fringe benefits, transportation and insurance expenses, clothing allowances, consultants' fees, and health care bills. But what about variables such as the better mental health of family members who participate in the Families First program? How do we attach a dollar value to the fact that some parents who participate in the program experience less anxiety and depression? Suppose that children who participate in the program improve their self-esteem and self-confidence. How can we measure that in dollars and cents?

The same problem arises in many cost–benefit analyses. For example, in Mt. Washington's program for men who batter, it's not hard to calculate the monetary value of fewer nights that the men spend in jail or prison. All we need to do is multiply the official per diem rate for a night at the state prison or local jail by the number of nights spent there. Similarly, it's not hard to figure the cost of the emergency room medical care for the men's spouses or partners. All we would need to do is obtain copies of the relevant bills. But how do we measure in dollars such things as the fear and emotional anguish that the men's spouses or partners experience, the psychological distress that children in these households suffer, or the psychological pain associated with separation and divorce as a result of domestic violence?

We encounter the same problem with Mt. Washington's substance abuse treatment program. We can readily calculate variables such as nights spent in a detox facility, wages lost because of substance abuse, and the costs of inpatient stays in a residential treatment facility and outpatient counseling. But how can we figure the monetary value of the emotional relief that people feel when they are sober or clean, or the shame that children may feel when their parents are known in the community as substance abusers? There are no simple answers to these questions. Clearly, one of the limitations of cost–benefit analyses is the difficulty we have quantifying the qualitative phenomena.

Now let's look at a cost–effectiveness analysis of the Families First program. Our main objective here is calculating the costs of the program, especially compared with those of other programs. Let's say that the program's budget during its first year was $125,000 (including staff salaries and fringe benefits, rent, utilities, etc.) and during that year the program served 45 families, including 63 children who were placed in foster care (24 of the 63 children) or were considered by the county department of social services to be at risk of being placed in foster care (39 of the 63 children). That means the program cost about $2777 per family ($125,000 divided by 45) or $1984 per child in foster care or at risk ($125,000 divided by 63). By the end of the first year, the evaluator estimates, the Families First program enabled 11 of the children in foster care to return to their families of origin and prevented 26 of the 39 at-risk children from being placed in foster care. Based on the evaluator's estimates, which included some pretty complicated accounting techniques, the Families First program saved the county social services department $2815 for each family served, for a total of $126,675. The evaluator's estimates took into account what it ordinarily costs the department to serve families with children in foster care or whose children are at risk of being placed in a foster home.

Notice that this cost–effectiveness analysis did not include any estimate of the harder-to-quantify benefits of the Families First program. That is, the analysis didn't take into account any of the variables I mentioned earlier, such as less demand on the county social services department staff as a result of fewer child abuse and neglect investigations, less demand for foster care and adoption services, fewer delinquent offenses committed by participating children, less demand for law enforcement agencies' involvement in these families' lives, lower incidence of substance abuse among these children and their parents, fewer special education services required at the children's schools, less demand for hospitalization and emergency health care, increased employment, and less demand for public assistance by the children's parents. You can probably see how complicated cost–benefit analyses can get, how hard it is to figure out what variables to include, and how to measure them.

POLITICAL ISSUES

Sometimes social workers have an idealized view of program evaluation, visions of "pure" and "objective" researchers (perhaps in white lab coats) who are seeking the pristine and virtuous ideals of knowledge and "truth." I guess this image comes from the portrayal of scientists we often see in the movies and on television. I have a feeling that the general public, including social workers, imagines that scientists work in ways and settings that are immune from political considerations. Oh, if only that were so. In fact, much of science in general, and nearly all social work research and evaluation, is permeated by politics.

To begin this discussion, I need to clarify what I mean by politics. (Have you heard the joke about how politics is a noble enterprise and how the term stems from two important root words: *polis*, meaning an ancient Greek city-state, and *ticks*, blood-sucking insects?) Politics is another one of those simple-sounding terms that mean different things to different people. One political aspect of program evaluation is the actual political arena, by which I mean federal, state, and local government. How does politics get involved in program evaluation? First, the political-party affiliations of elected officials—whether at the federal, state, or local level—can have a lot to do with the substantive issues that are researched and the funding that is available. If elected officials are deeply committed to the sorts of social problems that concern social workers, there is likely to be more interest in and opportunity for program evaluation. It's fair to say that generally when more liberal elected officials are in office, evaluations of social programs of interest to social workers are more prevalent. It stands to reason that elected officials interested in public spending to mitigate problems such as teenage pregnancy, poverty, substance abuse, domestic violence, and mental illness are more likely to support evaluations of social programs. This is true of elected officials in both the executive branch (presidents, governors, and mayors, for example) and the legislative branch of government (federal and state legislators and local city council representatives). When more conservative public officials are elected to office, it's not unusual to hear social work researchers groan that they're in for a dry spell.

Of course, there always are exceptions to the rule. Sometimes relatively conservative public officials don't stand in the way of, and even encourage, social spending and related program evaluations. But this seems to be fairly uncommon. What's more common, in my experience, is that in a conservative political climate, the funds available for social spending and program evaluation may go to traditionally conservative causes, for example, evaluating the impact of cuts in welfare benefits and enhanced workfare requirements or the impact of stiffer prison sentences on recidivism rates.

Politics can also rear its head in a very different way. Many program evaluations are funded by outside agencies, typically government agencies or foundations. As I said earlier, social workers often obtain their evaluation funding by submitting a proposal in response to a formal request for proposal (RFP). Because the proposals are usually reviewed by a panel of "experts" in the field, the social workers who submit such proposals usually are concerned about the "politics" of the review process. Applicants may worry about the ideological biases of reviewers, the repercussions of their past disagreements with one or more of the reviewers, or the effect of professional jealousy when certain applicants and reviewers "compete" with one another for recognition in the same field of expertise. Occasionally you'll hear applicants complain that a particular review process was "all political" or "wired" and that the review panel had its predetermined favorites. Even though these kinds of political considerations aren't inevitable, they're certainly not unheard of.

Also, as I mentioned in our discussion of ethical issues in chapter 4, many, although certainly not all, evaluation projects must be presented to institutional review boards (IRBs) for approval. To refresh your memory, IRBs are used by government, university, health care, and many other agencies to ensure that evaluation and research designs comply with prevailing standards for the protection of human subjects.

It is perhaps tempting to think that IRB reviews are entirely objective and that each proposal is judged solely on its methodological merits. However, although this may be true in many instances, it's certainly not true in all. Members of IRBs are human and thus have their own ideological biases and preferences concerning "appropriate" evaluation designs. It's not unusual to hear social workers speculate about reviewers' methodological biases and the need to take them into account when writing a program evaluation proposal.

Then, of course, there are the agency politics to be aware of that I mentioned earlier. How do you think the staff in many agencies feel when an administrator announces that the program they have worked in for some time, and on which their livelihood depends, will be formally evaluated? Quite understandably, they may worry that their jobs are in jeopardy or that they will be judged unfairly. The politics of program evaluation can be particularly toxic if staff members have a strained relationship with their administrator or believe that their administrator is merely using the evaluation to advance his or her own political goals, which may include shrinking or terminating the program.

Politics can also be present when funding agencies recruit outside researchers to evaluate a program, instead of allowing the agency staff to do it themselves. The funding agencies may be concerned that the agency's staff, who have a vested interest in the evaluation's outcome, won't be objective or may bias the evaluation's results in the program's favor. To avoid this possibility, the funding agencies may insist on a more "objective" outside evaluator.

This arrangement can lead to a complicated and politically charged relationship between the outside evaluator and the agency being evaluated. On the one hand, the program's staff need to cooperate, if for no other reason than that the funding agency requires such cooperation as a condition of the grant or contract. On the other hand, the program's staff may not want to cooperate because of their resentment of a group of outsiders peering over their shoulder and judging the quality of their work. At times this resentment is so intense that the program's staff are determined to sabotage the evaluation. In addition, they may feel that an outside evaluator has been retained essentially as a "spy" or, alternatively, to conduct an evaluation that will whitewash or sanitize well-known problems in the agency. Agency administrators may also pressure an outside evaluator to omit, revise, or reframe negative findings that, if included in the final report, would not reflect well on the agency. Obviously, this can be a very unpleasant atmosphere in which to conduct a program evaluation.

There's no magical way to deal with or avoid the possible political issues in a program evaluation. Not being naive about the influence of politics and having a range of diplomacy skills to deal with political dynamics can be enormously helpful. One advantage for many social workers is that they've been educated to understand the role of politics in the field (both uppercase "P" and lowercase "p" politics) and also the interpersonal skills required to navigate stormy political waters.

ETHICAL ISSUES

Although I've already discussed ethical issues pertaining to evaluation and research in general (chapter 4), several issues are worth reiterating or highlighting because of their special relevance to program evaluation. First, social workers need to be mindful of the ethical issues in program evaluations that include randomization procedures. There are complicated ethical issues in program evaluations that deliberately withhold services to a control group of clients who are otherwise eligible for services being provided as part of the evaluation. As a result, many program evaluations avoid true control groups and rely instead on comparison groups.

Second, social workers need to be aware that clients often agree to participate in the program evaluation not so much because they want to but because they fear missing out on services they want. Social workers should avoid even the slightest hint of coercion and should obtain potential participants' informed consent (unless the design is such that traditional informed consent is not necessary or appropriate and has been approved by an institutional review board). Nonetheless, social workers who bend over backward to avoid making clients feel like they face an ultimatum ("participate in my program evaluation or you won't get any of these wonderful services") may not be able to eliminate this potential problem completely. Some clients, no matter what social workers say, may feel coerced because of their situation. Imagine, for example, Mt. Washington clients who are ordered by the court to receive family services because of concerns about their neglect of their children. Suppose in the middle of the service delivery a family's social worker announces the availability of the Families First program, which will be far more demanding and time-consuming than the agency's ordinary services. How free will the parents feel to refuse the offer, particularly given their concern about losing custody of their children?

Social workers need to be careful about protecting the program evaluation participants' right to privacy and confidentiality. Participants in program evaluations aren't research subjects in the traditional sense, that is, people who had no relationship with the researchers before the data were collected and will not have a relationship with the researchers after the data are collected. In contrast, participants in program evaluations usually are clients in one way or another, and consequently, they may worry that the information they disclose to program evaluators will be given to others. Such participants may worry that staff members will find out their unflattering or critical answers to questions and that they will jeopardize their much-wanted involvement in the program being evaluated.

Also, because participants in a program evaluation often have problems—such as those involved in the Families First program—social workers need to be prepared to offer supportive services that are not part of the research or evaluation design. Sometimes program evaluators need to be social workers first and evaluators second. Should there be a crisis, social workers in the program evaluation need to put aside their research and evaluation agendas, at least temporarily, and turn to relieving the participants' distress.

Finally, social workers must handle program evaluation results responsibly. They need to report findings accurately and avoid omitting, camouflaging, or distorting important information to deceive funders or mislead colleagues. Often there's much riding on the results of a program evaluation, including the program's very future, the line staff's jobs, the viability of a popular and important intervention approach, or social workers' careers. Program evaluators sometimes have the power to shape what happens in this regard based on how they report the results.

II

DATA ANALYSIS

If you think we've had a good time so far, fasten your seatbelt. The fun's just about to begin. Now we find out what to do once we've gathered all the data we've been talking about. Think about it—you've spent weeks designing a research or evaluation project, constructing data collection instruments, and gathering the data. In front of you is an enormous pile of information on data collection sheets. What are you supposed to do with it?

To be honest, this is the part of the process that makes many social work students get that feeling of butterflies floating around in their stomachs. This is the moment in the course when my students tend to produce a zillion or so reasons that they need to do something else, like change their automobile tires, paint the house, clean the cat's litter box, or watch grass grow. It's a good thing I don't take it personally.

For years I've noticed that students become anxious when we approach the subject of data analysis. When I poll them (using only the most scientific of sampling and survey research techniques, of course), I find that they tend to fall into two groups. Group 1 is those students who have taken a statistics course, usually as an undergraduate, and (1) found it to be miserable, sadistic (on the instructor's part), and masochistic (on the student's part), (2) didn't understand much of what the instructor was talking about or what they read, (3) weren't convinced that the statistical concepts were relevant to anything even remotely related to their career interests, or (4) some combination of these, including the possibility of "all the above." Group 2 is those students who have not taken a statistics course but who have talked to students in group 1 about their experience. Frankly, it's rare that I find a student who has taken a statistics course, appreciated its relevance, and enjoyed the experience.

I know this may sound disingenuous, but I don't believe this is the way it needs to be. When I took my first statistics course as an undergraduate student, I—like most undergraduate students in statistics courses—had barely a clue to what was happening. I attended class dutifully (unlike some of my colleagues, I might add) and did my best to sort it all out. I learned most of the concepts, I think, but the truth is that my effort was largely wasted. The course was taught in such a way that the material seemed completely irrelevant. I really didn't understand how statistical concepts could be used in real life. The whole experience seemed like an endurance test, not unlike boot camp or the experience of pre-med students taking organic chemistry—something only to get through.

Not until years later did I figure out that many of these concepts can be remarkably helpful in social work. Time and time again, I have found that basic statistical concepts can indeed help social workers organize information efficiently and that some of the mathematical concepts provide an elegant way to comprehend a wide range of very practical social work phenomena. This is a necessarily abstract idea at this point, but I think you'll see what I mean as we proceed.

I have several aims to achieve in this chapter. First, for those of you who believe that you'll never understand statistical concepts, I am determined to present this material so that you will. Second, I will acquaint you with statistical tools that can help you—yes, really help you—organize the information you gather throughout your career. I have no illusions about the number of readers who will end up being sophisticated researchers and data analysts. I am well aware that many of you—though not all—place research and statistics close to or at the bottom of the list of favorite things to study in social work education. Nonetheless, I am convinced that every social worker, and I do mean every social worker, can find statistical and data analysis concepts useful and relevant to their work. The trick is presenting the material in a way that demonstrates this. Third, I will show you why understanding statistical concepts can enhance your thinking about and understanding of social work phenomena, even if you never use the statistics in their mathematical form. That is, I believe that many statistical concepts provide useful metaphors or ways of characterizing what happens when social workers do what social workers do.

In case you are wondering, I don't plan to go into a great deal of mathematical detail or present lots of complicated formulas here. Instead I'll give you brief overviews of a couple of formulas that I think communicate something useful. But I know from experience that too many can overwhelm students being introduced to statistical concepts for the first time. For those of you who enjoy mathematical detail, there are plenty of statistics books that can satisfy your curiosity. My main goal is to offer a clear, conceptually oriented overview of basic statistics and how they can make a difference in social work. This chapter is designed to get you oriented to statistical concepts.

In addition, I plan to limit my discussion to the statistics and data analysis procedures most important to typical social workers. I don't want to bore you with esoteric details of complicated statistical and data analysis techniques that have little or no relevance to the working lives of typical practitioners.

A Brief Road Map

Lots of different kinds of data are available for social workers to analyze. Some data are quantitative (in the form of numbers), and some are qualitative (in the form of words). Some data pertain to individual clients, as in single-case designs, and some pertain to small, medium, or large groups of people, organizations, or communities. Data may be obtained from observations of clients, case records, interviews, questionnaires, surveys, or existing data sets.

In fact, even one research or evaluation project can produce all or many of these different kinds of data. That's certainly true of Mt. Washington's Families First program. Let's take a closer look at some of the possibilities. Quantitative data might be collected in the form of periodic measures of the children's behavior. If each month the evaluator, Andrew R., administers a standardized child behavior assessment tool, which includes a series of items measured on a Likert scale, he needs to know how to analyze the quantitative data that the instrument produces. If Andrew R. spends time observing family dynamics in the participants' homes or interviews family members with a number of open-ended questions, he needs to know how to analyze these qualitative data. If Andrew R. focuses on an individual case and introduces interventions after collecting data during a baseline period, he needs to know how to analyze data associated with single-case designs. If Andrew R. administers a client satisfaction questionnaire to all the program's participants or summarizes information drawn from the clients' case records (for example, information concerning presenting problems, length of service, or number of missed appointments), he needs to know how to analyze aggregate data.

Another important distinction is between descriptive statistics and inferential statistics. As the term suggests, social workers use *descriptive statistics* when they simply want to describe something, quantitatively, about an individual, family, group of people, community, or organization. For example, if Andrew R. wants to summarize the Families First participants' ethnic/racial backgrounds, the kinds of services they received, or the general pattern of their responses to a number of client-satisfaction questions, he would use descriptive statistics. He will also use descriptive statistics if he wants to report information about the number of families in the Mt. Washington area living below the poverty line or in substandard housing.

Social workers use *inferential statistics* when they want to use data obtained from a sample to make inferences about the population from which the sample was drawn. Let's say that Andrew R. decides to administer in-depth client-satisfaction interviews to a 40 percent sample of Families First participants. He would like to interview all the participants, but his budget and the time available aren't large enough to be able to do this. Because Andrew R. knows something about probability and simple random-sampling techniques, he plans to use inferential statistics to analyze the data. In this way, he will be able to extrapolate from the sample data to the population (the entire group of program participants) from which the sample was drawn.

Social workers use *parameters* to describe the characteristics of a population and *statistics* to describe the characteristics of a sample. For example, the average age in a population is a *parameter*, but the average age in a sample drawn from that population is a *statistic*. Thus if Andrew R. collects data on the entire population of Families First participants, such as their age, gender, or history of substance abuse, he would use parameters to summarize the information. If Andrew R. collects the same data on a sample of Families First participants, he would use statistics to summarize the information. For simplicity's sake, I will use the term *statistics* throughout this chapter.

Social workers also must understand the three ways to analyze data (actually there are more, but to explore beyond the three that I will focus on here would get us into some very technical statistical procedures that are rarely used in social work). First, social workers can analyze variables one at a time. For example, Andrew R. may want to summarize the frequency with which school-age children in the Families First program are suspended from school, truant, or arrested by the police. When Andrew R. examines these variables one at a time, he does a *univariate analysis* (the Latin prefix *uni* means "one"). But after he presents the univariate information, he may want to see whether any variables are correlated with school suspensions, truancy, and arrests. For example, Andrew R. may want to explore whether variables such as age, gender, parents' family status (that is, whether children are being raised in a single-parent or a two-parent household), types of services received, or length of service are correlated with these variables.

Or Andrew R. may want to analyze the relationship between some of these variables two at a time. For instance, he may want to look at the correlation between types of services received and school suspensions, to see whether the children who received certain types of services (such as individual, family, or group counseling) had higher or lower rates of school suspensions. Or Andrew R. may want to examine the relationship between length of time in counseling and arrests. This sort of exploration, in which social workers examine the relationship between two variables at a time, is called *bivariate analysis* (the prefix *bi* means "two").

Then Andrew R. may want to see whether there is a significant pattern among a number of these variables. One possibility would be for him to explore whether certain combinations of variables—such as age, gender, race/ethnicity, types of services received, and length of service—are associated, as a group, with a particular outcome variable, such as school suspensions or arrests by the police. When social workers study the relationships among a number of variables (actually, three or more), they do what is called *multivariate analysis*. In this chapter I will look mainly at univariate and bivariate analyses, with a modest amount of information on multivariate analyses.

There's one other topic I want to explore before we get down to business: *levels of measurement*, a statistical concept with many implications for the kinds of analyses that social workers conduct. In short, there are four levels of measurement—nominal, ordinal, interval, and ratio—and every variable is associated with a particular level of measurement. You should understand this concept because the level of measurement you're working with determines which statistics you will use to analyze the data. I can't emphasize this enough. Social workers who are confused about the levels of measurement they're working with may end up selecting the wrong statistic, and this is a MAJOR PROBLEM. If you analyze data with the wrong statistics, guess what you end up with? Ever heard the term GIGO? I don't know its exact origins, but it stands for "garbage in, garbage out." That is, if you use the wrong statistics going into the data analysis, the results will be equally wrong.

Here's a brief summary of the four levels of measurement:

Nominal level. The *nominal level* is the most basic of the four. Social workers use nominal data when they classify information into two or more mutually exclusive (that is, nonoverlapping) categories. Nominal measurement is often referred to as the "lowest" level of measurement because it makes the fewest assumptions about the data. With nominal data we assume only that the categories differ from one another qualitatively. We make no assumptions about rank order among the categories, whether one is "better" or "higher" than another.

For example, Andrew R. may collect information about the racial and ethnic makeup of children participating in the Families First program. The appropriate categories, given the composition of the neighborhood, are African
American, Latino, Native American, white, and Southeast Asian (Cambodian,
Hmong, Laotian, and Vietnamese). Each child is placed into one of these categories, and Andrew R. then summarizes the frequency, or number of people,
in each one. Ethnicity, then, is a nominal variable.

Similarly, Andrew R. may classify the Families First clients as belonging to
one of several "service delivery" categories. The three possible options are families receiving family counseling only, families receiving family counseling and
parent education, and families receiving family counseling, parent education,
and substance abuse counseling. Families are placed in one of these categories
based on the staff's assessment of their needs. Data summarizing the number
of families in each of the three "service delivery" options are nominal level.

Ordinal level. When social workers rank-order information—from low to
high or small to large, for example—they are working with ordinal data, or on
an *ordinal level.* By definition, ordinal data imply some kind of rank. One type
of ordinal data is similar to nominal data, the only real difference being that the
categories of ordinal data are ranked. For example, one of the goals in the
Families First program is to reduce the frequency of children running away from
their residences, whether they are with their families of origin or with foster families. If Andrew R. places the children in foster care into one of three rank-ordered
groups based on the staff's assessment of the risk that the children will run
away—high, medium, and low risk—he will use an ordinal measure. Andrew R.
would also be using an ordinal measure if he classified families as high, medium,
and low priority with respect to their need for additional follow-up services.

Another way that ordinal data are used is by rank-ordering a group of people, organizations, communities, or whatever. If Andrew R. rank-orders a
group of children from "most aggressive" to "least aggressive," he is presenting
the information in ordinal fashion. Similarly, if Andrew R. rank-orders the
families in the program from "most progress achieved" to "least progress
achieved," he is presenting the information in an ordinal fashion.

With ordinal data, our only assumption is that there is some kind of rank
order among the different phenomena. We make no assumption about the
amount of distance between the various ranks. That is, the distance between
the family that made the "most progress" and "the next most progress" might
be much larger than the distance between this second family and the one that
follows it immediately in the rank ordering. Thus with rank ordering, all we
can say is that items or elements in the rank (whether persons, communities,

or organizations) are more or less than the others; we can't say anything about how far apart the items or elements are.

Interval level.   In various places throughout this book, I have mentioned the scales that social workers use to measure different things, such as clients' self-esteem, depression, relationships with parents or partners, or aggressive behavior. Scales can also be used to measure various aspects of organizational life (for example, job-related stress or morale among employees) and community life (fear of crime, social service needs). As I'm sure you recall from the earlier discussion of measuring instruments, some scales are standardized and some are nonstandardized, created by social workers for use in unique circumstances.

⟡ Many of the scales that social workers use are *interval-level* measures that use scales containing a number of equally spaced points or intervals. Examples are a 7-point scale, ranging from "happy" to "sad," that clients in a psychiatric program use to rate their current mood, and a 100-point scale, with various anchor points, on which a client's level of functioning is rated. Thus, like ordinal measures, interval-level measures have ranked scores, but unlike ordinal measures, interval-level measures have equally spaced points or intervals.

A good illustration of an interval-level measure that can be used in the Families First program is the Global Assessment of Functioning (GAF) scale cited in the *Diagnostic and Statistical Manual of Mental Disorders* (American Psychiatric Association 1994), known in shorthand as the *DSM*, the widely used (and controversial) classification of mental health problems that social workers and other professionals encounter. The American Psychiatric Association encourages mental health professionals who use the *DSM* to include in every diagnosis five major pieces of information about the client, one of which uses the GAF to assess the client's level of functioning. (Some of you may be familiar with the five "axes" that the *DSM* uses: clinical disorders and other conditions that may be a focus of clinical attention, personality disorders and mental retardation, general medical conditions that may be relevant to clients' mental disorders, clients' past and current psychosocial and environmental problems, and the Global Assessment of Functioning.)

The GAF is a 100-point scale, where lower scores indicate major problems in psychological, social, and occupational functioning and higher scores indicate superior functioning. Andrew R. may use the GAF as a tool to keep track of and evaluate the functioning of Families First clients. The scale has ten major anchor points to help practitioners locate an appropriate score. For example, scores ranging from 1 to 10 should be used when there is evidence of a "persistent danger of severely hurting self or others (e.g., recurrent violence) OR persistent inability to maintain minimal personal hygiene OR serious suicidal act with clear expectation of death." Scores ranging from 41 to 50 should be used when there are "serious symptoms (e.g., suicidal ideation, severe obsessional rituals, frequent shoplifting) OR any serious impairment in social, occupational, or school functioning (e.g., no friends, unable to keep a job)." Scores ranging from 81 to 90 should be used for "absent or minimal symptoms (e.g., mild anxiety before an exam), good functioning in all areas, interested and involved in a wide range of activities, socially effective, generally satisfied with life, no more than everyday problems or concerns (e.g., an occasional argument with family members)."

As a special example of an interval-level measure, consider the following: Andrew R. decides to pose a "summary" question to each family member every two weeks during their participation in the Families First program: In general, would you say that things in your life are

1. Excellent
2. Good
3. Fair
4. Poor

You might label this as technically an ordinal-level scale, because the four options are rank ordered. But this kind of scale, which includes options that intuitively seem to be equally spaced, is usually treated statistically as an interval-level scale. Similarly, scales that include options like "Strongly agree, Agree, Disagree, Strongly disagree," "A great deal, Some, Not very much," "All of the time, Most of the time, Some of the time, Rarely, None of the time," and "Very helpful, Somewhat helpful, and Not very helpful" are usually treated as interval-level measures.

This may seem like a trivial point, but it's not. The reason is that the statistical procedures we can use with interval-level data are more powerful and yield more information than do the statistics we can use with ordinal-level data. This will become clearer as we describe the specific statistical procedures.

Ratio level. *Ratio-level* data are similar to interval data. That is, ratio measures include rank-ordered scores that appear as equally spaced points or intervals on a scale. The main difference is that ratio-level scales assume an *absolute zero point*, meaning that the zero value on the scale indicates that nothing is being measured. In addition, ratio scales don't include any negative numbers. Ratio data are considered the "highest" level of measurement.

A few examples may make this clearer. First, let's consider a well-known interval-level scale, the household thermometer. Certainly this measurement device includes rank-ordered scores that appear on a scale with evenly spaced

points—the basic criteria for an interval-level measure. But does a typical thermometer, whether it measures temperature in Celsius or Fahrenheit, include an absolute zero point? Of course not. If a thermometer included an absolute zero point, a reading of zero would mean no temperature! As all of us know, the zero on a thermometer is a relative indicator of temperature, not an absolute zero.

Similarly, in goal attainment scaling, we can use a scale on which a –2 means much less progress than expected; –1, somewhat less progress than expected; 0, a goal met as expected; +1, somewhat more progress than expected; and +2, more progress than expected. With this commonly used scale, the zero doesn't mean no progress; rather, it's an arbitrary zero that indicates expected progress. We could certainly use a different scale if we wanted, even one without a zero.

Several ratio-level measures that might be useful in evaluating the Families First program are age, income, length of participation in the program, and number of missed appointments. Each of these satisfies the assumptions of ratio-level data; each variable has an absolute zero point (for example, zero income means absolutely no cash is coming in, and zero missed appointments means absolutely no appointments were missed) and equally spaced, rank-ordered scores. (You may be wondering about the concept of "zero" age. Although we would never record a person's age as zero, we all understand that this is not an arbitrary zero and that no negative values are possible. Hence a variable such as age is considered ratio level.)

Before I discuss specific statistical procedures, I want to warn you about a mistake that many social workers make—the sort of mistake that causes practitioners to gnash their teeth when they realize what they've done. Suppose Andrew R. wants to record the number of scheduled appointments that each client in the program missed. He asks a research assistant to read through each client's case records after services have been terminated, count up the number of missed appointments, and then check one of the following categories:

—— none
—— 1–3
—— 4–6
—— 7–9
—— 10 or more

Then when Andrew R. begins the data analysis, he decides to compare the average number of missed appointments for clients who were required by the courts to pay some amount for their services (a copay, if you will) and those for whom the courts made no such requirement. Andrew R. was curious to see whether there was a significant difference between the number of appointments missed by these two groups, hypothesizing that clients who were required to pay something for their services and those who risked being charged if they missed appointments had a greater incentive to avoid missing them. At this point, however, Andrew R. realizes that he cannot calculate the average number of missed appointments for the two groups, because for that calculation, he would have to have recorded the data at the ratio level. Unfortunately, Andrew R. collected the data at the ordinal level, where each rank includes a range of scores. There's no way he can compute an average for this information. As a rule, whenever it's appropriate, collect data on interval and ratio variables such as age, income, problem frequency, depression scores, and number of missed appointments in their raw, ungrouped form rather than in grouped categories. If necessary, you can always group the data later yourself. But if you first collect the data in grouped form, you can't treat them as interval or ratio level, and so you will forfeit the opportunity to use more powerful statistical techniques.

This doesn't mean that Andrew R. has no way to analyze these data, but the other options use less powerful and informative statistics. So, there's a substantial price to be paid if you don't collect data using the level of measurement required for the analyses you will want to conduct. This is another good reason that you should think through ahead of time, in detail, the kinds of questions you will want to be able to answer with the data and the kinds of data analyses you will want to carry out. If you collect the data at the "wrong" level (specifically, one that's "lower" than the one you will need to work with later on), you can't go back and fix the problem without collecting the data all over again. As a general rule, always collect data using the "highest" level of measurement. You can always convert ratio- or interval-level data to grouped, aggregate, or ordinal-level data. That's not a problem. But you can't go in the other direction. It just won't work.

Now we're ready to begin exploring specific statistical concepts and data analysis procedures. I have divided this discussion into four sections: (1) basic or foundation concepts relevant to different kinds of statistical procedures using quantitative data; (2) statistical tools that social workers use to analyze the quantitative data they collect when conducting single-case designs involving individual clients; (3) statistical procedures useful for aggregating quantitative data concerning groups of people, organizations, or communities; and (4) how social workers can analyze qualitative data.

Displaying Data

Once you've collected your data, it's often a good idea to look at it displayed in a graph, table, or chart. Although staring at the numbers spread out on a piece of paper or computer screen and summarizing them in a narrative style can be informative, a picture summarizing the numbers is sometimes worth a thousand words. Trends and patterns are often easier to spot when the data are displayed graphically.

It usually makes sense to begin with a *frequency distribution*, a summary of the number of cases corresponding to each possible value. If we're working with a nominal variable such as "type of service received," the frequency distribution will list how many people received individual counseling, family counseling, substance abuse counseling, and the like. It may also include the percentage of the total that each score represents (for example, if 43 of 135 people received individual counseling, that would be 32 percent of the total). If we're working with an interval variable such as a GAF score, the frequency distribution will show how many clients have a score of 0, 1, 2, 3, and so on, up to 100. If we're working with a ratio variable like age, the frequency distribution will show how many clients are 13 years old, 14 years old, 15 years old, and so forth.

Data that are classified into categories are easier to handle. You can imagine that frequency distributions for interval and ratio data are much more cumbersome, particularly if the variables have a wide range of possible values. One

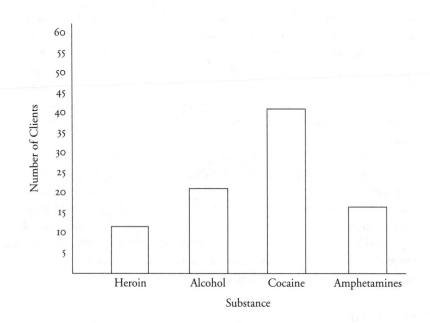

FIGURE 11.1   Primary Substance Abuse Problem (bar chart)

way to handle this problem is to group the interval or ratio data. For example, GAF scores can be grouped from 0 to 10, 11 to 20, 31 to 40, and so on. Age can be grouped from 11 to 15, 16 to 20, 21 to 25, 26 to 30, and so on.

The most common ways to display frequencies graphically are with bar charts, pie charts, histograms, and frequency polygons.

Bar Charts

The bars in bar charts are of equal width, each one representing a different nominal-level category. The height of each bar corresponds to the frequency count for that category. Therefore a category containing 22 people (for example, the number of Families First clients who have a problem with alcohol) has a bar that is twice as tall as a category containing 11 people (the number of clients who have a problem with heroin). The categories being measured are placed along one axis, and the frequency is placed along the other axis. Notice that the bars don't touch; the reason is that bar charts summarize the frequencies for nominal-level data and the categories don't have any direct relationship to one another (figure 11.1).

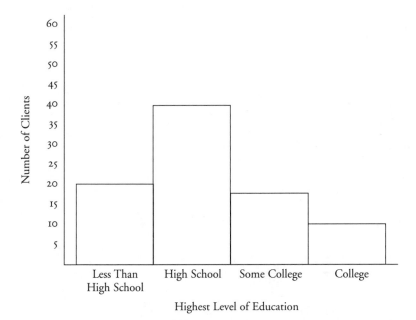

FIGURE 11.2   Client Educational Level (histogram)

Histograms

Histograms are somewhat similar to bar charts in that bars are used to indicate the frequency associated with different categories of a variable. Unlike bar charts, histograms can be used with ordinal data (and sometimes with interval or ratio data). Because the categories are rank ordered, usually from low to high, the convention is to have the sides of the bars touch each other, with no space in between. Figure 11.2 shows a histogram for the educational levels of Mt. Washington clients enrolled in the Families First program. You can see that about four times as many clients have a high school education as have a college education.

Frequency Polygons

Even though *frequency polygon* is a pretty fancy term, the concept is not all that complicated. A polygon is a two-dimensional figure having three or more straight lines. Actually, the frequency polygon is an extension of the histogram and provides a way to display patterns of ordinal, interval, or ratio data. All that's involved is placing a dot in the middle of the top of each bar of a his-

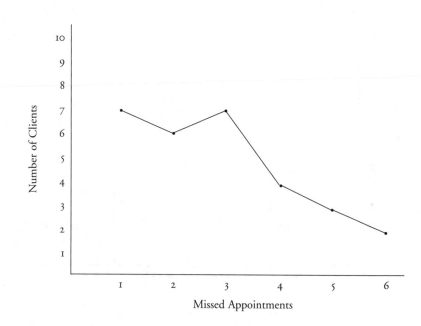

FIGURE 11.3   Number of Missed Appointments (frequency polygon)

togram and connecting the dots. If you were to delete the histogram, you'd be left with a graph. Figure 11.3 is a frequency polygon for the number of missed appointments for Families First clients.

Pie Charts

Pie charts are similar to bar charts. All you need to do is designate a pie "slice" for each category you're measuring and make the size of the slice pro- portionate to the percentage of the total for that category. For example, you could use a pie chart to display the data on Families First clients who have a substance abuse problem. These clients fall into one of four groups: alcohol abuse, cocaine abuse, heroin abuse, and abuse of more than one substance (polydrug abuse). If 40 percent of these clients are being treated for alcohol abuse, one slice, taking up 40 percent of the pie, is dedicated to this category. If 15 percent of the clients are being treated for polydrug abuse, a smaller slice, taking up 15 percent of the pie, is dedicated to this category (figure 11.4).

FIGURE 11.4 Substance Abuse Problems (pie chart)

MEASURES OF CENTRAL TENDENCY AND DISPERSION

Suppose that as part of his evaluation of the Families First program, Andrew R. asks his staff to record the Global Assessment of Functioning (GAF) scores when a client's participation in the program begins and again when the services are terminated. One of Andrew R.'s objectives is to compare the scores to see whether they changed. He knows that if the changes in the scores are significantly positive, he can't necessarily attribute them to the Families First program, since the design did not include a control group and therefore he can't rule out the influence of extraneous factors or plausible alternative explanations. Nonetheless, Andrew R. is understandably curious about changes in the scores.

How can he find out about these changes? Certainly he doesn't want to line up and summarize every single pair of scores; that's too time-consuming and inefficient. Rather, Andrew R. wants to figure out a way to summarize the overall pattern of changes in GAF scores from time 1 to time 2.

Measures of Central Tendency

As a first step, Andrew R. decides to summarize the "typical" or "average" cases. In statistical language, this is called a *measure of central tendency*. Social workers can use one of three main measures of central tendency. Which one is appropriate depends on the kind of data they're working with, specifically the level of measurement. Each measure of central tendency offers a different view of the data that helps identify patterns and themes; that is, each summarizes trends in the data in a different way.

TABLE II.I Service Delivery Categories

	Frequency	Percentage
Family counseling only	12	23
Family counseling and parent education	27	52
Family counseling, parent education, and substance abuse counseling	13	25
Total	52	100

The first measure of central tendency is the *mode*, which is used when data are grouped into categories, based on frequencies, and we want to know which category is the largest or contains the most cases. For example, if Andrew R. places Families First clients in several "service delivery" categories—families receiving family counseling only, families receiving family counseling and parent education, and families receiving family counseling, parent education, and substance abuse counseling—the mode is the category with the largest number of families in it. In table II.I, the mode is 27.

The mode can also be used with one type of ordinal data, those data placed into ranked categories such as high, medium, and low progress in the Families First program. Here, too, you should identify the mode to indicate the central tendency. The mode provides useful, although not very sophisticated, information about typical cases.

The second measure of central tendency is the *median*, which is used with ordinal data that have been rank ordered. If Andrew R. rank-orders a subgroup of parents in the Families First program from highest to lowest based on their GAF scores, the typical or median case would be the one right in the middle of the rank ordering. If Andrew R. rank-orders thirteen parents, for example, which would be the median case? The answer is the seventh case, since that's the one right in the middle. Table II.2 is an example of this kind of rank ordering with scores on the 100-point GAF scale where higher scores reflect higher levels of functioning. The median score is 44.

A more elaborate way to define the median is to say that it's the score at the 50th percentile. A *percentile* is the percentage of other scores that fall below that number. So if a client scores at the 63rd percentile on a standardized instrument, you can say that 63 percent of all the other scores fell below that client's score. Hence the median is the score in a rank-ordered set where 50 percent, or half, the scores fall below and 50 percent, or half, the scores fall above it.

Perhaps you're wondering how to treat an even number of scores. This is not an uncommon occurrence and is handled easily. If you have twelve scores,

TABLE 11.2   Rank Order of Parents' GAF Scores

Parent	Score
1. Allan F.	95
2. Carl E.	68
3. Judy S.	62
4. Sy S.	55
5. Jessica L.	54
6. Lisa D.	50
7. Eric N.	44
8. Brent C.	39
9. Paul R.	33
10. Jonah G.	30
11. Ellen H.	28
12. Shelley K.	26
13. Mark G.	15

for example, all you need to do is average the two middle scores (in this case the sixth and seventh) (that is, add them together and divide by two).

The third measure of central tendency is the one understood most intuitively: the *mean*, which is nothing more than the average of a group of scores (which is calculated by adding up all the scores and dividing by the total number of scores). You can probably see that it wouldn't work to calculate a mean for nominal or ordinal data. Such a calculation wouldn't make any sense. If Andrew R. categorizes Families First participants according to race and ethnicity, where African American = 1, Latino = 2, white = 3, Southeast Asian = 4, and so on, what would it mean to calculate an average in which, say, the mean = 2.4? That doesn't make much sense, does it? The numerical value associated with each of the racial/ethnic groups is nothing more than an arbitrary nominal designation, with no rank order or scale implied. A mean of 2.4 doesn't tell us anything.

As you may have figured out, you need to have interval or ratio data to calculate a mean. These are the only data with which you can add and divide to calculate an average. In the preceding display of GAF scores, for example, we have interval-level data, for which we can calculate the mean by adding up the thirteen scores and dividing by thirteen. The mean is 599 divided by 13 equals 46.08. Notice that the mean in this case is quite close to the median of 44, but this doesn't mean that the mean and median are interchangeable. In fact, in many situations the mean and median for the same distribution of scores are quite different. In general, the mean and median differ when the scores are not spread out somewhat evenly. Let's say that the GAF scores we just reviewed

TABLE 11.3   Rank Order of Parents' GAF Scores

Parent	Score
1. Allan F.	95
2. Carl E.	92
3. Judy S.	22
4. Sy S.	20
5. Jessica L.	18
6. Lisa D.	14
7. Eric N.	13
8. Brent C.	11
9. Paul R.	10
10. Jonah G.	9
11. Ellen H.	8
12. Shelley K.	6
13. Mark G.	4

were distributed very differently, fairly bunched up at the low end of the scale with just a couple of high scores, yet the overall ranking stayed the same. Table 11.3 shows the distribution.

In this instance, the median is 13 (the "middle" of the rank-ordered scores), and the mean is 322 divided by 13 equals 24.77. This is the sort of thing that can happen when a distribution contains one or more "extreme" scores or "outliers." *Extreme scores* and *outliers* are scores very different from the bulk of the other scores. When you calculate a mean, the extreme scores will "drag" the average down or "pull" it up, depending on where the extreme scores are located. If the extreme scores are unusually high, the mean will be pulled in that direction; if the extreme scores are unusually low, the mean will be pulled in that direction. Thus, when you're dealing with extreme scores, it's usually not a good idea to use the mean as the measure of central tendency, as the result will be a misleading mean.

Can you see why the median is a more sensible measure of central tendency to use when you have extreme scores? Ordinarily, the median provides a much more realistic measure of central tendency when you're dealing with extreme scores, reflecting more accurately the "typical" score in the distribution than the mean would.

Another way to say this is that the median is not sensitive to extreme scores in the same way that the mean is. Extreme scores have an immediate impact on the mean; they are factored right into the calculation. In contrast, extreme scores won't necessarily affect the median. Look at table 11.3. Suppose Allan F.'s GAF score was 24 instead of 95 and Carl E.'s score was 23 instead of 92. How would that affect the median? Not at all. Do you see why? Allan F.'s score would still be the highest, and Carl E.'s score would still be the second highest. Thus the scores' rank order wouldn't change a bit, and the median wouldn't change a bit.

But what would these two changes do to the mean? The mean would change dramatically, dropping from 24.77 to 14.00 and demonstrating how sensitive the mean is to extreme scores.

To summarize measures of central tendency for interval or ratio data, you should usually report both the mean and median. Sometimes it's a good idea to include the mode too if that piece of information is useful (although often the mode doesn't tell us much about interval and ratio data). Then your readers will have some information to help them picture the distribution. If the mean and median are very similar, we can assume that we don't have much of a problem with extreme scores or outliers. What would it mean if the mean were much higher than the median? It would indicate extreme scores at the high end of the scale, pulling up the mean. If the mean is a lot lower than the median, there must be extreme scores at the low end of the scale, dragging down the mean. When extreme scores are present, statisticians sometimes refer to the distribution as *skewed* (positively or negatively, depending on the direction of the extreme scores).

Measures of Dispersion

Certainly it's useful for Andrew R. to have some sense of the central tendency of GAF scores. But isn't it also important for him to know something about how scores are distributed *around* the measure of central tendency? It turns out that knowing the scores' central tendency is only one side of the coin. The other side—information about how the scores are distributed—is often just as important. Table 11.4 shows why. The column labeled Time-1 contains the same scores that appeared in table 11.3, and the column marked Time-2 contains a second set of scores for the same parents, obtained a number of weeks after the first set of scores.

Look carefully at these two sets of scores. Do they seem similar or different? I assume you concluded that they look quite different. The Time-1 scores are quite spread out, and the Time-2 scores are much more compact. If you were to summarize these two sets of scores, would you summarize them similarly or differently? Clearly, these two distributions call for different descriptions. But the mean for these two distributions is exactly the same: 24.77. That is, two very different distributions of scores can produce identical means. So it's always important to summarize the distribution of scores around the measure

TABLE 11.4   Two Distributions of GAF Scores

Parent	Time-1	Time-2
1. Allan F.	95	23
2. Carl E.	92	20
3. Judy S.	22	29
4. Sy S.	20	24
5. Jessica L.	18	22
6. Lisa D.	14	21
7. Eric N.	13	26
8. Brent C.	11	29
9. Paul R.	10	21
10. Jonah G.	9	28
11. Ellen H.	8	26
12. Shelley K.	6	25
13. Mark G.	4	28

of central tendency. Another way to put this is to say that it's important to report both the measure of central tendency and the *measure of dispersion*. One without the other is like telling only half the story. Reporting only the mean, for example, doesn't provide any information about whether the distribution is spread out or narrow. We need a measure of dispersion for that.

What's the best way to summarize the variability among scores, or their dispersion? There are basically three ways. The first, and most primitive, is to report the range. Technically the *range* is the difference between the highest and lowest scores in a distribution plus one, although most people think of the range less formally as the difference between the highest and lowest scores. What's the range for the Time-1 scores in table 11.4? (Answer: 95 minus 4 plus 1 equals 92.) What's the range for the Time-2 scores? (Answer: 29 minus 20 plus 1 equals 10.)

For those of you who are curious about the "plus one," the explanation is simple. Let's say the scores in a distribution are 3, 4, 2, 2, 4, 3, 5, 2. What's the range? The highest score is 5, and the lowest score is 2. Thus, the distribution has four possible scores: 2, 3, 4, and 5. An easy way to find the number of possible scores—the range—is to subtract the lowest number from the highest and add one (in this example, 5 minus 2 plus 1 equals 4).

Although the range is a useful piece of information, it has one major limitation. Look at table 11.5 and see if you can discover what the problem is. The problem is that the range doesn't tell us how the scores between the highest and lowest ones are spread out. Table 11.5 shows an extreme example of two distributions that have exactly the same range (94 minus 6 plus 1 equals

TABLE 11.5 Two Different Distributions, Same Range

Distribution 1	Distribution 2
6	6
47	8
46	20
48	34
47	42
46	49
47	57
47	65
48	71
48	82
94	94

89). Yet the scores are distributed very differently. That is, the range isn't very informative. Ideally, we would have a measure of dispersion that tells us something about the distribution between the highest and lowest scores.

A measure of dispersion is a number that summarizes the nature of the distribution of a set of scores. Let's think conceptually for a few minutes here without getting bogged down in any complicated math. Look at the two sets of scores in table 11.5. Do you see that the scores in distribution 1 tend to be bunched up in the vicinity of the middle of the range and that the scores in distribution 2 tend to be more spread out across the range? Wouldn't it be nice if we could come up with a number that summarizes how bunched up or spread out the scores are?

I'd like you to bear with me here as I walk through this process. This is the one of the few places in this chapter where I will spell out some of the mathematical steps in a statistic. My aim is to show you how intuitive statistics can be.

One way to describe the difference between distribution 1 and distribution 2 is to say that *on average,* in distribution 1 the scores are closer to the mean and in distribution 2 they are farther from the mean. That is, on average, in distribution 1 the distance between each score and the mean is less than it is in distribution 2. Thus it would seem easy simply to calculate the average distance in these two distributions between the scores and the mean as a way of summarizing how bunched up or spread out the scores are. In distribution 1 we could calculate the distance between each score and the mean, add up those distances, and divide by the number of scores for the "average distance." We could then do the same for distribution 2 and compare the two numbers.

This seems to make a lot of sense, except for one thing. Some of the scores are above the mean and some are below it, because by definition the mean is in the "middle." Hence the distances between some of the scores and the mean are positive (the scores are higher than the mean), and some are negative (the scores are lower than the mean). Guess what happens when we add up all these differences to calculate the "average distance"? We will always, always, always get a big fat zero. The distances pertaining to the scores above the mean and the distances pertaining to the scores below the mean will always cancel each other out, so to speak. As a result, when we add up all the distances in order to divide by the number of scores, we will always have zero as the numerator (the number above the line in a fraction) and the number of scores as the denominator (the number below the line in a fraction), and zero divided by any number is zero. The conclusion is that this won't help us summarize the distribution, although it certainly is appealing intuitively.

Fortunately, there's a way around this. Years ago a clever statistician figured out that if adding up all those positive and negative values created a problem, the easiest solution would be to get rid of the negative values. Now you can't just change all the minus signs to plus signs. That's too easy—and it also violates a mathematical rule. But it is OK to square each of the values. As you may recall from algebra, when you square two positive numbers, you get a positive number (+3 times +3 equals +9, +5 times +5 equals +25, +12 times +12 equals +144), and when you square two negative numbers, you also get a positive number (–3 times –3 equals +9, –5 times –5 equals +25, –12 times –12 equals +144). So the way to eliminate the problem of adding up positive and negative numbers that will always result in zero is to square each of the differences between the scores and the mean. That may seem like one of those smoke-and-mirrors tricks that a magician might use, but mathematically it's a legitimate procedure.

Let's make sure you haven't lost the forest now that we've spent some time looking at the trees. It's important not to lose sight of the big picture. What I've just described is a way to calculate the "average" (sort of) distance between a group of scores and the mean of the scores for First Families clients. To avoid the problem of adding positive and negative "difference" scores, or deviations, we can square each difference score, add those up (known in statistics as the *sum of the squares*), and divide that total by the number of scores. The result is called the *variance*. A distribution of scores that's spread out will have a much higher variance than will a distribution that's narrow or bunched up. You can see how this happens with the two distributions in table 11.4, which I've reproduced in table 11.6. You can see that distribution 1 (Time-1 scores) produces a

TABLE 11.6   Variance of Time-1 Scores

Parent	Time-1	Mean	Distance from the Mean (deviation)	Deviation Squared
1. Allan F.	95	24.77	70.23	493.23
2. Carl E.	92	24.77	67.23	451.99
3. Judy S.	22	24.77	−2.77	7.67
4. Sy S.	20	24.77	−4.77	22.75
5. Jessica L.	18	24.77	−6.77	45.83
6. Lisa D.	14	24.77	−10.77	115.99
7. Eric N.	13	24.77	−11.77	138.53
8. Brent C.	11	24.77	−13.77	189.61
9. Paul R.	10	24.77	−14.77	218.15
10. Jonah G.	9	24.77	−15.77	248.69
11. Ellen H.	8	24.77	−16.77	281.23
12. Shelley K.	6	24.77	−18.77	352.31
13. Mark G.	4	24.77	−20.77	431.39
Totals			0	2997.37

variance that is much smaller than the one produced by distribution 2 (Time-2 scores).

The sum of these squared deviations is 2997.37, which means that the variance is 2997.37 divided by 13 equals 230.57. Table 11.7 calculates the variance for the Time-2 scores:

In table 11.7 you can see that the distance between the scores and the mean is, on average, much smaller than it is in table 11.6. This means that the square of each deviation is smaller, on average, and therefore the sum of the squared deviations is smaller. In fact, the sum of the squared deviations for the Time-2 scores is 122.27, compared with 2997.37. The variance for the Time-2 scores is 122.27 divided by 13 equals 9.41, which is clearly much smaller than the variance for the Time-1 scores, 230.57. Simply by comparing the two variances, you can see how much more compact the Time-2 scores are than the Time-1 scores; on average, the Time-2 scores are much closer to the mean.

The only drawback to this approach is that the numbers we must use when we calculate the variance are often large and can be unwieldy. The reason is that squaring all those deviation scores can produce lots of big numbers, particularly when a distribution has a fair amount of variance, as with the Time-1 scores.

Well, statisticians have one last trick up their sleeves. The way to handle this annoying problem is simply to work with the square root of the variance rather than the variance itself. That is, after squaring each of the difference scores or deviations and adding up the numbers, we can return to the original unit of measurement by taking the square root of the sum of squared deviations.

TABLE 11.7   Variance of Time-2 Scores

Parent	Time-1	Mean	Distance from the Mean (deviation)	Deviation Squared
1. Allan F.	23	24.77	-1.77	3.13
2. Carl E.	20	24.77	-4.77	22.75
3. Judy S.	29	24.77	4.23	17.89
4. Sy S.	24	24.77	-.77	.59
5. Jessica L.	22	24.77	-2.77	7.67
6. Lisa D.	21	24.77	-3.77	14.21
7. Eric N.	26	24.77	1.23	1.51
8. Brent C.	29	24.77	4.23	17.89
9. Paul R.	21	24.77	-3.77	14.21
10. Jonah G.	28	24.77	3.23	10.43
11. Ellen H.	26	24.77	1.23	1.51
12. Shelley K.	25	24.77	.23	.05
13. Mark G.	28	24.77	3.23	10.43
Totals			0	122.27

(In case you've forgotten, the square root of a number is another number which, when multiplied by itself, gives you the original number. So the square root of 9 is 3, since 3 multiplied by itself gives you the original number, 9. The square root of 16 equals 4, the square root of 49 equals 7, and the square root of 100 equals 10.)

When you take the square root of the variance, the result is the *standard deviation*, which is nothing more than a direct indication of the amount of variation in a group of scores—a measure of dispersion. The standard deviation should be relatively easy to understand intuitively, in that it's computed by looking at the difference between each score in a distribution and the distribution's mean, squaring each of those differences to get rid of the minus signs, adding up all those "squared deviations," dividing that sum by the number of scores (which gives you the variance), and then taking the square root of the variance to get back to the original unit of measurement. Thus the standard deviation for the Time-1 scores is 15.18 (the square root of the variance, which is 230.57), and the standard deviation for the Time-2 scores is 3.07 (the square root of the variance, which is 9.41). Here, too, you can simply look at the two standard deviations (15.18 and 3.07) and quickly figure out that the distribution of Time-1 scores is much more spread out than the distribution of Time-2 scores.

How many times have you read a professional book or journal article, come across a reference to a standard deviation, thought to yourself "That's one of those things I don't understand and never will understand," skipped over that

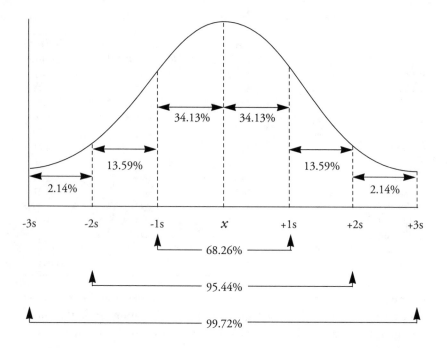

FIGURE II.5   Normal Curve and Percent of Scores Between Selected
Points Under the Curve

passage, and moved on? My hope is that this conceptual (and slightly mathematical) overview helps clarify what may have seemed like an incomprehensi-
ble topic. Now that you understand what a standard deviation is, you're better
able to figure out the meaning of the information presented in those reports.

The mere reference to a standard deviation does not necessarily tell you
whether a distribution of scores is large or small. For example, suppose I were
to tell you that a Mt. Washington social worker administered an instrument
measuring self-esteem to a group of school-age children in the Families First
program who are members of a support group and that the standard deviation
was 2.7. Would that tell you much? No, it wouldn't tell you much of anything
unless you knew more about the possible range of scores on this instrument.
If the scores could range from 1 to 10, this would be a pretty large standard
deviation. However, if the scores could range from 1 to 100, this would be a relatively small standard deviation. That is, you need to know the context of the
standard deviation in order to interpret it.

The standard deviation also has some other fascinating properties and uses.

Remember my brief discussion of the normal curve in chapter 5? I described an exhibit I once saw at Chicago's Museum of Science and Industry that demonstrated that Ping-Pong balls dropped on top of a series of pegs always fall in the pattern of a normal curve or *normal distribution*. A normal distribution, often referred to as a *bell curve* because of its shape (figure 11.5), is symmetrical, so if you folded it in half, the two halves would overlap very closely. One of the interesting things about life is that many phenomena are distributed in the form of a normal curve. For example, if we plotted, in order, the IQ scores of a random sample of Americans across the horizontal axis and the number of people with each score, or frequency, up and down the vertical axis, I bet it would form a normal curve. Also, if we were to plot something like the number of days per year that people eat in restaurants, it probably would form a normal curve.

When dealing with a normal curve, we know certain things about how the scores are distributed. First, 34.13 percent of all cases are between the mean and one standard deviation above the mean. Similarly, 34.13 percent of all cases are between the mean and one standard deviation below the mean. That is, in a normal distribution, 68.26 percent of all cases (or a little more than two-thirds) fall between one standard deviation above and below the mean. Second, 13.59 percent of the cases fall between the first and second standard deviations above the mean, and the same goes for the area between the first and second standard deviations below the mean. Another way to say this is that between the mean and two standard deviations above and below the mean are 95.44 percent of all the cases (34.13 percent + 34.13 percent + 13.59 percent + 13.59 percent). Finally, 2.15 percent of the cases fall between the second and third deviations above the mean, and the same goes for the area between the second and third standard deviations below the mean. Therefore, 99.74 percent of the cases (which is just about all of them) fall between the mean and three standard deviations above and below the mean.

Apart from all these statistical properties, the standard deviation is a concept that can help social workers think more clearly and precisely about their work, even if they never use it for any statistical purpose. Here's an example of what I mean. Suppose a Mt. Washington social worker, Florence I., facilitates two substance abuse treatment groups for parents enrolled in the Families First program, one on Tuesday evening and the other on Thursday evening. Because some people have dropped out of each group, Florence I. is considering combining them.

She is concerned, however, that the remaining members of the two groups may not function well together, in large part because of differences in their substance abuse histories and the severity of their problems. Florence I. has observed that even though the "average" member of each of the two groups has a similar substance abuse history (the typical client has had a problem with cocaine for about four years), the Tuesday evening group is much more varied than the Thursday evening group. According to Florence I., the Tuesday group includes a couple of members who have had a problem with cocaine for only several months and several members who have had a problem with cocaine for more than eight years, whereas in the Thursday group most of the members have had a cocaine problem for about four years. She doesn't really need to compute a standard deviation to be able to use this concept. She knows that the central tendency for the two groups is about the same (the "mean" profile, if you will) but the dispersions (the standard deviations, figuratively speaking) are quite different. Florence I. may want to take into account this difference when she thinks about combining the two treatment groups.

THE CONCEPT OF STATISTICAL SIGNIFICANCE

As I mentioned earlier, sometimes social workers need only descriptive statistics to summarize data (for example, when using frequencies, measures of central tendency, and measures of dispersion). At other times, however, social workers need to use inferential statistics to generalize to a population the results from a sample.

Thus far we've focused mainly on descriptive statistics. Now we'll look at some inferential statistics. To do this, we must understand the concept of statistical significance. The idea of statistical significance is a bit tricky, so please pay particularly close attention to the next passage.

Statistical significance is based entirely on probability theory, which has to do with statistical odds, such as the likelihood that you'll win the state lottery tomorrow, pick the right number at the roulette wheel in Las Vegas, drive your car during the next year without getting a flat tire, have your July 4 picnic rained out, and be offered the first job you apply for once you finish your social work education. In social work, probability is important when considering such things as the odds that clients' behavior will change, the grant we applied for will be approved, and the agency we work for will be sued for malpractice in a recent incident. Clearly, life is filled with situations in which statistical odds matter.

Statistical probability is important to social work evaluation and research because of the frequency with which we social workers use samples. Because of limited time and funding, we often gather data from samples rather than populations. When we do this and believe that the sample we use is representative of the population from which it was selected, we need to know that the result we obtained is not a fluke.

Even when we use the most sophisticated sampling techniques, there is always a possibility, although perhaps a remote one, that the results are due to chance. For example, imagine that Andrew R. randomly selects a sample of 50 case records from the entire population of 500 Mt. Washington case records. Let's say that the mean or average age of the 500 clients is 34.7. If Andrew R. randomly selects one sample of 50, the sample's mean age should be pretty close to 34.7. In fact, if he were to select multiple samples of 50 (not that there would be any practical reason for him to do this), the mean age for every sample should, in principle, be close to 34.7. We know, however, that every once in a while, because of the laws of probability, Andrew R. will get a sample with a mean age that is much lower or higher than 34.7 (like those stray Ping-Pong balls in the demonstration at Chicago's Museum of Science and Industry). We need to know in these situations how much higher or lower a sample's mean age would have to be to be *significantly* different.

The same idea applies when we examine relationships between variables. Suppose Andrew R. wants to examine the relationship between the number of missed appointments and parents' level of functioning as indicated by the GAF scale. We can use statistics to calculate this relationship, and we may want to know whether the result is statistically significant. That is, what is the likelihood, or probability, that the statistical relationship Andrew R. finds in his one sample between the number of missed appointments and parents' level of functioning really exists in the population from which the sample was selected?

Null Hypotheses

Statisticians have what may seem like a rather strange way of approaching this question: What is the probability that the statistical relationship found in this sample would have occurred by chance if, in fact, there was no statistically significant relationship in the population from which the sample was selected?

Let's walk through this slowly. As I mentioned before, when we select a sample, we really have no way of knowing for sure whether it's representative of the population from which it was selected. Of course, if we use careful sampling procedures, we will have more confidence than if we select a sample very casually. Nonetheless, there is always the possibility of sampling error. No matter how careful our sampling procedures, there is always a chance, albeit perhaps a remote one, that the sample we actually select is an aberration, like one of the very few Ping-Pong balls that ended up far away from the majority in the museum exhibit.

Since we can't know for sure how representative any particular sample is (unless we actually compare it with the population, which defeats the purpose of the sampling in the first place), the best we can determine is the *probability* that the sample results have occurred by chance. Since we can't prove directly that the sample results are representative of the population from which the sample was selected, we approach the problem indirectly, by determining the likelihood that the sample results would have occurred if they *do not* exist in the population. This is called testing the *null hypothesis.* That is, we attempt to disprove, or reject, the hypothesis that there is no statistically significant relationship in the population. If the result we obtain is very compelling or strong, we have enough evidence to "reject the null hypothesis" (that's how statisticians say it) and, therefore, to assert the *alternative hypothesis.* When we reject the null hypothesis, we are saying that we have statistical evidence that chance is an unlikely explanation and that the results are probably not due to sampling error.

To go back to our example, Andrew R. is interested in the relationship between the number of missed appointments and parents' level of functioning as indicated by their GAF score. The null hypothesis is that there is no statistically significant relationship between these two variables. If the results in the sample are sufficiently strong, he will have enough evidence to reject the null hypothesis and assert that there is evidence to suggest a statistically significant relationship between these two variables and that chance (sampling error) is an unlikely explanation of the results.

Statistical Significance

The term I just used—*statistically significant*—has a precise meaning. How strong, you might ask, does the statistical evidence need to be to reject the null hypothesis and assert that a significant relationship exists? Widely accepted norms or standards are used to determine whether a result is statistically significant. At a minimum, a statistically significant result is one that would occur by chance 5 percent of the time or less. Of course, we would prefer that results occur by chance zero or maybe 1 percent of the time. But statisticians and other professionals who perform statistical analyses are usually willing to tolerate up to a 5 percent probability that the sample results occurred by chance. In essence, if there is a 5 percent or less chance that a particular result is due to sampling error (a fluke, that is), we are willing to conclude that the result is, indeed, statistically significant. These percentages are known variously as *rejection levels, significance levels,* or *alpha levels.* As you probably realize, a .001 rejection level is more demanding than a .01 rejection level, and both are more demanding than a .05 rejection level.

Perhaps you've read professional publications and come across notations like ($p<.05$) or ($p<.01$). Does that look familiar? You may have seen this notation in a sentence like "The analysis demonstrated that the relationship between the two variables was statistically significant ($p<.01$)." In this example it means that the relationship between the variables is statistically significant at the .01 level or that this result would occur by chance (assuming the null hypothesis of no relationship between the two variables in the population from which the sample was selected) less than 1 percent of the time (the p stands for probability and the $<$ is the algebraic notation for "less than"). Another way of saying this is that we are willing to reject the null hypothesis and assert an alternative hypothesis with 99 percent certainty.

Two Types of Error

Because we always base our conclusions on probability, there is always the possibility, no matter how remote, that we're wrong. Actually, there are two ways for us to be wrong. One is that we would reject the null hypothesis, thereby asserting that a statistically significant relationship really exists when, in fact, the null hypothesis is true and shouldn't have been rejected. This is called a *Type I error*. If we use a rejection level of .01, for example, the likelihood of a Type I error is 1 percent. Thus, if Andrew R. concludes that a statistically significant relationship exists between the number of missed appointments and parents' level of functioning when it actually does not exist (suggesting that the sample Andrew R. used was an aberration), he would have made a Type I error. Of course, there's a 99 percent chance that this wouldn't happen.

In contrast, Andrew R. may *fail* to reject the null hypothesis, concluding that there is no relationship between the two variables when, in fact, there *is* a relationship. If he did this, he would make a Type II error.

There's a close relationship between Type I and Type II errors; they are not independent. That is, if we are determined to reduce the likelihood of a Type I error, we must increase the likelihood of a Type II error, and vice versa. The two go hand in hand. (It may help to think about a long, blown-up balloon. If you squeeze or narrow one end of the balloon, the other end will expand.) In some cases, it seems important to reduce the likelihood of a Type I error, such as when it would create a terrible problem if we rejected the null hypothesis by mistake. Imagine what would happen if the Mt. Washington staff rejected a true null hypothesis (a Type I error) concerning the effectiveness of a very expensive and time-consuming intervention. This would be enormously costly, given the time and resources that staff members might invest in an intervention that, in fact, was not effective. In this instance, it might seem wise to minimize the likelihood of a Type I error, even though the risk of a Type II error would rise (and the staff might miss a golden opportunity to use an intervention that they had erroneously concluded was not effective). Conversely, if the Mt. Washington staff were particularly concerned about failing to implement a compelling intervention or program, they might decide to minimize the likelihood of a Type II error, thereby increasing the risk of a Type I error. In sum, there's no simple solution to the tension between these two types of error. Social workers must use good judgment when deciding how to balance the relative costs and benefits. The *possibility* of error is inevitable, so all social workers can do is minimize the error and balance the trade-offs between Type I and Type II errors.

Statistical Versus Practical Significance

Occasionally social workers go overboard with the concept of statistical significance, assuming that if the words *statistical significance* appear, they always mean that the results are important in a practical sense. Although many statistically significant results do have practical relevance, some do not.

Why not? Sometimes social workers obtain statistically significant results for purely methodological reasons. For example, it's well known among statisticians that a large enough sample can produce statistically significant relationships between variables, even when the relationship is actually quite weak. That is, we can say that it's unlikely that the result occurred by chance (it's statistically significant) but that when push comes to shove, the result is pretty weak and doesn't have important implications for practice.

This means that social workers must be able to distinguish between statistically significant results that matter and those that don't. I wish there were some simple way to do this, but there isn't. In the final analysis, social workers must filter statistically significant results through their own screen, which consists of their knowledge of social work theory and practice. Does the result, though statistically significant, have practical, meaningful, and important implications for practice? If the answer is yes, it is appropriate to make a big deal of the statistically significant result. But if the answer is no, it's important not to exaggerate the relevance of a statistically significant result.

ANALYZING DATA IN SINGLE-CASE DESIGNS

Most of the time, social workers analyze what are called *aggregate data*, information about groups of people, families, couples, organizations, and communities. This information may be collected by surveys, questionnaires, interviews, examination of case records, or observation. Knowing how to present frequencies, measures of central tendency, and measures of dispersion when working with aggregate data is very useful.

But what about the data that social workers collect when they work with individual clients, particularly with single-case designs? For example, Andrew R. is working with a ten-year-old child in the Families First program, Jared D., whose behavior in school has been unmanageable, according to school officials. Jared's teacher reports that he is frequently disruptive and occasionally aggressive with other children. The school principal is beginning to think that he may need to be placed in an alternative school. Before taking this step, however, the principal was willing to have one of the social workers in the Families First program work with Jared and his family. The principal, the teacher, and Jared's parents agreed that if Jared's behavior didn't improve significantly in twelve weeks (to provide enough time for a modest baseline period and a reasonable intervention period), the principal would have him transferred to an alternative school.

The Families First social worker, Pam K., worked with the teacher to design an intervention strategy that included lots of behavioral principles, such as positive reinforcement. The teacher agreed to complete a simple "behavior assessment" form at the end of each day. The form contains one closed-ended and one open-ended item. The closed-ended item uses a Likert scale to summarize the quality of Jared's behavior (the item uses a 4-point scale where 1 = excellent, 2 = good, 3 = fair, and 4 = poor). This is followed by an open-ended item asking the teacher to describe Jared's behavior that day, significant events that may have affected the behavior, and any other relevant observations.

Pam K. and Jared's teacher agreed that the teacher would not introduce the behavioral intervention until ten additional school days had passed but that she would begin recording her observations the very next day. In this way, Pam K. would have a baseline and an intervention period.

What tools do we have for analyzing data collected as part of an AB design (or any other single-case design, such as an ABAB or multiple baseline design)?

In some instances, social workers may prefer simply to "eyeball" the data, that is, examine whether a client's status has changed over time without using formal statistical techniques. Social workers who use this approach should consider the following factors (Blythe and Tripodi 1989; Jayaratne, Tripodi, and Talsma 1988; and Parsonson and Baer 1978):

1. The reason for the intervention and the likelihood that the dependent variable will increase, decrease, or stay the same over time (the parties in

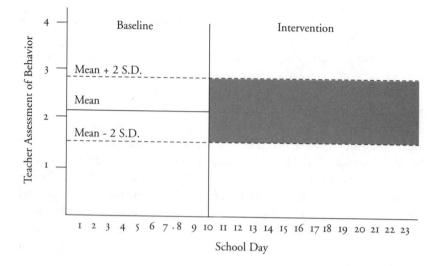

FIGURE 11.6   Shewart Chart

Jared's case hope that the frequency of his desirable behavior will
improve, of course).

2. The distance between the units of measurement that appear on the horizontal axis (usually some unit of time) and the vertical axis (the measure
of the dependent variable) (for example, it wouldn't make much sense to
have Jared's teacher complete the rating scale every five minutes; once a
day should suffice).

3. Agreement by the social worker and, preferably, the client (and, when
appropriate, other interested parties) on what would constitute meaningful and significant progress (ideally, Pam K., Jared, and Jared's teacher
would agree on the goal of their work together).

4. The pattern during the baseline period (ideally, a clear pattern would
emerge during the baseline period before the teacher introduces the
intervention with Jared; the pattern may show an increase, decrease, no
change, or fluctuation in the measure during the baseline period).

5. The pattern during the intervention period (again, the measure may show
an increase, decrease, no change, or fluctuation).

6. The comparison of the baseline data with the data for the intervention
period, especially changes in such factors as the severity, frequency, and
duration of the measure (for example, with the appropriate measures, the
parties in Jared's case could decide whether his behavior seemed to have
deteriorated or improved over time, whether the problematic behavior

occurred more or less frequently, and whether there was a change in the length of time of the problematic episodes).

Although this sort of visual inspection of data is sufficient in many circumstances, social workers may want or need to conduct a more thorough analysis of the data, usually to determine whether any significant changes in the client's status have occurred over time with respect to such things as the existence, severity, frequency, and duration of the problem. Fortunately, several useful statistical techniques are available to discover whether significant change has occurred over time. Because the specific procedures used can be a bit complicated, I will provide a brief conceptual overview here; those of you who are interested in more detail can consult several useful publications (Bloom, Fischer, and Orme 1995; Blythe and Tripodi 1989; Gottman and Leiblum 1974; Jayaratne 1978).

Shewart Chart

The Shewart chart explores whether there have been any statistically significant departures from the general pattern. For example, a Shewart chart could be used to determine whether Jared's behavior deteriorated or improved significantly on any particular days during the intervention period.

The first step when using a Shewart chart is calculating the mean and standard deviation for the observations during the baseline period (see figure 11.6). Thus if there are ten data collection "points" (in this case, days) during the baseline period, Andrew R. adds up on the 4-point scale the scores of the teacher's daily assessment of Jared's behavior and computes the mean. Since 1 = excellent and 4 = poor, the best possible score for the ten days would be 10 and the mean would be 1, and the worst possible score would be 40, with a mean of 4.

Using the procedures I just described, Andrew R. would also compute the standard deviation for the ten scores. If the standard deviation was small, it would mean that over the ten days, the teacher's assessments varied very little (of course, whether it varied very little at a "high" or a "low" level would be determined by the mean score). If the standard deviation was large, it would mean that over the ten days, the teacher's assessments varied considerably.

After the mean and standard deviation for the baseline period were computed, Andrew R. would graph the results. On the left-hand or vertical axis he would plot the four point values ranging from excellent (1) to poor (4), and along the horizontal axis he would plot the days. The first ten marks would correspond to the baseline period, and the subsequent marks would correspond to the intervention period.

Then Andrew R. would find where the mean was located on the vertical axis and would extend a straight line from that point horizontally across the graph. Next he would multiply the standard deviation times two and would mark that distance both above and below the mean on the vertical axis (put another way, there would be two points, one marked two standard deviations above and the other two standard deviations below the mean). Andrew R. would also extend straight lines across the graph horizontally from these two points.

Any data points during the intervention phase that fall *above or below* the two outside lines (the ones drawn from the mean ±2 standard deviations) are considered statistically significant or significantly different from the observations obtained during the baseline period; that is, they are likely to occur by chance less than 5 percent of the time. Conversely, any data points during the intervention phase that fall *between or within* the two outside lines are not significantly different from the observations obtained during the baseline period.

This technique can be useful because it can help you quickly pinpoint specific days (or any other observation time period) that are "unusually good" or "unusually bad." With this information, you can explore why things did or did not go well on those particular days. (We think of the data points that fall above or below the two outside lines as *outliers*. Outliers aren't necessarily good or bad; they merely are statistically significant and warrant attention. Whether the outliers constitute good news or bad news depends on the issues being explored.)

Binomial Test

Sometimes social workers feel a bit queasy when they see terms like *binomial*. But all that *binomial* means in this context is that the test is based on an algebraic expression that has two parts (hence the prefix *bi*). You use a binomial test when you want to look beyond individual outliers (as with the Shewart chart) at whether the *overall pattern* of results obtained during the intervention period is significantly different from the overall pattern of results obtained during the baseline period.

If Andrew R. wanted to use a binomial test to compare the baseline and intervention periods for Jared, he would begin by identifying the median (not the mean) of the scores that Jared's teacher reported during the baseline period. As with the Shewart chart, Andrew R. would draw a straight line horizontally from this point on the vertical axis across the graph (through the baseline and intervention periods). In this example, the lower scores correspond to desirable behavior (1 = excellent and 4 = poor), so scores below the median would be "successes" and scores above the median would be "failures" (to use the statistical

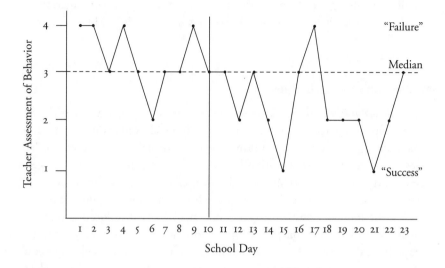

FIGURE 11.7   Binomial Test

jargon). All Andrew R. would need to do is count up the number of successes during the intervention phase out of the total number of observations during the intervention phase (see figure 11.7). Using a simple little table (trust me, it's really simple—see Blythe and Tripodi 1989:130), Andrew R. could quickly determine whether the number of successes during the intervention period constituted a statistically significant result. Therefore if there were eight observations during the intervention period (for instance, to see the extent to which Jared stayed in his seat), seven successes (scores below the median) would be required to achieve statistical significance (that is, in eight 30-minute observations of Jared in his classroom, he stayed in his seat in seven of them). That's quite a few, but it's what's required to rule out chance as an explanation. If there were twenty observations during the intervention period, fifteen successes would be required to achieve statistical significance. Similar values can be obtained for any number of observations during the intervention phase.

Once again, the minimum number of successes required to achieve statistical significance is based on probability theory. More specifically, the binomial test is based on what statisticians know about the frequency with which different results occur by chance when there are two options. The classic illustration of the binomial test is based on coin tosses and the probability that when flipped repeatedly, a fair, unbiased coin will produce various combinations of heads and tails. That is, binomial theory tells us the statistical likelihood that if we flipped an unbiased coin 50 times, we will get, say, 28 heads and 22 tails, or 31 heads and 19 tails.

Celeration Line Technique

The *celeration line technique* is merely a variation on the binomial test theme. The main difference is that the celeration line technique is used when the trend during the baseline period isn't consistent or stable but, rather, accelerates or decelerates. The celeration line technique takes into account the general trend during the baseline period (whether it is acceleration or deceleration) and factors that into the analysis of whether there was significant change during the intervention period (see figure 11.8). Instead of locating only the median during the baseline period and extending a line horizontally across the graph from that point, the celeration line technique requires calculating a couple of points in the baseline phase so as to factor in the extent of the acceleration and deceleration, extending that line across the graph (through the baseline and intervention phases), and, as with the binomial test, calculating the number of successes represented by points below the line during the intervention phase (or above, if higher rather than lower scores are desirable). In fact, the same binomial table is used to determine whether the number of successes during the intervention period is statistically significant (for additional details, see Bloom, Fischer, and Orme 1995; Blythe and Tripodi 1989; and Gingerich and Feyerherm 1979).

Correlation and Causality

I must remind you of a point I emphasized during our discussion of research and evaluation designs: correlation does not imply causation. Some designs, both group and single-case, control for extraneous factors (such as the effects of maturation, measurement, and contemporaneous events) better than others do. Program evaluations that include random assignment to experimental and control conditions control for extraneous factors and rule out plausible alternative explanations much more effectively than do program evaluations that include pre- and postmeasures with only one group. Single-case designs that contain reversals (for example, ABAB) or multiple baselines control for extraneous factors and rule out plausible alternative explanations much better than do simple AB designs.

All the designs in which Shewart charts, binomial tests, and the celeration line technique are used are of the AB variety. These designs permit you to com-

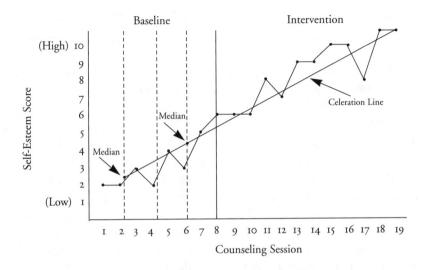

FIGURE II.8   Celeration Line Technique

pare what occurs during baseline and intervention phases, but they do not offer much control for extraneous factors. Consequently, you need to be careful not to assume that any statistically significant results associated with these three data analysis techniques provide evidence of *causal* relationships between the intervention and the outcome data during the intervention period. It may be tempting to infer a causal connection, but without more rigorous control for extraneous factors, this kind of inference isn't warranted.

ANALYZING AGGREGATE DATA

Now that we've looked at analyzing data collected from or about individual clients, we will explore the data analysis techniques used for grouped or aggregate data. In many, many situations, social workers need to analyze lots of data collected from interviews, surveys, questionnaires, observation, or the examination of existing or secondary data.

As I mentioned earlier, there are basically three broad types of analyses. We've already considered the first, which analyzes one variable at a time (univariate analysis). Frequencies, measures of central tendency (mean, median, mode), and measures of dispersion (range, variance, standard deviation) are suitable for univariate analyses.

But as you might imagine, there are many reasons that social workers may need to look beyond individual variables and explore relationships between and among variables. When they explore relationships between two variables at a time, they conduct bivariate analyses, and when they explore relationships among three or more variables, they conduct multivariate analyses.

Bivariate Analysis

Think about Andrew R.'s evaluation of Mt. Washington's Families First program, particularly the part of the evaluation that focuses on changes in family functioning. What kinds of variables might be relevant to this analysis? First are outcome measures. What might they include? Possibilities are changes in the participants' GAF scores and changes in the children's scores on the child behavior instrument. It's important to summarize this data one variable at a time. Andrew R. can present the frequencies, measures of central tendency, and measures of dispersion appropriate for this kind of interval-level data.

But wouldn't it make sense to see whether any variables are associated with these outcome measures? What might they be? Perhaps certain demographic characteristics are correlated with outcome, such as age, ethnicity, or gender. Perhaps certain features of the Families First program are worth looking at, such as the families' primary social worker, the degree of contact between clients and social workers, and the specific services that the program provided.

We don't want to go on a fishing expedition, in which we would identify every conceivable relevant variable and then correlate all of them two at a time. Because of the laws of probability, we'd probably come up with some statistically significant findings by chance, simply because we computed so many correlations. Instead, we need to explore correlations between pairs of variables based on what makes conceptual sense in practice theory or practice wisdom. In short, we should have a sound, good reason for every bivariate relationship we look at.

Hence the first step in bivariate analyses is identifying the important, relevant relationships to examine. Once we have this list—which may be short, medium, or long depending on our evaluation or research project—we should begin thinking about which statistical procedures are most suitable. As I explained at the beginning of this chapter, you should select statistics based on the variables' levels of measurement. For example, an analysis of the relationship between two nominal-level variables requires a different sort of statistical procedure than does an analysis of the relationship between two interval-level variables or between one ordinal- and one ratio-level variable.

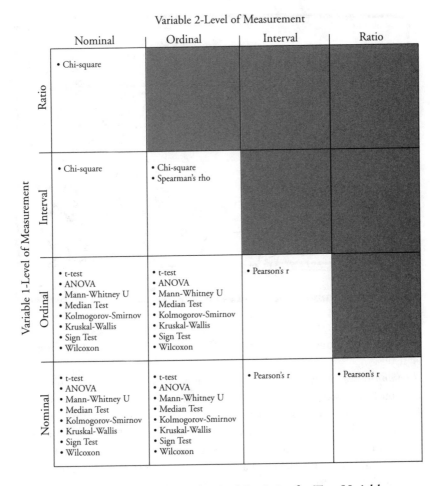

FIGURE 11.9   Commonly Used Statistics for Two-Variable
Combinations

My objective here is to give you a general overview of the menu of options.
If you know the range of possibilities, you should have a good idea of which
statistical procedure to use.

It's helpful to use the chart in figure 11.9. You'll see that the possible two-
variable combinations are (1) two nominal variables, (2) two ordinal variables,
(3) two interval variables, (4) two ratio variables, (5) one nominal variable and
one ordinal variable, (6) one nominal variable and one interval ratio, (7) one
nominal variable and one ratio variable, (8) one ordinal variable and one interval variable, (9) one ordinal variable and one ratio variable, and (10) one inter-

val variable and one ratio variable. Different combinations require different statistics.

Two nominal variables.   In many situations, you may want to explore the relationship between two nominal-level variables. One example from Andrew R.'s evaluation is the relationship between whether or not a family had a parent with a substance abuse problem and whether or not the family completed the Families First program. The first variable has four nominal categories: (1) no substance abuse problem, (2) a parent with an alcohol problem, (3) a parent with another drug problem (for example, cocaine, heroin), and (4) a parent using more than one drug (alcohol and cocaine). The second variable has two nominal categories: yes and no.

To analyze this relationship, Andrew R. places the data in a table with four rows (substance abuse status) and two columns (program completion), with each family positioned somewhere in this "four by two" table, or *crosstab* (figure 11.10).

To analyze this table statistically—to see whether there is a statistically significant relationship between these two variables—Andrew R. uses the *chi-square test* (pronounced "kai"-square). The abbreviation of chi-square is the Greek letter chi and the exponent of two, indicating squared: χ^2.

The formula for calculating chi-square is slightly complicated. Fortunately,

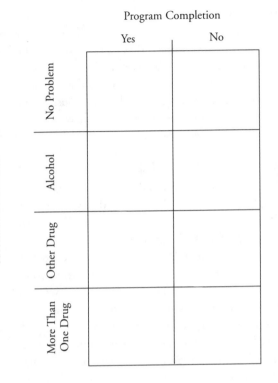

FIGURE 11.10   Crosstab

virtually no one computes this statistic by hand anymore, as lots of computer software packages are available to do this and other statistical calculations for us (perhaps the most widely used is the *Statistical Package for the Social Sciences*, or *SPSS*). Basically, the chi-square calculation compares the frequencies actually obtained (known as *observed frequencies*) with the frequencies that one would expect to obtain if, in fact, the null hypothesis is true, meaning there is no statistically significant relationship between the two variables (these are known as *expected frequencies*).

Although it's a bit more complicated than this, the chi-square formula essentially adds up the discrepancies between the observed and expected frequencies and determines how likely this sum is to occur by chance if the null hypothesis is true and there is no statistically significant relationship between the two variables. If you think about this for a moment, it should make sense intuitively. If the observed and expected frequencies are similar, it means that the actual results are similar to what we would expect if no relationship really existed between the two variables (consistent with the null hypothesis). If the observed and expected frequencies are different, it means that the actual results are different from what we would expect if the null hypothesis were true, that is, no relationship really existed between the two variables.

Before the advent of computer programs that calculate statistics, social workers would compute chi-square by hand and use a table in the back of a statistics book to determine whether the result were statistically significant. Here's how it worked. Let's say Andrew R. uses the chi-square formula and finds that the chi-square value is 10.2. By itself, this number doesn't mean much, so Andrew R. would then look in the back of a statistics book for a table entitled something like "Critical Values of Chi-Square." Down the left-hand side, he would see a heading labeled *df* with a series of consecutive numbers beginning with 1.

The symbol *df* stands for "degrees of freedom," another fairly abstract statistical concept. Crosstab tables—the kind of table from which chi-square is calculated—come in lots of different sizes: a two-by-two table (two rows and two columns), a three-by-six table (three rows and six columns), a seven-by-five table (seven rows and five columns), or you name it. A practical problem, however, is that the final chi-square result—which is basically determined by adding the differences between the observed and the expected frequencies for each cell of a table—is affected by the size of the table (that is, the number of cells). It's common sense that a table with six cells of numbers to add up is more likely to produce a smaller total than will a table with twelve cells of numbers to add up. Hence, the final chi-square value is likely to depend on the table's size.

To control for this, statisticians use the concept of *degrees of freedom*, the number of scores or values that are free to vary or the number of independent pieces of information in a table (the concept means something slightly different when used in conjunction with other statistics). When computing chi-square, degrees of freedom are determined by the number of rows in the table minus one times the number of columns in the table minus one: $df = (r-1)(c-1)$. Thus, in Andrew R.'s table, which has four rows and two columns, $df = (4-1)(2-1) = 3$. Andrew R. looks down the list of numbers in the chi-square table under the column headed *df* until he finds 3.

Then he looks to the right and, in most chi-square tables, finds several columns with headings like ".05," ".02," ".01," and ".001." These numbers indicate the rejection or significance levels that I discussed earlier. Under each heading is, for each of the different degrees of freedom, the specific chi-square values that need to be exceeded to conclude that a statistically significant relationship exists. Andrew R. finds the number at which the appropriate degrees of freedom and the critical value intersect, which is the number that his chi-square value needs to exceed for Andrew R. to conclude that a statistically significant relationship exists between the two variables.

There's one other thing that Andrew R. must consider. Chi-square tables usually list two sets of rejection or significance levels: one for a *one-tailed test* and another for a *two-tailed test*. One-tailed tests are used for making specific predictions about the direction of a statistical relationship (for example, that families in which at least one member has an alcohol problem are less likely to complete the program than are families in which there is no evidence of a substance abuse problem). In contrast, a two-tailed test is used when no prediction is made about the direction of the statistical relationship, only that some kind of statistically significant relationship does exist.

The distinction between one-tailed and two-tailed tests is important because the statistical cutoffs are different for each. In short, the statistical cutoffs for two-tailed tests are higher because a two-tailed prediction is weaker than a one-tailed prediction; with the latter, you must go farther out on a limb by making specific predictions concerning the direction of the statistical relationship. For example, if Andrew R. decides to use a one-tailed test with a rejection level of .05 and $df = 3$, his chi-square value will have to exceed 6.25 to be statistically significant. But if he decides to use a two-tailed test with the same rejection level and degrees of freedom, his chi-square value will have to exceed 7.82 to be statistically significant.

In our particular example, Andrew R.'s chi-square value is 10.2, which is clearly significant at the .05 level, regardless of whether he uses a one-tailed or a two-tailed test. What about the .01 rejection level? For a one-tailed test and $df = 3$, Andrew R.'s chi-square value needs to exceed 9.84, which it does. Therefore the relationship is statistically significant at the .01 level. But for a two-tailed test and $df = 3$, Andrew R.'s chi-square value must exceed 11.34, which it does not, so the relationship is statistically significant at the .05 level but not at the .01 level. Remember that we always prefer that relationships be statistically significant at the lowest possible level because this makes a stronger statement concerning the likelihood that the result is not due to chance factors.

Having said all this about using tables in the back of statistics books to determine whether a particular chi-square result is statistically significant, I should point out that computer programs for data analysis routinely indicate whether a result is statistically significant and, if so, at what level (.05, .01, .001, etc.). Thus although social workers now rarely need to look up a result in a table in a statistics book, I think it's useful to know how it works (and to remind you of what people like me had to do before computer programs were so accommodating).

There is one other important point about analyzing data in tables. Let me explain by telling a short story. A number of years ago, I got a phone call from a social worker who was very upset because of the response she got when she presented to her agency's board of directors the results of a needs assessment she had conducted. The project was designed to determine the social service needs of the area's elderly. Unfortunately, the social worker had calculated the percentages for several of the tables in the wrong direction, which meant that she had made a number of erroneous conclusions. The really painful part of the story is that the error wasn't discovered until one of the board members, who happened to know something about data analysis, saw the problem when the tables were projected onto a screen for the entire board to see.

It should be clear, therefore, that you need to understand how "to percentage" tables. There are basically two options: to percentage across the rows (using the row totals as the denominator) and to percentage down the columns (using the column totals as the denominator). Here's the widely accepted rule: In tables that treat one variable as an independent variable (or that treat a variable as a causal factor), always percentage in that direction and then compare the percentages in the other direction. Andrew R., for example, would treat the presence or absence of a substance abuse problem as the independent variable and the completion of the program as the dependent variable.

To percentage this table properly, Andrew R. would use the number of people in each "substance abuse" category as the denominator and the number of people who did or did not complete the program as the numerator. For example, if 60 families did not have a family member with a substance abuse problem and 40 of those families completed the program, Andrew R. would divide 40 by 60 and insert 66.67 percent in that cell of the table along with the frequency (40). He would then compare that percentage with the percentages computed for the other "substance abuse" categories. The point would be to see which of the substance abuse categories had the highest (or lowest) completion rates. If Andrew R. made the mistake of percentaging the table in the wrong direction (which I've seen happen on a number of occasions), he would end up comparing the percentages erroneously. It's *very* important for social workers to understand why they need to percentage tables in the proper direction. No one wants to be embarrassed by presenting and analyzing tables incorrectly.

Fortunately, living in a computer-dominated age means that social workers themselves don't actually have to calculate percentages, chi-square values, and other statistics. With the push of a few buttons, all this is done automatically. The challenge for social workers, and it's not a small one, is knowing which statistic to ask for and what percentages the computer should calculate. For instance, you must tell the computer whether to calculate row or column percentages. The computer doesn't have the capacity to figure this out (too bad).

Two ordinal variables.   If you're dealing with ordinal variables in which ranked categories are used (such as high, medium, low or 0 to 3, 4 to 7, 8 to 11), you use the chi-square test just as you would for two nominal variables. For example, if Andrew R. wants to examine the relationship between number of family sessions (in which the data are placed into ranked groups such as 0 to 1, 2 to 3, 4 to 5, 6+) and worker assessment of family risk (categorized as high, medium, or low), the chi-square statistic is appropriate. Andrew R. is working with a four-by-three table. How many degrees of freedom? Answer: (4 - 1) (3 - 1) = 6.

Two interval variables.   Over time, Andrew R. notices that those Families First clients who were functioning at a low level seem to be "down in the dumps" or blue much of the time. Andrew R. speculates that some of them may be clinically depressed and wonders whether addressing the clients' symptoms of depression may be associated with their functioning. To test his hunch, Andrew R. administers to all the Families First clients a fairly simple standardized depression scale. He then examines the statistical relationship between the clients' GAF scores and their scores on a standardized depression scale, two interval-level variables.

To conduct this analysis, Andrew R. uses a statistic called Pearson's *r*, or simply *r* (actually the formal name is Pearson's Product Moment Correlation Coefficient, but that's not the sort of phrase that just rolls off the tongue). Pearson's *r* is a very easy statistic to understand (although as with many statistics, the mathematical computation can be a bit intimidating). This *correlation coefficient*, as it's called, can range from +1 to –1. A coefficient of +1, which is called a *perfect positive correlation*, means that the two variables are perfectly correlated, so that higher scores on one variable are correlated with higher scores on the other variable. The flip side of the coin is that lower scores on one variable are correlated with lower scores on the other. If the GAF and depression scores are perfectly correlated, high GAF scores will be associated with high depression scores, low GAF scores will be correlated with low depression scores, and, to be thorough, medium GAF scores will be correlated with medium depression scores.

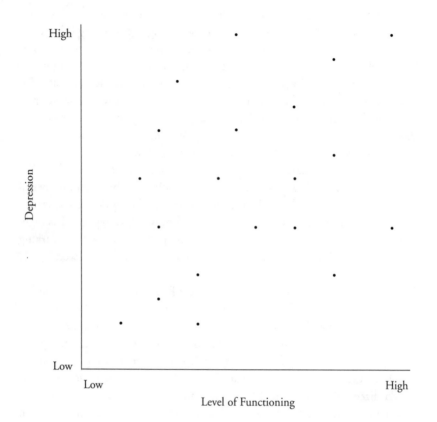

FIGURE 11.11   Scattergram

A correlation coefficient of –1, which is called a *perfect negative or inverse correlation,* also means that the two variables are perfectly correlated, but in this instance, high scores on one variable are associated with low scores on the other. That is, high GAF scores are associated with low depression scores, and low GAF scores are associated with high depression scores.

A correlation coefficient of zero means no correlation between the two variables. That is, knowing a person's value on one variable doesn't enable you to predict accurately the person's value on the other variable. In contrast, with a +1 or –1 correlation, knowing the value of one variable does permit you to predict with complete accuracy the value of the other variable—a stockbroker's dream. In between correlations of zero and +1 or –1 are lots and lots of possibilities. Correlations such as +.62 or -.54 are usually described as moderate correlations (although one is positive and one is inverse). Correlations of +.17 or -.19 are usually labeled weak correlations.

Which correlation coefficient is stronger, +.42 or -.58? Here's a hint—the correct answer has a 5 in it. Yup, the stronger coefficient is -.58. With correlation coefficients, the sign (positive or negative) has no bearing on the strength or weakness of the correlation. All that matters is the size of the number itself. The sign merely provides information about the direction of the relationship, that is, whether the relationship is positive or inverse.

I should add that Pearson's r coefficients are often reported without any significance level (for example, $p<.01$, $p<.05$), because with this particular statistic, a significance level can be very misleading. The principal reason is that a large sample can turn a tiny coefficient (for example, $r=.15$) into a statistically significant result. Well, a coefficient of .15 could hardly be considered *substantively* or *practically* significant under any circumstances. A finding of statistical significance with Pearson's r really means that the coefficient is significantly different from zero, and that's about all. As a result, the significance level is often omitted. The risk in including the significance level when reporting results is that readers who aren't familiar with this concept will exaggerate the substantive and practical significance of the coefficient.

Often when social workers calculate a Pearson's r (or, more accurately, have their computer calculate the coefficient), they display the data graphically using something called a *scattergram* (or *scatterplot*). A scattergram is a useful way to show how two variables are related to each other. A scattergram consists of two axes, with one variable on one axis and the second variable on the other (see figure 11.11). All the social worker (or the computer) does is find the point on the graph where each pair of scores corresponds to their intersection. For example, one of Andrew R.'s clients had a GAF score of 65 and a depression score of 40. Andrew R. finds where 65 falls on the axis where the GAF scores appear and where 40 appears on the axis where the depression scores appear, runs imaginary lines from each of these points toward the interior of the graph, and places a point where the two lines meet. If Andrew R. were to repeat this procedure for each pair of scores in his sample, he would end up with a swarm of points on the graph, one for each person in the sample.

What will the swarm of points look like if the correlation between the GAF scores and the depression scores is +.85? What will it look like if the correlation between the two variables is -.30? (see figure 11.12 for the answer).

Here are some general guidelines concerning the patterns you'll find with different coefficients. A coefficient of +1 or −1 will appear as a straight line at a

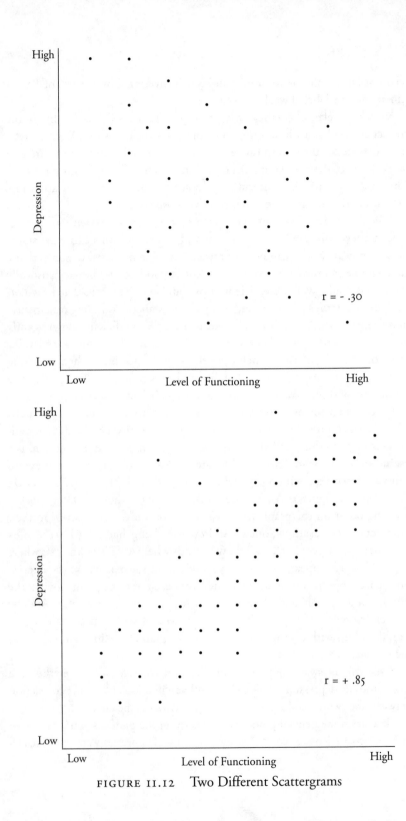

FIGURE 11.12   Two Different Scattergrams

45 degree angle (whether the line runs from the lower left to the upper right or from the upper left to the lower right depends on the way the scale values on the axes are numbered, from either lower to higher numbers or vice versa). The swarm of points for a coefficient of +.8 or -.8, for example, will approximate the direction of the straight lines you'd find with a +1 or –1, but the shape will be more elliptical. That is, the farther the coefficient is from +1 or –1, the more elliptical the swarm will become.

There are some exceptions to these patterns. For example, not all correlations that form a clear pattern resemble a line (called a *linear relationship*). Some resemble curves, or a *curvilinear relationship*. This would occur, for example, if Andrew R. finds that both very high and very low depression scores are correlated with moderate GAF scores and that moderate depression scores tend to be associated with high GAF scores. Displayed graphically, the swarm of points would look something like a horseshoe.

Sometimes you'll read in the professional literature a statement like "The clients' depression scores explained only 25 percent of the variance in the clients' GAF scores." This is "statistics speak" for a pretty simple idea. Let's say that Andrew R. is interested in what factors influence clients' level of functioning (measured by the GAF score). He noted that Families First clients' functioning varies considerably and is eager to know what accounts for this. In the language of statistics, Andrew R. wants to be able to explain the variance in GAF scores. To find out, he correlates the clients' depression scores with their GAF scores and finds that Pearson's $r = .5$, a moderate positive correlation. Using this number, he can easily calculate what statisticians call a *coefficient of determination*, that is, the percentage of the variance in one variable that is "explained" or accounted for by the other. All Andrew R. needs to do is to square the Pearson's r coefficient to calculate the coefficient of determination. In this instance, the coefficient of determination is 25 percent, meaning that the depression scores explain or account for 25 percent of the variance in the GAF scores. Of course, this also means that 75 percent of the variance in the GAF scores is unaccounted for, so there's more searching to be done.

I know I'm beginning to sound like a broken . . . compact disk (I almost said record, but I guess that's now an anachronism), but I need to remind you yet again of the important distinction between correlation and causation. Social workers sometimes make the mistake of assuming that a strong correlation coefficient is equivalent to evidence of a strong causal relationship between two variables. Not so. As I've said repeatedly, many things in the world are strongly correlated without any causal connection. A strong correlation is required to demonstrate that a causal relationship exists, but the correlation, by itself, does not imply causation. In Andrew R.'s case, however, it's not hard to imagine that the moderate correlation between depression scores and GAF scores may provide some evidence of a causal connection (although the size of the coefficient suggests that the relationship is not especially powerful). I can certainly understand how a person's depression could affect his or her level of functioning, and vice versa.

Two ratio variables. Suppose Andrew R. wants to look at the relationship between a client's age and the number of missed appointments. He's curious to see whether there's statistical evidence of a pattern he's noticed—that younger clients seem to miss more appointments. For example, younger clients may miss more appointments because they are more easily distracted by activities with friends. The staff thus may need to make a special effort to persuade younger clients to participate in their treatment.

In this instance, Andrew R. is dealing with two ratio-level variables, and here too he would use Pearson's r to analyze the strength and direction of the relationship. The statistic is interpreted in exactly the same way as with two interval-level variables. For example, a Pearson's r of -.74 means that, indeed, there is a strong inverse correlation between a client's age and the number of missed appointments—younger clients tend to miss more appointments (and, conversely, older clients tend to miss fewer appointments). For this sample, the clients' age explains 54.8 percent of the variance in missed appointments (-.74 squared = +54.8).

One nominal and one ordinal. Suppose that Andrew R. wants to examine the relationship between the presence or absence of a substance abuse problem (a nominal variable) and the social worker's assessment of future risk with respect to child abuse or neglect (an ordinal variable measured by high, medium, or low risk). He wants to see whether parents with a history of substance abuse tend to pose a greater future risk than do parents who don't have a substance abuse problem. In this situation, Andrew R. is working with "categorical data" best displayed in the form of a crosstab. Along one axis, he has categories of substance abuse (none, alcohol only, cocaine or heroin, etc.), and along the other axis, he has categories of risk. As with other crosstabulations, chi-square is the appropriate statistical procedure.

One nominal and one interval/ratio. One of the things that Andrew R. is curious about is whether the presence or absence of a substance abuse problem (for this analysis, the substance abuse variable is dichotomized simply as yes or no) is associated with the clients' GAF scores. That is, Andrew R. wants to see whether those clients with a substance abuse problem are more likely to have lower GAF scores, indicating a lower level of functioning. If this turns out to be the case, the Families First staff might consider focusing on the special needs of clients with a substance abuse problem.

For this analysis, Andrew R. is working with a two-category nominal variable (the presence or absence of a substance abuse problem) and an interval-level variable (GAF scores). This analysis calls for a *t-test* (also called a "difference between two means" test). The t-test basically compares the means of two groups of scores to determine whether they are significantly different from each other. The formula for this test produces a number (called—surprise!— *t*) that doesn't have much meaning until you use one of those tables found in the back of most statistics books.

As with chi-square, you look down the left-hand side of the table for the appropriate degrees of freedom. With this kind of t-test, known as an *independent groups t-test* (there's another type I'll describe shortly), the *df* equals the number of scores in group 1 plus the number of scores in group 2 minus two (or *N1* + *N2* - 2). Again, just like the chi-square table, you must decide whether to use a one-tailed or a two-tailed test and then identify the *t* value in the table that must be exceeded for different significance or rejection levels to conclude that there is a statistically significant difference between the two groups' means. Andrew R. uses a one-tailed test in this case, because he is speculating that individuals with a substance abuse problem are more likely to have lower GAF scores. (If he had no hunch as to which substance abuse category would have lower GAF scores, Andrew R. would use a two-tailed test.) If Andrew R. has 26 scores in the "yes" substance abuse group and 16 scores in the "no" substance abuse group, the *df* will be 40 (26 + 16 - 2). To reject the null hypothesis (no difference between the two groups' means) at the .05 level, Andrew R.'s *t* value must exceed 1.684. To reject the null hypothesis at the .01 level, the *t* value must exceed 2.423. Again, with the advent of sophisticated computer programs that calculate these statistics in an instant (literally), social workers rarely need to consult a statistics book to determine whether a result is statistically significant. The information is routinely included on the computer printout.

A second type of t-test is the *correlated-groups t-test* (also referred to as a *matched-groups t-test*). Social workers use this t-test to compare two groups of scores in which each pair of scores is somehow matched. The most common circumstances are the comparison of Time-1 scores and Time-2 scores for the same people and the comparison of scores for two groups of people who have been carefully matched (for example, when social workers use matched groups to compare experimental and control conditions because random assignment is not possible). Because the scores in group 1 are not entirely independent of the scores in group 2 (that is, there's a close connection between the scores in each pair), we need to use a different mathematical equation that takes into account this interdependence. The degrees of freedom also are different from those in the independent-groups t-test (equal to the total number of pairs of scores in the sample minus 1, or $N - 1$). Once you obtain the t value, you can determine whether the result is statistically significant in the same way I described for the independent-groups t-test. That is, you look in the table of t values, find the appropriate degrees of freedom, decide whether to use a one- or a two-tailed test, and find the t value that needs to be exceeded to reject the null hypothesis at different significance levels.

Now let's make things a bit more complicated. Let's say that Andrew R. doesn't simply want to compare the GAF scores of families in which a parent has a substance abuse problem and families in which neither parent has a substance abuse problem. Rather, he wants to make finer-grained comparisons among four groups: (1) families in which a parent has primarily a serious alcohol problem, (2) families in which a parent has primarily a cocaine, heroin, or other nonalcohol problem (for example, methamphetamine), (3) families in which a parent has a serious problem with more than one substance (for example, alcohol and cocaine), and (4) families in which neither parent has a serious substance abuse problem. In this situation, a t-test won't do because the formula for this statistic allows for only two sets of scores. We need a statistical procedure that examines differences among three or more groups. It's called *analysis of variance* (abbreviated with the acronym *ANOVA*).

Analysis of variance is a procedure that compares the means of three or more groups. Mathematically there's much more to it, but this is the basic idea. Like the t-test, ANOVA examines means and determines whether they show evidence of statistically significant differences. The ANOVA formula produces an *F statistic*, which is calculated by dividing what's called the *between-group variance* by the *within-group variance*. Briefly, between-group variance measures the differences among the means of the different groups you're comparing. Within-group variance takes into account how much variation there is within each group. Perhaps you can picture how these two types of variance relate to each other. If the means of several groups are far apart, the between-group variance (the numerator) will be large. If there is little variation within each group (a small standard deviation, indicating little spread among scores), the within-group variance (the denominator) will be small. This means you'd have a relatively large numerator divided by a relatively small denominator, resulting in a relatively large value for F. If we plotted these groups on a graph, we'd see several distinct groups with considerable distance between the means and with little overlap among their scores. In Andrew R.'s case, this would mean that the four groups' GAF scores do differ.

In contrast, suppose you have several groups whose means are fairly close together and whose scores vary a great deal. This means that the between-group variance (the numerator) is relatively small and the within-group variance (the denominator) is relatively large. A smaller number divided by a larger number produces a relatively small value for F. If we plotted these groups on a graph, we'd see considerable overlap among them, in part because the means are fairly close together and their scores overlap.

This means that larger F values reflect greater differences among groups when comparing their means. However, as with the t-test, a particular F value doesn't mean much without knowing the relevant degrees of freedom. With ANOVA, there are actually two separate degrees of freedom: the between-groups degrees of freedom equals the number of groups minus 1, and the within-groups degrees of freedom equals the total sample size minus the number of groups. As with t-tests and chi-square, you can look in a statistics book for the F value that needs to be exceeded, given the respective degrees of freedom, to conclude that there is a statistically significant difference among the groups. Of course, widely available computer software packages also provide this information instantly.

The simplest ANOVAs have one independent variable and one dependent variable, as in Andrew R.'s situation. This is called a *one-way ANOVA*. Often, however, social workers want to analyze the relationship between two or more independent variables—all categorical variables—and one interval or ratio-level variable. For example, Andrew R. may want to add gender or ethnicity to his analysis.

Fortunately, there's an easy way to handle this with ANOVA. Instead of a one-way ANOVA, social workers can conduct two-way ANOVAs (which have two categorical independent variables), three-way ANOVAs (three categorical independent variables), and so on. These ANOVAs produce lots of useful information, including an F value for each of the independent variables (called the *main effect*) and F values for the interaction among the variables (called the *interaction effect*). For example, if Andrew R. includes the variables of substance abuse status and gender in his analysis of GAF scores, the computer will generate an F value for substance abuse status, an F value for gender, and an F value for the interaction of substance abuse status and gender.

You may have figured out that finding a statistically significant F tells you only part of the story, only that there is evidence of statistical significance among the groups. The F value doesn't tell you where, exactly, those differences are. In Andrew R.'s situation, for example, there may be a statistically significant difference between the GAF scores of parents who have an alcohol problem and those who don't, but not between the GAF scores of parents who have an alcohol problem and those who have a cocaine, heroin, or some other non-alcohol problem.

Fortunately, there's an easy way to pinpoint such statistically significant differences: a statistical procedure called *post hoc comparisons*, which the computer can calculate easily and quickly. Post hoc comparisons indicate where the statistically meaningful differences are once you have a statistically significant F value. (You may be wondering why you don't simply conduct multiple t-tests to see where the statistically significant differences exist between different pairs of groups. For technical reasons, this is considered a statistical indiscretion. Post hoc comparisons are considered more appropriate.)

You've probably noticed that in my discussion of t-tests and ANOVA, I haven't distinguished between interval- and ratio-level data. The reason is that for nearly all statistical analyses, there's no meaningful difference between interval and ratio data. Both use equal-interval scales; the only major difference is that ratio-level variables include an absolute, rather than an arbitrary, zero point. Whether the zero is arbitrary or absolute doesn't have any bearing on the statistical procedures we're reviewing here. Hence statistical procedures that are suitable for interval-level data also are suitable for ratio-level data, and vice versa.

One ordinal variable and one interval/ratio variable. When you want to examine the relationship between ordinal data in the form of two ranked groups (for example, more aggressive versus less aggressive) and an interval or ratio variable, you should use the t-test (almost always the independent-groups t-test, because you'll be comparing two different groups of people). When you want to examine the relationship between ordinal data in the form of three or more ranked groups (for example, high, medium, low) and an interval or ratio variable, you should use ANOVA. That is, categorical data—whether nominal or ordinal—should be handled in the same way in these situations.

One interval and one ratio variable. A good example of one interval and one ratio variable is Andrew R.'s analysis of the relationship between the clients' age (ratio) and their GAF scores (interval). Since interval and ratio data are treated in much the same way, this combination should be analyzed using Pearson's r.

Multivariate Analysis

One of the things social workers know well is that life is very complicated. When we address issues such as poverty, mental illness, domestic abuse, substance abuse, child abuse and neglect, and crime, we routinely cite many factors that need to be confronted. Often we must look beyond the relationships between two variables and examine the relationship among multiple variables. Just think of the variables that affect poverty. The possibilities include unemployment, lack of education, racism and discrimination, mental illness, and physical disabilities. Similarly, we know that crime rates are affected by substance abuse, unemployment, marital conflict, gambling, and poverty. Although in many instances, we must conduct bivariate analyses, often we need multivariate analyses.

Of the many esoteric multivariate procedures, the one that social workers are most likely to encounter is *multiple regression*, used for examining the relationship between a number of independent or predictor variables and a single dependent or criterion variable. The general assumption with multiple regression (there are some technical exceptions to the rule) is that all the variables are measured at the interval or ratio level. (There's a way around this restriction if you want to include a nominal variable such as gender or ethnicity. What you do is create *dummy variables*. No kidding, that's the formal name.) Using multiple regression, you can determine how much of the variance in the criterion (or dependent) variable is accounted for by the predictor (or independent) variables considered as a group and also the relative influence of each of the predictor variables while controlling for the influence of all the others. For example, Andrew R. could treat the clients' GAF scores as the criterion variable and variables such as age, depression scores, and severity of substance abuse problem (rated on an interval-level scale) as predictor variables. The predictor variables shouldn't be selected at random, of course. Rather, social workers should consult the relevant literature, theoretical frameworks, or other concepts when choosing predictor variables to include in the analysis.

The typical computer program that conducts multiple regression analysis gives social workers the choice of entering all the predictor variables at one time, one by one, or step by step. Sometimes social workers merely want to know how much of the variance in the criterion variable is explained by the entire group of predictor variables. Or they want to see whether any particular variable or combination of variables adds a significant amount of explained variance beyond what is explained by other predictor variables that have already been considered (this is known as *stepwise regression*).

Multiple regression produces several important statistical pieces of information. First, it produces *beta* (ß) *coefficients*, one for each of the predictor variables. Beta coefficients indicate the relative contribution of each variable. The larger the beta is, the more influence a variable will have on the criterion variable, in a statistical sense, controlling for the influence of the other predictor variables. For example, if Andrew R. discovers that age has a beta of .36 and depression has a beta of .24, he can conclude that age has a greater impact on GAF scores than does depression.

Multiple regression analysis also produces an R^2 coefficient. R^2 tells us what percentage of the variance in the dependent variable is accounted for by the group of predictor variables. The range for R^2 is 0 to 100. If Andrew R. finds that the R^2 for his combination of variables is .47, he can say that the group of variables accounts for 47 percent of the variance in the clients' GAF scores. Both beta coefficients and R^2 are accompanied by rejection or significance levels (for example, $p < .01$) that indicate whether the coefficients are statistically significant.

Several other multivariate procedures I will mention only briefly. *Discriminant analysis* is much like multiple regression in that it's used when social workers want to look at the relationship between multiple predictor variables and a single criterion variable. The main difference is that with discriminant analysis, the criterion variable is nominal or ordinal (for example, completion of the Families First program versus noncompletion, a subsequent report of child abuse or neglect versus no subsequent report).

Factor analysis is a "data reduction" technique and is used when social workers want to gather data on lots of variables and reduce them to a more manageable number of items that provide a comparable measure. For example, Andrew R. constructs a lengthy client satisfaction instrument to be used in the Families First evaluation. By using factor analysis, he finds that certain items are redundant and that he can reduce the number of items on the instrument without losing any of its key content. The factor analysis may also reveal certain patterns in the responses, that some items tend to be highly correlated.

Finally, remember that with an analysis of variance, you can examine the influence of more than one independent variable on a single dependent variable (namely, two-way ANOVA, three-way ANOVA, and so on). There's also a statistical procedure, *multiple analysis of variance* (*MANOVA*), that enables social workers to examine the influence of nominal or ordinal variables on more than one interval- or ratio-level dependent variable. For example, Andrew R. might use MANOVA to see the effect of variables such as substance abuse status or gender on two dependent variables, such as GAF and self-esteem scores.

Nonparametric Statistics

Most of the statistics that social workers routinely use require certain technical assumptions. For example, statistics such as the t-test, Pearson's *r*, ANOVA, and multiple regression use the normal distribution or the normal probability curve. Inferential statistics that make such assumptions about the distribution of the data in the population from which samples are drawn are called *parametric statistics*.

In many situations, however, social workers can't make the assumptions that certain parametric statistics require. In these circumstances, social workers often rely on *nonparametric statistics* to analyze their data. *Nonparametric tests* make no assumptions concerning the distribution of data in a population, so they are sometimes referred to as "distribution-free tests of significance."

There are lots and lots of different nonparametric statistics, so I will offer a brief overview of only those that social workers are most likely to use.

Mann–Whitney U-test. The *Mann–Whitney U-test* is a statistic that is similar to the t-test and is used when assumptions for the t-test can't be met. Suppose Andrew R. wants to see whether there is a significant difference between the "risk scores" that Families First social workers assign to families in which at least one parent has a substance abuse problem and the risk scores for families in which no parent has a substance abuse problem. If the distribution of the data is a problem, precluding the use of a t-test, Andrew R. can use the Mann–Whitney U-test, which examines the order or rank of all the people in the two groups. If there were no significant difference between the groups (the null hypothesis), we would expect members of the two groups to alternate in their rank ordering. If someone from the first group had the highest risk score, we would expect someone from the second group to have the next highest, someone from the first group to have the third highest, and so on. This pattern would show that group membership (the presence or absence of a substance abuse problem) didn't make a significant difference in the risk scores; the ordering would be random. The Mann–Whitney U-test basically determines whether the pattern is sufficiently different from this random distribution to achieve statistical significance.

Median test. The *median test* is another statistic that can be used to compare two groups. It requires an interval- or ratio-level dependent variable. You begin by dividing the sample into cases whose scores fall below the median and cases whose scores fall above the median. The median test assumes that if there is no significant difference between the two groups of people (or agencies, communities, and so on) with respect to the dependent variable, the percentage of cases above the median and below the median for each of the two groups should be about the same. So, if Andrew R. compares the GAF scores of individuals with a substance abuse problem and the GAF scores of those without a substance abuse problem, he should find roughly the same percentage of scores above and below the median in the first group as in the second.

Kolmogorov–Smirnov test.   The *Kolmogorov–Smirnov test* is similar to the median test. The major difference is that the Kolmogorov–Smirnov test takes into consideration the dispersion, the shape of the distributions, and several other pieces of information, as well as where the two groups' scores fall in relation to the overall median.

Kruskal–Wallis test.   If the Mann–Whitney U-test is analogous to the t-test, the *Kruskal–Wallis test* is analogous to ANOVA. Thus, if Andrew R. wants to compare the risk scores of three or more groups, rather than simply the scores of the "substance abuse" and "no substance abuse" groups, the Kruskal–Wallis test would be appropriate. The data for the groups are handled in much the same way as data are handled in the Mann–Whitney U-test. That is, all the scores are rank ordered. After this is done, the ranks for each of the groups are totaled. The assumption is that if there are no significant differences among the groups (the null hypothesis), the totals for the groups should be the same or similar. Kruskal–Wallis tests whether the totals of the ranks differ so much from one another that they achieve the level of a statistically significant difference.

The sign test.   The *sign test* is useful when you want to look at the relationship between two sets of *paired* scores (similar to the t-test for correlated groups). Suppose Andrew R. wants to see whether there is a significant difference between the Time-1 and Time-2 GAF scores of a group of Families First clients. Each client would have a Time-1 and Time-2 score. If for some reason the assumptions for the t-test could not be met, Andrew R. could use the sign test. If the Families First intervention made no difference (the null hypothesis), we would expect that half the changes from Time-1 to Time-2 would be in the positive direction and half would be in the negative direction. There are criteria for determining whether the number of changes in one direction is high enough to be statistically significant.

Wilcoxon matched-pairs signed-rank test.   The *Wilcoxon matched-pairs signed-rank test* is similar to the sign test, but in addition to considering the *direction* of change from the first set of scores to the second, the Wilcoxon test also takes into account the *magnitude* of the difference between each pair of scores.

Spearman's rho.   *Spearman's rho* is a useful statistic when you want to compare two sets of ranks. For example, Andrew R. may want to see whether there

Dear Mom + Dad:

Chi there! Tau r U? I really Likert social work school. It wasn't an error for me to come here. This sure is the right mode for me and I'm having a whole range of experiences. For a nominal phi U could be here, too.

The professors aren't mean; this place suits me to a t. But when I'm away from U for a long interval, and the frequency of our contact goes down, it sure tests the strength of our relationship.

My mood isn't really linear and can be hard to predict; sometimes I feel like I'm regressing. I can't explain all this variation.

Write often! I love having your letters dispersed throughout the semester.

Mean Median Mode X̄ Ø X̄ Ø, Buffy

degree of freedom diploma MY DREAM

P. S. I really love my social work research + evaluation course. See how much I've already learned!

is a strong correlation between the rank of a subgroup of Families First clients with respect to the quality of parent–child relationships and the rank of the same clients with respect to the risk of future child abuse or neglect. Or Andrew R. may want to see whether the rank of this subgroup with respect to the risk of child abuse or neglect before a particular intervention is significantly different from the subgroup's rank following the intervention. Spearman's rho is essentially a correlation coefficient indicating the extent to which the two rank orders—whether they are the same people ranked on two different variables or the same people ranked at two different times on one variable—are the same or different. If the two sets of ranks are the same, the Spearman's rho coefficient will equal +1. If the two sets of ranks are completely opposite (the highest-ranked case on one variable is the lowest-ranked case on the other variable, and so on), the coefficient will equal –1. If there is no correlation, the coefficient will be 0.

Although this isn't an exhaustive (although it may be an exhausting) summary of all available statistical procedures, it does touch on many of the most commonly used procedures. You can see that there are lots of possibilities. The trick is understanding what kind of data you're working with and what kinds of questions you want to explore with your data. Once you decide this, you can review the assumptions associated with the various statistics and select the one that's right for your situation. Since some of the assumptions and procedures can get pretty technical, you may want to consult with someone who has studied statistics extensively.

ANALYZING QUALITATIVE DATA

Statistical procedures for analyzing quantitative data are very handy in many situations that social workers encounter, but sometimes social workers want to collect qualitative information. Hence we should look at the best way to analyze this kind of data.

Unlike our approach to quantitative data, there are no precise formulas for analyzing qualitative data. There are some widely accepted procedures, but no exacting formulas into which we enter our data. Instead, analyzing qualitative data requires lots of subjective judgment and interpretation.

In many circumstances, social workers may collect qualitative data. Practitioners may build in a number of qualitatively oriented questions in surveys, questionnaires, and interviews (for example, "Tell me in your own words, what it is like being a single parent?"). They may collect qualitative information when they observe clients or other individuals (for example, when social workers observe the interactions between staff and residents in a group home). In addition, qualitative data are useful when conducting ethnographic or naturalistic research and making content analyses of historical documents. In my experience, social workers are most likely to gather qualitative data when administering surveys, questionnaires, and interviews and observing interactions among people (most often clients).

As part of his evaluation of the Families First program at Mt. Washington, Andrew R. conducted in-depth interviews with a carefully selected subsample of twenty-five families. He arranged to interview as many family members—meeting together as families—as possible. The purpose of the interviews was to assess their reactions to the program and to ask them for feedback about the most and least helpful aspects of the services they received. Andrew R.'s interview instrument included a number of closed-ended questions that yielded quantitative data requiring statistical analysis. But some of the questions were open-ended and required qualitative data analysis. One question, for instance, was, "Are there specific aspects of the Families First program that you think should be changed? If so, what are they?"

During the interviews, most of which lasted about one to one and a half hours, Andrew R. took lots of detailed notes on the family members' responses. At the end of the process, he had a mountain of paper that needed to be organized and analyzed. This is the typical scenario when surveys, questionnaires, or interviews contain open-ended, qualitatively oriented items. Social workers end up with lots and lots of paper with lots and lots of words on them, and somehow all this information must be sorted out, organized, analyzed, and presented coherently.

The following are the steps I like to follow when faced with this kind of task:

1. If the data are gathered from an interview, reread your notes and edit them as soon as possible afterward. Sometimes social workers hastily write down the respondents' comments and then can't read their writing or remember their abbreviations. You can probably picture yourself scribbling comments sideways in the margin, drawing arrows going every which way, crossing out words, and abbreviating phrases to save time. Then if you wait a few days or weeks before rereading your notes, there's a good chance you'll end up scratching your head a lot, trying to reconstruct the interview and figure out what you wrote and why. The challenge is even greater if you've held a number of other interviews in the interim. The standard advice in this business is to reread and edit your notes immediately after an interview if possible and, if that's not possible, as soon as you can. Some professional evaluators and

researchers actually instruct their staff to sit in their cars or offices and edit their notes immediately after conducting an interview.

2. Once all the data have been collected, pick out the noteworthy themes and patterns and significant departures from these themes and patterns (the exceptions). This should sound like a familiar idea. Using the language of quantitative data analysis, and a little bit of analogy, what I'm talking about here is looking for *central tendencies, dispersion,* and *outliers.* Although we don't use quantitative statistics to do this, the concepts are much the same. For example, Andrew R. will want to review all the respondents' comments, find out whether there are any recurring observations, themes, and patterns with respect to aspects of the Families First program that the clients would like to see changed (central tendencies), the extent to which the clients' comments varied (dispersion), and any unusual comments that warrant reporting (outliers).

3. To identify central themes and patterns, and variations around them, first read once through all the respondents' comments for each question to get a general feel for their observations and a sense of the broad context; second, go back to the first respondent's comments, read through them, and, on a separate piece of paper or on the computer, begin listing the noteworthy points; and third, read through the remaining respondents' comments one by one, adding to the list of noteworthy points and putting a check mark next to any point that is repeated. By the end of this process, which can take a lot of time, you should have a detailed summary of all the respondents' major points and, in effect, a frequency distribution of their comments.

4. When writing up these results, begin by summarizing the range of responses (for example, some respondents had no suggestions to offer, and some suggested major changes in the Families First program), and then describe the most obvious themes and patterns (starting with the comments that were repeated most often and moving to those comments made less often), how the respondents' comments varied with respect to these themes and patterns (the dispersion), and any noteworthy exceptional comments (the outliers). It's helpful to include quotations to illustrate points and to add some life to the discussion.

Let's apply these steps to Andrew R.'s interviews with Families First clients:

1. Shortly after conducting the interviews, Andrew R. reads through and edits his notes.

2 and 3. Andrew R. then identifies the major themes and patterns, and the variations on these patterns, by listing the respondents' major points, indicating the number who made similar comments. Here's an example of the respon-

dents' suggested changes for the Families First program (in descending order of frequency):

Social workers should be more accessible by telephone (12).
Social workers should provide more advanced notice before visiting clients in their homes (10).
Social workers should offer a more thorough explanation of the program's goals and services (7).
The program should help parents and children learn how to get along better (5).
Social workers should be more courteous to clients (2).

4. The following shows how these results could be written up in a narrative style:

Program participants were asked whether they believe aspects of the Families First program should be changed. Fifteen of the respondents (60 percent of the total) stated that aspects of the program should be changed and offered specific suggestions. The most common suggestion, made by 12 of these 15 respondents, concerned the respondents' wish that social workers be more accessible by telephone. These respondents reported feeling frustrated that social workers are often hard to reach when crises arise and that it often takes a long time for them to respond to telephone messages. A typical comment was made by one mother who said, "I like my social worker just fine, but she sure is hard to get ahold of. Maybe she should carry a beeper or something. There have been lots of times when I needed her and no one knew where to find her. Sometimes a couple of days would pass before she returned my call."

Nearly as many respondents (10) said that they would like more notice from staff members before they visited the respondents' homes. Most of these respondents (8) reported feeling caught off guard when social workers called to say they would be stopping by shortly. Several of this group (4) said that they felt that their social worker was paying a surprise visit to see whether the respondents were "doing anything wrong." As one father observed, "Isn't it just common decency to let people know when you're coming over? Aren't we entitled to get ready, clean the place up a little, just like normal people? Are we really that different? Sometimes this program makes me feel like a child who needs to be watched."

About half those who suggested changes in the program (7) expressed a need to know more about the program's goals and services, particularly when they began participating in the program. All these individuals said that they felt in the dark for a while, that it took them some time to figure out what they were trying to achieve and what services would be available. One mother said, "It took me a long time to understand what, exactly, [the program] was trying to do for us. Why couldn't they just spell it out in the beginning what we would need to do to get our kids back? For a long time I felt like this was some silly guessing game." Another mother, who was attempting to retain custody of her son, commented, "My worker seemed like a know-it-all, somebody who was going to tell me what to do but who wasn't going to clue me in or involve me in any of the decisions. I ended up liking her OK, but not for a long time. It sure would have helped if she had sat down with me at the very beginning and laid it all out—what she wanted me to accomplish and all that."

One-third of the respondents who suggested possible changes (5) said that they wanted more practical advice about how to get along better with their children. All of them said that their inability to manage their children's behavior was the primary reason for the family's problems and the reason that they were participating in the Families First program. These respondents reported learning some new skills, but all said they felt the need for more. Typical comments were:

"I just need to know more about what to do when X throws one of his temper tantrums. I'm still not very good at it." (mother of a nine-year-old)

"I feel like I'm still bearing down on X and Y all the time. I know I criticize them too much. I don't think the program helped me very much in that department. I sure wish I could do something about this." (father of a six-year-old and an eight-year-old)

"My daughter is very aggressive. When something doesn't go her way, she ends up pushing and hitting a lot. I tried to get my social worker to help me more with this, but she thought we should pay more attention to other things. I feel kind of disappointed about this." (mother of a seven-year-old)

One of these respondents made a comment that stood out from the others. This mother of two boys who had been placed in foster care said that she felt that she learned so little about how to handle her children that she had decided that she was "not fit to be a parent. I thought they would teach me how to be a better parent. Either they need to do a better job of teaching or I'm not teachable."

Only two of the respondents who suggested changes in the program said that social workers needed to be more courteous. Both respondents recounted incidents when, in their judgment, their social workers were rude and insulting. One respondent noted, "There was this one time when I was late for one of our appointments. Boy, you would have thought [the social worker] had just caught me beating my kid. She started yelling at me about how I need to be more responsible, how this is the sort of thing that got me in trouble in the first place. I couldn't believe she treated me like that. Maybe she was just having a bad day." The other respondent made a similar observation: "[The social worker] was nice most of the time, but there were times when he seemed kind of mean and, how do you say it, impatient. It's hard to describe, but at times he would sort of yell at me when he thought I wasn't really paying attention or trying hard enough to work on the stuff we talked about. Sometimes he reminded me of my father."

Social workers who summarize qualitative data in this way need to be concerned about the reliability of their interpretations of the data. After all, if only one person is summarizing and interpreting the data, there is always the possibility of bias. Although having one or two other people examine the data doesn't guarantee "objectivity," this kind of reliability check does minimize the likelihood that the social worker's judgment is biased.

The second type of qualitative data analysis I want to comment on pertains to information that social workers collect when they observe people. In family intervention programs, for example, social workers may conduct therapy sessions while a colleague observes the family's interactions behind a one-way mirror (with the family's permission, of course). In these circumstances, the observer usually begins with some kind of conceptual framework, with a list of categories of information that will be recorded. Using a structured recording guide, the observer may keep a running tally of the frequency of certain interactions (which is a form of quantitative data) and also take notes, in narrative form, describing the family's interactions (both verbal and nonverbal interactions). Once the observer has completed and edited all her notes, she should read through them looking for themes and patterns (central tendencies), variation within these themes and patterns (dispersion), and noteworthy exceptions (outliers).

This general approach—in which social workers identify themes and patterns, and exceptions to them, in qualitative data—can be used in many evaluation and research projects, such as analyzing tape recordings of clinical sessions, examining the professional literature for a specific topic, assessing changes in issues addressed over time, observing how an agency's board of directors functions at its meetings, or evaluating social work educators' teaching style (this last one hits pretty close to home).

12

PREPARING RESEARCH AND EVALUATION REPORTS

Now we will assume that Andrew R. has gathered and analyzed all the relevant data on the Families First program. What should he do with it?

First, Andrew R. must write up his results, but this isn't as simple as it may seem. The reason is that there are various ways to prepare research and evaluation reports, depending on the audience and the uses to which the report will be put.

There are three basic types of research and evaluation reports:

1. *Reports prepared for internal use.* Often social workers conduct research and evaluation projects exclusively for their own agency's use. The results of needs assessments, client satisfaction surveys, single-case designs, and cost-benefit analyses, for example, may be of use to no one other than the social workers and their agency-based colleagues directly involved in the issues on which the project is based. For instance, if Mt. Washington's administrators are interested in the views of minorities and people of color in the surrounding community concerning the agency's mission and practices, the survey results would be for in-house use only, to help the staff improve the agency's delivery of services.

2. *Reports prepared for funding sources, licensing or regulatory agencies, or other public or private organizations.* Funding agencies typically require grantees and contractors to submit final reports describing their projects and findings (sometimes funding agencies require interim or progress reports, too). Although these reports may be of some use to the agency staff who prepare them, it's not unusual for them to complete reports only or primarily because doing so is a condition of a grant or contract. In these instances, social workers may have little or no control over the report's format or content, although

sometimes social workers who prepare reports for funders do have considerable discretion.

In addition, licensing or regulatory agencies or other public or private organizations may sponsor or require a research or evaluation project for which a final report is submitted. For instance, if Mt. Washington were sanctioned by a national accreditation body because of evidence that it had not tried hard enough to serve minorities and people of color in the surrounding community, the results of the agency's survey might be shared with the accreditation team as evidence of the Mt. Washington staff's efforts to address the problem. Or if a state licensing body was concerned about the number of complaints it had received from Mt. Washington clients about the agency's services, the Mt. Washington staff might conduct a consumer satisfaction survey and share the results with licensing officials.

3. *Reports prepared for scholarly publication.* One of the hallmarks of a profession is its members' commitment to disseminating knowledge to colleagues. In principle, social workers should be actively engaged in research and evaluation and sharing the results via books, professional journals, and computer-accessed sources (for example, the Internet and World Wide Web).

Social workers use widely accepted formats to prepare research and evaluation reports, although their length and level of technical sophistication (for instance, the amount of data analysis and statistical details) vary depending on the intended audience and purpose.

THE COMPONENTS OF A REPORT

Introduction/Problem Statement

The first section of the report describes the subject or issues addressed in the project. This section should be concise and give readers an overview of the project's background, the reasons for conducting the project, the relevant research literature and theory, and the specific questions, issues, or hypotheses that the project was designed to address, though they aren't necessarily discussed in this particular order. A common strategy is to begin with a brief statement about the core issues and the reasons that they needed to be investigated. This is followed by a summary of the relevant research literature and theory, finishing with an overview of the specific questions, issues, or hypotheses addressed.

The length of this section varies according to the nature of the report. If the project is complicated and leads to a lengthy report, this section may be thirty

pages long. However, if the manuscript is being written for submission to a professional journal that imposes a twenty-page limit, this section is usually about four pages.

Summarizing relevant literature can be a real challenge, one that often leads to a common "mistake." In chapter 13, I explain how to locate the relevant literature, but for sake of our discussion here let's assume that the literature you want to cite is already in hand. You've examined it thoroughly and want to highlight a few published articles and unpublished reports and manuscripts that are germane to the project. The mistake—and I can't tell you how many times I've seen it—is summarizing the literature one publication at a time in serial fashion. It's hard to imagine anything more boring for a reader to have to review. Consider a research report prepared by Andrew R. that begins with a discussion of the importance of home-based services and family reunification programs. He describes the problem and explains its relevance to the Mt. Washington Family Service Agency. He then begins his overview of the relevant literature before presenting the specific research and evaluation questions and issues. Andrew R. found nine important journal articles and research monographs to use in his report and summarizes them using the following writing style (these are hypothetical citations):

Washington (1994) evaluated a home-based services program involving fifty-four families. All the families were referred by the county social service department following reports of suspected abuse and neglect. The services consisted of family counseling and crisis intervention services. Washington found that . . .

Lincoln (1992) reports on the results of a family reunification program that extensively used paraprofessionals. The paraprofessionals received training from a local family service agency to enable them to provide a range of supportive services. Lincoln found that . . .

Taft (1989) presents the results of a longitudinal study of sixteen families who were mandated by court order to participate in an intensive home-based family preservation program. The study was designed to monitor the extent to which the families met a range of goals. Taft found that . . .

Harding (1990) summarizes the findings of a survey of directors of family preservation programs. The survey asked the program directors to report on intervention approaches and models that, in their judgment, were particularly effective with highly dysfunctional families and parents at risk of abusing and/or neglecting their children. Harding found that . . .

Madison (1991) conducted a secondary review of the research and evaluation literature related to family preservation and family reunification programs. The primary purpose of this publication was to provide a comprehensive overview of program models and to explore patterns in the research results associated with different intervention approaches. Madison found that . . .

Roosevelt (1993) evaluated a family reunification program sponsored by a partnership between a county family court and a private community mental health center. This publication provides a case study of the ways in which courts and social service agencies can collaborate in an effort to assist at-risk families. Roosevelt found that . . .

Hoover (1994) conducted in-depth interviews with both parents and children who successfully completed a six-month family reunification program operated by a family service agency funded by a state child welfare agency. The interviews were designed to compare and contrast different family members' perspective on the program. Hoover found that . . .

I don't know about you, but I find this style of presentation to be quite tedious. I can tolerate only so much of these serial listings of relevant publications. Doesn't this strike you as a rather monotonous way to share the information with readers? I'm not suggesting that the individual publications are monotonous or tedious. Actually, these publications seem rather interesting, but isn't there a more engaging and effective way to convey the information?

The trick with literature reviews is to *synthesize* the various summaries into coherent prose, to weave together the different synopses to give readers a sense of patterns, tendencies, and exceptions to these patterns and tendencies. Wait a minute! Didn't we just talk about the idea of identifying patterns, themes, and exceptions? Of course we did, when discussing measures of central tendency and dispersion and again when analyzing qualitative data. It's really the same.

Here's how most experienced social workers summarize literature without torturing their readers. The first thing to do is cite all the publications that you want to describe. Next prepare a brief, and I mean brief, summary of each one, on index cards, pieces of paper, or the computer. Although most of us depend heavily on the computer these days, for this sort of task some people still like to use paper or index cards, because they can spread them out on a table for easy examination. In my own work I find that when I have a long list on the computer, it's hard for me to keep track of what's where, since I can't fit all the information on one screen.

After writing the brief summaries of the publications, look through them for natural groupings, themes, and patterns. For instance, Andrew R. might find publications focusing on the effectiveness of different intervention approaches, on tools to measure family functioning, and on factors correlated with client outcome. Once you have settled on the broad categories, line up the literature summaries of each topic and decide how to best characterize the *overall* themes, patterns, and "central tendencies" reflected in each group's publications. Then figure out which theme or topic to address first, second, third, and so on. From there you can prepare a paragraph or so for each theme or topic, beginning with a general summary of the overall pattern (for example, you might lead with a sentence like "A number of studies have found that families that receive family counseling in conjunction with parent education services have more favorable outcomes than do families. . . . "), followed by sentences referring to specific studies and their findings: "Eisenhower (1990) and Coolidge (1992), for instance, found that when this combination of services is provided to single parents whose children have been placed in foster care because of abuse or neglect, reunification was more successful than when these services were provided independently. . . . These findings were corroborated by

Bush (1994) and Clinton (1996), both of whom found similar results with two-parent families." You might then conclude each section's overview with a mention of noteworthy exceptions: "In contrast, Humphrey (1994) reported mixed results when she compared the relative effectiveness of family counseling, parent education, and the two combined. Unlike, Bush and Clinton, Humphrey found that when parent education is provided by itself, the reunification rate tends to. . . . "

At the end of the literature review, you could summarize the major points and acknowledge noteworthy limitations in your literature search. Examples of limitations are the absence of recent empirical research on the subject, lack of attention in the literature to unique issues related to the subject, or consistent methodological flaws in the research on which much of the literature is based.

Presenting a literature review in this way is far more effective, efficient, and helpful than a serial listing of various publications. It helps readers grasp important themes and patterns, along with important exceptions. Instead of requiring them to draw connections among the various publications based on discrete summaries, this kind of literature review helps readers see the big picture.

Method

The second section is a detailed overview of the research methodology, in which you tell your readers exactly how you gathered the data. You should include information about the overall research design, key variables, sampling procedures, data collection instruments, data collection procedures, validity and reliability issues, significant limitations, and any relevant ethical issues. The summary of the overall research design should describe the use of experimental or quasi-experimental procedures (for example, use of a pre-test, post-test control-group design, an ABAB design, or a self-administered survey) and the specific steps that you took to implement the procedure (for example, procedures used to randomly assign clients to experimental and control groups, the length of baseline and intervention phases in a single-case design, or procedures used to distribute a survey instrument). Identify key variables, and offer clear, precise definitions (that is, operational definitions, to use the technical term).

The summary of sampling procedures should describe how you carried out your probability sampling (for example, random or stratified random sampling) or nonprobability sampling (for example, availability, quota, purposive sampling) and how you generated the sample (for example, how you used a table of random numbers or a lottery to create a random sample, how you used specific criteria to select individuals for a purposive sample) and the final sample size.

Sometimes it's hard to know how much detail to provide concerning the data collection instruments. Generally speaking, the method section should offer only a modest amount of detail. For example, if Andrew R. developed a client satisfaction survey, he doesn't need an item-by-item description of the entire instrument. Instead, the custom is to summarize the instrument's overall organization, the content of major sections, and the ways in which closed- and open-ended items were used. Many writers also give examples of different types of items, to give readers a sense of the instrument's format and content. Sometimes they include the entire instrument as an appendix in a research or evaluation report. Of course, if you're writing a manuscript for submission to a professional journal, you should not include the entire instrument; it would be too long.

If you used a standardized instrument, you should summarize the content, format, scoring procedures, and any relevant validity and reliability issues.

Once you have described the data collection instruments, you should discuss the specific procedures you used for gathering the data. Without going into too much detail, answer the "who, what, when, where, and how" of the data collection. Who helped with the data collection? What data did these people collect? When were the data collected (usually phrased like "The survey was administered between September and December 1997" or "The interviews were conducted at the beginning of the clients' admission to the group home and at the time of their discharge"). What setting(s) was used to collect the data (for example, the social worker's office, the clients' homes, the day room of a psychiatric facility)? What procedures were followed (this might include details of the oral explanation given before the clients completed an evaluation tool, how surveys were distributed throughout a large social service agency, or the procedures used to record clients' behavior observed through a one-way mirror).

It's also important to identify any relevant validity and reliability issues. For example, if there were special challenges related to content or face validity or if special steps were taken to enhance interrater reliability, mention them here. If you conducted a reliability test of two observers' data recordings, summarize the results. Many standardized instruments come with summaries of the results of reliability tests that have been carried out, and these results are usually reported in the method section (for example, alpha coefficients as an indicator of an instrument's reliability).

Toward the end of the method section, it's customary to cite any important limitations. Limitations might be possible sampling bias or error, misinterpretation of instructions on a questionnaire, the likelihood that respondents provided socially desirable answers to interview questions, or inaccurate data contained in agency records.

You also should acknowledge pertinent ethical issues. This is where you describe how you handled unique confidentiality issues, informed consent procedures, or special steps to address "protection of human subjects" concerns.

Results (or Findings)

The "results" section attracts the most attention, and given its potential impact, it's important that the results be presented in a comprehensive, concise, and, above all, clear manner. I have two pieces of advice: Don't provide too much detail, and don't provide too little detail.

It takes quite a bit of skill to know just how much detail to include in this section. Once again, if you're preparing a fairly lengthy research report for in-house use or submission to an external agency, you may have room to include lots of details, tables, figures, quotations, and so on. But if you are preparing the manuscript for submission to a professional journal, you may have to be a bit ruthless in your omissions. Sometimes you must choose among a number of important, and perhaps even vital, pieces of data.

As with the literature review, you should avoid a detailed, serial listing of every morsel of information. Instead, you need to look for major themes and patterns to emphasize. Although some individual results may be worth noting and discussing, if you have limited space it's important to focus on major findings and trends in the data. Esoteric details should either be omitted or relegated to footnotes.

It's best to present quantitative results in an overview of statistical techniques used and to include statistical results that substantiate your key points. Be sure to include appropriate statistical coefficients, significance levels, sample sizes, degrees of freedom, and so on. Often it makes sense to use tables and figures (for example, histograms, bar charts, pie charts) if they help illuminate an important point. The best way to learn how to organize tables and figures is to thumb through empirically based articles published in well-known journals. These journals have high standards for the presentation of quantitative results and take great care to use tables and figures properly.

Ordinarily, it's a mistake to include a detailed explanation of the statistical procedures used in quantitative data analysis. Most of the time, the statistical results are based on routine procedures, so it's not necessary to take up space describing them. Although this can be a problem for readers who aren't familiar with statistics, this is the custom. Once in a while you will find a fairly detailed explanation of a statistical procedure, but this usually happens when new or little-known procedures are used.

There are various ways to organize the content of the results section. A common format is to begin with an overview of the sample's characteristics (assuming there was some kind of sample), followed by a summary of key results associated with the major topics addressed. It's best to organize the topics into a logical sequence for presentation of the results. For data obtained from interviews, surveys, or questionnaires, simply follow the sequence of the items or questions.

The results section is *not* the section in which you speculate about the meaning of the findings and their implications for practice. That comes later. In the results section, you want to limit yourself to a *descriptive summary* (as opposed to an evaluative discussion or interpretation) of the results.

Discussion

The first three sections of a research or evaluation report follow a fairly tight script. Although the specific content necessarily varies from report to report, the sequence of general topics is pretty predictable. It's in the final section, the discussion section, where you can become creative and express your own ideas.

The main purpose of the discussion section is to highlight the major findings and explore their implications for practice. Here's another common mistake: Sometimes social workers use the discussion section to reiterate what they just stated in the results section. But there's no point killing trees for the paper it takes to say something twice. It's also boring to read the same thing twice. Instead, use the discussion section only to underscore major findings. Trust your readers to remember what they just read.

Once you have covered the major findings, you can explore their meaning. First, you might speculate about why the results came out as they did. Were they expected or unexpected? What factors explain these results? This is where you can offer your own opinions about the findings.

Second, identify the practical relevance of the results. For example, Andrew R. should explore the implications of the findings for social workers in family preservation and family reunification programs. How can clinical social workers, supervisors, and administrators use the results? Do the results suggest that services ought to be designed in ways that differ from popular program designs? Are there implications for the kinds of staff that should be hired for these programs? How generalizable are the results to other settings and circumstances?

Third, it's usually helpful to draw connections between the results and the literature cited in the first section of the report. Are the results consistent or inconsistent with what other researchers or evaluators have found? If the results are inconsistent, why might that be? Do these inconsistencies have any special implications?

After this discussion, you should acknowledge any significant limitations in the project's design, data collection procedures, and data analysis. This is where you mention problems with, for example, extraneous factors, attrition in the sample, or inaccurate case records. It's best to be honest about any aspects of the project that may limit the findings' relevance. Honesty is the best policy. Not only is professional integrity important; you certainly don't want anyone to accuse you of camouflaging or hiding anything.

Finally, it's customary to close the discussion section with a brief statement about what questions or issues remain to be addressed in light of the project's results. This may include some speculation about reasonable next steps, such as other research or evaluation projects.

Depending on the nature of the research or evaluation project, it may also be appropriate to make specific recommendations based on the project's results. A discussion section at the end of a report on a needs assessment may include recommendations of what needs to be addressed next and possible strategies (for example, implementing a new program, lobbying for new legislation, convening a task force). A discussion section at the end of a program evaluation report may recommend changes and ways to improve the delivery of services. Including practical, focused recommendations is important, given that social work is an action-oriented profession whose practitioners engage in research and evaluation to meet people's needs and promote social change.

Occasionally, social workers prepare an *executive summary* of a project's results, particularly when the full report is quite long. If social workers hope that their results will be reviewed by their colleagues, especially "busy" colleagues, it's usually a good idea to write a separate, very brief report (perhaps five pages or so) that summarizes the project and key findings. Sometimes an executive summary accomplishes just as much as the full report, and the full report is always available for those who want more detail.

PREPARING MANUSCRIPTS FOR PUBLICATION

Preparing manuscripts for publication in a professional journal is a unique skill. Most social workers haven't received any training in writing for publication and learn only by trial and error.

For a number of years I served as editor in chief of the *Journal of Social Work Education*, published by the Council on Social Work Education. In that position I read every manuscript submitted for publication, assigned them to members of the editorial board for their review and assessment, and made final decisions about acceptance or rejection. Based on that experience and my own experience submitting manuscripts for publication and receiving colleagues' feedback, I've come up with a number of suggestions to help social workers who want to write for publication:

Look at the journals to which you want to submit your manuscript. It's rare that only one journal is appropriate for a manuscript; usually at least two are suitable. Ask yourself several questions: Are the topics addressed in recent issues similar to the one I'm writing about? (If not, find a journal that's more appropriate.) Is my subject matter suitable for this particular journal? Are the articles in recent issues exclusively quantitative or qualitative, or is there a mix of the two? (If your article is qualitative, it's probably best to avoid journals whose articles are nearly always quantitative.) What kind of literature do the journal's writers draw on? Is the literature interdisciplinary, or does it tend to come from one particular field? (If you're interested in an interdisciplinary journal, write your article with that audience in mind. Don't refer exclusively to the social work profession.) What is the journal's audience? Do its authors tend to write for academicians or practitioners? (Anticipate what kind of articles your audience will be interested in. If your article contains lots of complex, technical statistical detail, the average practitioner may not be interested.) Are the journal's authors from various fields or one particular field? In general, how good is the fit between my manuscript and the journal's readers?

There are lots of journals to choose from. Sometimes you will want to submit your manuscript to journals edited primarily by and for social workers, such as *Social Work, Social Service Review, Families in Society, Health and Social Work, Social Work in Health Care, Social Work in Education, Journal of Social Work Education, Administration in Social Work, Social Work with Groups, Affilia, Social Work Research,* and *Research on Social Work Practice.* You should also consider submitting your manuscript to journals that reach broader audiences or audiences with specialized interests related to social work. Examples are *Hospital and Community Psychiatry, Professional Psychology: Research and Practice, Journal of Counseling and Development, Journal of Drug Issues, American Journal of Orthopsychiatry, International Journal of Group Psychotherapy, Family Coordinator, American Journal of Psychotherapy,* and *American Journal of Hospice Care.* If you're not familiar with the range of journals published in and related to social work, you can find a comprehensive list in the journals reviewed by *Social Work Abstracts,* published by the National Association of Social Workers.

Pay close attention to the instructions for authors. Every journal gives some kind of instructions to authors. They may not appear in every issue because of space constraints, so you may have to look through several issues to find them. The instructions usually include information about the appropriate subject matter (the journal's mission and audience), appropriate manuscript length, format for citing literature, number of copies to be submitted, details concerning the review process (procedures and typical waiting time), and the journal's mailing address.

Pay very close attention to these instructions, particularly those related to manuscript length and style. If the instructions say "manuscripts should be no longer than twenty pages," DON'T, DON'T, DON'T send in a thirty-page manuscript. That's a sure way to get the editor to push the reject button. It may be exceedingly difficult to squeeze everything you want to say into the pre-scribed number of pages, but that's what you have to do. If the instructions tell you to "follow the APA (American Psychological Association) style for the cita-tions," don't use a different citation format. Remember that journal editors typically have lots of manuscripts to choose from; in fact, the more selective journals may accept only 15 to 20 percent of submitted manuscripts. A manu-script that doesn't comply with the instructions provides an easy excuse to look at the next submission in the pile.

There's widespread agreement in the field that writers should submit a manuscript to only one journal at a time. Otherwise, journal staff and review-ers could spend enormous amounts of time on a manuscript that will be accepted first by another journal. Simultaneous submission to various journals is therefore considered out and out unethical. Of course, you can send your manuscript to a second journal if it was rejected by the first one.

Make sure your topic is important. I know this seems obvious, but you should recognize that what seems important and compelling to you may not seem so important or compelling to manuscript reviewers and journal editors. Reviewers sometimes make comments like "this is an interesting discussion, but the paper doesn't address a topic of vital concern to the profession" or "five years ago or so this topic was compelling, but interest has waned since then; I don't think our readers will be very interested."

Avoid "show and tell." This is a common problem. Understandably, many social workers are proud of the work they do and the programs and services they offer, and often they want to publicize their good work. As a result, many journals receive a steady stream of manuscripts that describe what appear to be interesting and important programs and services. The fatal flaw, however, is that these manuscripts don't report the evaluation of the programs or services being described. In addition, such manuscripts may lack in-depth literature reviews. Most journals simply won't publish descriptive overviews.

Make sure the literature review is up-to-date. You must take time to conduct comprehensive and thorough literature reviews. Some reviewers begin their assessment by flipping to the references to see how current they are. An out-of-date reference list is a red flag, and a big one.

Don't pad the references with gratuitous citations. It can be tempting to include lots of citations to the literature to create the impression that you spent gobs of time reading the relevant publications. But the standard rule is to list only those citations that you've actually used. Don't try to create false impressions. It can backfire if the reviewers decide you're trying to impress them.

Include sufficient methodological details. If your project involved some kind of data collection, be sure to explain in detail the research design, key variables, sampling procedures, data collection instruments and procedures, validity, reliability, and ethical issues. Reviewers might feel nauseated if important methodological details are omitted, particularly if they want to know exactly what procedures you used to sample a population or collect the data. Believe me, you don't want a nauseated reviewer reading your manuscript.

Get good statistics consultation. Here's an example of another kind of comment you don't want to read in a review: "The author seems to be confused about the data analysis. In table 3, he (she) presents the results of a t-test conducted with an ordinal-level dependent variable. Also, on p. 12, the author presents the results of a chi-square, but the table clearly has too many cells with low expected frequencies. Finally, on p. 13, the author seems to be confused about the difference between statistical and substantive significance. He (She) reports a Pearson's r of .13 ($p<.01$) and makes strong statements about this statistically significant result (note that this correlation explains less than 2 percent of the variance). The author may want to consult with a knowledgeable colleague about the data analysis carried out in this project."

Another problem to avoid is including an unnecessarily technical and arcane discussion of statistical procedures and techniques. Unless the journal to which the manuscript is being submitted is known for featuring this kind of detail, discussions of this sort are likely to turn off reviewers.

Don't let the tail wag the dog. Sometimes social workers gather a modest amount of data and think, "Gee, maybe I can write this up as a journal article." The result looks something like this (assuming a twenty-page manuscript): pages 1–7 are the introduction, problem statement, and literature review; pages 8–10 describe the methodology; pages 11–12 summarize the modest results; and pages 13–20 discuss the relevant issues. Typically in these manuscripts, the writers cover a number of issues in considerable detail, but the data themselves seem tangential and secondary. In a sense, the data offer the "excuse" needed for the rest of the paper.

Generally, it's not a good idea to organize an entire manuscript around a modest amount of data. Rather, the data should be the centerpiece. The narrative surrounding the data should enhance and supplement the results; it shouldn't overshadow them.

Edit, edit, edit. Nothing annoys a reviewer or journal editor more than a poorly written or sloppily edited manuscript. Poor writing and editing create a bad impression that can bias a reviewer from page 1. It can be tedious, but it's important that you read and reread your manuscript for problems with overall organization, grammar, sentence construction and syntax, clarity, and spelling. Be as concise as possible and avoid any terminology that might be insensitive with respect to gender, sexual identity or orientation, race, and ethnicity. Fortunately, most reviewers are tolerant of occasional mistakes and oversights; we all make them.

Many reviewers and editors prefer that authors avoid professional jargon as much as possible, as it can be slippery and vague. I think it's best to use simple, clear language that a broad audience can understand. I'd also suggest avoiding words that may be unfamiliar to readers. This isn't a place to show off (Do you know what *sesquipedalian* means?).

Once you've finished your first draft, you might ask a trusted and conscientious colleague or two to read through it carefully. Don't pick people who are so nice that they won't give you constructively critical feedback. You want honest and balanced comments; otherwise, there's no point in having colleagues review your paper.

Years ago one of my mentors advised me to write as if I were a *New York Times* reporter, relying on straightforward, clear, declarative sentences. I think that was good advice. The prose may not be exciting, but it's effective.

Be patient. The review process takes time, often much more than writers are prepared for. While I was a journal editor, I sometimes received telephone calls from writers who couldn't understand what was taking so long. Why, they asked, does it take twelve to sixteen weeks to read a twenty-page paper and make a decision? What's the big deal? Well, when you walk through the process, you can see how a review could take that long. The first week or so can be eaten up while the office staff logs in the manuscript and sends it, or an abstract, to the journal editor (who may be out of state) for his or her initial review. The journal editor—who, by the way, probably has a full-time job doing other things—may take another week or so to review the material and assign the paper to several reviewers. The journal editor then gets back to the office staff (usually the journal's managing editor) with the reviewers' names. The office staff then prepare rating sheets and mail the manuscript to the reviewers; this can take another week. That means we're now up to three or four weeks. Assuming the postal service didn't eat the mailing (actually, I've had remarkably good luck with the mail), the reviewers may be given three or four weeks to read the paper, complete the rating form, and type up their comments (by the way, the author's identity is withheld from reviewers to enhance the likelihood of an unbiased assessment). Unfortunately, it's not unusual for one of a manuscript's reviewers to be tardy, because of professional demands, illness, or personal distractions. These things happen, and they add to the time needed to complete the review. Also, keep in mind that reviewers often are appointed to editorial boards because they are accomplished people—read "busy."

After the completed reviews are sent into the journal's office, it may take a week for the office staff to collate the material and mail to the editor. Then the editor needs time to read the entire manuscript carefully, read the reviewers' assessments, and make a final decision. Depending on what's going on in the editor's professional and personal life, this step could take a couple of weeks. After the editor makes a final decision, he or she mails back the manuscripts and the editor's own rating sheet to the office staff, who then prepare a letter to the author.

When you add all this up, it's not hard to see why the process can easily take three months or so. That can be very frustrating for the authors, but the review process for manuscripts submitted to journals that are selective and conscientious is time-consuming, pure and simple.

Social workers also need to be patient once a manuscript is accepted for publication. Particularly with the "better," more selective journals, the lag between acceptance and actual publication can be a year or more.

Don't be defensive. It's rare for a manuscript to be accepted after the first review. It happens, but not often. Actually, there are four possibilities: outright acceptance, acceptance with minor revisions required, outright rejection, and rejection with an invitation to revise the manuscript based on the reviewers' comments.

It's very common for authors to receive some kind of rejection letter. Although it's tempting to grumble and complain about the reviewers' unfair assessment, it's usually wise to take a deep breath and read the reviews carefully and with an open mind to see whether they may contain useful and legitimate points. Reviewers aren't always right, of course; they're human, they often disagree with one another, and they can misinterpret authors' comments or make errors in judgment. More often than not, however, reviewers offer thoughtful observations worth considering. If you can summon up the energy to revise a manuscript, taking into account the reviewers' comments, there's a reasonably good chance—although certainly no guarantee—that a manuscript that you've been encouraged to revise and resubmit will be accepted. Be sure to respond to all the reviewers' comments, even if you end up saying that you disagree with some of them. The last thing you want to do is ignore the reviewers' suggestions, as that would just about ensure getting a rejection letter.

A Good Example

Now that I've described preparing an evaluation or research report, I think it would be a good idea for us to take a look at a real one. The following is an article that I discovered when I conducted a literature search on the subject of family reunification. It appears in the journal *Research on Social Work Practice* (vol. 5, no. 3, 1995, pp. 259–282). I present it here to give you an example of a published social work research report. In chapter 13, I refer back to this same article in my discussion of critiquing and assessing the quality of research and evaluation reports.

Examining Family Reunification Services: A Process Analysis of a Successful Experiment[*]

Robert E. Lewis (*Utah Department of Human Services*)
Elaine Walton (*Ohio State University*)
Mark W. Fraser (*University of North Carolina*)

This article describes the central elements of a family-based reunification service that was found to be effective in reducing foster care placements in Utah. In addition, the article assesses the relation between types of services and program outcomes.

No matter what their size or constitution, families bear primary responsibility for caring for the young and the old. This principle underpins the recent emergence of family-based services in child welfare, mental health, aging, commu-

---

[*]"Examining Family Reunification Services: A Process Analysis of a Sucessful Experiment," by Robert E. Lewis, Elaine Walton, and Mark W. Fraser, first appeared in *Research on Social Work Practice* 5, no. 3 (July 1995): 259–82 (copyright (c) 1995 by Sage Publications). Reprinted by permission of Sage Publications, Inc.

nity nursing, and other human and health services (Whittaker 1991). In spite of its popularity, the resurgence of family-oriented practice is far from new in social work. In child welfare, Kadushin once argued, "We always act on the supposition that until proven otherwise, the best place for the child is in his [or her] own home, cared for by his [or her] own parents" (1980:75).

Practitioners, policymakers, advocates, and scholars have sought to create child welfare services that strengthen and support families while concomitantly protecting children from abuse and neglect. Even under conditions of maltreatment, few children choose to live anywhere other than in their own homes (Wald, Carlsmith, & Leiderman 1988). Across families separated by the placement of a child in foster care, groups homes, or other substitute care services, most children and their parents both envision and work toward reunification. And, in fact, somewhere between 50 percent and 75 percent of the children placed out of their homes will return to their homes (Committee on Ways & Means 1991; Fanshel, Finch, & Grundy 1989; Goerge 1990; Grigsby 1990). Reunification is a natural and normal aspect of providing family-based services in child welfare settings.

But many reunifications fail. Too frequently, reunification occurs without resolution of the problems that necessitated placement. Although absence from the home may remove a child from immediate risk of maltreatment, it does little to change the habitability of a home, to improve a parent's disciplinary or anger management skills, or to help a caretaker think and act responsibly in her/his parenting role. In the absence of a service designed to strengthen families and promote reunification, it is not surprising that, across the nation, 20 percent to 40 percent of all reunified children are placed again in foster care (Goerge 1988; Maluccio, Krieger, & Pine 1988; Rzepnicki 1987; Tatara 1992; Wulczyn 1991).

THE FAMILY REUNIFICATION PROJECT

In recent years, renewed emphasis has been placed on enabling families to reunify successfully (Goerge 1988; Lahti 1982; Stein, Gambrill, & Wiltse 1978), and the purpose of this article is to examine a service that was found to be effective in promoting reunification. In 1983, the Utah State Department of Human Services implemented a brief intensive family preservation service (IFPS) (Callister, Mitchell, & Tolley 1986; Lantz 1985) and later participated in a major evaluation of these services, the Family-Based Intensive Treatment (FIT) Project (see Fraser, Pecora, & Haapala 1991). The IFPS was adapted from the approach used by Homebuilders™. The treatment model was based on social learning theory and includes the provision of concrete services, crisis intervention, and skills training (Lewis 1990, 1991a).

Because of the promise of the FIT and other projects in preventing the placement of children out of their homes (see, e.g., Feldman 1991), a follow-up experiment was initiated in 1989. The follow-up experiment, known as the Family Reunification Project (FRP), applied the FIT family preservation technology to the problem of reunification.

The FRP was evaluated by comparing randomly assigned treatment and control groups of children in foster care. Cases were followed for 12 months after conclusion of the intervention. Routine foster care services were provided to the control group children and their parents. In contrast, the treatment group of children and their parents received a 90-day family-strengthening, reunification service based on the FIT family preservation model. When identified as a *treatment* case, foster children's cases were transferred from the foster care worker to the FRS treatment worker. Treatment workers had an initial goal to return the child home within 15 days. This involved considerable early involvement in gaining agreement on a reunification plan with the child, parents, juvenile court judges, guardians ad litem, school authorities, and other agencies working with the child or family. Treatment work was usually initiated with the child and family separately, but as soon as possible involved the entire family with the child in place in the home. During the course of treatment, in addition to treatment activities, workers continually monitored and assessed the safety of the child at home, and in some cases recommended and arranged re-removal. At the end of the 90-day treatment period, workers staffed each case with their supervisor and clinical team, where children were at home, to determine if the case should be closed, referred to a protective supervision worker, or other action taken.

Significant differences were found between the two groups in rates and duration of out-of-home care subsequent to FRP treatment. At the end of the 90-day treatment period, 92.9 percent of the treatment children were home as compared to 28.3 percent of the control children. At 6 months after service completion, 70.1 percent of treatment children were home, compared to 41.5 percent of the control children. At 12 months after the treatment concluded, 77.2 percent of treatment children had returned home, whereas 49.1 percent percent of control children had returned home. Treatment children also returned home sooner than control children. Comparing children home at the end of the 12-month follow-up, treatment children averaged 54.7 days until permanently reunified with their parents; control children averaged 117.0 days (for details, see Walton, Fraser, Lewis, Pecora, & Walton 1993).

Because the experiment was distinguished by careful measurement of the family reunification service itself, a process analysis was undertaken to identify the core elements of family-based reunification services. In addition, the ways in which specific services were differentially provided and the relative contribution of various services to successful reunification were examined. Thus the primary aim of this article is to explore the central processes of a promising intervention that was designed to reunify families subsequent to an out-of-home placement.

METHOD

The FRP was evaluated by a team of researchers from the Social Research Institute of the Graduate School of Social Work, University of Utah, and the Utah Department of Human Services, with funding from the Children's Bureau of the U.S. Department of Health and Human Services. The study took place in four locations of the Office of Social Services, Utah Department of Human Services. Cases began to be served in July 1989, with the last of the 12-month follow-up data collected in November 1991.

The overall study design was experimental, comparing two randomly assigned groups of foster children. One group ($n = 57$) was assigned to receive an in-home reunification intervention, whereas the other group ($n = 53$) received routine child welfare services. Only one child per family was included in the study, assigned at random within the family if siblings appeared in the original sample frame. The two groups of children and their families were compared on a variety of measures including client and family characteristics, details of service delivery, worker characteristics, and case outcomes. The families were tracked for 12 months following completion of reunification services (see Walton 1991 for other methodological details). Using only the families in the experimental group, further data were collected to describe the way in which a variety of services were differentially employed and to identify services associated with successful family reunification. These data are the basis for this report.

Participants

The treatment group children studied were primarily Anglo-American (86.0 percent). They ranged in age from 1 to 17 years. The most frequent reason for the out-of-home placement was neglect (31.6 percent), followed by disruptive behavior by the child (22.8 percent), sexual abuse (15.8 percent), and physical abuse (12.3 percent). The number of prior placements ranged from one to six, with a mean of 2.8 placements. The combined total time in all previous placements ranged from 1 to 88 months, with a mean of 11.1 months. At the time of their inclusion in the study, most of the children were in foster homes (73.7

percent) as opposed to other settings, and had been in that specific setting for an average of 7.2 months.

The typical family targeted for reunification consisted of four persons, with the primary caretaker a female (91.2 percent) who was divorced or separated (54.4 percent). The mean age of the primary caretaker was 33.7 years. She or he averaged 12 years of education. During the previous 5 years, these families had changed residences an average of 3.4 times, and most (75.5 percent) of the families rented their homes. A slight majority (52.6 percent) of the families had at least one employed adult, and more than half had an annual income of less than $10,000. A majority (66.7 percent) of the parents identified themselves as members of the predominant religion in Utah—the Church of Jesus Christ of Latter-day Saints (Mormon). More than half (54.4 percent) of subject families, however, indicated that religion was not important to them.

Data Collection

Caseworkers who participated in the FRP collected data describing the services that they provided. These caseworkers received the same training and supervision as routine family preservation workers. Procedural differences for reunification workers included: (a) They carried an average of six cases for 90 days, and (b) they carried full foster care case responsibilities, while sharing an additional reunification treatment responsibility.

In this analysis, a Goal Checklist and a Worker Case Termination Survey were used. The former was employed by all FRS workers to set goals initially with their families and to record at service completion the degree to which these goals were achieved. The instrument and goal-setting methodology were developed in connection with the FIT project by a working group of evaluators, IFPS therapists, and supervisors. (Specific goals addressed are listed later in this article in table 4.) Goal achievement was rated on a 5-point scale with anchors ranging from *No progress* to *Totally achieved.*

The Worker Case Termination Survey was modified from instruments also originally developed by working staff and evaluators for the FIT project. This instrument contained the following types of service measures: reports of in-person, phone, and collateral hours spent for the case; hours spent providing concrete services (including providing transportation, direct provision of other concrete services, and enabling activities to help the family improve skills to access concrete services); and the level of usage of a range of clinical techniques. A total of 73 separate clinical activities were measured and are listed later in this article as part of table 1. FRP workers summarized their activities in response to this instrument based on daily contact notes contained in the agency case records.

Limitations

For several reasons, caution should be exercised in interpreting FRP findings. First, service and goal data were collected at the close of treatment and were based on worker report. The length of time before scoring may have introduced some error into the data, although agency requirements specify weekly case monitoring and recording. All service-related data were collected within 1 week of the close of FRP services for each participating family.

Second, workers and families jointly selected multiple treatment goals, and workers provided many different services in meeting these goals. This service contracting, planning, and reporting approach did not allow for specifying relationships between specific services and case goals. For this analysis, all services constituting the cluster of interventions provided in each case were assumed to contribute to each case goal.

Third, program evaluation was initiated at the same time as the start of the experimental reunification services. Thus findings are partially based on a service approach that may not have been fully stabilized. Mitigating this effect, however, was the fact that in most cases reunification workers and their supervisors had prior experience with the FIT family preservation treatment model.

RESULTS

The data were analyzed to determine the degree to which the various services were differentially utilized. Services were examined by category and frequency of use. The categories of analysis included the relative use of various clinical interventions, the degree to which concrete services were provided, the amounts of contact time with families, and service goal setting and achievement. Correlates for success and failure in family reunification were estimated.

Clinical Elements of Reunification Services

Seventy-three clinical service activities were specified in the treatment model and examined in the FRP (see table 1). This list of interventions was originally developed for the FIT Project with input from a panel of family preservation services supervisors and therapists serving in the Homebuilders^{TM} program in Washington State and the Utah Department of Human Services family preservation program (Fraser, Pecora, & Hoapala 1991:67–68).

Clinical services were distinguished from concrete services in that the former did not involve provision of tangible assistance. Rather, clinical interventions were aimed directly at improving personal functioning, coping, or life-

TABLE I   Clinical Services Provided to Treatment Cases (n = 57)

	Proportions of Contacts[a]		Cases Served	
	Mean	SD	Number	Percentages
Listen	6.88	2.64	57	100.0
Build relationships	5.81	3.45	57	100.0
Offer support/understanding	5.42	3.12	55	96.5
Build hope	4.82	3.23	53	93.0
Give encouragement	4.81	3.00	55	96.5
Build self-esteem	4.18	2.75	51	89.5
Clarify problems	4.12	2.66	54	94.7
Reframe family situation	4.04	3.01	52	91.2
Set treatment goals	3.86	2.91	56	98.2
Monitor clients	3.84	3.61	45	78.9
Make treatment plans	3.28	2.35	55	96.5
Help parents improve child compliance	3.23	2.48	49	86.0
Do problem solving	3.16	2.51	51	89.5
De-escalate conflict	2.98	2.52	53	93.0
Teach anger management	2.98	2.88	45	78.9
Teach use of natural consequences	2.91	2.40	50	87.7
Provide reinforcers	2.86	3.02	41	71.9
Manage anxiety/confusion	2.84	2.99	40	70.2
Teach use of reinforcement	2.71	2.53	45	78.9
Clarify family rules	2.75	2.41	49	86.0
Defuse crisis	2.75	2.54	49	86.0
Build routine in family	2.67	2.36	46	80.7
Consult with other service	2.63	2.23	48	84.2
Teach ways to handle frustration	2.67	2.59	43	75.4
Clarify family roles	2.56	2.51	47	82.4
Teach negotiating skills	2.44	2.52	43	75.4
Refer to other counseling	2.42	2.84	38	66.7
Reduce client self-criticism	2.37	2.34	43	75.4
Implement pleasant events	2.37	2.73	36	63.2
Manage depression	2.33	2.29	41	71.9
Teach use of environmental controls	2.32	2.20	46	80.7
Teach listening	2.37	2.30	43	75.4
Teach time-out	2.19	2.27	40	70.2
Values clarification	2.26	2.47	45	78.9
Build conversation skills	2.29	2.33	41	71.9
Teach how to give and accept feedback	2.16	2.43	35	61.4
Teach impulse control	2.14	2.58	34	59.6
Use RET concepts/techniques	2.05	2.21	42	73.7
Teach assertiveness concepts	2.05	2.38	39	68.4
Teach problem-ownership concept	2.05	2.32	35	61.4
Teach "I" statements	1.96	2.09	40	70.2

	Proportions of Contacts[a]		Cases Served	
	Mean	*SD*	*Number*	*Percentages*
Refer to other social services	1.89	2.30	39	68.4
Teach territorial concepts	1.81	2.60	29	50.9
Teach how to accept "no"	1.77	2.21	31	54.4
Advocate with schools	1.75	2.13	38	66.7
Teach/implement family council	1.70	2.03	37	64.9
Refer to informal helping network	1.68	2.23	32	56.0
Teach how to track behaviors	1.68	2.14	31	54.4
Teach process of change	1.67	2.12	32	56.0
Teach fair fighting	1.61	2.26	32	56.0
Teach "no-lose" problem solving	1.61	2.22	28	49.1
Meet with other providers	1.60	1.73	33	57.9
Teach child development	1.51	1.75	39	68.4
Track behaviors	1.49	2.17	26	45.6
Teach use of leisure	1.46	1.71	35	61.4
Build skill to protect from sex abuse	1.35	2.04	28	49.1
Help improve academic skills	1.33	2.02	28	49.1
Develop informal supports	1.30	1.88	29	50.9
Implement crisis card	1.09	1.86	24	42.1
Teach job-hunting skills	1.09	2.06	23	40.4
Teach time management	1.07	2.12	19	33.3
Track emotion frequency/intensity	1.07	2.21	18	31.6
Use relaxation therapy	.98	1.26	29	50.9
Teach money management	.98	1.62	20	35.1
Provide literature	.96	1.22	35	61.4
Recognize suicide potential	.91	1.98	16	28.1
Attend-testify in court	.88	1.05	35	61.4
Use behavior rehearsal-role play	.86	1.23	27	47.4
Teach appropriate sexual behavior	.75	1.46	19	33.3
Advocate with utilities	.67	1.53	16	28.1
Teach use of journal	.51	1.51	10	17.5
Use multiple-impact therapy	.30	1.02	6	10.5
Provide paper-pencil tests	.26	1.04	6	10.5

[a]This is a 10-point scale, with 10 = 100% of the contacts including the particular intervention, 9 = 90%, 8 = 80%, and so on.

skill levels of individual clients. In addition, they often focused on interpersonal relationships and the climate of the home.

From the list of 73 clinical service activities, workers rated the proportion of client contacts in which each clinical technique was used. In the FRP, the most frequently used clinical activity was Listening, reported to be employed as a major clinical strategy in 68.8 percent of all service contacts. Several other Rogerian-type relationship-building techniques were also frequently employed as were activities associated with building a treatment contract and developing service plans. Wide use was also reported of various techniques for (a) improving child compliance and behavior, (b) conflict reduction and crisis resolution, (c) problem solving, (d) the enhancement of self-esteem, and (e) management of affective problems. Fifty-seven (78.9 percent) of the services were reported as being used in at least half of the cases studied.

To further the understanding of the application of these clinical services, several aggregate scales were developed from the specific measures. Various combinations of service variables were grouped using principal components factor analysis, with both orthogonal and oblique rotations. The composition of the scales was then further refined using the internal reliability statistic alpha. Five scales were identified: (a) Relationship Building/Treatment Contracting, (b) Crisis-Conflict Management, (c) Self-Esteem Building/ Mood Management, (d) Skill Building/Behavioral Treatment, and (e) Outside Resource Involvement, along with one 2-variable index Time-Money Management (table 2). Alpha coefficients for three of the scales were in the high .90s and the other two were approximately .85, indicating acceptable levels of internal consistency for the scales. Relationship Building/Treatment Contracting was used significantly more than any other set of services, with reported average usage in 47.8 percent of all contacts and with 96.3 percent of cases. For the other scales, average usage across contacts was in the 20 percent to 25 percent range. The factor-based groupings of services tended to be utilized in about two-thirds of the cases, except for Crisis-Conflict Management interventions, which were present in nearly 80 percent of the cases. Time-Money Management interventions were used with a little less than a third of the families.

One high-use single variable, Do problem solving, did not load with any scale or index and appeared to represent an independent service component not embodied in the composite measures. Do problem solving was reported as being used in 31.6 percent of client contacts and at some point in nearly 90 percent of the cases.

TABLE 2 Clinical Services Summated Scales and Indices (n = 57)

Scale or Index Name	Number of Variables	Alpha Reliability	Cases Served		
			Mean of Proportion Contacts[a]	Mean	Percentage
Relationship Building/ Treatment Contracting	9	.957	4.78	54.9	96.3[b]
Clinical services: Listen, build relationships, offer support/ understanding, give encouragement, build hope, clarify problems, reframe family situation, set treatment goals, make treatment plans					
Crisis/Conflict Management	5	.942	2.70	44.8	78.6[b]
Clinical services: De-escalate conflict, teach anger management, defuse crisis, teach ways to handle frustration, teach impulse control					
Self-Esteem Building/ Mood Management	6	.859	2.35	37.7	66.1[b]
Clinical services: Build self-esteem, manage anxiety/confusion, reduce client self-criticism, manage depression, teach use of leisure, recognize suicide potential					
Skill Building/Behavioral Treatment	34	.975	2.07	37.2	65.2[b]

TABLE 2 *(Continued)* Clinical Services Summated Scales and Indices (n = 57)

Scale or Index Name	Number of Variables	Alpha Reliability	Cases Served		
			Mean of Proportion Contacts[a]	Mean	Percentage
Clinical services: Monitor clients, help parents improve child compliance, provide reinforcers, teach use of natural consequences, teach use of reinforcement, build routine in family, clarify family rules, clarify family roles, implement pleasant events, teach use of environmental controls, teach negotiating skills, teach listening, teach time-out, values clarification, build conversation skills, use RET concepts/techniques, teach assertiveness concepts, teach how to give and accept feedback, teach problem-ownership concept, teach "I" statements, teach territorial concepts, refer to informal helping network, teach/implement family council, teach how to accept "no," teach how to track behaviors, teach process of change, teach "no-lose" problem-solving, teach child development, track behaviors, teach fair fighting, track emotion frequency/intensity, implement crisis card, use relaxation therapy, teach appropriate sexual behavior					
Outside Resource Involvement	4	.852	2.06	37.7	67.5[b]
Clinical services: Consult with other service, refer to other counseling, refer to other social services, develop informal supports					
Time/Money Management	2	.818[c]	1.02	19.5	34.2[b]
Clinical services: Teach time management, teach money management					
Major single variable not included in scale or index (Do problem solving)	1	—	3.16	51.0	89.5

[a]Proportion of contacts: This is a 10-point scale, with 10 = 100% of the contacts including the particular intervention, 9 = 90%, 8 = 80%, and so on.
[b]Average of the percentages of cases served.
[c]Correlation coefficient.

Concrete Elements of Reunification Services

Concrete services have been identified as an important component of family preservation services (Frankel 1988; Jones 1985) and are given a central role in the Homebuilders™ model (Haapala & Kinney 1979; Kinney, Haapala, & Booth 1991; Lewis 1991a, 1991b). Three categories of concrete assistance were identified in the FRP. These included: (a) providing transportation, (b) doing concrete services, and (c) enabling concrete services. Providing transportation is a specific kind of tangible helping that in the FIT study was afforded a majority of cases (Lewis 1991a). A second concrete service dimension, Doing services, provides other kinds of direct tangible help. These Doing services may include providing financial assistance, food, household goods, and other specific resources, or helping with housework or child-care. A third concrete services dimension, Enabling, refers to efforts by the worker to help and train clients to acquire needed resources by their own efforts. When a worker coached a parent through an employment or food stamp application, it was scored as an enabling concrete service. Concrete services were reported by workers in terms of hours spent in each of these three categories of activity.

As shown in table 3, workers reported an average of 3.2 hours of time transporting clients, 3.3 hours performing Enabling activities, and 2.2 hours per case in direct provision of tangible assistance (Doing). Concrete service provision time totaled an average of 8.7 hours per case, but there was substantial variation across cases ($SD = 7.6$ hours). The number of hours reported for concrete service provision ranged from zero in one case to 46 in another. Across all cases, nearly one-fourth of total case time (23.1 percent) involved provision of concrete services.

A high proportion of cases involved the use of concrete services. Providing transportation and Doing services were each used in more than 70 percent of the cases studied. Enabling services were given in more than 80 percent of the cases, and at least one type of concrete service was provided in 93 percent of cases.

CONTACT TIME IN THE FAMILY REUNIFICATION PROJECT

Workers reported an average of 37.6 hours in direct service time per case (table 3). This total included 29.2 hours in face-to-face contacts and 8.4 hours of telephone contact time with family members, constituting a case average of about 3 hours of direct service time per week. In addition, workers spent an average of 9.3 hours per case in collateral contacts, staffing time, and paperwork.

TABLE 3   Service Provision Time (n = 57)

					Usage	
Variable	Mean	SD	Percentage of total	Percentage of total direct service hours	Number	Percentage
In-person contact hours						
—1st 2 weeks	8.63	7.60	62.5			
Phone hours—						
1st 2 weeks	2.25	2.55	16.3			
Total direct service hours						
—1st 2 weeks	10.88	9.80	78.8			
Other[a] hours						
—1st 2 weeks	2.93	2.09	21.2			
Total hours per case						
—1st 2 weeks	13.81	10.71	100.0			
Concrete service hours						
—transportation	3.19	3.94	36.7		40	70.2
Concrete service hours						
—doing	2.21	2.10	25.4		41	71.9
Concrete service hours						
—enabling	3.30	5.65	37.9		47	82.5
Total concrete service hours	8.70	7.63	100.0	23.1	53	93.0
Total in-person contact hours	29.23	14.66	62.3		57	100.0
Total phone hours	8.39	5.78	17.9		56	98.2
Total direct service hours	37.61	16.65	80.2		57	100.0
Total other[a] hours	9.28	5.41	19.8		56	98.2
Total hours per case	46.89	18.65	100.0		57	100.0

[a] Collateral contacts, case staffings, and paperwork.

Service time was loaded toward the initial days of a case. Nearly 30 percent of the total time was expended during the first 2 weeks of services (or about 15 percent of the standard 90-day service period).

REUNIFICATION SERVICE GOALS

Several researchers have identified service goal achievement as a crucial element in the success of family preservation (AuClaire & Schwartz 1986; Nelson, Emlen, Landsman, & Hutchinson 1988; Willems & DeRubeis 1981). In the FIT Project, service goal achievement significantly buffered placement risk

TABLE 4   Service Goal Usage and Achievement (n = 57)

Service goal	Goal Usage		Achievement	
	Number	Percentage	Mean	SD
Increase parenting skills	47	82.5	3.28	1.06
Establish trust and working relationship	37	64.9	3.89	.91
Increase self-esteem	37	64.9	3.65	.86
Increase communication skills	33	57.9	3.33	1.14
Increase anger management skills	32	56.1	3.06	1.08
Improve school performance	26	45.6	3.73	1.08
Increase compliance with house rules	25	43.9	3.64	.91
Increase use of community resources	20	35.1	3.90	.91
Decrease anxiety, worry, and fear	19	33.3	3.05	.78
Decrease depression or suicide thoughts	17	29.8	3.35	.70
Improve household physical condition	17	29.8	3.53	1.23
Decrease running away	14	24.6	3.29	1.38
Decrease drug or alcohol use	14	24.6	3.36	1.28
Increase social support network	13	22.8	3.39	1.12
Decrease delinquent or illegal behavior	12	21.1	3.33	1.16
Increase appropriate sexual behavior	10	17.5	3.20	1.03
Mean goal achievement	57	100.0	3.47	.81

factors (Fraser, Pecora, & Lewis 1991:220–21). Even modest goal achievement had a strong suppression effect on risk factors for service failure.

With families, reunification workers set service goals at the beginning of treatment and documented the degree to which the goals were achieved at the end of the 90-day service period. Goal achievement was measured on a 5-point scale: 1 = *No progress*; 3 = *About half achieved*; 5 = *Totally achieved* (2 and 4 were not anchored).

Given the relatively short term of service, the extent of goal setting was surprisingly ambitious. Families and workers set an average number of 6.4 goals. The most common goal was Increase parenting skills, which was set in more than 80 percent of the cases (see table 4). Four other goals were established in more than half of the cases: (a) Establish trust and working relationships, (b) Increase self-esteem, (c) Increase communication skills, and (d) Increase anger management. On the other hand, the goals Decrease running away, Decrease drug and alcohol use, Increase social support network, Decrease delinquent or illegal behavior, and Increase appropriate sexual behavior were set in less than one fourth of the cases.

Goals having the highest average achievement rates were Increase use of community resources (3.90), and Establish trust and working relationships

(3.89). Lowest achievement rates occurred for the goals Decrease anxiety, worry, and fear (3.05), and Increase anger management skills (3.06). Mean goal achievement, aggregated across all the goals, was 3.47, well above the *about half achieved* level. The standard deviation for mean goal achievement was relatively small (.81). Based on these figures, it appears that reunification workers consistently recognized at least a moderate degree of success in relation to specific outcomes anticipated in their treatment plans.

REUNIFICATION SERVICES ASSOCIATED WITH SUCCESS

For the purposes of this analysis, child-focused service success was defined two ways: (a) being reunified at home at the end of the 12-month follow-up period, and (b) returning home and remaining home throughout the follow-up period. The second was a more conservative measure of success because there was no allowance for recidivism.

Within the treatment group only, service variables significantly related to these success measures are shown in table 5. Of all the service-related measures, only a group of goal-achievement measures was related in a substantial way to success. Differences between the success and failure groups with regard to mean goal achievement were significant (for children returning and remaining home, $p < .001$; for children home at the 12-month follow-up, $p < .01$). Individual goals linked to success included Increase communication skills, Increase parenting skills, Increase anger management, Improve school performance, and Increase compliance with house rules).

A small group of specific clinical techniques was associated with service outcome. Children were more apt to remain in or be returned to out-of-home care when there was treatment emphasis on problem clarification, crisis intervention, and conflict management. Additionally, service failure occurred more often when a substantial amount of caseworker time was devoted to providing transportation or when levels of telephone time with clients were high. All of these variables may be indicators of greater severity of child or family problems. This is consistent with findings in the underlying study that identified that number of prior placements experienced by a child, various child behavioral problems, indications of child depression, and families that required more concrete services, that had less living arrangement stability, and that absorbed greater expenditures of emergency funds were associated with failure in FRS (Walton 1991). It appears that caseworkers may have focused on a small number of relatively high-risk families. The workers spent time with these families endeavoring (unsuccessfully) to find solutions to trying prob-

TABLE 5 Service Measures Significantly Associated with Return Home of Foster Children

Relationship	Group	N	Mean[a]	SD	t	p	Direction
Foster children returning home and staying home							
Clinical services							
Clarify problems	Failure	19	5.68	3.00	-3.05	.005	Failure
	Success	38	3.34	2.11			
Reframe family situation	Failure	19	5.16	3.29	-2.05	.045	Failure
	Success	38	3.35	1.93			
Defuse crisis	Failure	19	4.37	3.27	-3.05	.006	Failure
	Success	38	1.95	1.59			
De-escalate conflict	Failure	19	4.26	3.23	-2.41	.024	Failure
	Success	38	2.34	1.82			
Clinical scale							
Crisis/conflict management	Failure	19	3.76	3.10	-2.13	.044	Failure
	Success	38	2.10	1.56			
Goals							
Increase communication skills	Failure	16	2.75	1.06	3.26	.003	Success
	Success	17	3.88	.93			
Increase parenting skills	Failure	16	2.75	1.06	2.60	.013	Success
	Success	31	3.55	.96			
Improve school performance	Failure	10	3.20	1.14	2.12	.045	Success
	Success	16	4.06	.93			
Mean goal achievement	Failure	19	2.95	.85	3.76	.000	Success
	Success	38	3.72	.66			
Service time							
Total phone hours	Failure	19	10.79	6.36	-2.30	.025	Failure
	Success	38	7.18	5.15			

TABLE 5 *(Continued)* Service Measures Significantly Associated with Return Home of Foster Children

Relationship	Group	N	Mean[a]	SD	t	p	Direction
Concrete service hours—transportation	Failure	19	5.37	5.20	-2.58	.017	Failure
	Success	38	2.11	2.60			
Foster Children Home at 12-Months' Follow-Up							
Clinical services							
Clarify problems	Failure	14	5.43	2.90	-2.19	.033	Failure
	Success	43	3.70	2.46			
Goals							
Increase communication skills	Failure	12	2.58	1.16	3.27	.003	Success
	Success	21	3.76	.89			
Increase parenting skills	Failure	12	2.50	1.09	3.24	.002	Success
	Success	35	3.54	.92			
Increase anger management skills	Failure	9	2.33	1.00	2.61	.014	Success
	Success	23	3.35	.98			
Improve school performance	Failure	8	3.00	1.20	2.54	.018	Success
	Success	18	4.06	.87			
Increase compliance with house rules	Failure	8	3.13	.99	2.08	.049	Success
	Success	17	3.88	.78			
Mean goal achievement	Failure	14	2.84	.92	3.65	.001	Success
	Success	43	3.67	.67			
Service time							
Concrete service—hours transportation	Failure	14	5.21	5.47	-2.29	.026	Failure
	Success	43	2.53	3.11			

[a]Mean—for clinical measures the measure is proportion of contacts with service used, a 10-point scale with 10 = 100% of the contacts including the particular intervention, 9 = 90%, 8 = 80%, and so on. For goals the measure is a rating on a 5-point scale of achievement, with 5 = *fully achieved*, 1 = *not achieved*. For service time, the measure is in hours.

lems, to resolve crises, to mediate family conflict, and to acquire needed resources.

A set of 28 clinical services associated with success cases is presented in table 6. These are clinical techniques that met the following criterion: on a goal-by-goal basis where mean goal achievement was 3 or above (where 3 = *about half achieved*), these services must have been used in at least 25 percent of case contacts for at least three-fourths of the goals. Thus this set of 28 services may be thought of as core reunification services regardless of the goals selected.

Ranked according to the average proportion of contacts for cases with mean goal achievement of 3 or above, the first five services were associated with the summed scale Relationship Building/Treatment Contracting, as were nine out the first 12 variables. Nine other core interventions were from the Skill Building/Behavioral Treatment dimension. The solitary service, Do problem solving, was present among the more highly used interventions. Four of the services associated with Crisis /Conflict Management were included, along with three services from the Self-Esteem Building/Mood Management group and two interventions from Outside Resource Involvement.

Variation in service usage was not large across goals. For example, for the service Listen, the variation was from .69 to .83, a range of .14. For Build relationships, the range was .15, and for Offer support/understanding, there was a range of .16. Based on these observations it appears that a single, though multifaceted, reunification service was provided consistently across cases.

DISCUSSION

Applications to Social Work Practice

The family reunification service model described in this article appears to be a synthesis of three major treatment or practice approaches. First, the model was grounded in Rogerian theory (Kinney et al. 1991; Pray 1991; Rogers 1961). The use of relationship-building clinical skills, aimed at forming working attachments with clients and setting treatment expectations, was a constant theme running through every worker's endeavors. These activities functioned to promote client cooperation and utilization of specific treatment regimes.

Behavioral interventions constituted a second theoretical base for the model. Diverse approaches incorporated into the treatment model included training clients in mood and self-management skills to relieve anxiety, control anger, improve self-esteem, and lessen depression. Parenting training approaches were used to improve communication and child management

TABLE 6 Average Proportion of Contacts with Clinical Services Used for Services Associated with Success Cases[a]

Service	Service Goal[b]																Mean Goal Achievement
	1	2	3	4	5	6	7	8	9	10	11	12	13	14	15	16	
Maximum n =	34	27	39	23	22	35	16	15	23	10	13	11	19	9	10	8	45
Listen	.76	.70	.69	.73	.73	.71	.73	.74	.74	.73	.75	.83	.80	.71	.82	.76	.67
Build relationships	.66	.63	.58	.67	.65	.56	.60	.65	.62	.63	.63	.71	.63	.59	.74	.60	.57
Offer support/ understanding	.64	.59	.55	.60	.61	.54	.64	.64	.59	.58	.55	.69	.59	.53	.67	.60	.54
Build hope	.57	.56	.50	.59	.57	.52	.62	.65	.55	.60	.53	.70	.60	.58	.68	.56	.49
Give encouragement	.57	.55	.51	.57	.55	.53	.61	.62	.55	.58	.55	.70	.60	.57	.73	.59	.49
Build self-esteem	.47	.45	.44	.50	.48	.48	.51	.49	.44	.55	.61	.61	.49	.49	.57	.60	.45
Reframe family situation	.47	.52	.42	.47	.51	.42	.56	.53	.46	.55	.48	.59	.51	.53	.66	.54	.40
Monitor clients	.42	.45	.37	.42	.45	.32	.41	.43	.32	.33	.42	.41	.35	.39	.57	.60	.40
Clarify problems	.47	.50	.42	.48	.48	.41	.58	.54	.45	.49	.49	.61	.52	.51	.67	.54	.39
Set treatment goals	.40	.43	.38	.47	.44	.38	.48	.49	.42	.42	.42	.51	.46	.43	.49	.46	.37
Help parents improve child compliance	.31	.36	.31	.39	.39	.34	.36	.35	.38	.40	.38	.46	.37	.46	.49	.54	.33
Make treatment plans	.39	.40	.33	.41	.34	.35	.44	.40	.33	.30	.45	.44	.35	.46	.31	.33	
Provide reinforcers	.32	.39	.31	.38	.39	.29	.39	.39	.32	.32	.30	.43	.29	.36	.51	.48	.33
Do problem solving	.32	.36	.32	.40	.38	.32	.38	.38	.34	.37	.44	.42	.34	.37	.45	.44	.32
Build routine in family	.25	.34	.27	.33	.34	.28	.37	.29	.31	.29	.32	.36	.30	.34	.42	.43	.30
Manage anxiety/ confusion	.31	.36	.30	.41	.37	.29	.38	.41	.31	.51	.37	.51	.33	.48	.50	.43	.29
Clarify family rules	.28	.32	.29	.34	.41	.27	.27	.37	.33	.30	.34	.39	.29	.33	.38	.44	.29

TABLE 6 (*Continued*) Average Proportion of Contacts with Clinical Services Used for Services Associated with Success Cases[a]

Service							Service Goal[b]										Mean Goal Achievement
	1	2	3	4	5	6	7	8	9	10	11	12	13	14	15	16	
Teach use of reinforcement	.28	.33	.31	.28	.35	.28	.32	.31	.32	.26	.31	.36	.28	.27	.39	.45	.29
Consult with other service	.30	.30	.27	—	.29	.27	.36	.39	.28	.26	.33	.37	.41	.29	.39	.39	.29
Clarify family roles	.27	.31	.26	.29	.34	—	.28	.29	.26	.26	.26	.36	—	.29	.41	.34	.28
Teach use of natural consequences	.27	.34	.27	.34	.33	.27	.33	.26	.32	—	.31	.35	.30	.33	.34	.44	.27
Refer to other counseling	.26	.34	.27	.32	.28	.26	.32	.30	.26	.31	.35	.42	.33	—	.40	.38	.27
De-escalate conflict	.31	.31	.27	.33	.32	—	.31	.32	.31	.33	.28	.33	.29	.31	.32	.34	.25
Manage depression	.27	.28	—	.31	.25	.25	.29	.31	—	.39	.26	.34	—	.29	.33	—	.25
Teach anger management	.30	.29	—	.37	.30	—	.29	.33	.27	.25	.27	.29	.27	.27	.34	.25	.24
Teach use of environmental controls	.27	—	.27	.33	—	.27	.30	.25	.37	.37	.30	.28	.25	.28	.36	.34	.22
Defuse crisis	.30	.28	.25	.31	.30	—	.30	.31	.29	.29	.26	.34	.30	.28	.29	.28	.22
Teach ways to handle frustration	.29	.28	—	.31	.30	—	.31.	.32	.29	—	.28	.30	.25	.30	.37	—	.22

[a]For cases where Goal achievement = 3 or above (goal at least half achieved). Services listed where, for at least three-fourths of the goals, proportion of contacts with the intervention utilized was 25% or above.

[b]Services goal: 1 = Establish trust and working relationship; 2 = Increase communication skills; 3 = Increase parenting skills; 4 = Increase anger management skills; 5 = Improve school performance; 6 = Increase self-esteem; 7 = Decrease anxiety, worry, and fear rules; 8 = Decrease depression or suicide thoughts; 9 = Increase compliance with house rules; 10 = Decrease running away; 11 = Improve household physical condition; 12 = Increase social support network; 13 = Increase use of community resources; 14 = Decrease delinquent or illegal behavior; 15 = Decrease drug or alcohol use; 16 = Increase appropriate sexual behavior.

skills. In addition, some activities emphasized the didactic presentation of information, including steps in family problem solving. Workers assisted parents in establishing contingencies, monitoring child behaviors, and implementing other family-focused behavior change strategies.

A third major component of the reunification model was the use of concrete services. As in the FIT Project, three categories of concrete assistance were defined in the FRP: (a) providing transportation, (b) direct provision of tangible help (Doing), and (c) helping or coaching clients to acquire needed assistance themselves (Enabling). Concrete services were provided to more than 90 percent of the families and represented nearly one-fourth of the total direct service time. These figures appear to confirm the position of concrete service provision as a substantial aspect of the reunification service model.

The findings suggest that the major elements of the original family preservation intervention model were deployed successfully in reunification; however, several differences in emphasis were identified and warrant further investigation (a preliminary comparison is provided in Lewis 1994). Isolating these differences may have important implications for program implementation, staffing decisions, and training focused on reunification. For example, study of these adaptations might answer questions about the interchangeability of family preservation and reunification staff. Can workers carry both kinds of cases equally well or should reunification be treated as a separate specialty? The type and quality of supervision and training needed by reunification workers is also of concern. Would changing supervision and training to conform specifically to reunification improve effectiveness? In a broader sense, we argue that focusing additional study on adaptations that occur in innovative projects can produce practice- and management-related information that often helps to further define critical ingredients for both the design and implementation of new programs. This has been the purpose of this article.

For the most part, workers delivered the same services utilizing the same amount of direct contact time both to families who were able and to families who were not able to reunify. Clinical services were provided consistently across cases, with some clinical services being used more frequently than others. Concrete services were applied more selectively by workers in response to differential needs. It was difficult, however, to differentiate between success cases and failure cases on the basis of services delivered. In a few cases, workers invested extra effort in apparent response to difficult problems, and those higher-risk cases often resulted in failure. As in the FIT Project, goal achievement was the primary correlate of service success. Future research should address the correlates of goal achievement, for goal achievement appears to be a proximal outcome measure that mediates family risk factors and more distal outcomes such as child out-of-home placement.

In this project, reunification workers carried full responsibility for foster care casework while providing reunification services. Their duties included such tasks as working with foster parents to resolve problems in the placement, obtaining needed medical resources for the child, working with juvenile court officials, and preparing court documents. The impact of concurrently carrying foster care and reunification responsibilities may have had an effect on the types and amounts of therapeutic activity in which these workers engaged. Without the foster care case management role, for example, services might have been of shorter duration and greater intensity. Future research should assess different service lengths and staff models.

Given the mixed findings from recent studies of placement prevention services (see, e.g., Feldman 1991; Schuerman, Rzepnicki, Littell, & Chak 1993; University Associates 1993; Yuan, McDonald, Wheeler, Struckman-Johnson, & Rivest 1990), the alternative of providing family-based services to promote the reunification with the parents of children already in foster care warrants further investigation. Moreover, because provision of this service does not require estimating risk of placement and the acceptance for service only of families thought to be at imminent risk, a reunification service may be more efficient than a family preservation service in changing foster care utilization rates across states. Data from the process analysis both define central elements of reunification services and indicate that this approach, like family preservation, may not be effective in remediating the problems of all families. Although no single service is likely to be unvaryingly successful with the broad constellation of problems and conditions that affect families, reunification services offer a promising alternative to existing placement prevention programs.

References

AuClaire, P. & Schwartz, I. M. (1986). *An evaluation of the effectiveness of intensive home-based services as an alternative to placement for adolescents and their families.* Minneapolis, Minn.: Hennepin County Community Services Department and the University of Minnesota, Hubert H. Humphrey Institute of Public Affairs.

Callister, J.P., Mitchell, L., & Tolley, G. (1986). Profiling family preservation efforts in Utah. *Children Today* 15(6): 23–25, 36–37.

Committee on Ways and Means, U.S. House of Representatives. (1991). *Overview of entitlement programs; background material and data on programs within the jurisdiction of the committee on ways and means: 1991 green book*. Washington, DC: U.S. Government Printing Office.

Fanshel D., Finch, S.J., & Grundy J.F. (1989). Foster children in life-course perspective: The Casey family program experience. *Child Welfare* 69: 391–402.

Feldman, L. H. (1991, December). *Assessing the effectiveness of family preservation services in New Jersey within an ecological context (final report)*. Trenton, N.J.: Bureau of Research, Evaluation, and Quality Assurance, New Jersey Division of Youth and Family Services.

Frankel, H. (1988). Family-centered, home-based services in child protection: A review of the research. *Social Service Review* 62: 137–57.

Fraser, M. W., Pecora, P. J., & Haapala, D. A. (Eds.) (1991). *Families in crisis: The impact of intensive family preservation services*. New York: Aldine.

Fraser, M. W., Pecora, P. J., & Lewis, R. E. (1991). The correlates of treatment success and failure for intensive family preservation services. In M. W. Fraser, P. J. Pecora, & D. A. Haapala (Eds.), *Families in crisis: The impact of intensive family preservation services*, 181–224. New York: Aldine.

Goerge, R. M. (1990). The reunification process in substitute care. *Social Service Review* 64: 422–57.

Goerge, R. M. (1988). Cumulative effects of a child's placement in substitute care. Unpublished doctoral dissertation, University of Chicago.

Grigsby, R. K. (1990). Reuniting children with their families after foster care: An exploratory study of the family restoration process. Unpublished doctoral dissertation, University of Pennsylvania.

Haapala, D. A. & Kinney, J. M. (1979). Homebuilder's approach to the training of in-home therapists. In S. Maybanks & M. Bryce (Eds.), *Home-based services for children and families*, 248–59. Springfield, Ill.: Charles C. Thomas.

Jones, M. A. (1985). *A second chance for families: Five years later, follow-up of a program to prevent foster care*. New York: Child Welfare League of America.

Jones, M. A., Neuman, R., & Shyne, A. W. (1976). *A second chance for families: Evaluation of a program to reduce foster care*. New York: Child Welfare League of America.

Kadushin, A. (1980). *Child welfare services*. New York: Macmillan.

Kinney, J. M., Haapala, D. A., & Booth, C. (1991). *Keeping families together: The homebuilders model*. Hawthorne, N.Y.: Aldine.

Lahti, J. (1982). A follow-up study of foster children in permanent placements. *Social Service Review* 56: 556–71.

Lantz, B. K. (1985). Keeping troubled teens at home. *Children Today* 14(3): 9–12.

Lewis, R. E. (1990). Service-related correlates of treatment success in intensive home-based child welfare services. Doctoral dissertation, University of Utah, Salt Lake City.

Lewis, R. E. (1991a). What are the characteristics of intensive family preservation services? In M. W. Fraser, P. J. Pecora, & D. A. Haapala (Eds.), *Families in cri-*

sis: The impact of intensive family preservation services, 93–108. New York: Aldine.

Lewis, R. E. (1991b). What elements of service relate to treatment goal achievement? In M. W. Fraser, P. J. Pecora, & D. A. Haapala (Eds.), *Families in crisis: The impact of intensive family preservation services*, 225–72. New York: Aldine.

Lewis, R. E. (1994). Application and adaptation of intensive family preservation services to use for the reunification of foster children with their biological parents. *Children and Youth Services Review* 16: 339–61.

Maluccio, A.N., Krieger, R., & Pine, B.A. (1988). *Promoting family reunification through agency-school collaboration: Project summary*. West Hartford, Conn.: U.S. Department of Health and Human Services, Office of Human Development Services, Administration for Children, Youth and Families.

Nelson, J. P. (1985). An experimental evaluation of a home-based family-centered program model in a public child protection agency. Unpublished doctoral dissertation, University of Minnesota.

Nelson, K. E., Emlen, A., Landsman, M. J., & Hutchinson, J. (1988). *Family-based services: Factors contributing to success and failure in family-based child welfare services: Final report*. Iowa City, Iowa: National Resource Center on Family Based Services, School of Social Work, University of Iowa.

Nelson, K. E. & Landsman, M. J. (1992). *Alternative models of family preservation*. Springfield, Ill.: Charles C. Thomas.

Pray, J. E. (1991). Respecting the uniqueness of the individual: Social work practice within a reflective model. *Social Work* 36(1): 80–85.

Rogers, C. (1961). *On becoming a person*. Boston: Houghton Mifflin.

Rzepnicki, T. L. (1987). Recidivism of foster children returned to their own homes: A review and new directions for research. *Social Service Review* 61: 56–70.

Schuerman, J., Rzepnicki, T. L., Littell, J. H., & Chak, A. (1993). *Evaluation of the Illinois Family First Placement Prevention Program: Final report*. Chicago, Ill.: Chapin Hall Center for Children.

Stein, T.J., Gambrill, E. D., & Wiltse, K. T. (1978). *Children in foster homes: Achieving continuity of care*. New York: Praeger.

Szykula, S. A. & Fleischman, M. J. (1985). Reducing out-of-home placements of abused children: Two controlled field studies. *Child Abuse and Neglect* 9: 277–83.

Tatara, T. (1992). *Child substitute care population trends—FY82 through FY91: A summary*. VCFS Research Notes, No. 6. Washington, D.C.: American Public Welfare Association.

University Associates. (1993, March). *Evaluation of Michigan's Families First program*. Lansing, Mich.: Author.

Wald, M. S., Carlsmith, J. M., & Leiderman, P. H. (1988). *Protecting abused and neglected children*. Stanford, Calif.: Stanford University Press.

Walton, E. (1991). The reunification of children with their families: A test of intensive services following out-of-home placement. Unpublished doctoral dissertation, University of Utah, Salt Lake City.

Walton, E., Fraser, M. W., Lewis, R. E., Pecora, P. J., & Walton, W. K. (1993). In-home, family-based reunification services: an experimental study. *Child Welfare* 72: 473–88.

Wells, K. & Biegel, D. E. (1991). Conclusion. In K. Wells & D. E. Biegel (Eds.), *Family preservation services: Research and evaluation*, 241–50. Newbury Park, Calif.: Sage.

Whittaker J. K. (1991). The leadership challenge in family-based services: Policy, practice, and research. *Families in Society: The Journal of Contemporary Human Services* 72: 294–300.

Willems, D. M. & DeRubeis, R. (1981). *The effectiveness of intensive preventive services for families with abused, neglected, or disturbed children*. Trenton, N.J.: Bureau of Research, New Jersey Division of Youth and Family Services.

Wulczyn, F. (1991). Caseload dynamics and foster care reentry. *Social Service Review* 65: 133–56.

Yuan, Y. T., McDonald, W. R., Wheeler, C. E., Struckman-Johnson, D., & Rivest, M. (1990). *Evaluation of AB1562 in-home care demonstration projects, Volume 1: Final report*. Sacramento, Calif.: Walter R. McDonald & Associates.

Authors' Note : Correspondence may be addressed to R. E. Lewis, Utah Division of Family Services, 120 North 200 West, POB 45500, Salt Lake City, UT 84145–0500. The Family Reunification Project was made possible through a grant award by the Children's Bureau of the U.S. Department of Health and Human Services.

13

LOCATING AND CRITIQUING LITERATURE

As a social worker conducting research and evaluation, you need to know how to locate and critique professional literature and other documents (I'm using the term *literature* very broadly to include traditionally published documents and other information or reports, including those that may be available on the Internet and the World Wide Web). Theoretical discussions and findings from prior research can have an enormous influence on the way you go about your own projects. For one thing, you don't want to repeat what others have done, unless a particular project bears replicating for some reason. Also, discussions in the literature may help you refine and narrow your focus, particularly with respect to key concepts and variables. In addition, locating summaries of relevant research and evaluation efforts may help you identify useful methodological tools and avoid pitfalls that your colleagues have encountered.

Locating and critiquing literature are art forms.

LOCATING RELEVANT LITERATURE

There are several ways to go about locating literature. First, you need to decide what kind of literature you are looking for. Let's imagine you're Andrew R. who wants to track down information about family reunification and family preservation programs. What are the possible sources? I can think of seven: (1) books, (2) chapters in books, (3) articles published in professional journals, (4) government documents and publications, (5) encyclopedias, (6) monographs published by private agencies and organizations, and (7) unpublished material (for example, evaluation reports or position papers).

Be sure not to limit yourself to the most obvious libraries, that is, college or university libraries that are easily accessible. Social workers should know that in many communities other specialized libraries are available. Many state houses, for instance, have excellent reference libraries and knowledgeable librarians. Law libraries can often be found in court houses, and libraries focusing on mental health may be found in big public and private hospitals. Also, the U.S. government funds many clearinghouses that contain valuable information on topics such as aging, poverty, criminal justice, child welfare, substance abuse, housing, and mental health. Just ask a knowledgeable reference librarian to help you find them.

There are various ways to find literature from each of these sources. Let's consider them one by one.

Books

Not too long ago I would have briefly mentioned card catalogs and assumed that everyone knew how to use them. But I can't remember the last time I used a card catalog since the advent of computerized records in libraries.

There are basically two ways to locate relevant books. The first is to go to your library's automated or computerized catalog and use authors' names, if you know them, or subject headings to find books in that library and in area libraries (and perhaps even check on the circulation status). Right now, I'm going to stop writing this section and go to my library's computerized database to see what book titles I can find. Fortunately, I don't have to traipse over to the library; I can log on to the computer right from my office. Although libraries' systems vary somewhat, they all follow the same basic principles.

First I enter my library's automated system and type in the words "family preservation" and "family reunification" under the subject headings (these are known in the library trade as *key words*). But there's nothing. So now I'll enter the term "family," and the computer says there are 4901 entries! If I review all of them, I'll never make it home in time to . . . vacuum the house, take out the garbage, and mow the lawn. On second thought, maybe I *will* look through all of them. Let's glance at some of the headings under this topic: Family: African East, Family Allowances, Family and Television. . . . This isn't working at all; I thought I had the perfect excuse to get out of all those household chores.

Obviously my first search was too narrow and my second search was too broad. Time to pursue plan B.

Now I enter "Family Programs" under the subject heading, and finally we're getting somewhere. Here are several references that popped up on the screen:

Fraser, M. W., Pecora, P. J., and Haapala, D. A. (Eds.), *Families in crisis: The impact of intensive family preservation services.* New York: Aldine, 1991.

Kinney, J. M., Haapala, D. A., and Booth, C. *Keeping families together: The homebuilders model.* New York: Aldine, 1991.

Nelson, K. E., and Landsman, M. J. *Alternative models of family preservation.* Springfield, Ill.: Thomas, 1992.

Schuerman, J. R., Rzepnicki, T. L., and Littell, J. H. *Putting families first: An experiment in family preservation.* New York: Aldine, 1994.

Another potential resource is *Books in Print,* available at libraries and bookstores. *Books in Print* provides comprehensive listings of all books published, organized by author and topic.

Chapters in Books

Finding relevant chapters in books is much trickier. As far as I know, there's no centralized listing of book chapters. Generally speaking, you need perseverance and luck as you search for chapters that appear in books that you've tracked down or discover citations of book chapters that appear in other literature you read on the subject.

I always advise social workers to try to find book chapters (or journal articles) with titles like "Family Reunification: The State of the Art" or "Family Preservation: A Summary of the Literature." Finding a recent book chapter that provides a comprehensive review of the literature is like hitting oil. There's certainly nothing wrong with taking advantage of other people's labor, as long as it's in the public domain.

Articles Published in Professional Journals

Social workers usually get most of the literature they use from professional journals. Even with the necessary time lag in journal publication, journal articles often provide the most recent information about a given subject. I predict that before long the time lag will shorten dramatically as journals provide nearly instant access to articles on the Internet and the World Wide Web.

To locate journal articles, first look up relevant citations in various "abstracts." Abstracts are published periodically throughout the year and contain brief summaries of articles in a long list of journals. The organizations that publish these abstracts employ staff who read and summarize articles in journals relevant to the abstracts' general focus (social work, psychology, sociology, education, women's studies, health care, etc.). You can locate relevant citations by using the author and/or subject headings or key words that appear in the abstracts' index. Most of the abstracts provide guides to conducting a search, including how to select key words. For each article there is a short paragraph summarizing the content and listing the article's author(s), title, the journal in which it was published, and the journal's volume number, issue number, year of publication, and pages.

For social workers, the pertinent abstracts are *Social Work Abstracts, Psychological Abstracts, Sociological Abstracts, Women's Studies Abstracts, Public Affairs Information Service Bulletin, Index Medicus, Dissertation Abstracts International, Child Development Abstracts and Bibliography, Social Sciences Index,* and *ERIC*. The *Readers' Guide to Periodical Literature* also is a useful tool for locating literature in many magazines and journals, although its focus is much broader than that of the other abstracts.

If a particular citation seems relevant, all you do is find that journal in your library, flip through the pages, and you're in business. In truth, I've made the process sound much easier and simpler than it usually is. Here's a brief list of the top ten frustrations that Andrew R. and the rest of us might encounter: (1) The library is closed when you go there because of a power failure, a leaky roof above the main floor, or some holiday you didn't even know existed; (2) you can't figure out where in the library the abstracts are located and you're embarrassed to ask the reference librarian; (3) sixteen other people from your class are standing in line waiting to use the same set of abstracts; (4) a good friend walks by and convinces you that it would be far more fun to sit out on the library's lawn and chat—even though you're in Minnesota and it's February and the wind chill index is 20 degrees below zero; (5) someone has removed the volumes you need from the shelf, placed them on a nearby table, and is draped over them, sound asleep; (6) you locate the volumes you need but don't find any helpful subject headings in the index; (7) you find helpful subject headings but none of the citations seems particularly relevant; (8) you find a citation that seems perfect, only to discover that your library doesn't subscribe to the journal in which the article appears; (9) you find a citation that seems perfect, only to discover that although your library subscribes to the journal in which the article appears, the article was written in a language you've never heard of; and (10) you find a citation that seems perfect, only to discover that although your library subscribes to the journal in which the article appears and the article was written in English, the one volume you need is missing from the shelf.

A second way to find journal articles is to use the CD-ROMs that the publishers of abstracts make available (CD-ROM stands for "Compact Disk-Read Only Memory"). Many libraries regularly receive updated CD-ROMs and load them into computers in the reference section. You can then search very rapidly by authors' name, subject heading, and title, without having to thumb through those heavy books of abstracts.

If you're concerned that the most recent CD-ROM may not be current enough, you may be able to make an "on-line" search through one of the abstract publishers. This will give you up-to-the-minute access to citations. This kind of search is available through, for example, *Social Work Abstracts, Index Medicus* (*Medline*), *Psychological Abstracts* (*PsycInfo*), *Family Resources, Child Abuse and Neglect,* and *Sociological Abstracts.* The disadvantage of this very appealing option is that it often is expensive. The cost is usually based on the amount of computer time required, telephone line charges, and the length of the printout or number of citations. Sometimes social workers can get grants to pay for an on-line search.

Another way to conduct on-line searches that won't cost you any money (unless your own institution assesses a charge) is through the computerized search services to which many libraries subscribe. I currently have access through my library to a couple of terrific options: Expanded Academic Index ASAP (EAI) and First Search. The first search option provides access to citations of publications in almost two thousand "scholarly and general interest journals," with weekly updates. The second provides access to citations of books, journal articles, theses, films, computer software, and so on.

At this point I'm going to push a few buttons on my computer keyboard to get into EAI. Now I've clicked on that option, and the computer is asking me to choose whether I want an author, title, or subject search. I'll choose subject, and I'm typing in "family preservation." Frankly, I don't expect much, but I'll give it a try. It worked. Here are just a few examples of citations that popped up on my screen:

> Scannapieco, M., and Jackson, S., "Kinship care: The African American response to family preservation." *Social Work,* March 1996, vol. 41, no. 2, pp. 190ff.
> Skibinski, G. J., "The influence of the family preservation model on child sexual abuse intervention strategies: Changes in child welfare worker tasks." *Child Welfare,* September–October 1995, vol. 75, no. 4, pp. 975ff.
> Smith, M. K., "Utilization-focused evaluation of a family preservation program." *Families in Society,* January 1995, vol. 76, no. 1, pp. 11ff.
> Warsh, R., Pine, B. A., and Maluccio, A. N., " The meaning of family preservation: Shared mission, diverse methods." *Families in Society,* December 1995, vol. 76, no. 11, pp. 625ff.

Now I'll try the term "family reunification" for the subject heading and I get . . . absolutely nothing.

Let's see what the First Search option produces. I get a menu giving me choices among major subject headings, such as Arts and Humanities, Business and Economics, Conferences and Proceedings, Education, Medicine and Health, Public Affairs and Law, and All Databases. To be on the safe side, I'll pick All Databases, even though this might result in an excessively broad search. But I figure it's worth a try. I'll try "family preservation" for the subject heading, and I hit pay dirt a second time. Here are a few examples of the diverse citations available through this search service:

> The Program, *Family Preservation Program County Commission Report* (FY 1994–95). Denver, Colo.: Author.
> Rossi, P. H., *Evaluating family preservation programs: A report to the Edna McConnell Clark Foundation.* Amherst, Mass.: Social and Demographic Research Institute, University of Massachusetts, 1991.
> Schuerman, J. R., Rzepnicki, T. L., and Littell, J. H., "Putting families first: An experiment in family preservation," *Social Work*, vol. 41, no. 4, 1996, pp. 425ff.
> Tracy, E. M., *Social support resources of at-risk families: Implementation of social support assessments in an intensive family preservation program.* Ph.D. thesis, University of Washington, 1988.

Notice that the First Search service generates listings from a wide range of sources, including journals, dissertations, and agency monographs.

What's really remarkable, and is becoming more widespread, is that many of the journals in the social sciences are making their articles available on line, meaning on the Internet, the computer-based information network. Thus, not only can I find relevant citations, but in many instances, although not all, I also can pull up the article itself just by pushing another button on the keyboard.

A nifty way to locate references to journal articles is to use something called *Social Science Citations Index (SSCI)*. This is a very valuable tool that many social workers don't know about. Basically, if you know an "important" author's name, *SSCI* can give you citations to all the journal articles written by this person *and* the citations that appear in this person's publications. That's a good way to find out what people who've published literature have to say on a subject, and as an added bonus, you can take advantage of that person's literature search and get an instant bibliography. *SSCI* also can give you a list of all the publications citing the person whose work you consider to be important. So, if Paula Gitlin is an important author on the subject you want to study, you can find out who has cited Paula Gitlin in their work. That would help you broaden your search to include works by others who have written on the topic.

Government Documents and Publications

College and university libraries typically employ reference librarians specializing in government documents and publications. These people are worth their weight in gold. Sometimes the biggest challenge is finding them. I have a recurring image of these reference librarians sitting at their desks completely camouflaged by piles and piles of government reports and other documents. But if your reconnaissance mission is successful and you're able to find one of these MVPs (most valuable person), explain exactly what kinds of government publications you're looking for. For instance, Andrew R. is looking for government-funded reports or program summaries on family reunification and family preservation programs. He may also want information on household characteristics or poverty data pertaining to the broader community in which the Mt. Washington Family Service Agency is located. These data typically appear in reports published regularly by the U.S. Bureau of the Census.

I've always been a bit intimidated when I've tried to track down government documents. There's so much to know about what exists, how to find out what exists, and how to find what exists once you know that it actually exists. So it makes sense to take full advantage of the knowledge that reference librarians who specialize in this area have accumulated. In a heartbeat, they can rattle off names of or produce documents such as *Monthly Catalogue of U.S. Government Publications, United States Government Manual,* and *Monthly Checklist for State Publications.* What a skill.

Encyclopedias

Social workers sometimes overlook the fact that good, solid overview articles are available in a number of different encyclopedias. The most relevant to social workers is the *Encyclopedia of Social Work,* published by the National Association of Social Workers. It's available in print form and on CD-ROM. In addition, there are specialized encyclopedias, such as the *Encyclopedia of Bioethics, Encyclopedia of Psychology, Encyclopedia of Applied Ethics,* and *Encyclopedia of Crime and Justice.* On occasion I have even found useful information related to social work in the *Encyclopedia Britannica.*

Monographs Published by Private Agencies and Organizations

As with book chapters, there's no simple way to find monographs and reports published by private agencies and organizations. Social workers often discover such publications by word of mouth or by chance encounters with references to them in other literature. Whenever I try to locate this kind of literature, I contact colleagues who know a lot about the subject and ask them what unpublished literature they know about. Chances are, if you can find a colleague who has been paying attention to the literature on the subject for quite some time, he or she will be familiar with nearly every major report that's available. Although it's always possible that even the best-informed colleagues haven't heard of some important report, it's likely that if you contact enough knowledgeable colleagues, you'll end up with a comprehensive list.

Unpublished Material

Finding relevant unpublished material works much like finding reports and monographs published by private agencies and organizations. Good luck.

CRITIQUING EMPIRICALLY BASED LITERATURE

For the sake of discussion, let's assume this story has a happy ending: you've actually found the very article you've been looking for, a summary of an empirical evaluation of a family preservation program. The article happens to be the one presented in chapter 12 by Lewis, Walton, and Fraser, "Examining Family Reunification Services: A Process Analysis of a Successful Experiment" (what a remarkable coincidence). Terrific. You read it to see whether the article's content is relevant. It is. Fine. Now you have to decide whether the quality of the research reported on in the article is good enough to cite and to use in your own work.

It's at this point that we get to use much of what we've covered in this book. This is the ribbon on the package. We get to apply all this knowledge to an assessment of an actual research and evaluation report.

There's considerable consensus among social work researchers concerning the criteria to consider when assessing the quality of empirically based literature (see, for example, Campbell and Stanley 1963; Tripodi, Fellin, and Meyer 1983). Although various authors' lists vary, they contain some common elements. Here's a summary of the questions I think are most helpful for social workers to consider:

Introduction/Problem Statement

- Are the issues and questions addressed in the research stated clearly and precisely?
- Are the study's variables defined and operationalized clearly?
- Is the literature review comprehensive?

- Does the literature review draw connections among prior studies and theoretical discussions?
- If the study tested specific hypotheses, are they stated clearly and precisely?
- If the study examined the relationship between independent and dependent variables, and perhaps antecedent and/or intervening variables, were the relationships among these variables stated clearly and precisely?
- Does the author acknowledge important factors, if any exist, that might bias his or her approach to the study?
- Does the study address important issues or questions?

Method

- Does the study contain a clear overview of its overall design?
- Was the research design appropriate given the author's aims?
- Is the study's time frame clearly stated?
- Are the sampling procedures clearly described?
- Is the sample appropriate and adequate in light of the author's aims?
- Are the data collection methods and instruments described clearly?
- Were reasonable efforts made to minimize data collection error?
- Are the concepts of validity and reliability discussed thoroughly?
- Is there a clear summary of the design's limitations?
- Is there a comprehensive overview of relevant ethical issues?

Findings

- Are the sample's characteristics described thoroughly?
- Were the appropriate statistical analyses conducted?
- Were the qualitative data analyzed appropriately?
- If the study explored causal relationships among variables, was the author careful to avoid equating correlation with causation?
- Were the findings reported thoroughly?
- Were the findings reported clearly?

Discussion

- Are the study's major findings reiterated?
- Does the author draw conclusions based directly on the study's findings?
- Does the author draw connections between the study's findings and the results of prior research?
- Does the author acknowledge the extent to which the study's limitations affect the findings' implications?
- Are the implications of the study's findings spelled out?
- Does the author recommend reasonable and appropriate next steps?

Let's walk through this list and apply the criteria to the Lewis, Walton, and Fraser article. I will organize this assessment around the article's major sections: Introduction/problem statement (unlabeled, which is usually the case in journal articles), Method, Results, and Discussion. (Let me say at the outset that I think this is a very impressive article. But it's always possible to find some aspects of even the most competently written article that, in the reviewer's judgment, might have been presented differently. This is true even of my own work!)

Introduction/Problem Statement

Are the issues and questions addressed in the research stated clearly and precisely? The study's primary purposes are stated clearly: (1) to identify the key service delivery features of a family-based reunification program that was found to be effective in reducing foster care placements and (2) to identify the relationship between different types of services/worker activities and the program's outcomes. In the authors' words, "a process analysis was undertaken to identify the core elements of family-based reunification services. In addition, the ways in which specific services were differentially provided and the relative contribution of various services to successful reunification were examined. Thus the primary aim of this article is to explore the central processes of a promising intervention that was designed to reunify families subsequent to an out-of-home placement."

Although this is a clear statement of the study's purposes, I think it would help to define the term *process analysis*. It may be clear to some, but I suspect that it's not clear to many. I assume the authors have in mind a detailed analysis of the activities that workers engaged in and how they spent their time with clients. It would help to spell this out.

Are the study's variables defined and operationalized clearly? In general, the variables are stated clearly. The authors briefly summarize the intervention, the Family Reunification Project (FRP), which applied the Family-Based Intensive Treatment (FIT) model. In addition, they explain how a number of other variables were measured. For example, they describe how goal achievement was measured on a five-point scale and how "child-focused service success was defined two ways: (a) being reunified at home at the end of the 12-month follow-up period, and (b) returning home and remaining home throughout the follow-up period."

Another good example of the authors' explication of variables concerns the variable *concrete services*. They describe in considerable detail the concrete services in this study: providing transportation, performing specific services (for example, offering financial assistance, food, household goods), and enabling particular services (for example, coaching a parent through an employment or food stamp application).

My one modest concern is that the authors provide only a one-sentence summary of the intervention program: "The treatment model was based on social learning theory and includes the provision of concrete services, crisis intervention, and skills training." Later on in the method section, they state that caseworkers in the family reunification program carried an average of six cases for ninety days and had full foster care case responsibilities while sharing additional reunification treatment responsibilities. Given the key role of this intervention in the study, I think it would be useful to have a more detailed overview of the theoretical underpinnings of the "independent variable" and the specific methods of implementing the model (for example, exactly how social learning principles were implemented and why, and the crisis intervention and skills training components that were used). This kind of information would help readers fully appreciate the nature of the intervention and its possible application to their own settings and circumstances. It's possible, of course, that the journal's editor deleted some of this detail because of space limitations.

Is the literature review comprehensive? As far as I can tell, the authors did a fine job of citing the relevant literature. Although I am not an expert on the subject of family reunification, I can tell, based on my general familiarity with literature on the subject, that the authors cited well-known literature.

My one concern is that this introductory section doesn't explain the emergence and evolution of the concept of reunification itself. When did the concept first appear? How have definitions of the concept changed over time? Has reunification always been a major service goal in the child welfare field, and has this changed over time? In other words, I think it's important for readers to have a grasp, at least a minimal one, of the historical context of the contemporary concern about reunification.

In addition, I think readers should know something about the range of intervention models that exist or that have been tested concerning reunification. Although the model tested by the authors is a popular one, it's not the only one. The authors state, in fact, that "in recent years, renewed emphasis has been placed on enabling families to reunify successfully." Why did this occur "in recent years"? What was happening before this time? What approaches have been tried? Readers might like a brief overview of these issues, along with citations of relevant literature.

Does the literature review draw connections among prior studies and theoreti-

cal discussions? Notice that the authors, quite appropriately, don't review the relevant publications one by one. Rather, they make important conceptual points and cite the publications that support their observations.

For example, in the opening paragraph, the authors observe that our society continues to recognize the essential role of the family in caring for children and the elderly. They cite Whittaker's 1991 article in *Families in Society* and Kadushin's 1980 book, *Child Welfare Services*, to support this point. They don't say something like "We located two publications that discuss the importance of the family in modern society. The first publication is by Whittaker. He says that. . . . The second publication is by Kadushin, who says that. . . . " Instead of summarizing relevant publications one by one, the authors make their conceptual point and cite those publications that support it. Good.

Similarly, in the article's third paragraph, the authors note that many attempts to reunify children placed in foster care with their birth families did not succeed. At the end of the paragraph, the authors cite five publications that support their statement. This citation lets readers know that they can review these publications to learn more about unsuccessful reunification efforts. Again, fortunately, the publications aren't summarized one by one.

That's not to say that it's never appropriate to summarize the details of a publication; in fact, it's not unusual to read a literature review that does just that. For example, in this article the authors might have included a paragraph that began "There are three comprehensive longitudinal studies of families that participated in reunification programs. Two of the three were considered qualified successes, and the third was considered a failure, overall. The first study, conducted by Smith and Jones (1994), investigated thirty-seven families referred to a family service agency by [details of the program and the study's results would be placed here]. . . . In the second study, conducted by Black and White (1995), the authors followed twenty-eight families for six years to document [details of the program and the study's results would come here]. . . . " I don't have a problem with this, because the overview is still organized around ideas and flows coherently.

Sometimes authors want to describe a few publications in some detail but aren't able to because of space limitations. Because most journals impose strict limits on article length, authors have to cut descriptive detail in the introductory section that they would have preferred to retain but might be able to include in a longer research report.

If the study tested specific hypotheses, are they stated clearly and precisely? The authors didn't test specific hypotheses, so this has no bearing on the quality of the study. In fact, in social work the majority of research and evaluation projects don't test specific hypotheses. That's more common in the kind of theoretically oriented research found in fields such as psychology and sociology. More often than not, social workers identify research questions and issues to address, not hypotheses per se. In the Lewis et al. article, the authors spell out several research questions pertaining to key elements of the family reunification service, the ways in which services were provided to clients, and correlations between various services and reunification success.

If the study examined the relationship between independent and dependent variables, and perhaps between antecedent and/or intervening variables, were the relationships stated clearly and precisely? This study seems to have had two purposes: to generate descriptive data concerning elements of the delivery of family reunification services and to explore possible causal connections between features of the service delivery and the reunification success or failure. With respect to the latter, the authors clearly state their intent to investigate the ways in which aspects of the service delivery (for example, how the workers spent their time, the focus of their efforts) contributed to successful reunification. Obviously, this suggests that the authors planned to explore causal relationships.

Although the authors clearly stated their intentions, I think it would help to acknowledge that they were able to examine the possible causal relationships only by calculating correlations between service delivery characteristics and successful/unsuccessful reunification. That is, they could not randomly assign workers and clients to different service delivery conditions and determine whether the clients in the different groups had significantly different reunification rates (unlike in the first phase of the study, reported in a separate publication, in which families were randomly assigned to a treatment group based on the FIT family preservation model and a control group that received routine foster care services). Consequently, the authors could not control completely for a variety of possible extraneous factors that might explain statistically and substantively significant correlations between service delivery–related variables and successful/unsuccessful reunification. I don't consider this a major flaw in the design or in the article. I just think it would be useful to explain this limitation more explicitly to help readers better understand the study's implications.

Does the author acknowledge important factors, if any exist, that might bias his or her approach to the study? In the first paragraph of the method section, the authors are careful to disclose their professional affiliations. Although part of the research team was associated with the human service department responsible for the intervention, I don't see any reason to be concerned about significant bias.

Does the study address important issues or questions? It seems clear that the study does address important issues. Family reunification is a crucial goal in the child welfare field, as parents and children who are separated can suffer life-long trauma. Thus it's essential that social workers learn more about what factors improve the chances of successful family reunification.

Method

Does the study contain a clear overview of its overall design? The article clearly explains the overall design, that is, that the data were collected from agency staff who worked with families in the Family Reunification Project. The study was not based on an experimental design.

Was the research design appropriate, given the author's aims? Given the descriptive data the authors wanted to collect concerning the ways in which the caseworkers spent their time with clients, the design was appropriate. In an ideal world it would have been nice if the authors could have used an experimental design to investigate the impact of various service delivery–related variables on reunification success rates (that is, the causal relationship). Not surprisingly, and as is typical, the authors had to rely on correlational data to explore this relationship. This is understandable in light of the logistical and ethical constraints of using experimental and control or comparison groups, random assignment of clients, and so on.

Is the study's time frame stated clearly? The authors supply both the date when cases included in the study began to be served and the date when the last follow-up data were collected.

Are the sampling procedures spelled out clearly? The authors do not state whether all families whose children were placed in foster care by the state agency during the data collection period participated in the study or whether they used a sample. We do know that the study relied on cases from four locations of the state office of social services, but we don't know which ones or how representative they were of the agency's various offices. These kinds of details would be helpful to know.

The authors state clearly that only one child per family was included in the study and describe the procedures used to select the child when siblings appeared in the original sample.

Is the sample appropriate and adequate in light of the author's aims? I have no quarrel with the sampling approach. I would simply like to know somewhat more about it.

Are the data collection methods and instruments clearly described? The authors provide a brief overview of the data collection instruments' content and format; some of this information appears in the narrative, and some appears in the tables. The article doesn't contain many details about the instruments' development, but these details probably appear in other publications generated from this study. In addition, the article doesn't spell out the caseworkers' instructions about completing the instruments (for example, what definitions they should use for various terms), where the caseworkers completed the instruments (in their offices or some other location), and when the instruments were completed (exactly when after the cases were closed). This information would help readers decide whether the data collection procedures had any bearing on the results.

Were reasonable efforts made to minimize data collection error? It's difficult to know what efforts were made to minimize data collection error. However, because most of the data were collected directly from caseworkers, my guess is that there was minimal data collection error. That's not to say that the caseworkers' reports didn't contain inaccurate information (for example, their estimates of the amount of time they spent engaged in various activities), but the data collection effort itself didn't seem to create much opportunity for error (in contrast to, for instance, projects that depend heavily on data from case records, which could be filled with errors).

Are the concepts of validity and reliability discussed thoroughly? In the section on data collection, the authors don't directly discuss issues related to the instruments' validity and reliability. Ideally, the article would explain some of the steps the authors took to enhance content and face validity and to assess the instruments' reliability. Rather, they state only that the instruments were developed by a "working group" of evaluators, program staff, and supervisors. Of course, page limitations may have limited the authors' ability to address these issues, and they may be covered amply in other publications that grew out of this study. But readers who aren't familiar with these other publications and read only this one article wouldn't see that information.

Are the design's limitations clearly summarized? The authors include a separate subsection on limitations in the method section of the article, in which they list several limitations. The first pertains to relying only on workers' subjective reports for service- and goal-related data. The second limitation concerns possible bias or inaccuracy that might result from waiting until the close of treatment to obtain the workers' assessments. Third, the intervention was provided in a way that prevented the researchers from linking specific services and specific case goals, thus requiring them to state that "all services constituting the cluster of interventions provided in each case were assumed to contribute to each case goal." Finally, the program evaluation and the experimental reunification program started at the same time; consequently, the "findings are partially based on a service approach that may not have been fully stabilized."

This is a fine summary of possible limitations. As I suggested, however, I think it would have been helpful to add a statement concerning the limitations of correlational analysis when exploring possible causal relationships. In addition, I would have liked a more detailed comment about the possibility, although not necessarily the probability, that the workers exaggerated their reports of the kind of activities they engaged in and the amount of time they spent on various goals, in part because the workers knew they were being evaluated by the researchers (a form of socially desirable response and perhaps a manifestation of what's known as the *Hawthorne effect*, in which the researchers' very presence affects the behavior of the people they are observing).

Is there a comprehensive overview of relevant ethical issues? The study reported in this article did not involve major ethical issues. The earlier component of the study—which involved the random assignment of families to experimental and control groups—clearly did entail important ethical issues, but since that methodology was not germane to the Lewis et al. article, a full discussion of ethical issues wasn't warranted.

Findings

Are the sample's characteristics described thoroughly? The authors provide a clear and comprehensive summary of the sample's characteristics. This information is ordinarily presented at the beginning of the results section, although sometimes, as in this article, the data are presented in the methods section. The summary of the sample includes useful information about ethnicity, age, reasons for the out-of-home placements, the number and amount of time spent in prior out-of-home placements, placement settings, family size and residence, and parents' marital/relationship status, education, employment, income, and religion.

Were the appropriate statistical analyses conducted? All the statistical analyses seem appropriate for the levels of measurement of the variables and the questions that the researchers were addressing. In table 1, for example, the authors report on the mean proportion of client contacts in which a number of different services were provided. Standard deviations also are supplied with each mean. Both the mean and the standard deviation are appropriate because the data are ratio level (proportion of contacts); it also makes sense to present both a measure of central tendency (the mean) and a measure of dispersion (the standard deviation). With this information, we can easily see which clinical services were provided most often (the higher means), which ones were provided least often (the lower means), which ones were provided in varying proportions across cases (the higher standard deviations), and which ones were provided in roughly the same proportion across cases (the lower standard deviations).

The factor analysis reported in table 2 also seems appropriate, given the authors' wish to create scales that include combinations of different services. One concern I have, however, is that they don't have a summary, even a brief one in a footnote, of the concept of factor analysis. Although some social workers are familiar with this statistical technique, my guess is that most of them are social work academicians or researchers and that the majority of practicing social workers are not familiar with factor analysis. The omission of a brief explanation or overview of this statistical procedures therefore limits many readers' understanding of the study's methodology and results.

Table 5 is a good example of the appropriate use of a t-test to determine whether there is a statistically significant difference between the means of two groups. In this case, the authors compared the means indicating the proportion of contacts in which various services were used for successful and unsuccessful reunification cases (the two groups being compared). The table appropriately reports the sample size (N) for each group, the means and standard deviations for each group, the t-test result, and the significance level (the p value). The t-test is appropriate here because the authors were comparing two groups on a ratio-level variable (the t-test for independent groups makes sense here, right?). Many tables of this sort also include the relevant degrees of freedom (df), although this table doesn't.

Were the qualitative data analyzed appropriately? This study did not gather qualitative data.

If the study explored causal relationships among variables, was the author careful to avoid equating correlation with causation? This article generated a considerable amount of descriptive data concerning the activities that workers engaged in during their work with clients, but it also explored possible causal relationships between various service measures (for example, emphasis on clarifying problems, defusing crises, managing conflict, improving school performance, increasing anger management skills) and reunification failure or success. The authors found that several variables were correlated with successful reunification (in particular, variables related to goal achievement, such as increased communication and parenting skills, improving school performance, and increasing compliance with house rules).

I'm certainly willing to believe that these statistically significant associations provide some evidence of a causal relationship between the goal-achievement variables and successful reunification. But there is always the possibility that these statistically significant results are evidence of correlation more than of causation. That is, those cases in which a substantial portion of the contacts with clients focused on goal achievement may have been clients who were functioning better to begin with and could focus on very specific goals. Therefore, a significantly higher success rate for these cases could be a result of the fact that they were more amenable to the family reunification intervention in the first place, which is why the workers spent more time on specific goals.

I'm not saying this is a likely explanation, but it is a possible one. As a matter of principle, I think it's a good idea to acknowledge the possibility of spurious correlations and extraneous factors when using correlational data to suggest the existence of a causal relationship.

Were the findings reported thoroughly? The findings are reported thoroughly and comprehensively, virtually without exception.

Were the findings reported clearly? I think the authors' overview of the results is very clear. Although some readers, especially those without much experience reviewing the results of empirical research, might find the tables and numbers somewhat intimidating and confusing, my guess is that most readers would find the overall presentation to be quite clear and understandable.

Discussion

Are the study's major findings reiterated? The authors do a fine job of highlighting the study's major findings without repeating the details that appear in the findings section. The discussion is lean and avoids redundancy.

Are the author's conclusions based directly on the study's findings? The authors' conclusions are based directly on the study's findings. Their assertions about the major elements and successful aspects of the family reunification program are grounded in the study's results. The authors don't make claims that can't be supported by their data.

Does the author draw connections between the study's findings and the results of prior research? I particularly like the way the authors discuss their findings in the context of prior research. They are careful to point out that their results must be interpreted in light of "the mixed findings from recent studies of placement prevention services." They then cite the various studies that, when considered as a group, yield mixed results.

Does the author explain how the study's limitations may affect the findings' implications? Many research reports include a brief statement in the discussion section concerning noteworthy limitations. Typically these statements alert readers to the reasons that the findings, or portions of them, need to be considered carefully in view of the limitations or taken with a grain of salt, so to speak. Although the authors acknowledged several limitations in the method section, a brief reiteration would be helpful in the discussion section, I think.

I am concerned that the authors don't mention that the generalizability of the study's findings may be limited by the fact that 66.7 percent of the parents identified themselves as members of the Mormon Church. Although this figure may not be unusual in Utah, where the study was conducted and where the Mormon Church is very prominent, it's highly unusual compared with the religious orientation of families in reunification programs elsewhere in the nation. The sample's religious orientation, with all the related lifestyle and values implications, seems to have considerable bearing on the study's external validity.

Does the study spell out the implications of its findings? The authors' summary of the study's implications is especially helpful. They explain how the intervention model synthesizes three major treatment approaches: Rogerian principles, behavioral techniques, and the use of concrete services. As an aside, it might have been helpful if they had mentioned these concepts and approaches, and their relationship to the study, in the introductory section of the article. This may have helped readers better understand the conceptual foundation of the intervention model.

The authors also note that the findings have implications for the program's implementation (the extent to which workers can carry both family preservation and family reunification cases simultaneously and with comparable effectiveness), staffing decisions (the interchangeability of family preservation and family reunification staff), and training related to reunification (focusing training on specific goals whose achievement seems to be correlated with reunification success).

Does the author recommend reasonable and appropriate next steps? The authors concisely summarize those issues and questions that warrant further attention, such as the need to investigate further the correlates of goal achievement, the impact of different lengths of service and staffing models, and the relative benefits of providing family-based services to reunify parents and their children who have been placed in foster care.

CLOSING THOUGHTS

You've now had an introduction to key topics in social work research and evaluation. My hope is that this book has helped you appreciate the importance and relevance of research and evaluation skills in social work, because the ability to understand core research and evaluation concepts and to apply them in practice is essential to effective and ethical social work. It should be clear to you by now that research and evaluation skills are as pertinent to, and as much a part of, practice as is any other social work skill. In the final analysis, as a social worker you need to understand the problems you address and the effectiveness of your efforts. Social work research and evaluation skills will help you do this.

Here's one more hope I'd like to share with you, that from time to time throughout your career, you'll revisit the ideas, concepts, and skills we've discussed. You may not need these tools every day, but I can assure you there will be times when they'll come in handy, for example, when it's time to assess a client's problems and monitor that client's progress during intervention, design a clinical or program evaluation for a grant application, conduct a needs assessment for your agency's five-year strategic plan, or interpret the results presented in an important research publication. At those times, the material we've reviewed together will help.

In the end, research and evaluation skills enable social workers to pursue their most important goal: to help people in need, address people's problems in living, and promote social justice.

REFERENCES

American Psychiatric Association. 1994. *Diagnostic and Statistical Manual of Mental Disorders*. 4th ed. Washington, D.C.: American Psychiatric Association.

Anastasi, A. 1997. *Psychological Testing*. 7th ed. Upper Saddle River, N.J.: Prentice-Hall.

Andrulis, R. S. 1977. *Adult Assessment: A Sourcebook of Tests and Measures of Human Behavior*. Springfield, Ill.: Thomas.

Asch, S. E. 1956. "Studies of Independence and Submission to Group Pressure." *Psychological Monographs* 70: 416.

Atherton, C. R., and D. L. Klemmack. 1982. *Research Methods in Social Work*. Lexington, Mass.: Heath.

Bloom, M., and J. Fischer. 1982. *Evaluating Practice: Guidelines for the Accountable Professional*. Englewood Cliffs, N.J.: Prentice-Hall.

Bloom, M., J. Fischer, and J. G. Orme. 1995. *Evaluating Practice: Guidelines for the Accountable Professional*. 2d ed. Boston: Allyn & Bacon.

Blythe, B. J., and T. Tripodi. 1989. *Measurement in Direct Practice*. Newbury Park, Calif.: Sage.

Campbell, D. T., and J. C. Stanley. 1963. *Experimental and Quasi-Experimental Designs for Research*. Chicago: Rand McNally.

Cautela, J. R. 1990. *Behavior Analysis Forms for Clinical Intervention*. Cambridge, Mass.: Cambridge Center for Behavioral Studies.

Chun, K., S. Cobb, and R. French. 1975. *Measures for Psychological Assessment: A Guide to 3,000 Original Sources and Their Application*. Ann Arbor: University of Michigan, Survey Research Center, Institute for Social Research.

Ciarlo, J. A., T. R. Brown, D. W. Edwards, T. J. Kiresuk, and F. L. Newman. 1986. *Assessing Mental Health Treatment Outcome Measurement Techniques*. DHHS Publication No. (ADM)86–1301. Rockville, Md.: National Institute of Mental Health.

Conn, L. K., and D. P. Crowne. 1964. "Instigation to Aggression, Emotional Arousal, and Defensive Emulation." *Journal of Personality* 32: 163–79.

Conoley, J. C., and J. J. Kramer. 1990. *The Tenth Mental Measurements Yearbook.* Lincoln, Neb.: Buros Institute of Mental Measurements.

Craft, J. L. 1990. *Statistics and Data Analysis for Social Workers,* 2d ed. Itasca, Ill.: Peacock.

Crowne, D. P. 1959. "The Relation of Self-Acceptance Behavior to the Social Learning Theory Construct of Need Value." Ph.D. diss., Purdue University.

Crowne, D. P., and D. Marlowe. 1964. *The Approval Motive.* New York: Wiley.

Edwards, A. L. 1957. *The Social Desirability Variable in Personality Assessment and Research.* New York: Dryden.

Festinger, L., and J. N. Carlsmith. 1959. "Cognitive Consequences of Forced Compliance." *Journal of Abnormal and Social Psychology* 58: 203–10.

Fischer, J., and K. Corcoran. 1994a. *Measures for Clinical Practice: A Sourcebook:* Vol 1. *Couples, Families, Children.* 2d ed. New York: Free Press.

Fischer, J., and K. Corcoran. 1994b. *Measures for Clinical Practice: A Sourcebook:* Vol. 2. *Adults.* 2d ed. New York: Free Press.

Fredman, N., and R. Sherman. 1987. *Handbook of Measurements for Marriage and Family Therapy.* New York: Brunner/Mazel.

Gillespie, D. F. 1995. "Ethical Issues in Research." In *Encyclopedia of Social Work,* vol. 19., pp. 884–93. Washington, D.C.: National Association of Social Workers.

Gingerich, W., and W. Feyerherm. 1979. "The Celeration Line Technique for Assessing Client Change." *Journal of Social Service Research* 3: 99–113.

Gottman, J. M., and S. R. Leiblum. 1974. *How to Do Psychotherapy and How to Evaluate It.* New York: Holt, Rinehart and Winston.

Grinnell, R. M., Jr., ed. 1981. *Social Work Research and Evaluation.* Itasca, Ill.: Peacock.

Grotevant, H. D., and C. Carlson, eds. 1989. *Family Assessment: A Guide to Methods and Measures.* New York: Guilford.

Hersen, M., and A. S. Bellack, eds. 1988. *Dictionary of Behavioral Assessment Techniques.* Elmsford, N.Y.: Pergamon.

Holman, A. M. 1983. *Family Assessment: Tools for Understanding and Intervention.* Beverly Hills, Calif.: Sage.

Hudson, W. W. 1982. *The Clinical Measurement Package: A Field Manual.* Homewood, Ill.: Dorsey Press.

Hudson, W. W. 1992. *The WALMYR Assessment Scales Scoring Manual.* Tempe, Ariz.: WALMYR Publishing.

Jayaratne, S. 1978. "Analytic Procedures for Single-Subject Designs." *Social Work Research & Abstracts* 14: 30–40.

Jayaratne, S., and R. Levy. 1979. *Empirical Clinical Practice.* New York: Columbia University Press.

Jayaratne, S., T. Tripodi, and E. Talsma. 1988. "The Comparative Analysis and Aggregation of Single-Case Data." *Journal of Applied Behavioral Science* 24: 119–28.

Kadushin, A., and J. Martin. 1988. *Child Welfare Services*. 4th ed. New York: Columbia University Press.

Kestenbaum, C. J., and D. T. Williams. 1988. *Handbook of Clinical Assessment of Children and Adolescents*. New York: New York University Press.

Laird, J. 1993. "Revisioning Social Work Education: A Social Constructivist Approach." *Journal of Teaching in Social Work* 8: 1–10.

Levin, H. M. 1983. *Cost-Effectiveness: A Primer*. Beverly Hills, Calif.: Sage.

Levine, C. 1991. "AIDS and the Ethics of Human Subjects Research." In F. G. Reamer, ed., *AIDS and Ethics*, pp. 77–104. New York: Columbia University Press.

Levitt, J. L., and W. J. Reid. 1981. "Rapid-Assessment Instruments for Practice." *Social Work Research & Abstracts* 17: 13–19.

Lewis, R. E., E. Walton, and M. W. Fraser. 1995. "Examining Family Reunification Services: A Process Analysis of a Successful Experiment." *Research on Social Work Practice* 5: 259–82.

Maddox, T. 1997. *Tests: A Comprehensive Reference*. 4th ed. Austin, Tex.: Pro-Ed.

McCubbin, H. I., and A. I. Thompson, eds. 1991. *Family Assessment: Inventories for Research and Practice*. 2d ed. Madison: University of Wisconsin Press.

McDowell, I., and C. Newell. 1996. *Measuring Health: A Guide to Rating Scales and Questionnaires*. 2d ed. New York: Oxford University Press.

McReynolds, P. 1984. *Advances in Psychological Assessment*. San Francisco: Jossey-Bass.

Mullen, E.J., and J.L. Magnabosco, eds. 1997. *Outcomes Measurement in the Human Services*. Washington, D.C.: NASW Press.

National Association of Social Workers. 1996. *Code of Ethics*. Washington, D.C.: National Association of Social Workers.

National Commission for the Protection of Human Subjects of Biomedical and Behavioral Research. 1978. *The Belmont Report: Ethical Principles and Guidelines for the Protection of Human Subjects of Research*. Washington, D.C.: National Commission.

Orcutt, B. A. 1990. *Science and Inquiry in Social Work Practice*. New York: Columbia University Press.

Parsonson, B. S., and D. M. Baer. 1978. "The Analysis and Presentation of Graphic Data." In T. R. Kratochwill, ed., *Single-Subject Research: Strategies for Evaluating Change*, pp. 101–65. New York: Academic Press.

Polansky, N. A., ed. 1960. *Social Work Research*. Chicago: University of Chicago Press.

President's Commission for the Study of Ethical Problems in Medicine and Biomedical and Behavioral Research. 1982. *Making Health Care Decisions: The*

Ethical and Legal Implications of Informed Consent in the Patient–Practitioner Relationship. Vol. 3. Washington, D.C.: U.S. Government Printing Office.

Reamer, F. G. 1993. *The Philosophical Foundations of Social Work.* New York: Columbia University Press.

Reamer, F. G. 1994. *Social Work Malpractice and Liability.* New York: Columbia University Press.

Reamer, F. G. 1995a. "Ethics and Values." In *Encyclopedia of Social Work.* 19th ed., pp. 893–902. Washington, D.C.: National Association of Social Workers.

Reamer, F. G. 1995b. *Social Work Values and Ethics.* New York: Columbia University Press.

Reid, W. J. 1987. "Social Work Research." In *Encyclopedia of Social Work.* 18th ed., pp. 474–87. Silver Spring, Md.: National Association of Social Workers.

Reid, W. J., and A. Smith. 1981. *Research in Social Work.* New York: Columbia University Press.

Richmond, M. 1917. *Social Diagnosis.* New York: Russell Sage Foundation.

Rosenberg, M. J. 1965. "When Dissonance Fails: On Eliminating Evaluation Apprehension from Attitude Measurement." *Journal of Personality and Social Psychology* 1: 28–42.

Rosenberg, M. J. 1969. "Conditions and Consequences of Evaluation Apprehension." In R. Rosenthal and R. L. Rosnow, eds., *Artifact in Behavioral Research*, pp. 279–349. New York: Academic Press.

Rosenthal, R., and K. L. Fode. 1963. "The Effects of Experimental Bias on the Performance of the Albino Rat." *Behavioral Science* 8: 183–89.

Rosenthal, R., and L. Jacobson. 1968. *Pygmalion in the Classroom: Teacher Expectation and Pupils' Intellectual Development.* New York: Holt, Rinehart and Winston.

Rosenthal, R., and R. L. Rosnow, eds. 1969. *Artifact in Behavioral Research.* New York: Academic Press.

Sherman, E., and W. J. Reid, eds. 1994. *Qualitative Research in Social Work.* New York: Columbia University Press.

Sigall, H., E. Aronson, and T. Van Hoose. 1970. "The Cooperative Subject: Myth or Reality?" *Journal of Experimental Social Psychology* 6: 1–10.

Strickland, B. R., and D. P. Crowne. 1962. "Conformity Under Conditions of Simulated Group Pressure as a Function of the Need for Social Approval." *Journal of Social Psychology* 58: 171–81.

Thomas, C. B., J. H. Koivumaker, F. D. Miller, J. E. Dewhirst, G. A. Fine, M. Taylor, and R. L. Rosnow. 1974. "Evaluation Apprehension and the Interpretation of Test Correlations." Unpublished manuscript, Temple University.

Thomas, E. J., M. Yoshioka, and R. D. Ager. 1994. "Spouse Enabling Inventory (SEI)." In J. Fischer and K. Corcoran, eds., *Measures for Clinical Practice: A Sourcebook*: Vol. 1. *Couples, Families, and Children.* 2d ed., pp. 177–82. New York: Free Press.

Thomas, E. J., M. Yoshioka, and R. D. Ager. 1996. "Spouse Enabling of Alcohol Abuse: Conception, Assessment, and Modification." *Journal of Substance Abuse* 8: 61–80.

Touliatos, J., B. F. Perlmutter, and M. A. Straus, eds. 1990. *Handbook of Family Measurement Techniques.* Newbury Park, Calif.: Sage.

Tripodi, T., P. A. Fellin, and H. Meyer 1983. *The Assessment of Social Research: Guidelines for the Use of Research in Social Work and Social Service.* 2d ed. Itasca, Ill.: Peacock.

Tyson, K. 1995. *New Foundations for Scientific Social and Behavioral Research.* Boston: Allyn & Bacon.

Weber, S. J., and T. D. Cook. 1972. "Subject Effects in Laboratory Research: An Examination of Subject Roles, Demand Characteristics, and Valid Inference." *Psychological Bulletin* 77: 273–95.

Weinbach, R. W., and R. M. Grinnell Jr. 1995. *Statistics for Social Workers.* White Plains, N.Y.: Longman.

Zimbalist, S. E. 1977. *Historic Themes and Landmarks in Social Welfare Research.* New York: Harper & Row.

INDEX